America agination

America in the British Imagination

1945 to the Present

John F. Lyons

palgrave
macmillan

AMERICA IN THE BRITISH IMAGINATION

Softcover reprint of the hardcover 1st edition 2013 978-1-137-37678-7

First published in 2013 by
PALGRAVE MACMILLAN®
in the United States—a division of St. Martin's Press LLC,
175 Fifth Avenue, New York, NY 10010.

Where this book is distributed in the UK, Europe and the rest of the World, this is by Palgrave Macmillan, a division of Macmillan Publishers Limited, registered in England, company number 785998, of Houndmills, Basingstoke, Hampshire RG21 6XS.

Palgrave Macmillan is the global academic imprint of the above companies and has companies and representatives throughout the world.

ISBN 978-1-137-37679-4   ISBN 978-1-137-37680-0 (eBook)
DOI 10.1057/9781137376800

Library of Congress Cataloging-in-Publication Data

Lyons, John F., 1960–
America in the British imagination : 1945 to the present / John F. Lyons.
pages cm
Includes bibliographical references.

1. Great Britain—Civilization—American influences.
2. Great Britain—Social life and customs—1945–
3. Great Britain—Social conditions—1945– 4. Popular culture—Great Britain—History—20th century. 5. Great Britain—Relations—United States. 6. United States—Relations—Great Britain.
7. United States—Civilization. I. Title.
DA589.4.L96 2013
941.085—dc23   2013026832

A catalogue record of the book is available from the British Library.

Design by Integra Software Services

First edition: December 2013

10 9 8 7 6 5 4 3 2 1

For Enrico, Michele and Giorgia

Contents

Acknowledgments

There are a number of people in Britain and in the United States who have played a crucial role in bringing this book to publication. I would like to thank Diane Shutts of the Joliet Junior College (JJC) library for searching far and wide for my eccentric requests and the rest of the library staff for their wonderfully professional and friendly service. I am particularly appreciative of the financial help provided by JJC that has allowed me to present my findings at various academic conferences. The *Best of British* magazine and Terry Guntrip at Whirligig (http://www.whirligig-tv.co.uk) were gracious enough to publish my request for interviewees. A special thanks to Chris Chappell at Palgrave Macmillan for showing an enthusiasm for the book from the beginning.

Thanks to those who agreed to be interviewed either in person, by telephone or by email: Jon Denton, Phillip Dick, Liz Fiorani, James Graham, Raymond Johnston, Ray Kennedy, Mary Lyons, Michael Lyons, Patricia McManus, Roderick McNeill, Patrick Mills, Mary Minnock, Davina Neal, Peter O'Neill, Brian O'Sullivan, Christine Paine, Michael Penny, Gareth Rowlands, Nik Skeat, Barbara Smith, Sheryl Smithson, Alan Stepney, Paul Wood and Gary Younge. Limitation of space, I am afraid, means that the words of some of the interviewees are not included in the study but their views have still been valuable in influencing the content of the book.

I would like to express my great appreciation to Anthony Maravillas and David Reid for commenting on earlier drafts of the book and to the commentators and audiences at the 1st California and Northwest World History Association Conference in Portland, Oregon; the 8th Annual Meeting of the Northwest World History Association in Vancouver, Canada; and the 1st Mid-West World History Association Conference in Chicago, Illinois, who helped me rethink some of my ideas and prodded me in new directions. A special thanks to the anonymous reviewers at Palgrave Macmillan for their insightful comments.

Finally I would like to thank my extended family for sustaining me during the time it took to research and write the book. Mike, Mary, Dorothy, Mike and Eddie have supplied fun, kindness and encouragement while Enrico, Michele and Giorgia have provided friendship, stimulating conversations and child care. Joanie and Sinead have given me enormous support while I complete the book and are always a constant source of love and affection. Fair play to all of you!

Introduction

In 1943, English writer George Orwell entered a tobacconist in London and was confronted by two American soldiers "sprawling across the counter, one of them just sober enough to make unwanted love to the two young women who run the shop, the other at the stage known as 'fighting drunk.'" The inebriated GI immediately turned his attention to Orwell. "Wharrishay is, perfijious Albion. You heard that? Perfijious Albion. Never trust a Britisher. You can't trust the b—s," he loudly stated. "Can't trust them with what?" Orwell wearily asked. "Wharrishay is, down with Britain. Down with the British. You wanna do anything about that? Then you can—well do it," the soldier responded, sticking his chin in the air. Orwell declined the invitation and left the store in a rage. "This kind of thing is not exceptional. Even if you steer clear of Piccadilly with its seething swarms of drunks and whores, it is difficult to go anywhere in London without having the feeling that Britain is now Occupied Territory," Orwell complained.[1]

Young Margaret Tapster enjoyed a completely different experience with the American GIs stationed in London during World War II. The soldiers she met were generous with their supply of exotic goods like nylons and chewing gum and with their seemingly unlimited supply of perfume and cigarettes. They also brought the exuberance of the jitterbug and swing music to staid Britain and an enormous sense of fun and adventure to women like Tapster. One American in particular held her affections. Southerner Sergeant Kurt Wagner Jr. would tenderly kiss her while he told her about his home and his mother and father, who he promised Margaret would meet once the war was over. She would, alas, never meet Wagner's parents. After a night of heavy bombing, Sergeant Wagner's body was found amongst the rubble of an apartment block, his heart pierced with shrapnel and his body lying next to the unconscious air raid warden that he had carried from a burning building.[2]

The differing attitudes toward the American presence in Britain of Eton-educated George Orwell, a middle-aged man and prominent intellectual, and Margaret Tapster, a young working-class woman, proved a precursor to the divisions in British society that would appear in the aftermath of the war. The military occupation during World War II would be replaced in the postwar years with an occupation of the mind as American economic, political and cultural influence in Britain increased dramatically. Because of a shared language, cultural ties and historical traditions, and a close political and military relationship between the two governments, the impact of the United States on Britain proved stronger than on almost any other country. American culture was popular in Britain since the beginning of the twentieth century but increased affluence in Britain, the rise of the mass media and the strength of the US economy helped to escalate the American influence in the postwar years. Although most, like Margaret Tapster, embraced the American presence, others, like George Orwell, expressed resentment at the loss of Britain's world power status to the United States and at the American imports, which they saw as intrusive and as a symbol of Britain's decline.

America in the British Imagination, 1945 to the Present, seeks to answer a series of interrelated questions pertaining to the US presence in Britain. How extensive and significant was the American imprint on postwar Britain? Why did large sections of the British population embrace American culture? How did the United States change British society? The cinema, literature, television and music that journeyed across the Atlantic did not just transform the British landscape, but they also provided a window on the United States through which Britons developed a view of America and Americans. What view of Americans, American society and the foreign policy of the US government did the British obtain from the media and popular culture? How much did opposing opinions of the United States depend on class, gender, political persuasion and generational cohort? This book suggests that British attitudes toward the United States fluctuated widely and intensified or waned depending on developments both in the United States and in Great Britain. In general, British views of America and its people transformed from admiration of the United States in the immediate postwar years, to cynicism in the 1970s, to anger during the closing years of the twentieth century, and then to a growing indifference in more recent years.

Despite the tremendous impact America has had on the British landscape since 1945, historians have paid surprisingly little attention to the United States' influence on Britain. There has been no comprehensive study on the subject, and recently published histories of postwar Britain manage to virtually omit American cultural, political and social influence on the country.[3] Those that have written on the subject largely suggest that US influence on Britain has been less than transformative.[4] Richard Pells in his study of American influence on Europe since World War II, for example, suggests that Europeans have assimilated some aspects of American culture without losing their own identity and that the United States has not changed Europe to any great degree. American films, television, consumer goods and tourists have flooded Europe since the end of the war, but, Pells argues, they have "not significantly altered the values or behavioral patterns of most people in Western Europe" and that "the 'Americanization' of Europe is a myth." Pells, a frequent American visitor to Europe, concludes that Europeans "have been successful in preserving their distinctive cultural characteristics despite the efforts of Washington to persuade them to embrace the American model."[5] Similarly, Adrian Horn suggests that in the 1950s "with the exception of American rock 'n' roll music young people were not overly influenced by American popular culture."[6] By examining jukeboxes, the catering establishments in which they were located and the dress style of the young people who listened to them, Horn believes that "the period was not, as has been commonly thought, one where young people significantly adopted American popular cultural influences, except, that is, in the area of popular music."[7]

The British certainly rejected and transformed aspects of American culture but Pells and Horn try too hard to minimize the influence of the United States on Britain. Pells views Britain as part of a homogeneous Europe, but Britain has always been more receptive to American economic, political and cultural practices than any other European country. By concentrating on one provincial region, Lancashire, Horn, not unexpectedly, finds less American influence on British youth than he would have if he had focused on the capital, London. Still, no matter which part of the country he had studied, a receptive British youth were exposed to American TV programs, billboards, glossy magazines and movies, which make it untenable to say that the United States did not alter traditional British customs. Britain may not look exactly like America, but it is impossible to dismiss American influence on British business practices, retailing, architecture, music and fashion. Both Pells and Horn highlight the strength of British traditions but they underestimate the willingness of British people to embrace American customs and of British politicians and business elites to adopt US practices and change local conditions.

A more nuanced and balanced view of American influence on Britain is found in the recent work of historians Victoria de Grazia and H. L. Malchow, who emphasize the changes America brought to Britain. De Grazia argues that American consumer society, or what she calls the Market Empire, displaced "Europe's old regime of consumption" in the twentieth century. She believes that American salesmanship and mass production of goods replaced the European emphasis on class differentiation and specialization in retailing.[8] In a similar vein, Malchow deeply enriches our understanding of the Swinging Sixties in Britain by suggesting that the United States enjoyed a substantial influence on the culture and politics of middle-class Londoners in the 1960s. Malchow focuses on the growing personal contact between intellectuals on both sides of the Atlantic from the mid-1950s to the mid-1970s "with the object of repositioning American culture and its agents as central to any narrative of Britain in this era—and beyond."[9]

This book builds on the insights of De Grazia and Malchow by recognizing the willingness of Britons to embrace American imports rather than their stubbornness to maintain British traditions. When American culture reached Britain, blending did occur, but to really understand postwar Britain we need to recognize the impact of the United States on the country and to identify the aspects of British society that are derived from the United States. Unlike De Grazia, who focuses on the period before World War II, this book concentrates on British society since 1945, the period when American influence was at its peak. Rather than spotlight only one aspect of American influence or only one specific British region, as Malchow does, the book examines the myriad ways the United States shaped Britain as a whole.

In addition to utilizing the body of literature on Americanization, this book draws on the studies of political scientists and journalists who discuss the negative image of America and Americans under the umbrella of "anti-Americanism." A host of books, especially those that appeared since the tragic events of September 11, 2001, suggest that in Britain and the world there is an enduring blanket dislike of Americans and everything American or, as political scientist

Andrei Markovits suggests, a "resentment, hate, negativity, and mockery that has nothing to do with criticism of any policy or action."[10] Because authors like Markovits, who emphasize an enduring irrational hatred for America, are at a loss to explain why the intensity of anti-Americanism is sometimes low and sometimes high, a whole wealth of recent literature concludes that the actions and policies of the US government such as unfair trade practices and unpopular military adventures leads to outbreaks of anti-Americanism around the world. Replacement of indigenous cultural traditions by the US mass entertainment industry and the uncaring environmental and industrial relations practices of US companies provoke further hostility to the United States.[11]

The term "anti-Americanism" is too broad and unhelpful for unraveling attitudes toward the United States of America. Anti-Americanism is a catch-all phrase to describe a variety of opinions that varies from opposition to the policies of the United States government, aversion to Americans as individuals, dislike of aspects of American society or disapproval of American cultural influence. Some Britons supported US foreign policy but held prejudices against individual Americans while others intensely disliked aspects of American society but admired the music or films emanating from the country. *America in the British Imagination, 1945 to the Present,* carefully distinguishes between these differing views.[12] In addition, the anti-Americanism literature does not take account of the admiration of the United States in Britain and elsewhere. Anti-Americanism is well studied but there is little attempt to explain why some people were so positive about America and some so negative. Rather than focus only on episodes of animosity toward the United States, this book asks, why did so many people admire aspects of the United States and what did they appreciate about America in particular?

America in the British Imagination, 1945 to the Present, sets out to restore America to British history by examining the American influences on postwar Britain, how Britons imagined the United States and how they responded to the America they imagined. The book is a balance of economic, political, cultural and social history, and examines famous Americans who have shaped British society such as Henry Ford, Marilyn Monroe, Elvis Presley, Milton Friedman, Bill Clinton and Steve Jobs and those less famous ones who also played a part in bringing American influences to Britain. The study ventures on to the dance floor, into the living rooms of working-class Britons, into the cabinet rooms of the Houses of Parliament and into the comfort of the movie theater to see how the giant across the Atlantic has influenced the British. Famous and less famous Britons, from Michael Caine to John Lennon, from Margaret Thatcher to Tony Blair and from David Hockney to Martin Amis, took inspiration from the United States they imagined and changed Britain in the process.

This study not only revises traditional views of Anglo-American relations but it also draws on a variety of new or under-utilized sources. The book analyzes British popular music, television programs, literature and movies to understand how Britons imagined the United States of America. *America in the British Imagination,* however, is mostly told from the perspective of those who have lived in an Americanized Britain and allows these people to express their opinions on the America they encounter. While it has been difficult to unearth working-class sources in the past, this is not the case for postwar Britain. Famous people reminiscing about their youth, the growth of self-publishing and the interest in working-class studies means that many evocative memoirs and autobiographies have now been written by working-class people. I supplement these by undertaking a number of interviews that provide a window into the variety of British views of the United States. Memories can be distorted by time, and individuals often do not possess enough critical detachment from events they experienced, so other contemporary data has also been consulted including diaries, newspapers, polling data and political speeches to understand British views of the United States. By drawing on these varied sources, this book provides new stories and fresh angles to look at familiar issues in British history, from the political changes of the 1950s to the nature of Thatcherism, from the Swinging Sixties to the rise of New Labour.

The first chapter of the book outlines the extent to which the United States influenced postwar Britain. The vigor of the US economy and American businesses, the trade policies of the American government and developments in mass communications disseminated American products and culture into Britain. From eating habits to leisure pursuits, from business practices to political ideals, Britons eagerly adopted ideas and practices emanating from across the Atlantic. Yet they did not forsake British culture and America did not remake Britain in its own image as many people adopted American culture but mixed it with British and even European influences. Inspired by European and British traditions, the hybrid forms that emerged in Britain, however, still betrayed the American influence.

Chapter 2 examines the reaction of the British people to the America they encountered in 1945–1963. Britons' imagined view of the United States was shaped by the temper of the times, political persuasion, class, age and gender. Conservative and upper-class Britons expressed anxiety at the changes brought to Britain by American culture and at the prospect of America replacing Britain as a world power. Conservatives greeted American popular culture with disdain, believing that it was undermining standards through a general leveling down and contaminating of British traditions. The socialist left expressed concern at US foreign policy, the detrimental impact of American popular culture on working-class militancy and the inequalities of American society. For women, younger people and the working classes, more than for men, the older generation and the upper classes, however, all that was pleasurable in life appeared to come from the United States. Most Britons believed that America was affluent, modern, exciting and rebellious and offered opportunities unavailable in class-ridden Britain.

The 1960s saw a change in British perceptions of the United States. Britons still admired America and American culture but, as Chapter 3 demonstrates, Britain became the center of popular culture in the 1960s and the standard of living of most Britons rose substantially, consequently they revered the United States less. The civil rights movement exposed racial divisions in the United States and the war in Vietnam showed a darker side to US foreign policy. Many left-wing intellectuals treated American foreign policy with cynicism but most Britons cared considerably less about events in Southeast Asia. Most criticism of the United States was directed at what seemed like the increasingly violent and immoral nature of US society. By the 1970s, imported TV programs and Hollywood movies exposed the seedy underbelly of American urban life and Britons developed a more negative and cynical view of the United States.

Since the colonial period, British conservatives were highly critical of what they saw as uncultured Americans and of the society that they had created but, as Chapter 4 shows, by the 1980s members of the Conservative Party became America's most fervent supporters. Disillusioned by the planned economy and the generous welfare state developed by the Labour Party, Conservatives like Margaret Thatcher, who became Prime Minister in 1979, looked to the United States as a model as they sought to remake British society. Prime Minister Thatcher and President Ronald Reagan cemented a relationship based on free-market politics, anticommunism and nuclear brinkmanship, which provoked enormous opposition from many in Britain. Britons railed against the aggressive foreign policy of the US government and feared that the social problems of urban America were coming to Britain.

Prime Minister Margaret Thatcher left office in November 1990 but Labour Party leader Tony Blair, who became prime minister in 1997, maintained his predecessor's fixation with the free-market economy of the United States. As Chapter 5 elucidates, Blair eroded further the generous welfare state by replicating the US model of minimal government assistance and introduced American ideas of presentation into British politics. This, together with the heightened supremacy of the United States after the end of the Cold War and the increased American influence on Britain, provoked a nationalistic wave of resentment against America and Americans.

Chapter 6 focuses on the aftermath of the terrorist attacks of September 11, 2001. The twenty-first century began with the most pervasive wave of hostility to America ever seen in British history, provoked by the military adventures of President George W. Bush and the unstinting support of Bush's policies by Prime Minister Tony Blair. By the end of the decade, however, this latest wave of opposition to American power receded to be replaced by a growing indifference to America. Change of political leadership on both sides of the Atlantic, increased global influences on Britain and a weakened America led Britons to become less concerned with the United States.

George Orwell and Margaret Tapster had no inkling that the GIs they met in London would be in the vanguard of an American incursion that would have such a huge impact on British life. From political beliefs to business practices, from music to clothing and from movies to food, America exported its culture to a receptive British public. As the American presence increased, Britons would pay greater attention to the colossus that seemed to dominate not only Britain but also the world. The dropping of the first atomic bomb, the assassination of President John F. Kennedy, the launching of the Apollo mission and the fall of the Twin Towers in New York City, all mesmerized the British public. So too did the America that Britons imagined through the movies, music, literature and TV programs that became such a vital part of British life.

1

The Architect of Modern Britain: The Influence of the United States on Britain, 1945–1963

Many in Britain in the 1950s expressed dismay at the American influence creeping into the country. "America mostly pays the piper and calls for most of the tunes," J. B. Priestley, the English playwright and novelist, suggested in 1955.

> There is no longer any point in leaving Leicester Square and Coventry Street in order to describe Broadway, which merely has more electric light, newer Hollywood films, larger cafeterias. English readers have not to be conducted across the Atlantic now to observe the American style of urban life: it can be discovered in the nearest town. It is now the great invader.[1]

English author and journalist Harry Hopkins saw the American imprint everywhere.

> From hula-hoops to Zen Buddhism, from do-it-yourself to launderettes or the latest sociological catch phrase or typographical trick, from Rock 'n' Roll to Action Painting, barbecued chickens roasting on their spits in the shop windows to parking meters, clearways, bowling alleys, glass-skyscrapers, flying saucers, pay-roll raids, armoured trucks and beatniks, American habits and vogue now crossed the Atlantic with speed and certainty that suggested that Britain was new merely one more off-shore island. Strip-tease clubs completed the "Fordisation" of sex, supermarkets of shopping and Wimpy bars of eating. As if by some automatic process every successful American stereo or gimmick duly appeared in British version—a Dors for a Monroe, a Steele for a Presley, a Shirley Bassey for an Eartha Kitt.[2]

As Priestly and Hopkins observed, the United States of America exerted a profound influence on twentieth-century Britain. Since the end of World War II, this influence deepened as the United States easily outpaced Britain as an economic power, greater affluence allowed Britons to purchase even more American products and developments in mass communications further disseminated American culture to Britain. Britons of course maintained many of their old traditions, adapted and remade the American culture they consumed and were influenced by other parts of the world besides the United States. Yet, the American stamp on British society was unmistakable. Britons adopted American production and business methods, enthusiastically bought American products and submerged themselves in American cinema, fashion, music and literature. The United States played a crucial role in the development of a modern consumer society as American-style supermarkets and retail methods took root in Britain.

US Influence on Britain

The United States of America and Great Britain emerged victorious from the bloodiest conflict in human history but with their economic and diplomatic power moving in different directions. The United States comprised 6 percent of the world's population in 1945 but produced 55 percent of its steel, 70 percent of its oil and 60 percent of its manufacturing output.[3] By 1959, 71 percent of the world's largest firms were American owned.[4] Most Americans shared in this wealth. Median family income adjusted for inflation nearly doubled between 1946 and 1960. Home ownership soared and suburbs grew as young couples moved into sprawling modern houses with long driveways and spacious garages housing huge cars fresh off the production line. Nearly every one of these households possessed an array of consumer products including refrigerators, televisions and washing machines.[5] Reflecting its economic strength, the United States pushed the boundaries of knowledge and human excellence. US universities were amongst the best in the world and the nation produced literature, music, art, science and architecture that was admired and copied all over the world. Unsurprisingly, in 1956 the United States overtook Germany as the country with the largest number of Nobel Prize winners.[6]

In contrast to the rising fortunes of the United States, the old economic powers of Europe including Britain lay in ruins. As World War II came to a close in 1945, Britain faced severe economic problems that would persist throughout the immediate postwar years. Nazi bombing campaigns had destroyed more than 200,000 homes during the war and made another 250,000 uninhabitable. Even though Britain was a victor in the war, shortages and rationing persisted until 1954. Britain faced the task of rebuilding its industry and administering its large Empire, even though the costs of the war meant the nation was almost bankrupt. Starting with India in 1947, Britain quickly granted independence to all of its major colonies.[7]

With Britain virtually on its knees, the United States used its military strength to confront the Soviet Union in a mounting Cold War, which further spread its influence across the globe. The United States held a monopoly on nuclear weapons until 1949, had the largest defense budget in the world, and deployed its armed forces around the world, including to the United Kingdom where 40,000–50,000 American servicemen were stationed in the early 1950s. In 1949, the United States took the lead in forming the North Atlantic Treaty Organization (NATO), a military alliance headed by the United States to defend Europe from the Soviet threat, with Britain becoming one of the organization's original 12 members.[8] The US government and private agencies sponsored programs in Europe to promote a positive image of the country and to counter communist propaganda. President Eisenhower established the United States Information Agency (USIA) in 1953 as an independent federal agency whose job it was to impart a favorable view of the United States abroad. The USIA, whose motto was "telling America's story to the world," sponsored educational exchanges, conferences on American history, art exhibitions, tours of musicians and performances of plays.[9]

As the world's most powerful and prosperous nation, the United States took the lead in creating international economic institutions and laying the ground rules for the global economic order. In 1944, delegates from 44 Allied nations met in Bretton Woods, New Hampshire, to establish rules for global commercial and financial relations. The leader of the US delegation and the primary mover behind the conference was Harry Dexter White, an American economist and senior US Treasury department official. Because of White's prodding, the conference established the dollar as the principal currency of international exchange, tying the other currencies to the dollar and linking the dollar to the price of gold. The conference established the International Monetary Fund (IMF) to lend money to nations with trade deficits, and the International Bank for Reconstruction and Development (IBRD), better known as the World Bank, to provide long-term loans to developing countries. These organizations were headquartered in Washington DC and dominated by US finance and personnel. Ironically, Harry Dexter White, the main architect of US economic dominance, was subsequently found to be a Soviet spy who passed secret information to Stalin's regime during World War II. On August 14, 1948, White appeared before the House Un-American Activities Committee and three days later he died of a heart attack.[10]

As part of its desire to rebuild the economies of Western Europe and combat communism, the United States provided the British government with much needed financial assistance. In 1941, the United States began to supply Britain with essential war-time material under the Lend–Lease program. At the end of the war, the US government agreed to write off all war-time debts and to supply the British government with a US$3.75 billion loan at 2 percent interest, which Britain finally paid off in 2006. Under the 1948 European Recovery Program, or Marshall Plan, named after US Secretary of State George C. Marshall, Britain received a further US$2.7 billion in aid, more than any other European nation. The financial assistance supplied by the United States helped to stabilize the British economy, relax austerity measures and rebuild the infrastructure of the country.[11]

The US government's activist stance continued as it helped to introduce American products into Britain by promoting free trade. The United States pressured Britain and other countries into reducing protective tariffs and restrictive quotas, believing that America's powerful corporations, using up-to-date manufacturing technology, would be able to produce cheaper and better made goods than their competitors and, therefore, dominate world trade. Under the Lend–Lease agreement, at Bretton Woods and in negotiations over the postwar loan for Britain, the United States had pressed for an end to imperial preferences, which was established in Ottawa in 1932 to create trade barriers to those outside of the British Empire. The General Agreement on Tariffs and Trade (GATT), a multilateral agreement signed in 1947, sought to reduce tariffs and other trade barriers further. Tariffs slowly fell but the British government continued to use import quotas against American manufactured goods until the late 1950s and the imperial preference system ended only when Britain joined the European Economic Community (EEC) in 1973. Still American products saturated the British market. US companies such as Esso, Hoover, Singer, Kellogg's, Wrigley, Heinz, Kraft, Coca-Cola, Harley-Davidson, Campbell's and Kodak became household names in Britain.[12]

US companies had a long history of investing in Britain, and the investments accelerated in the postwar years. In 1856, J. Ford and Company established a vulcanized rubber factory in Edinburgh and many other American companies subsequently followed their lead by investing in the UK. Woolworths, the US "five and dime" store, which offered a myriad of cut-priced merchandise under one roof, opened its first British outlet in Liverpool in 1909 and followed this with one on Oxford Street, London, in 1924. By 1914, 70 US manufacturing subsidiaries or jointly owned Anglo-American concerns operated in the United Kingdom, employing about 12,000 workers. Leading companies like Gillette, Hoover, Remington and Firestone—all established factories in and around London in the interwar years and General Motors took over British automakers Vauxhall in 1925. In 1950, US companies invested US$847 million in Britain but by 1960 the figure had risen to US$3,231 million.[13]

Aggressive marketing aided American companies in selling their products in Britain. Eye-catching packaging, expert salesmanship and slick and expensive advertising helped American products reach a mass market. American businesses used billboards, advertisements in magazines and newspapers and later television commercials to entice consumers to buy their products. American advertising agencies established outlets in London and British agencies employed American personnel and incorporated American techniques of consumer research, opinion polls and market testing into their work.[14] In 1960, five of the 12 largest advertising agencies in Britain were American-owned. The "Marlboro Man" enticed people to buy cigarettes with the promise of rugged individualism, masculinity and adventure in the Wild West, while the sophisticated elegance of Max Factor cosmetics tempted women to believe they could share in the glamour of Hollywood. "The American ballyhoo, which Britain has so much enjoyed mocking, is gradually winning," journalist Anthony Sampson wrote in the early 1960s. "The most obvious manifestation of this is the advance of advertising."[15]

Government support for free trade, and state-of-the-art marketing, may have been important for the success of American consumer goods in Britain, but their ability to produce innovative products contributed more toward American success. In the 1840s, Charles Goodyear, for example, developed the vulcanization of natural rubber and started the rubber industry, a product that has become a major component of modern life. Alexander Bell may have been born in Scotland but he immigrated to the United States where he invented the telephone in 1876 and established Bell Telephone Company. Bell demonstrated the telephone to Queen Victoria in January 1878 and established premises in London to distribute the device.[16] Thomas Edison made important technological innovations in motion pictures and the phonograph record player. The Wright Brothers, Wilbur and Orville, invented the first powered airplane in 1903, Eugene Polley invented the first wireless TV remote control in the mid-1950s and Gregory Pincus developed the first contraceptive pill launched in Britain in 1961. America gave Britain and the world other important inventions such as aerosols, safety razors and tea bags. The expression "the best thing since sliced bread" would not have been possible without the bread-slicing machine invented in the 1920s by Otto Rohwedder, a jewelry store owner from Iowa.[17]

British children in particular had much to thank the United States for. After President Theodore, or Teddy, Roosevelt refused to shoot a bear on a hunting trip in 1902, an American company started to produce stuffed toy bears calling them "Teddy's Bears" to honor the president's action. The toys became a success and Ideal Novelty and Toy Company began to produce the Teddy Bear in the United States and abroad. Teddy Bears became the bed-time companion for children throughout Britain and a ubiquitous presence in children's stories. A. A. Milne bought his son, Christopher Robin Milne, a Teddy Bear from Harrods in London in 1921 and was thus inspired to write Winnie-the-Pooh. The comic strip character Rupert the Bear made its debut in the 1920s, and Sooty and Paddington Bear made theirs in the 1950s.[18] Monopoly, a board game originating in the United States in the interwar period, began to be produced in Britain by Waddington's with London place names replacing the original New York ones. The word game Scrabble was introduced into Britain from the United States in the 1950s as were Yo-Yos and Hula Hoops.[19]

Washington's support for free trade, expensive and innovative advertising and the American genius for invention would not have led to the successful import of American culture into Britain without the unprecedented affluence of the 1950s, which provided a market for American products in Britain. By July 1957, only 1.2 percent of the British workforce was unemployed. Material wealth seemed to be improving for most members of society as real incomes rose by 20 percent between 1951 and 1961. Household income increased as more women too started earning. In 1931, only 10 percent of married women were in the workforce; by 1951 the figure had risen to 21.7 percent and by 1961 to 29.4 percent.[20] In 1958, the government abolished hire purchase restrictions. This meant that a buyer who could not afford to purchase a product could now pay a percentage of the price as a deposit and pay off the rest in monthly installments. In 1950, there were 2,307,000 cars and vans on the road in Britain; this figure doubled to 5,650,000 in 1960. Only 4.3 percent of the population owned a television in 1950, but this had risen to 39.8 percent in 1955 and to 81.8 percent in 1960.[21] In 1942, 3.6 percent of families owned washing machines, and in 1958 the number jumped to 29 percent.[22] *Which?* magazine began publication in 1957 to help consumers choose from the vast array of enticing goods on offer. The Ideal Home Exhibition, established in 1908 to display new home inventions and designs, enjoyed a record attendance of 1.5 million visitors in 1957. In July 1957, Conservative Prime Minister Harold Macmillan told an audience that "most of our people have never had it so good. Go around the country, go to the industrial towns, go to the farms and you will see a state of prosperity such as we have never had in my lifetime—nor indeed in the history of this country." Most believed he was right.[23]

American goods poured into Britain but American production methods also changed how British goods were made. Henry Ford developed the concept of mass production in the early years of the twentieth century, which revolutionized the way goods were produced in every nation in the world including Britain. Ford, born in Michigan in 1863, became an engineer, designed cars and established the Ford Motor Company. Ford employed unskilled workers to perform specialist tasks along a moving conveyor belt in his car assembly plant in Detroit. He may not have invented the assembly line but the Ford Company perfected the concept, lowering manufacturing costs and prices. Ford's "implementation of the moving assembly line" in 1913 "made 'Fordism' the most imitated concept in businesses around the world," argued historian Douglas Brinkley.

> With the implementation of mass-production methods, including the moving assembly line on the eve of World War I, Henry Ford and his associates set in motion a second industrial revolution. Additionally, it was Ford's opinion—that the *work* should move while the worker stood still—that forever changed the way things are made, and even the way people think.[24]

Ford opened its first assembly plant in Britain in Manchester in 1911 and built the largest automobile factory outside the United States in Dagenham, London, in 1931. British government and company representatives journeyed across the Atlantic to learn from the manufacturing successes of the assembly line. On their return home, they encouraged British companies to adopt mass-production techniques. The ubiquitous nature of Ford's assembly line in Britain was evident in the pessimistic vision of the future created by English writer Aldous Huxley in his 1932 novel, *Brave New World*. The calendar in the story is dated in years "After Ford" (A.F.), instead of exclaiming "Oh my Lord," the characters cry "Oh my Ford," London's Big Ben is renamed "Big Henry" and people gain wisdom from Ford's autobiography *My Life and Work* (1922), which is treated as holy writ.[25]

Frederick Winslow Taylor may not be as famous as Henry Ford, but as the innovator of scientific management he was equally important in influencing industrial production in Britain. Taylor, born in Pennsylvania on March 20, 1856, worked as an engineer at a steel mill where he sought to improve worker productivity. Taylor, like Ford, detested labor unions and wanted management to gain complete control over workers and the work process while work became more routinized. He studied and timed workers as they performed a task and devised ways to remove unnecessary motions from the work routine. Taylor then taught other workers to follow the machinelike process and to become more efficient. He died on March 21, 1915, but Taylor's ideas had by then begun to travel across the Atlantic. Some British industrialists visited the East coast and Midwest to study the ideas of Taylor. American management consultancy firms headed to Britain to spread the concept of scientific management. Companies like Campbell's Soups, Kodak, General Electric and J. Lyons and Co. adopted Taylor's ideas as they became established industrial practice in the interwar years.[26]

The United States not only dramatically altered how goods were produced but how they were sold as well. More than anyone else, Harry Gordon Selfridge helped American retail methods take root in Britain and in the process helped turn shopping into an enjoyable leisure experience. British shopkeepers paid little attention to retailing techniques in the early years of the twentieth century. Shops hid goods in glass cabinets only to be handled by surly staff. "When you go into a shop they treat you indifferently," Scottish-American industrialist Andrew Carnegie noted when he visited London in 1900. "You are scowled at if you ask for goods out of the ordinary, and you are made to feel uncomfortable if you do not buy. These shop people drive away more customers than they attract. What London needs is a good shaking up."[27] Selfridge, born in 1858 in Ripon, Wisconsin, was the man to shake it up. In 1879, he began to work for Field, Leiter and Company (later it became Marshall Field and Company), a leading Chicago retailer. He worked his way up through the firm to become manager and then junior partner in the flagship department store in State Street Chicago, and then proprietor of the Schlesinger and Mayer store (later Carson Pirie Scott). Selfridge focused on extensive advertising and eye-catching shop window displays to entice people into the store. Once inside, Selfridge made shopping a pleasurable leisure activity rather than a laborious task. He displayed merchandise on island counters on a brightly lit open-plan sales floor so that customers could browse on their own without any intrusion from pushy sales staff. Selfridge made the store visually pleasing and opened a restaurant for customers.

After a visit to London in 1906, Selfridge decided that the city needed a store based on the Marshall Field model. He subsequently built the first great "Cathedral of Shopping" in Britain when he opened a department store on Oxford Street, London, in 1909. The store covered six acres of floor space with five upper floors and a basement and included a restaurant, a library, a hair dressing salon and a staff of nearly 2,000 people. Selfridges sold all manner of goods, pleasingly displayed for the customers to handle. Unsurprisingly, the store became one of the most visited in Oxford Street. A penchant for gambling, frivolous spending, much of it on his many mistresses, and poor business decisions led Selfridge to die in near-poverty in England in 1947 after having brought American-style retail methods to Britain.[28]

The opening of US-style self-service supermarkets in Britain in the early 1950s further transformed shopping habits and played a crucial role in the development of a modern consumer society. Britons traditionally shopped for food in specialized merchants such as bakers, butchers and fishmongers in which the staff handled the goods. Developments in the United States would change this. Clarence Saunders opened a self-service store in Memphis in 1916 and then a chain of them with the unlikely name of Piggly Wiggly across the United States[29] Retailers and government officials journeyed to the United States to see the self-service stores in action and industry journals carried glowing reports of their success. There were just ten self-service shops in Britain when Tesco became the first major British company to imitate the self-service stores of the United States when it launched its first in St. Albans in 1947. In 1956, there were over 3,000 self-service stores in the United Kingdom; by 1962 there were 12,000.[30] Sainsbury's became the leader in self-service supermarkets (a store with more than 2,000 square feet of selling space) after the managing director, Alan Sainsbury, visited the United States in 1949 as part of a Ministry of Food drive to promote improvements in food retailing methods. Sainsbury opened their first purpose-built self-service supermarket in Eastbourne in 1952. By 1959, there were 286 supermarkets in Britain, and in 1961 there were 572. Self-service supermarkets changed the look of the high street by undermining the profitability of specialized face-to-face neighborhood shops and by offering customers a range of products under one roof.[31]

In addition to self-service supermarkets, American food outlets began to leave their imprint on the British high street when Wimpy became the first American restaurant chain to travel across the Atlantic. In 1954, the first Wimpy Bar opened at a Lyons Corner House Restaurant in central London. J. Lyons and co licensed the brand from Eddie Gold, who was running 12 restaurants in Chicago. The name Wimpy was inspired by the burger eating Popeye cartoon character J. Wellington Wimpy. Originally, Wimpy operated a separate fast-food section within the Lyons Corner House Restaurants, but the success soon led to the opening of independent Wimpy restaurants. By 1969, the company had opened 460 outlets in Britain offering exotic American food and drink. "We thought the food in the Wimpy Bar was wonderful—burgers, cokes, milkshakes," claimed Ron Staples from Newport. "It was so different, it was what we didn't have at home."[32]

Convenience foods originating in the United States helped transform the British diet. Cornflakes arrived in Britain in 1924 when Kellogg's set up offices in London and opened its first British manufacturing plant in Manchester in 1938. Cornflakes and other cereals almost completely replaced traditional breakfast foods such as bread and porridge.[33] Canned pork and beans, first consumed in farming communities in the United States, were brought into Britain by Heinz in 1905 and in 1928 the company established their first factory in Harlesden. Combined with a tomato sauce and served on toast, baked beans became a staple in the United Kingdom.[34] Tomato ketchup, another American invention, became a permanent fixture on dinner tables across Britain. Spam, a canned meat derived from shoulder pork ham made by the Hormel Foods Corporation, was first introduced into Britain during World War II to feed Allied troops, and became a favorite luncheon meat in postwar Britain.

Another American, Clarence Birdseye, had a lasting impact on the eating habits of the British because of his innovations in the frozen food industry. Birdseye was born in New York in December 1886. After college, he entered the fur trade business and while in Canada he was intrigued to see that the Eskimos were able to maintain a fresh food supply by quickly freezing food in the depth of the cold Arctic winter. He concluded that rapid freezing in extremely cold temperatures, a process called "flash freezing," could be used to preserve the taste and appearance of the food for months. Birdseye returned to the United States and in the early 1920s he invested in a frozen food plant where he froze vegetables and fish. Thanks to Birdseye, every imaginable type of fruit, vegetable, meat and fish was now preserved and available all the year round. None became as popular as fish fingers introduced into Britain by Birds Eye in 1955. In its first year, 600 tons of fish fingers were sold in Britain. Clarence Birdseye died in 1956 but he lived on as white bearded sailor Captain Birds Eye who first appeared on packaging and in television commercials for fish fingers in 1967. A poll undertaken in 1993 found Captain Birds Eye to be the most recognized captain in Britain after Captain James Cook.[35]

A further important American influence was in the area of architecture and design which changed the look of the British urban landscape. New York-style hotels and apartments were built in the West End of London to accommodate wealthy Americans such as William Waldorf Astor, Emerald Cunard, Consuelo Vanderbilt and Wallis Simpson who became major figures in London high society between the wars.[36] Selfridge's London store, designed by Chicago architect Daniel Burnham, became a model for commercial buildings throughout Britain when it opened in 1909.[37] Office buildings built in central London in the 1950s and 1960s with the large glass windows and concrete box shapes were partly inspired by American modern architectural designs.[38] In the postwar years, Bowling alleys, an import from the States, appeared in every British city. The first American-style launderette opened in Britain in 1949. By 1970 there were 7,000 in the country.[39] Parking meters, invented by Carlton Magee in 1935 and initially used in his home town of Oklahoma City, first came into use in Mayfair, London, in July 1958.[40] The first Milk Bar, styled to look like American drug stores, opened in London in 1935 and by 1938 there were more than a thousand in the country. Milk bars, which sold milk drinks to customers sitting on stools at a bar, vied with traditional snack bars and coffee bars for the business of young people in the postwar years.[41] Many of the counter tops and tables in these bars were made from Formica, an easily cleaned material invented by Daniel O'Connor and Herbert Faber in the United States in 1913. The first stated British factory producing Formica opened in 1951, and Formica became a fixture of surfaces in eating establishments and in household kitchens across the land.[42]

The United States changed British art as New York City became the center of the art world after World War II. Abstract expressionism, the controversial postwar American art movement made famous by Jackson Pollock, Mark Rothko and Willem de Kooning, was particularly innovative and controversial. The London Institute of Contemporary Art showed Pollock's work for the first time in London in 1953. In 1956, *Modern Art in the United States* and, in 1959, *The New American Painting* exhibits, both from the Museum of Modern Art in New York, visited the Tate Gallery in London and introduced a whole range of abstract art to a British audience. British painters like Rodrigo Moynihan, Patrick Heron and Alan Davie incorporated abstract ideas into their work.[43] "Young students had realized that American painting was more interesting than French painting," stated British artist David Hockney, first exposed to the work of Jackson Pollock at the Whitechapel Gallery in London in December 1958. "American abstract expressionism was the great influence. So I tried my hand at it."[44] A newer generation of American artists often described as both abstract and pop artists such as Jasper Johns and Robert Rauschenberg further influenced British artists. "In Britain, a weak, indigenous Fine Art tradition was effectively swamped," British art critic Peter Fuller lamented.[45]

For those interested in the written word, the United States provided a wealth of exciting literature. American Marvel and DC comics entertained British children with their color and their superheroes. Stories of the Wild West appeared in boy's comics while the *Buffalo Bill Wild West Annuals*, which began publication in 1948, sold more than 300,000 copies per annum by the mid-1950s.[46] Detective stories written by US writers like Dashiell Hammett and Raymond Chandler and Western novels by Louis L'Amour and Zane Grey provided exciting stories of individuals fighting heroically against authority. American authors like Edgar Allan Poe, William Faulkner, Eugene O'Neill, Sinclair Lewis, Herman Melville, Mark Twain, Scott Fitzgerald, John Steinbeck, Henry James, T. S. Eliot and Ernest Hemingway found a substantial audience in Britain because of their exotic settings and intriguing characters. The writing seemed fresh as the authors used concise, clear descriptions rather than the overly long and elaborate prose found in British novels. The J. D. Salinger's "*The Catcher in the Rye* was in a different league," English poet and author John Lucas, a student at Reading University in the late 1950s, believed. "No novel, before or since, has had such a strong or lasting impact on a whole generation of readers as Salinger's did on the generation which came of age in the 1950s." The main character Holden Caulfield, who railed against conformity and the "phonies" in his life, "provided a useful word to point at those telling the young to grow up, love the bomb, and settle for a life of placid, unadventurous normality."[47]

The so-called Angry Young Men literature of the 1950s, which enunciated a growing discontent with the British class structure, betrayed a variety of American literary influences. John Osborne's ground-breaking play *Look Back in Anger*, which opened at the Royal Court Theatre in London in May 1956, was influenced by the plain-talking style of Tennessee Williams. Arthur Miller's *Death of a Salesman* and *Crucible* played in London in the 1950s inspiring a generation of British playwrights to focus on social issues.[48] Kingsley Amis' *Lucky Jim* (1954), John Braine's *Room at the Top* (1957) and Alan Sillitoe's *Saturday Night and Sunday Morning* (1958) and *The Loneliness of the Long Distance Runner* (1959) all used characters and dialogue reminiscent of American detective novels and Hollywood movies to describe men trapped because of their working-class background. The authors of these plays and books found the language and characterization in American culture that they wanted to use to express anger against British snobbery, class inequality and conventional morality.[49]

Jazz music, which originated at the beginning of the twentieth century in the black communities of the southern United States and particularly in New Orleans, became an integral part of British popular music. A mix of African and European music traditions, jazz merged blues music with the sounds of marching bands to create a uniquely American music. Jazz was an intricate and sophisticated sound but one that emphasized improvisation and was looser and freer than the more rigid European classical music. Jazz reached Britain in 1919 when the Original Dixieland Jass Band played the Hippodrome in London and the Southern Syncopated Orchestra performed at London's Philharmonic Hall. Other performers visited the country after World War I to play in hotels and clubs and soon ignited British imitators. Subsequently, "sweet" jazz, played mostly by white British big bands or orchestras, began to dominate dance halls and the radio airwaves. Singers who often fronted the bands and bandleaders, such as Billy Cotton, Victor Silvester, Joe Loss and Ted Heath, became major stars. "Hot" jazz, less commercial music played mainly by African-Americans, was only heard on imported recordings. In the 1940s, American GIs brought swing music to Britain, which, with its frenzied rhythms, made stars of Benny Goodman, Artie Shaw and Glenn Miller.[50]

From the 1920s to the end of World War II, jazz music was principally a medium of dance. Hotels were initially the center of jazz dancing, but the Hammersmith Palais de Danse, which opened in 1919, became the first of a whole host of new luxurious dance halls built in every major town in the interwar period to meet the growing demand for dance venues. Many people went dancing two or three times a week in hotels and the palais de danse, but also in club halls throughout the land. "For everyman that danced two years ago, eight or nine dance now," claimed the *Daily Mail* in February 1922. British dance bands played cover versions of original American ragtime music and dance-goers enthusiastically adopted new dances from the United States. The Charleston in the 1920s and then the Jitterbug during the World War II swept through the dance halls of Britain. Jazz dancing revolutionized popular dance in Britain by emphasizing animated and individually expressive body movements rather than the restrained and restricted forms of traditional dancing. Soon British dancers adapted and transformed these wilder dances to suit the more sedate sounds of the big bands.[51]

The luxurious elegance of the palais de danse added to the enjoyment of the music and dancing. After depositing their coats in the cloak room, the customers entered a large elegant hall with soft inviting sofas that edged the dance floor. The dancers held each other close as the music floated down from the orchestra dressed in neat uniform suits playing a variety of brass instruments on a raised stage. The spacious balcony above held spectators overlooking the dancers below who moved slowly across the spacious floor. "The large mirrored sphere rotated gently above us, sending hundreds of sparkling slivers of silver light cascading over the walls and floor like glittering sequins," recalled Maureen Reynolds, a regular visitor to the Palais in Dundee. "With the tuneful strains of the band wafting over us, the effect was magical. It was like dancing in the middle of the universe, surrounded by exploding stars. For me, the Palais was love at first sight and I was determined to visit this wonderful place again."[52] As big band jazz declined in popularity after World War II, the age of the palais-de-danse became a distant memory.

In the postwar years, jazz bifurcated into bebop and traditional, or trad jazz, both of which favored smaller groups of musicians rather than big orchestras. Bebop, exemplified by Charlie Parker and Dizzy Gillespie, laid the ground for the modern jazz of Miles Davis and Thelonious Monk. The music was complicated, noncommercial and designed for serious listeners who tapped their feet to the music but refused to dance. John Dankworth and Ronnie Scott pioneered bebop music in Britain while Ken Colyer, who spent some time in New Orleans, returned to the United Kingdom in the early 1950s becoming a pioneer in the trad jazz revival. Colyer, along with Humphrey Lyttelton and George Melly, took their influence from the Dixieland jazz of the first decades of the twentieth century to produce a more energetic sound that encouraged dancing. In London clubs, pubs and dance halls, enthusiasts danced wildly, seeking to recreate the excitement of 1920s' America as an escape from the austerity and constraints of 1950s' Britain.[53] Young people from the local offices and shops descended on the London Jazz Club in Oxford Street to dance with abandon. "Many had got bored with the polite shuffling that passes for dancing at the palais, drifted into the Jazz Club one night, stayed to become regulars . . . to dance with dangerous vigour," the *Picture Post* reported.[54] Bebop and modern jazz remained a minority interest, but trad jazz became all the rage in the 1950s and early 1960s as some stars like Acker Bilk, Kenny Ball and Chris Barber entered the British charts.

In the early 1950s, America continued to dominate British popular music. Between November 1952, when the *New Musical Express* published the first record chart in the United Kingdom, and December 1959, there were 94 number ones in Britain, of which 62 percent came from the United States.[55] The songs of Bing Crosby, Frank Sinatra, Perry Como, Nat King Cole, Frankie Laine, Fats Waller, Ella Fitzgerald and Peggy Lee became staples of family sing-alongs in the 1950s. To chart in the 1950s, new British acts had to cover American songs. English singer Jimmy Young, for example, enjoyed hits with covers of Nat King Cole's "Too Young" (1951) and Perry Como's "More" (1956) while Marion Ryan made a career out of covering American songs including Perry Como's "Hot Diggity" (1956) and Peggy Lee's "Mr Wonderful" (1957). Irving Berlin, Cole Porter and the songwriting duo Richard Rodgers and Oscar Hammerstein dominated the London stage as they wrote some of the most successful musicals of the postwar years. The youthful exuberance of *Oklahoma!* and *Annie Get Your Gun,* which combined engrossing stories, memorable songs, elaborate scenery and costumes and spectacular dancing, contrasted sharply with the drab modest fair that appeared on the British stage. *Carousel, Guys and Dolls, Kiss Me Kate, Paint Your Wagon, South Pacific* and *The King and I* became popular in the early 1950s, carrying on the American domination of the British stage.[56]

American country and western music began to gain a large following in Britain in the 1950s. Western films and hit musicals ignited an interest in American square dancing in the early 1950s. Local halls held barn dances or "hoedowns" with music provided by an accordionist and a caller instructing the dances to "take your partner," "take hands," and "link arms."[57] "Many of our readers are becoming devotees of square dancing, which is such good fun," *Woman's Weekly* noted in January 1952.[58] Clothing companies responded to the boom by producing plaid shirts, which allowed men to "enjoy simple yet vigorous fun as square dancing," and by selling women's cotton blouses, full skirts and shoes called "Square Dancers" to capture the "mood of square dancing," the company suggested.[59] American Forces Network radio broadcast country and western songs to an eager audience in Britain. Liverpool, in particular, enjoyed a strong interest in the music gaining the name "the Nashville of the North." US servicemen and British seamen on Atlantic merchant ships nicknamed "Cunard Yanks," brought country and western records from the United States into the port of Liverpool. More importantly, the huge Burtonwood American Air Base at nearby Warrington became an outlet for live shows of US country musicians and a source for American country records. The large Irish population in Liverpool was especially receptive to a music that had its roots in traditional Celtic music. A number of local bands formed playing Jimmie Rodgers and Hank Williams songs and the country influence found its way into the emerging Merseybeat bands.[60] "A lot of the merchant seaman did bring records back" from America, Billy Hatton of the Liverpool band the Fourmost recalls. "They were mainly country and western records, but they got people interested in American music. Liverpool record stores started ordering in music from the States, and a lot of Liverpool people got into rock 'n' roll through country stuff." Carl Perkins, who bridged the divide between country and western and rock 'n' roll became enormously popular. "In Liverpool Carl Perkins was more important than Elvis," Hatton concluded.[61]

Skiffle, a term originated in 1920s' America to refer to impromptu music making, became all the rage in 1950s' Britain. Skiffle bands adopted the songs of American blues and folk artists like Leadbelly and Woody Guthrie. Musicians played acoustic guitars or banjos with rhythmic accompaniment provided by homemade instruments, such as a washboard played with thimbles and an upright bass made from a tea chest and a broom handle. Skiffle was popularized by Glasgow-born Anthony Donegan who took the name Lonnie from blues musician Lonnie Johnson and went on to have a huge hit with Leadbelly's "Rock Island Line" in 1956. Needing only a single acoustic guitar and someone who could keep a basic rhythm on the washboard or other improvised instrument, this simple style was accessible and affordable to cash-strapped young Britons unable to afford expensive musical instruments. Subsequently, thousands of groups formed around the country and performed in coffee houses, youth clubs, halls and church fetes. Skiffle music became so popular that the British Broadcasting Corporation (BBC) broadcast the *Saturday Skiffle Club* on the Light Programme radio station from June 1957. The skiffle craze soon petered out but it introduced many Britons to American folk and blues music and gave some future stars of British rock their first experience in a band.[62]

Skiffle was quickly surpassed in the British affections by the new sound of rock 'n' roll. Rock 'n' roll derived from African-American rhythm and blues music and began to cross over to an enthusiastic young white audience in the mid-1950s. The British press warned that in the United States the music inspired "riots, rape and alcoholism among the youngsters. Mayors have banned 'rock' concerts in several towns. Many disc jockeys won't play it any more."[63] Journalist Patrick Doncaster in the *Daily Mirror* helped to settle nerves by insisting that rock 'n' roll would not catch on in Britain. "I think we have little need for fear about rock 'n' roll troubles here. Teenagers do not compare with America's. American newspapers regularly report teenagers fighting, slaying, getting drunk without the aid of music of any kind. Rock 'n' roll is just another excuse."[64] The music was introduced into Britain by a rather overweight 30-year-old white man with a kiss-curl, Bill Haley, and his band, the Comets. In December 1954, Haley's "Shake Rattle and Roll" entered the British charts at number 13. In 1955, Haley's "Rock Around the Clock," heard on the opening credits of the movie, *The Blackboard Jungle,* remained on the British charts for 19 weeks and for a further 11 weeks the following year. Two more films featuring the music of Bill Haley were hits in Britain, *Rock Around the Clock* in 1956 and *Don't Knock the Rock* in 1957.[65] Haley was not the first American rock 'n' roll act to tour Britain, that distinction belonged to Pat Boone who played his sanitized versions of hits to British audiences in December 1956, but when Haley arrived in February 1957 his visit generated huge excitement with crowds and the media following his every step.[66]

Rock 'n' roll music appealed to teenagers because of its raucous sound and defiant attitude. The young could relate to the lyrics that dealt with the everyday lives and problems of adolescents and the not-so-subtle sexual innuendo. Many rock 'n' roll lyrics were simple, incomprehensible, or plain gibberish but the words were less important than the music and the attitude of the performers, which delighted the young. Teenagers loved the simple riffs and chugging rhythms of the music that exuded aggression, energy and defiance. Rock 'n' roll stars had attitude, epitomized by the swagger, bravado, sexually suggestive dancing and raucous antics of Little Richard and Jerry Lee Lewis. While the big bands and popular balladeers of the decade were staid and restrained, rock 'n' roll was full of raw power and its amplified electric guitars and exhilarating rhythms touched people on an emotional level. In turn, rock 'n' roll was condemned by adults because it seemed to solicit a frenzied and sometimes violent response in British teenagers. Bill Haley's "Rock Around the Clock" was used on the opening credits of *The Blackboard Jungle*, a film about juvenile delinquency. On top of this, members of the audience caused disturbances at the showing of *Blackboard Jungle* in 1956, gaining sensational press coverage. Rock 'n' roll and teenage delinquency became joined in the public mind.[67]

Bill Haley may have blazed the trail but Elvis Presley captured the imagination of the British public like no other rock 'n' roll artist. Presley, born in East Tupelo, Mississippi, on January 8, 1935, moved with his poverty-stricken family to Memphis, Tennessee, when he was 13 years old. At the crossroads of American music, Elvis absorbed the sounds of gospel music in the Church and country and western and rhythm and blues music on the radio and in the local clubs. In 1953, 18-year-old Elvis entered Sam Phillips' Sun Studios to make a sample recording. Phillips spotted his unique talent and asked Presley to record "That's All Right (Mama)," which was released as his first single in 1954. In May, 1956, his debut single in the United Kingdom "Heartbreak Hotel" entered the charts and in the summer of 1957, Presley reached number one in Britain with "All Shook Up." Backed by a driving rhythm, his raucous, sensual voice morphed into howling and yelling. John Peel, later a radio DJ, first heard Presley's "Heartbreak Hotel" on BBC radio's *Two-Way Family Favorites* as a teenager. "Heartbreak Hotel," he said,

> had the effect on me of a naked extraterrestrial walking through the door and announcing that he/she was going to live with me for the rest of my life . . . .There was something frightening, something lewd, something seriously out of control about "Heartbreak Hotel," and alarmed though I was by Elvis, I knew I wanted more.[68]

Once they saw magazine photos of the exotically named star, Britons noticed that Presley had great film star looks and a flamboyant style of dress; wearing brightly colored shirts and suits, not the traditional dark suits and white shirts worn by most performers. Movie newsreels of Elvis revealed a wild stage show that included the overtly sexual swiveling of his hips. Bill Haley was rather overweight and slightly balding, but Elvis, ten years his junior, was younger and slender, with his top lip fixed in a permanent sneer, his hair long and greased back framed by long sideburns.[69]

As an added attraction, the older generation and the middle classes despised Elvis. Patrick Doncaster in the *Daily Mirror* suggested that his singing was "a gurgle of breathless spasms that could mean anything from choking to insanity. . . .I think this rhythm is about as musical as the flushing of a sewer."[70] "His lyrics were sub-literate, truculent aphrodisiacs helped out with rutting noises, animal grunts and groans," *Daily Mail* journalist Peter Lewis opined. "He manipulated his hips and guitar together into an explicit paraphrase of the sexual act."[71] And British youngsters loved him for that. They dressed like him, cut their hair like him, talked like him and hung pictures of him on every available space of their bedroom walls. [72]

Elvis Presley and rock 'n' roll inspired a whole generation of Britons to sing. Cliff Richard, Billy Fury, Adam Faith and Marty Wilde borrowed the look and sound of American rock 'n' roll stars, particularly Elvis, and sang in fake American accents. "I wanted to be like Elvis and I practiced hard," admitted Cliff Richard. "I played his records and sang along to them, curling my lip, thrusting my hips and combing my hair into a quiff like his."[73] Television pop shows like *Six-Five Special*, which began on the BBC in 1957 and *Oh Boy*, which debuted on Independent Television (ITV) the following year, showcased the rising British rock 'n' roll stars. Much of their output consisted of inferior cover versions of American rock 'n' roll hits but some British acts recorded bona fide classics. Cliff Richard's "Move It," Vince Taylor and His Playboys' "Brand New Cadillac," both of which charted in 1958, and Johnny Kidd and the Pirates 1960 hit "Shakin' All Over" became rock 'n' roll standards.

In the late 1950s, some youngsters gravitated to American blues music, as the stars of rock 'n' roll left the scene, once again leaving the pop music charts full of tepid music. Elvis Presley joined the Army, Chuck Berry and Jerry Lee Lewis found their careers waning because of personal problems and scandals, Little Richard abandoned rock 'n' roll to devote his life to religion, and Buddy Holly tragically died in a plane crash. Unimpressed with the bland music that now dominated the charts, some youngsters were drawn to blues music because of the emotional delivery and heartfelt honesty of the singing, the hypnotic rhythm of the music and the wailing of the harmonica. The skiffle boom introduced many to the music. Blues was then spread by a small group of specialist jazz record shops that began to stock blues records, by enthusiasts importing albums by mail-order from America and by disc jockeys on the American Forces Network. The visits of blues stars like Josh White, Lonnie Johnson, Big Bill Broonzy and Muddy Waters produced much excitement among the small but growing number of blues enthusiasts. To cash in on the growing demand, American labels specializing in black music such as Atlantic, Chess and Specialty licensed their music to Decca's London American, Stateside and Pye International labels in the United Kingdom. Blues enthusiasts Alexis Korner and Cyril Davies started the first blues club, the Blues and Barrelhouse Club, in a Soho, London, pub called the Roundhouse in the mid-1950s. The club hosted Alexis Korner's Breakdown Group, later renamed Alexis

Korner's Blues Incorporated, Britain's first blues band. At one time or another, the group was backed by future stars of British rock such as Ronnie Wood, Charlie Watts, Jack Bruce and Ginger Baker and teenage fans performed with the group, including Mick Jagger, Brian Jones, Keith Richards, Rod Stewart, John Mayall, Eric Clapton and Jimmy Page.[74]

Since the interwar period, Britons had enthusiastically adopted new dances from the United States but no dance penetrated the mainstream and revolutionized the way Britons danced like the Twist. Chubby Checker's "Let's Twist Again" entered the British charts in December 1961 staying for 77 weeks and peaking at number two. Checker visited the country appearing on television shows with accompanying female dancers. The women, who danced alone swiveling their hips from side to side, caused a sensation setting off the Twist dance craze. The Twist was not universally welcomed, as a 14-year-old schoolboy, Jeff Dexter, found out when he attempted the Twist in the Lyceum ballroom in London.

> In with the record was a picture of the foot movements and how you were supposed to do it. So I followed the instructions, did the Twist and got barred from the Lyceum for being obscene. Everybody was still jiving at the time. To dance apart, bend over backwards, twist your bum around—that was just an outrage in a Mecca ballroom.[75]

The Twist may not have been the first dance where couples danced independently, but it was the one that became the most influential and set a trend that helped to end the practice of twirling couples holding hands and of the male dancer leading and the female following. Youngsters danced separately, in groups, or as couples with eyes closely following the sexy movements of their partner's body. The Twist especially liberated women who no longer needed to wait for a partner to ask her to dance but could join with other girls in a group.[76]

If American music became a major form of entertainment in Britain, so too did the concept of moving pictures, which first came to Britain in the 1890s. In the immediate postwar years, Britons became obsessed with movies. Annual cinema admissions rose from 903 million in 1934, to 1,027 million in 1940 and to a peak of 1,635 million in 1946. Many people attended twice or more a week. Cinema attendances in Britain in 1952 were five times as large as for theatre, football, cricket and racing combined. There were 3,000 cinemas in Britain in 1926 rising to just fewer than 5,000 in 1938. Hollywood dominated British theatres. In 1925, 95 percent of films shown in Britain were American and the early 1960s some three-quarters still originated in the United States.[77] Big-budget Hollywood films were technically brilliant and featured characters and values the audience could identify with. American films simply looked good with huge luxuriously furnished houses, big cars, exotic and modern-looking skyscrapers, expansive freeways, and healthy and extremely good-looking men, women and children. Technicolor displayed in Hollywood films, which was a new innovation in the 1950s, was such a contrast with the drabness of everyday life and with the black-and-white of British television, newspapers and films. The spectacle and driving plots provided an escape from the staid realities of life. "My friend Jill and I used to go to the cinema every Monday," recalled one woman.

> Films always used to lift our spirits. I remember in 1956, at the time of Suez, we were so depressed—we thought it was going to be another full-time war. But we went to see *Guys and Dolls* at the Empire, Leicester Square, and thoroughly enjoyed it. When we came out the crisis was over, and I've always felt kindly towards that film.[78]

People's fascination with American movies often started as children in Saturday morning pictures. All the major movie theatres launched Saturday morning cinema clubs for children, with the Odeon Children's Cinema Club and the ABC Minors Club being the two most successful. The clubs showed cartoons, a vintage comedy short, an episode of a serial like *Flash Gordon*, *Lassie*, *Zorro*, *Roy Rogers*, or *The Lone Ranger*, and a feature film, usually an adventure or Western film from the United States. The Walt Disney cartoons, which became popular in the interwar period and continued after the war, introduced Britain to Mickey Mouse and Donald Duck. A compere often encouraged children to scream and shout, boo and hiss, all the way through the shows. In the early 1960s, some 300,000 children attended Saturday morning pictures every week in the United Kingdom.[79]

It was not just what was on the screen that enticed people off the street; it was the pleasurable experience found in the movie theatre itself. Some cinemas were local "flea pits," but many were "picture palaces" that supplied a luxurious experience for cinema goers, far warmer and more comfortable than the homes they lived in. The Astoria Theatre in Finsbury Park, North London, exemplified the dream palace experience. Built in 1930, the plain exterior could not prepare the cinema goer for the opulence of the interior. A customer stepped into an Art Deco style circular foyer with a cafe and a spectacular goldfish-filled fountain in a star-shaped pool. Customers paid their money to the uniformed cashier, gave their ticket to an attendant and walked down a corridor entering a carpeted auditorium. Cinema goers were guided to their plush seat by usherettes armed with torches in the darkness and catered to by women who walked down the aisle of the cinema with trays hung with a ribbon around their necks selling chocolate and ice cream. Here people could sit back in their comfortable seats, luxuriate in the warmth and view the opulence surrounding them. Audiences were seated in a mock Mediterranean courtyard with Spanish-style balconies and twinkling stars and passing clouds in the black ceiling above them. The stage, spanned by a huge decorous arch, was equipped with a Wurlitzer organ that supplied musical interludes. Once the red satin curtain drew back and the lights went down, a beam of light from the projection room at the back of the theater cut through the cigarette smoke of a crowded cinema and opened onto a huge screen at the front. In communion with the other 3,000 attendees, and yet in the privacy of the darkness, families with children, couples and groups of young friends could forget about the worries of home, work or school, as they watched stars literally bigger than life on the screen.[80]

Britons did not just watch American movie stars on the silver screen, they also imitated their make-up, clothes and hair. Women avidly read magazines to keep up with the latest fashions of the Hollywood stars. In the 1920s, cosmetics such as mascara, rouge and lipstick made by American companies Max Factor, Elizabeth Arden and Helena Rubinstein spread to the United Kingdom courtesy of movie stars. Suntans, once considered the unfortunate outcome of manual labor, now reflected Hollywood glamour and led to the popularity of sun lotions and sunglasses.[81] One study of teenage girls undertaken in 1953 found "the amazing extent to which the minutiae of the cloths and hair arrangements of an American actress may affect the spending habits of a child in a mining village in Durham or a girl in a tenement in central London."[82] One woman remembered: "You got girls that imitated Dorothy Lamour, Hedy Lamarr, Rita Hayworth. Ginger Rogers was a favorite of most girls and she made a film about a girl with a sweater, I don't know the title, but you know all the girls afterwards started wearing sweaters, it was amazing."[83]

As they reached puberty, Britons found new Hollywood stars to idolize, and few could resist the allure of Marilyn Monroe. Monroe, born Norma Jeane Mortenson in California in June 1926, was idolized by both men and women. With her striking blond hair, full red lips and curvaceous body, men lusted after her while women, who often lived a life of dull domesticity, envied her glamour and open sexuality that seemed out of step with the conservative 1950s. Monroe had comedic qualities but she also played tragic characters that gained the audience's sympathy. She displayed a vulnerability that the audience identified with as she continually met men who wanted to control or use her but Monroe exhibited an exuberance and vibrancy that suggested she would persevere. Monroe imitators abounded, including Diana Dors who became known as "the English Marilyn Monroe" but no British female actress exhibited the same star quality and joy to live as the 1950s' icon.[84]

Young men also modeled their appearance and behavior on American stars. Wally Whyton remembered as a young man in the late 1940s and early 1950s wandering the cloths shops in the West End of London looking for American-style cloths because "everyone wanted to look like a Yank."[85] British gangsters tried to dress and act like mobsters they saw in Hollywood films, adopting American words including ok, yeah and hi. "They got their dress sense from watching movies starring James Cagney and Humphrey Bogart," remembers Colin MacFarlane in Glasgow who compared the movie icons to local football legends.

> They copied the patter, the body language, the gaze, the threatening tones and the humour of their Hollywood heroes. Some of the Glasgow heavies had even visited New York and come back speaking in pseudo-American accents. To Celtic supporters, Jock Stein was the hero; to Rangers fans, it was John Greig; to Glasgow's gangsters, it was Al Capone.[86]

The Hollywood image spread its appeal beyond gangsters. In 1946, Cecil Gee, a men's cloths shop in London, launched an "American Look," based on suits worn by film stars like Cary Grant and Clark Gable in the 1930s: pinstriped suits with broad-shouldered, double-breasted, wide-lapel jackets. Cecil Gee imported shirts with long pointed collars from the United States, hand-painted ties and wide-brimmed American hats. Soon, "there were queues all along his block, and halfway along the next."[87] The hand-painted ties seemed particularly fashionable. "Everybody has them, stockbrokers, clerks, teen-agers and the middle-aged," noted Cecil

Gee. "These ties are about the only way a man can put his personality across these drab days."[88]

Teddy Boys were the first of a number of postwar youth subcultures that took inspiration from the United States. The name "Teddy Boy" is derived from the Edwardian style of dress that had become fashionable amongst the affluent in some parts of London in the late 1940s. Working-class youth appropriated the long Edwardian coats with velvet collars to break free of the dowdiness and uniformity of postwar British life. Many added velvet collars and cuffs to the long drape jackets of the American zoot suits to look like the Edwardian coat. The long velvet trimmed jackets looked similar to the ones sported by Hollywood gunfighters and gamblers in a saloon and working-class youths started to mimic this look. They wore shoelace ties with a fancy ornament pulled up to the neck and long sideburns made famous by Wild West heroes like Wyatt Earp and Wild Bill Hickok. Teddy Boys dressed in trousers so tight they were referred to as drainpipes, brocade waistcoats and suede shoes with thick rubber soles first worn by British soldiers in North Africa, known as "brothel creepers" because of the activities of some of those who wore them. Hairstyles were influenced by American film stars like Tony Curtis whose hair was swept back with Vaseline or Brylcreem to form a quiff at the front and swept around the ears to form a duck-like tail at the back, usually referred to as a DA (Duck's Arse).[89]

Teddy Girls, much fewer in number than Teddy Boys, adapted the look of Teddy Boys to create their own unique style. They wore waist coats, tailored jackets with velvet collars, hats and high-necked blouses with turn-down collars to which they added neckbands and cameo brooches; the look rounded off with back-combed hair. Trousers were not a common sight on women in the 1950s but some wore rolled-up jeans or toreador pants while others wore pencil skirts.[90] Tricia Dempsey from Lambeth, London, recalled the cloths she wore:

> Teddy girl two-piece costume, it was a finger-tip drape, cut of the coat, and it cost me 13 guineas from Brixton market. It was a lot then. Took me six months to pay for it. And a flat beret. All the girls, all the Teddy girls, wore the berets with a great big hat pin with a pearl in it, and string pearls all tied up and that horrible pan-stick make up, thick brown and great big thick lips, cerise pink, you know? You think of it now. That sickly pink![91]

Sheila Francis remembers that living in a Welsh village she had less access to the clothes than youngsters living in major cities and that her fashion choice was frowned upon by her parents: "I managed to buy a black coat and trousers in a jumble sale, and my bootlace tie *was* a bootlace. Clothes were sneaked out, and you dressed in a secluded place near the bus stop."[92]

Fewer teenage girls adopted the subcultural look of the Teddy Boys but more embraced American College and high school fashions seen on teenagers in American movies. After seeing Natalie Wood in the film *Rebel without a Cause*, Liverpool-born Cilla Black "Americanised" herself "by wearing flat shoes, short white socks, a sticky-out skirt and pony tail, and a shirt and sweater borrowed from one of my brothers."[93] Others tended to wear tight-fitting cardigans, low-cut tops, silk neck scarves, calf-length wide-flared hoop skirts with layers of petticoats underneath and wide belts. Some sported American-style pump shoes and others wore tight trousers reaching to mid-calf. Young women adapted this look to suit individual tastes. In Dundee, rock 'n' roll fan Mae Stewart remembered how she used to go dancing wearing

> a blouse (preferably with a mandarin collar), a black straight wrap-over skirt, black stockings with filled-in black heels and a black seam... and the mandatory black bopper shoes. These were flat velvet pumps.... I even used to paint one eye with green eye shadow and one eye with purple eye shadow, and then put a strand of purple and green nylon hair through my hair and tie it all in a multi coloured ponytail.[94]

Janet Johnson, a teenager from Yorkshire, dressed up to go dancing on Saturday evenings at the Museum Hall in Selby. "Fine-knitted sweaters, often a button-through cardigan worn back-to-front, were fashionable," she remembered many years later. "Our skirts were full, with yards of pink frilly tulle beneath, and our waists were nipped in tightly with wide elastic belts. On our feet we wore short, white socks and flat, ballerina-style shoes made of velvet." In contrast to the boys who spent hours combing and preening their slick back hair, Janet was "happy with my maintenance-free ponytail."[95]

As the Teddy Boy look declined in the late 1950s, the love of America was replicated in another youth subculture, the Rockers. The affluence of the late 1950s and the growth of hire purchase led to a boom in the sale of British bikes like Norton, Vincent and Triumph. The roadside cafés, petrol stations and roadside stops became the meeting areas of young motorcycle enthusiasts. Originally called "Leather Boys," because of the leather jackets they wore, or "Ton-Up Boys," for their tendency to speed at up to 100 miles per hour, they eventually gained the name "Rockers" due to their allegiance to rock 'n' roll music. "Much of what the original Leatherboys held most dear was American," says author Johnny Stuart. They listened to rock 'n' roll music, especially Gene Vincent and Eddie Cochran when pop was replacing rock 'n' roll music in the charts. Rockers were partly inspired by Marlon Brando in the 1953 film *The Wild One*, which focused on the motorcycle gangs of the United States.[96] Although *The Wild One* was banned from British screens for 15 years, the posters and photos of Marlon Brando in his leather jacket astride his motorcycle influenced many young British men. Rockers wanted an escapist thrill, a way to live out a fantasy of freedom and independence, while projecting a masculine and rebellious attitude. Rockers wore black leather or PVC jackets, denim jeans, leather boots, wide leather belts, a scarf tied tightly around the neck and mouth in the style sported by American cowboys and peak caps worn by Brando in *The Wild One* photos.[97]

Rocker girls were far fewer in number than boys. Many girls could not afford to buy the prohibitively expensive bikes while others did not like the dirt, the discomfort, or the danger associated with motorcycle culture. "The Rocker scene was very much a man's world—a world tailored to meet their requirements," wrote Rocker Johnny Stuart. "And while the girls screamed, it was blokes who provided the stuff that screams are made of. A few girls, it's true, were into bikes with the same passion as Ton-up Boys themselves. One or two of them even owned and rode their own machines." Unable to afford a bike, Rocker girls generally rode pillion. They wore leather jackets, tight skirts and plenty of lipstick and other makeup. Rocker girls wore bouffant hair and then moved to the Beehive, a woman's hairstyle that literally resembled a beehive, which originated in the United States in the 1950s, and became famous through the all-girl singing group, The Ronettes.[98]

As Hollywood's grip on the nation waned in the 1950s, it was replaced in the public imagination by television. The BBC began television broadcasts in November 1936 from their studio on top of Alexandra Palace in North London. Only 15,000 British households had televisions in 1947, but this rose to 1.4 million by 1952. The 1953 Coronation of Elizabeth II spurred a further growth in television ownership. By 1956, 5.7 households had televisions in the United Kingdom and by 1964 this figure had risen to 14.2 million. With the introduction of commercial television in Britain in 1955, American Westerns, comedies and crime series filled the television screens of Britain as broadcast companies found it more profitable to import American television programs rather than make their own. American TV programs were fast paced and kept the audience in suspense as they advanced the story over weekly episodes of the series. Home-grown versions of American shows such as *What's My Line* and *This Is Your Life* gained large audiences in Britain.[99]

Television Westerns were particularly admired in the 1950s. "When I was a lad, in England in the 1950s, life during the school holidays seemed to largely revolve around American Western shows on the television," Rupert Cornwell remembered.

> How avidly we watched them on the crackly old black-and-white sets of the day: *Gunsmoke*, *The Lone Ranger*, *Hopalong Cassidy*, with Cassidy in his black suit, *The Cisco Kid* and, closing out that blessed era, the first series of *Bonanza* and *Rawhide*, with the young Rowdy Yates in the last named played by an impossibly fresh-faced Clint Eastwood.

Cornwell, like many British children, adored the show *Davy Crockett*, starring Fess Parker, which appeared on the ITV channel, and the film *Davy Crockett, King of the Wild Frontier*, released in Britain in 1956. The filmmakers promoted the film in the United Kingdom by selling Crockett merchandise, especially the coonskin cap and buckskin clothes, which became the latest fad amongst schoolchildren. "The Parker/Crockett phenomenon was extraordinary," Cornwell remarked. "Every other child wanted a Crockett buckskin shirt, Crockett-style moccasins and a toy Crockett rifle. Most of all, they wanted a coonskin cap," remembered Cornwell. "The Ballad of Davy Crockett," the theme song of both the television show and the film, became a hit in the UK for Bill Hayes and Tennessee Ernie Ford. The tune "and its words, in those drab post-war years in England, made America sound the most exotic and heroic place on earth," Cornwell suggests.[100]

Children, brought up on a diet of Wild West films and television series, acted out their fantasies in their homes and in the streets. "Cowboy films were popular viewing on the new televisions that everyone had started to acquire, and us kids would charge out next day to re-enact an exciting episode of *Rawhide*, or *Wagon*

Train, right down to the last blood-curdling yell," remembered Jules Evans of her youth in 1950s' Hertfordshire. "Round and round we raced on imaginary horses; being shot time after time, but still heroically managing to gallop on until at last a painful death by Indian arrows, which we played out in full with loud groaning, and rolling around in pretended agonized glory."[101] Children sported cowboy outfits with cardboard hats, waistcoats, silver six-shooter cap-guns in double holsters strapped to their legs and long-barrel shotguns. John Walsh in London would sit on a chest of drawers in the spare room, "six-guns holstered around my waist, long ropes of reins tied around the mirror supports, my juvenile bottom posting up and down on the glass top, my weedy heels spurring the frisky walnut sides as I rode into Dodge City... or galloped away from hordes of yelping Cheyenne savages."[102] Julie Walters used the back of the sofa as a horse. "In my imagination I was the boy from *Champion the Wonder Horse*, trekking across the prairie and then sitting down to beans and coffee with the folks from *Wagon Train*."[103] Girls found their own female heroes in Annie Oakley and Calamity Jane. Carolyn Kay Steedman remembers "playing Annie Oakley by myself all summer long in the recreation ground, running up and down the hill in my brown gingham dress, wearing a cowboy hat and carrying a rifle. Saturday-morning pictures confirmed it all: women worked hard, earned their own living; carried guns into the bargain."[104]

America's contribution to British life was political as well as cultural as a number of American liberal intellectuals directly inspired the development of British social democracy in the postwar years. Adolf Berle's and Gardiner Means' *The Modern Corporation and Private Property*, published in 1932, and James Burnham's book *The Managerial Revolution*, published in 1941, had a huge impact on British social democracy. Both books argued that a separation of ownership and control had occurred in major corporations. The widening dispersal of share-holding, and the supposition that managers were not simply concerned with maximizing profit, held out the hope of a gentler and fairer form of capitalism. As government oversight of the economy and trade union bargaining could now limit the excesses of capitalism, there was no need for more public ownership. "The thesis of Burnham's Managerial Revolution seems to have been taken over by Labour spokesmen and Labour theoreticians, lock, stock and barrel," an American observer wrote in 1950.[105] Equally important to the development of social democracy was Harvard economist John Kenneth Galbraith's book *The Affluent Society*, published in 1958. "[Galbraith] had immense impact in persuading Labour people that the wastefulness and inhumanity of capitalism could better be removed, not by nationalization or state management but by egalitarian social policies to eliminate class divisions," wrote historian Kenneth Morgan.[106]

American intellectuals greatly shaped the work of Labour Party politician Anthony Crosland who wrote the highly influential *The Future of Socialism*, published in 1956. Crosland, who enjoyed an extended stay in the United States, admired the social equality and lack of a hereditary upper class he found there. He believed that the United States offered greater opportunities than did Britain, where birth and social class largely determined chances in life. Anthony Crosland's *The Future of Socialism* was influenced by Adolf Berle who convinced him that the severance of corporate ownership and management had transmuted the capitalist system. With the widespread ownership of property and rising affluence, Crosland believed that class preoccupations were diminishing in Britain and the Labour Party had to develop a classless appeal. Crosland and many others in the Labour Party thought that economist John Maynard Keynes's demand management would provide full employment, a progressive income tax would help to ensure greater equality and generous public spending would ensure economic security and freedom from want. He, and other reformers like Labour leader Hugh Gaitskell, helped to move the Party away from socialist rhetoric and calls for increased nationalization toward an acceptance of capitalism. Crosland believed that capitalism could be successfully managed to allow economic growth and that increased productivity would lead to improvements in the living standards of the poorer sections of society.[107]

The Limits of US Influence

Notwithstanding the changes that the United States brought to postwar Britain, the influence of the United States on Britain was hardly all-pervasive. British pubs prospered in every village and neighborhood. The corner shop and local greengrocers, butchers, bakers and fishmongers played a far greater role than American-style supermarket in the life of most Britons. In 1961, there were 572 supermarkets in Britain but still about 150,000 independent food retailers.[108] American foods may have been prevalent in Britain but so too were traditional British fair of fish and chips, steak and kidney pie, toad in the hole, bangers and mash, Sunday roast with Yorkshire pudding and spotted dick for desert. The number of British men and women who adopted American styles of clothing was small. British dress styles remained more formal than American ones, with more men wearing shirts and ties and women sporting skirts rather than trousers. While American production methods influenced some British employers, older industries of coalmining, shipbuilding, iron and steel and cotton remained largely unaffected by American innovations. Worker resistance to Taylorism and conservative management in Britain slowed the implementation of Taylorist methods. British craft workers maintained greater influence over the labor process than American employees.[109]

For all of the adulation bestowed on American entertainment stars in Britain, home-grown idols remained popular. American golfers, boxers, tennis players and Olympic athletes became famous in Britain, but the only US sports team that was popular in Britain was the Harlem Globetrotters, an exhibition basketball team that combined sport and comedy and who first played in London in 1951. Football, cricket and rugby remained the major participatory and spectator sports in Britain, not American football, baseball, or basketball. Radio, which was the most popular form of entertainment for all families for most of the 1950s, was dominated by British shows and personalities. Domestically produced television programs always enjoyed higher ratings than most US imports. Although Hollywood stars were admired and emulated in 1950s' Britain, so too were British movie actors. The thousands who voted in the annual *Picturegoer* polls in the 1950s, regularly voted Jack Hawkins, Alec Guinness, Kenneth Moore and Dirk

Bogarde as their favorite stars.[110] The top 12 box-office films in Britain in 1959 were all made in Britain.[111]

The leisure time of British people was still built around many traditional pastimes unaffected by American influence. In 1941, George Orwell wrote of an

> English characteristic which is so much a part of us that we barely notice it, and that is an addiction to hobbies and spare time occupations, the *privateness* of English life. We are a nation of flower-lovers but also a nation of stamp collectors, pigeon-fanciers, amateur carpenters, coupon-snippers, darts players, crossword-puzzle fans. All the culture that is most truly native centres round things which even when they are communal are not official—the pub, the football match, the back garden, the fireside and the "nice cup of tea."[112]

Children read British books like Kenneth Grahame's *The Wind in the Willows,* A. A. Milne's *Winnie the Pooh,* Richmal Crompton's *Just William,* J. M. Barrie's *Peter Pan,* Lewis Carroll's *Alice's Adventures in Wonderland* and the books of Beatrix Potter, Enid Blyton and C. S. Lewis. Some boys read Marvel comics but most still bought British ones like *Beano, Dandy, Eagle, Rover, Hotspur* and *Wizard* while girls read *Girl, Bunty* and *Judy.* War games between Germans and the British were just as popular as Cowboys and Indians. Children played traditional games like knock-down ginger, tag, hide and seek, hopscotch, marbles, conkers, football, cricket, skipping and traditional hand-clapping games. They played with toys produced by British companies. Frank Hornby, an English inventor, produced three of the most popular toys in twentieth-century Britain: Meccano, a model construction kit; Hornby Model Railways; and Dinky Toys, a collection of toy vehicles.[113]

Not only were Britons still enjoying traditional leisure activities, but they were also modifying much of the American culture they encountered. The British dance bands played music that was more sedate and romantic and less focused on improvisation than American-based jazz. "The leading dance bands hardly ever played what the minority critics and connoisseurs would have called jazz. They had created an almost entirely new musical form," jazz historian James Nott concluded. Stars like George Formby and Gracie Fields combined music hall and Lancashire folk with American songs and music.[114] Dancers eliminated the wilder elements from American dances like the Charleston, modifying them into what became known as "The English Style."[115] To remain successful in Britain, American advertising agencies had to adapt their style to domestic cultural traditions, sensibilities and humor. "American advertising tended to hit viewers over the head until they submitted," D. Richard Truman, a Canadian working in advertising in London, maintained. "British culture relied on dialogue and humorous verbal persuasion, with generous dollops of absurdity, the famed-double-entendre and self-deprecation. Humor and sexual tease were two of the most powerful ingredients for selling products in the UK, but not in the U.S."[116]

The United States was not the only foreign country to influence the customs and leisure pursuits of the British. Britain had a long history of immigration from Europe; in the postwar years a new influx of immigrants from Europe arrived in Britain. In 1951, 160,000 people in England and Wales were born in Poland and

33,000 in Italy. There were about 430,000 Jews in Britain, many fleeing continental Europe. In 1951, 627,000 people in England and Wales were born in Ireland and over the next ten year another 400,000 emigrated from the Irish Republic. European Jews, the Irish and the Polish turned Judaism and Catholicism into mass religions in Britain and played a role in all facets of British life.[117] British youths eschewed the quaint Lyons tea shops, which seemed so outdated, and spent much of their leisure time in the bustling, music-filled, Italian-owned coffee bars serviced by chrome-plated Gaggia espresso machines. In1960, there were 2,000 coffee bars in Britain with 500 in Greater London alone.[118] American words may have entered the British vocabulary but so did words like "nosh," a Yiddish word for food, and "mush," a Romany word for man, which many Londoners adopted.[119]

Greater affluence allowed many to travel across the English Channel to Continental Europe and to return with European tastes. Anthony Sampson in his book *Anatomy of Britain*, published in 1962, noted the influence of foreign holidays on Britain.

> Britain has come out of dowdy isolation and responded to gay foreign influences—Italian shoes, French fashions. . .and people are bringing back new tastes like wine drinking; wine sales in Britain have doubled since 1939. . . .Tastes in food are more adventurous, and foreign restaurants—Chinese, Italian, Indian, and even vegetarian—have proliferated over big towns, notably in the North. Spaghetti Bolognese has become a staple lunch-time food for thousands of secretaries.[120]

The cook books of Elizabeth David, including *Book of Mediterranean Food* first published in 1950, *French Country Cooking* in 1951, *Italian Food* in 1954 and *French Provincial Cooking* in 1960, brought the Mediterranean diet to Britain.[121] In the postwar years, France, not the United States, remained the center of the fashion industry. French fashion designer Christian Dior's New Look collection of dresses introduced in 1947 set the tone for the dress of British women for the next decade.[122] French actress Brigitte Bardot was as admired and as influential as any American star, while actress Audrey Hepburn, originally from Belgium, and French actresses Leslie Caron and Juliette Greco were major fashion influences on young Britons. When asked to name their favorite actresses in early 1963, the four members of the Beatles revealed the extent of European influence. John Lennon chose Juliette Greco and Italian Sophia Loren, Paul McCartney picked Brigitte Bardot and Juliette Greco, and George Harrison and Ringo Starr chose Brigitte Bardot.[123] The number of non-British and non-US films shown in Britain increased from 48 in 1950 to 112 in 1960, while the number of US films fell from 260 to 142 during the same period.[124] "French cloths, French food, French anything were rated as inherently superior to their Anglo-Saxon equivalents," Mary Evans found when she was a pupil at a grammar school in the late 1950s.[125]

The fact that British football clubs were starting to participate in Europe-wide competition in the 1950s was symbolic of the increased influence of Europe on Britain. Wolverhampton Wanders, English champions three times in the 1950s, played in a series of midweek friendlies in 1953 and 1954 against top European sides Dynamo Moscow and Honved of Hungary. Friendlies between British and European clubs soon gave way to competitive games. Birmingham City was the first English club to play in a European competition when they played in the Inter-Cities Fairs Cup in 1955. Scottish club Hibernian became the first British representative in the European Champion Clubs' Cup, or European Cup, launched in 1955–1956. The following year, Manchester United became the first English team to enter the competition. The allure of the exotic and the foreign brought huge crowds to British grounds. Over 135,000 in the stadium, and millions more on television, watched Spanish side Real Madrid defeat West Germany's Eintract Frankfurt 7–3 at Glasgow's Hampden Park in the 1960 European Cup Final. New Leeds United manager Don Revie was so enthralled by the style of Real Madrid that his team adopted their all-white kit and in the 1960s' Manchester City changed their away strip to red-and-black striped shirts to replicate the colors of Italian side AC Milan.[126]

Two of the youth cultures that emerged in the late 1950s demonstrated both American and European influences. A younger generation, who had not lived through World War II nor held the anti-European prejudices of the older generation, adopted European styles. Beatniks, for example, were mostly young middle-class University and art school students who had little unifying philosophy but exhibited a fascination for Europe and an appreciation of the bohemian life. They admired American beat writers like the novelists Jack Kerouac and William Burroughs, and the poet Allen Ginsberg, who focused on those characters outside the mainstream of society and drew relatively explicit portrayals of sexual behavior, drugs and crime. Yet, many middle-class Beatniks looked to Paris as much as the United States for inspiration. Britons admired the bohemianism of Left Bank intellectuals and men adopted their black clothing, baggy trousers, poloneck sweaters, beards, duffel coats, scarves and cigarette smoking. Existentialists Simone De Beauvoir and Jean Paul Sartre and the café life of Paris held as much fascination for Beatniks as the beat writers and the jazz musicians of San Francisco and New York. "I would depart in spirit," Sheila Rowbotham, for example, reminisced of her days as a student, "Simone de Beauvoir's *The Mandarins* took me to Paris, I travelled to San Francisco with Jack Kerouac and dropped in to Chicago and New York when I listened to blues and jazz." French singer and actress Juliette Greco, with her fringe, dark eye make-up and black clothing became a fashion icon to be emulated by middle-class girls.[127] Rowbotham wore her hair "long and straight" and sported a "smart beatnik outfit: high heels, black stockings, C&A tight black jumper over a dark, pleated skirt in muted greys and blues."[128] The films of Jean Cocteau, the existentialism of Sartre and de Beauvoir and the look of Juliette Greco meant that "there was glamour in all things French," recalled Joan Bakewell a student at Cambridge University.[129]

While Teddy Boys and Rockers took their look and musical tastes from America, another youth cult, the Mods, joined Beatniks in incorporating influences from Europe. Mods, or Modernists because of their devotion to modern jazz, began to appear around the jazz clubs of Soho in central London toward the end of the 1950s. Mods were obsessed with clothes more than music and wanted to adopt the sophisticated look they found in the clothes of the jazz musicians and increasingly in Europe. Mods admired the look of Italian immigrants and tourists and of French and Italian film stars they saw in photos and on the big screen. "We wanted that lifestyle, we wanted a girlfriend that looked like Jean Seberg and live the way they did in those films and from that came wanting to know everything about it," an early Mod, Dicky Dodson, remembered. "We moved totally away from the American stuff which we now considered too showy and wanted to be French," Dodson recalled.[130] Another Mod, Johnny Moke, found inspiration in Europe. "We did go to all those foreign movies, and didn't understand a word. We watched the way they smoked a cigarette, how they buttoned their shirts and jackets, which shoes they wore."[131] "Our sporting heroes ranked alongside our cinema heroes," Graham Hughes remembered. "Not English footballers or cricketers like most other teenagers were into, we adopted cyclists. Instead of Stanley Matthews, I had Louie Kean Balvet and Fausto Cockpee."[132] Writing in 1961, journalist T. R. Fyvel noted "the Italian style," which

> was taken up by steadily increasing numbers of working-class boys. The main components of the style were short jackets, fully draped at the back and at first often broadly striped on the Italian pattern. The trousers were narrow; shirts could be coloured as well as white and cuffs and handkerchiefs were prominently shown. The new shoes were finely pointed on the Italian model and in London called Pickers or Pointers.

The look was topped off with Italian- and French-style short crew-cut haircuts without oil or grease. Mods also adopted Italian Vespa and Lambretta motor scooters to add to the European look. "What was novel was that English working-class youths had now discovered Europe and were ready, indeed eager, to know what was being worn by young people on the Continent," T. R. Fyvel noted.[133] "U.S. influence has declined somewhat from its initial supremacy," noted author Colin MacInnes in 1958 "because the American 'hero' has been increasingly replaced by European models." This may "hint at a certain degree not of 'anti-Americanism' so much as growing indifference to America."[134]

Female Mods were far more numerous than Teddy Girls and female Rockers. They modeled their look on French stars like Jean Seberg, Juliette Greco and Brigitte Bardot. A *New York Times* reporter in London was astonished to see the French influence on women in this "once staid city." "British women never have looked more daring nor more alluring," he remarked in October 1959. "This can be attributed in part to prosperity and to Brigitte Bardot." The reporter noted, "young girls ringed their eyes with black like the vamps of the twenties and pouted provocatively through white lipstick." They "walk around in knee-short, bouffant skirts, sweaters, spindly heels and Brigitte Bardot-influenced hairdos."[135] The look evolved to sporting short straight hair, trousers or ski pants and flat shoes. "By 1963 I was a sixteen-year-old mod," revealed Janet Ardern from Middlesex who, like many other Mods, took her admiration for Europe far beyond clothing. She spoke French, watched French and Italian movies, attended French plays and Italian operas, and listened to modern jazz. "I lapped up all these experiences eagerly, keeping notes and sketchbooks, lists and diaries, pictures cut from magazines." Ardern, like many Mods, was trying to break away from her working-class roots and these European influences offered new horizons. Ardern went on to study architecture at college. "By the time I was eighteen, I was a fully formed cultural elitist, and had soaked up more art cinema and been exposed to more of the operatic repertoire than anyone else in my year at college." Ardern later changed her name to Janet Street-Porter and became a prominent television producer.[136]

It was clear, as the lifestyle of Ardern attests, that by the end of the 1950s Europe played a larger part than previously in influencing British society as immigration and foreign travel helped to bring French and Italian style to a receptive British public. But, as contemporaries like J. B. Priestly and Harry Hopkins noted, the Americanization of British life was far more pervasive. The economic dominance of the United States in the postwar period, the growing affluence of the British population and the technological innovations in mass communications brought many Britons into greater contact with American culture. The working classes attended dance halls, cinemas and eating establishments in greater numbers and bought more records, radios and televisions, all of which were important conduits of American ideas and products into Britain. The United States influenced the way Britons danced, the way they spoke, the food they ate and the clothes they wore. The mass-production, consumer economy with its sophisticated sales and advertising techniques journeyed across the Atlantic to Britain to change how British people worked and shopped. Even British politics displayed the ubiquitous influence of the United States. As we will see in the next chapter, however, the extensive American influence on British society induced both wild admiration and intense dislike of the United States of America.

2

Terra Incognita: The United States in the British Imagination, 1945–1963

David Jones, born in January 1947 in Brixton, London, was besotted with the United States of America. As a child he played Cowboys and Indians and developed a keen interest in the mythical American West. Jones fell in love with rock 'n' roll upon hearing "Tutti Frutti" by Little Richard: "my heart nearly burst with excitement," he recalled. "I'd never heard anything even resembling this. It filled the room with energy and color and outrageous defiance. I had heard God." In 1958, Jones' older brother Terry returned home from three years' service in the Royal Air Force and introduced his younger sibling to jazz music and to the writers of the beat generation. David listened to American football on American Forces Network radio and at the age of 13 he wrote to the US Embassy requesting information on the game, receiving a helmet, a set of shoulder pads and a football in return. The young Jones also joined a baseball team, the Beckenham Blue Jays, but never mastered the game. "I think he liked the game because it was associated with the United States," opined teammate Philip Laing. Jones joined a number of rhythm and blues bands and began to play the saxophone after reading Jack Kerouac's novel *On the Road*. He loved Hollywood movies, particularly the 1960 release *The Alamo*, based on the Battle of the Alamo fought in Texas in 1836, and especially admired the Texan rebel Jim Bowie played by Richard Widmark. Jones became a singer in a local band and, to avoid confusion with another Englishman with the same name, Davy Jones, who later found fame with the Monkees, he decided to change his name. In 1965, David Jones adopted the name David Bowie in homage to Jim Bowie.[1]

David Jones' infatuation with the United States was mirrored by millions of others in postwar Britain, yet historians have been quick to see widespread hostility to America in 1950s' Britain. Raphael Samuel suggested that "the most virulent Anglocentrism of the war and postwar years" was directed at the United States. Antipathy to America "was still running strongly in the 1950s, notwithstanding NATO and the Anglo-American alliance, and was a unifying bond in the Tory party, after the debacle of Suez, as well as a leading component of the 'Socialist foreign policy' demanded by the Labour Left."[2] Meredith Veldman saw "anti-American" sentiment in the Campaign for Nuclear Disarmament (CND). "Nationalism and imperialist nostalgia played an important role in shaping the Campaign's protest and in strengthening its anti-Americanism," Veldman asserted. There was "a concern to preserve and protect essential British or English characteristics that were seen as threatened by Americanisation and standardization."[3] Mark Garnett and Richard Weight in their *Guide to Modern British History* suggest that: "Hostility towards Americanisation was directly related to the growing political and economic power of the United States and it reached a peak in the 1950s."[4]

Undoubtedly, some Britons were less than enamored with the United States. Many conservatives believed that it was culturally inferior to Britain and was bringing profound and unwanted changes to British society. The left expressed hostility to US foreign policy and to the inequalities that plagued American society. However, by focusing too much on the views of middle-class intellectuals, and by misreading legitimate criticisms of American Cold War policy and of American society as "anti-American," historians have been too eager to describe the postwar years as a period of intense hostility to America. Overall, admiration for US foreign policy, culture and society was the norm rather than the exception in postwar Britain.

Britain and the United States in the Postwar Years

In the immediate postwar years, British views of the United States were rarely shaped by direct contact with Americans or America and the sources of information about the colossus across the Atlantic remained limited. The first regular transatlantic flights only began in 1958 and even then most of the business people, politicians and cultural ambassadors that visited Britain only stayed in London and a select number of historic towns and merely a minority of British people came into contact with the visitors.[5] Because of the high cost of the trip, unfavorable exchange rates and government restrictions on how much currency British residents could take out of the country, few Britons visited the United States in the immediate postwar years. British immigration to the United States slowed as Canada, Australia and New Zealand made concerted efforts to attract British immigrants with offers of financial incentives and subsidized passages. Most children learned about Britain and Europe, not the United States, in school and college. Coverage in the media emanated from correspondents residing on the East Coast and concentrated on diplomatic news or the bizarre and sensational. Therefore, a majority of Britons established a view of the United States based on images contained in Hollywood movies, television programs, comics, novels and music that flooded into Britain. Even here, the coverage was geographically limited, and regional stereotypes prevailed. In the summer of 1957, Americans Doris and Edward Bernays in their visit to Britain found that many people "think of the U.S.A. as solely Hollywood-New York-Chicago, with a vague area of gunmen called the West and quaint people called Hillbillies in the mountains." California enjoyed the glamorous image of Hollywood and beaches while New York, the city that never sleeps, was inevitably seen as the real America, and Chicago as the city of gangster violence.[6]

Britons voiced resentment against Americans because of the actions of the United States government during and immediately after World War II. Many believed that the United States should have entered the war earlier and, when they did join the conflict, Britons took exception to the GI occupation of their land during the war and suggested that Americans were "overpaid, oversexed, and over here." The steep price the United States charged Britain for essential war-time supplies under the Lend–Lease program, and the way they abruptly ended the initiative only six days after the war with Japan had ended, convinced many that the US government wanted to push Britain into a crippling debt. "Not many people in this country believe the Communist thesis that it is the deliberate and conscious aim of American policy to ruin Britain and everything that Britain stands for in the world. But the evidence can certainly be read that way," *The Economist* stated in August 1947.[7] Fred Vanderschmidt, *Newsweek*'s London correspondent, suggested that "in the year 1947, one out of three Englishmen were more or less antagonistic to anything that came from America."[8]

> Our precarious economic position today is in no small measure due to the fact that, in addition to the enormous financial calls upon us during the war years, we had to devote so much of our resources to pay for munitions of every kind to the U.S.A. which emerged from this war, as it did from the first, the richest and most powerful country in the world,

bemoaned one Briton some nine years after the war had ended.[9]

The United States faced further resentment and anger as it surpassed Britain as a world power. Many expressed concern about Britain's financial dependence on the United States, which was confirmed when the United States loaned Britain US$3.75 billion at the war's end and provided a further US$2.7 billion in Marshall Aid. More felt humiliated because Britain increasingly depended on US military power for its security. "Perhaps the main reason" for the British animosity toward the United States "is the fantastic change that has taken place in the comparative status of the two nations," *Daily Mirror* columnist Cassandra surmised in May 1954. "The United States is the richest and the most powerful nation on earth. Britain used to be exactly just that. She no longer is. We have in material terms fallen far, far behind and psychologically, this bitter pill sticks in our throats."[10] By the mid-1950s, as author William Clark noted, "anti-American feeling in Britain has risen steadily in the last ten years."[11]

Conservative and Upper-Class Views of the United States

Some sections of British society were acutely antagonistic to the United States, particularly British conservatives who supported the maintenance of the British Empire and felt aggrieved by the US call for the self-determination of peoples.

In December 1945, the Tory right wing voted against the American loan in the House of Commons because it was conditional on Britain giving up Empire trade preferences.[12] The *Daily Express*, owned by imperialist Lord Beaverbrook, opposed closer economic ties with America in case it weakened the Empire. Since his early years, Conservative politician Enoch Powell despised Americans because of their opposition to the British Empire; his resentment increased as Britain became economically and militarily dependent on the United States and Britain's Empire collapsed. "I just don't like America, or Americans," Powell openly declared. "It is like saying you like sugar in your tea. *De gustibus non est disputandum.*"[13]

Anti-US feeling increased during the Suez Crisis of 1956, when many imperialists thought that the US government should have supported the British initiative in the Middle East. In July 1956, President Gamal Abdel Nasser of Egypt nationalized the Anglo-French controlled Suez Canal and in response French, British and Israeli troops occupied the Canal Zone. US president Dwight D. Eisenhower condemned the invasion while prodding Prime Minister Anthony Eden to call off the military adventure. "Our prime enemy in the Middle East is not Communism but the United States," Conservative MP Paul Williams pronounced in February 1957. Conservatives in the constituency of Beckenham protested against the adoption of a prospective parliamentary candidate on the grounds that he was American born. The candidate was finally adopted but the local party president condemned the actions of his colleagues and "their mean, low, and despicable anti-Americanism," the *Daily Mirror* reported in March 1957.[14] "Some Conservatives never forgave the Americans, and the fact that anti-Americanism lingered on in some generally right-wing circles when I was Prime Minister must be in part attributed to this," remembered Margaret Thatcher.[15]

Conservative resentment toward the United States did not start in the twentieth century but dated back to the colonial period. Visitors to the American colonies found the people uncultured and vulgar. While the upper-class travelers eschewed active money making as beneath them, and reveled in the trappings of birth and title, Americans demonstrated an enthusiasm for business, which Britons condemned as materialism. The British upper classes saw themselves as custodians of a superior culture while the colonies comprised deported criminals, political and religious misfits and the unwanted lower classes. After the colonists achieved independence, British visitors along with elites from other Western European countries saw the United States as an inferior country overly obsessed with wealth at the expense of the arts. "During the thirty or forty years of their independence, they have done absolutely nothing for the Sciences, for the Arts, for Literature, or even for the statesman-like studies of Politics or Political Economy," wrote Sidney Smith, one of the founders of the *Edinburgh Review*, in 1820.

> In the four quarters of the globe, who reads an American book? or goes to an American play? or looks at an American picture or statue? What does the world yet owe to American physicians or surgeons? What new substances have their chemists discovered? or what old ones have they analyzed? What new constellations have been discovered by the telescopes of Americans?—what have they done in the mathematics? Who drinks out of American glasses? or eats from American plates? or wears American coats or gowns? or sleeps in American blankets?[16]

As the United States celebrated its centenary in 1876, it had become a great industrial power but conservatives remained concerned by the cultural backwardness of Americans. "I have struck a city—a real city—and they call it Chicago," writer Rudyard Kipling stated at the end of the nineteenth century. "Having seen it, I urgently desire never to see it again. It is inhabited by savages."[17]

The attack on American culture continued in the interwar years, as conservative critics denounced the importation of Hollywood movies and jazz music. F. R. Leavis, an English cultural critic, worried that British cultural standards were being undermined by superficial and vulgar mass culture made with commercial ends in mind.[18] Moral guardians decried the rhythmic nature of jazz music as primitive and its strong association with provocative dancing as a threat to proper codes of behavior in Britain. The *Daily Mail* in the spring of 1926 described the Charleston dance as "degenerate," "negroid," and "a series of contortions without a vestige of grace or charm, reminiscent only of negro orgies."[19] Hollywood too encouraged a perceived decline in moral standards. In March 1933, Sidney Dark, editor of the *Church Times*, declared that cinema goers had "all sorts of intellectual and moral poison pumped into them without any kind of interference. Judging by the output of Hollywood, to describe that city as a cesspool, would be complimentary."[20] In the postwar years, conservative elites continued to criticize American culture for leading to a decline in moral standards. "[A] great many films, particularly of American origin, have moments when they might said to be glorifying false values," B. Seebohm Rowntree and G. R. Lavers suggested in *English Life and Leisure*, a survey of English culture in the late 1940s. The authors believed

> that the constant repetition of scenes of rather vulgar and ostentatious luxury, and the constant suggestion that "having a good time" can only mean dining and drinking champagne in expensive restaurants, and living in rooms of absurdly large dimensions, must have a deleterious effect upon a nation that has, above all, to realize that its future lies in plain living, hard work and in unsophisticated pleasures.

Not only American films but American periodicals also concerned Rowntree and Lavers. American magazines "dealing with sex and with crime stories in a grossly sensational way, is thoroughly undesirable. The illustrations in these magazines are in bad taste, the literary style is bad, and the advertisements are sensual, suggestive, and unpleasant. We would like to see their import prohibited."[21]

Conservatives condemned American jazz, movies and literature for lowering the morals of the young but rock 'n' roll music caused the greatest consternation. Many criticized the music because of its overt sexuality, its rudimentary musicianship and simplistic lyrics. "Mr Elvis Presley, now only twenty-one, whose combination of a hill-billy style of wailing with bodily contortions that are supposed to suggest the 'fundamental human drive' took him even beyond the peaks of popularity enjoyed most recently by the tearful Mr Johnny Ray and Mr Frank Sinatra," *The Times* suggested in September 1956.[22] Racist attitudes toward the music may have been less evident in Britain than in the United States but was hardly absent. In the spring of 1956, British band leader Ted Heath who just returned from a tour of the United States, helped to settle nerves in Britain by insisting that rock 'n' roll would not catch on in Britain. "It's primarily music for coloured folks, played by coloured bands. It includes a great deal of jumping up and down and crazy antics which I do not feel would be acceptable here."[23] "It is tribal. And it is from America," the *Daily Mail* editorial of September 5, 1956, pronounced of rock 'n' roll. "It follows ragtime, blues, Dixie, jazz, hot cha-cha and the boogie-woogie, which surely originated in the jungle. We sometimes wonder whether this is the Negro's revenge."[24] Sir Malcolm Sargent, conductor of the BBC orchestra, believed that there is "nothing new or wonderful about it. Rock and roll has been played in the jungle for centuries."[25]

This denigration of American popular culture inevitably led to criticism of individual Americans and of American society. In 1956, a leading psychiatrist noted that Americans call women "baby, honey, sugar, sweetie-pie. All these expressions indicate that the Americans are immature—so immature that they are still at the baby stage when love means food."[26] Mary Evans remembered when she was a pupil at a grammar school in the late 1950s and early 1960s that teachers celebrated European arts and literature but derided American culture.

> [The] United States remained largely foreign, a rather crass country glimpsed more or less entirely through the advertisements in the *National Geographic* magazine. In discussions about where we would travel to (if we all had the luck to be air hostesses when we grew up) it was generally agreed, and endorsed by the staff, that the United States would not be interesting as it "had no history." So "having no history" was a major qualification to be considered as a serious country.[27]

In 1952, writer Evelyn Waugh decried "Americans are cowards. They are almost all the descendants of wretches who deserted their legitimate monarch's for fear of military service."[28] At a cocktail party in Chelsea, a 26-year-old former public school boy told the *Daily Express* reporter: "isn't the food tasteless . . . and the television must be ghastly". He thought even less of the etiquette of the American people. "[T]hey have really no manners . . . they fumble everything . . . and they are so uncultured and ignorant."[29] Arthur Veysey, *Chicago Tribune* correspondent in Britain, lived in London for 11 years and could not wait to return home.

> There are a couple of million Englishmen it would be a pleasure never to see again. Most of these belong to or cater to the so-called upper classes. As a group they are becoming a psychological case. They or their forebears once ran Britain and strode the world like lords. Today their rule in England is challenged, and abroad they tend to be either fiddlers or beggars. America is top dog now and they can't accept the change.[30]

Even though Britain was militarily and economically weaker than the United States, a sense of superiority prevailed among British elites. The British upper classes needed to maintain a disdainful attitude to Americans to compensate for their loss of power and status. In Washington DC to negotiate the repayment of war debts, Lord Halifax told John Maynard Keynes, "It's true they've all the money bags. But we've got all the brains."[31] British journalist William Clark believed that Britain's wisdom and know-how would allow them to mentor the inexperienced United States. "Britain has a great deal to offer the partnership both in experience of world affairs and in her experiments at organizing modern society for man's happiness and progress."[32] In the summer of 1953, Oxford-educated former MP Harold Nicolson wrote that he was "frightened that the destinies of the world should be in the hands of a giant with the limbs of an undergraduate, the emotions of a spinster and the brain of a pea-hen."[33] "The European looks upon the American GI in Europe or Asia as a good-natured blunderer, benevolent but oh so immature, impatient and belligerent," American Father John Sheerin complained in June 1953. This view is even more common among diplomats, Father Sheerin suggested. "They claim we cannot be trusted in our political judgments because we are too young as a nation, too pitifully unversed in the game of politics."[34] Brian Magee, who left Oxford to study at Yale in the mid-1950s, summed up the prevailing upper-class view of Americans: "In the face of all evidence to the contrary we cling fiercely to the faith that Americans are culturally inferior—not because they are but because we deeply need to believe they are."[35]

These assertions of American cultural inferiority spread beyond conservative elites. In a Europe-wide survey undertaken in 1948–1949, 34 percent of Britons believed that the United States was "uncultured," higher than the European average of 30 percent.[36] Mass observation studies undertaken in 1947 found

> two sharply contrasting and yet fundamentally similar groups of opinion. In the one the American is immature emotionally and intellectually; he is boastful and flamboyant, bad mannered and full of intolerance to any minority group. But in the other he is simple and ingenuous, impulsive and uninhibited, friendly, kind hearted and generous. In either case his likeness to a child is stressed with notable frequency.[37]

The British saw Americans "as overgrown children and America as the 'kid sister' who must be taken by the hand and led," historian Jacques Freymond claimed in 1954.[38] In 1955, only 15 percent of Britons believed the United States was "cultured." Six years later even fewer, 11 percent, held the same opinion.[39]

The Left and America

While the conservative elites of the nineteenth century saw the United States as corrupt and vulgar, the political left in Britain believed that the US was a "beacon of freedom." British liberals condemned slavery in the United States but believed that the new nation was a living example of the virtues of republicanism, with its separation of church and state, religious tolerance and constitutional protection of individual rights. Reformers like the Chartists who sought the extension of the franchise in Britain spoke approvingly of the growth of male working-class suffrage and public education in the United States in the first half of the nineteenth century. British radicals of the nineteenth century saw the United States as a land where workingmen could enjoy political freedom and correspondingly pursue greater economic opportunities. "The great body of the aristocracy and the commercial classes are anxious to see the United States go to pieces," Charles Francis Adams, US ambassador to Britain during the American Civil War, wrote in December 1862. But, "the middle and lower class sympathise with us" because they "see in the convulsion in America an era in the history of the world, out of which must come in the end a general recognition of the right of mankind to the produce of their labor and the pursuit of happiness." After the War ended, British radical John Bright, MP, suggested America was a bastion of democracy. "There is no country in which men have been so free and prosperous," Bright declared.[40]

The British left became more critical of the US government and society when the country evolved into an industrial giant and an imperial power and socialism became a strong component of British radicalism. While radicals had previously praised the political liberty found in America, they now criticized its social and economic inequalities. The socialist left denounced the control of American industry by unscrupulous robber barons and monopolies, and the anti-union ferocity of American employers who in collusion with the local and national governments fought bloody battles with labor. Left-wing visitors to the United States who previously marveled at their political freedoms now noted the poverty and unemployment of the inner cities. "A quarter of a century ago the American Republic was the guiding star of advanced English political thought. It is not so now," English radical William Clark suggested.

> It is not merely a question of machine politics, of political corruption, of the omnipotent party boss... Over and beyond this is the great fact of the division between rich and poor, millionaires at one end, tramps at the other, a growth of monopolies unparalleled, crises producing abject poverty just as in Europe.[41]

The Great Depression in the United States convinced many on the left that Stalin's Russia was economically superior to US capitalism and the Soviet sacrifices in World War II drew further admiration from many.[42]

America's aggressive pursuit of the Cold War further strained relations between the Labour left and the United States. At the war's end, leftist MP Michael Foot warned that America was "arrogant, self-confident, merciless and convinced of its capacity to dictate the destinies of the world."[43] Between 1945 and 1947, the left wing of the Labour Party gathered around Aneurin Bevan, a minister in the Labour government, wanted Labour to develop a foreign policy based on the concept of a Third Force. Third Force ideas suggested that Britain could follow a middle path between the United States and the Soviet Union and align with countries that combined political democracy with a socialist economy. The left antipathy to the United States subsided with the imposition of the Marshall Plan but the Korean War, which broke out in the summer of 1950, further ignited left opposition to the United States as many resented Prime Minister Clement Attlee's decision to send British troops to Korea and feared that war would derail spending on social programs. In 1952, Labour MP Hugh Gaitskell believed that "hostility to America is fairly widespread in Britain today and has certainly increased since the outbreak of the Korean War." Gaitskell confirmed that "hostility to America is strongest on the left."[44] The Korean War ended in 1953, but left-wing resentment to the United States emerged again in the late 1950s as many feared that the country would become a target of Soviet missiles when the United States located nuclear weapons in Britain as part of the NATO alliance. The left-wing-led Campaign for Nuclear Disarmament (CND) gained considerable support because of its opposition to the nuclear proliferation begun by the American government. Launched in early 1958, CND wanted all countries to "Ban the Bomb" but urged Britain to unilaterally discharge its nuclear weapons and remove American weapons from British soil.[45]

The anticommunist scare in the United States drew further criticism from the British left. The House Un-American Activities Committee and Republican Senator Joseph McCarthy launched a crusade against communist influence in the US government after China fell to the communists in 1949. Soon Hollywood, the schools and other institutions came under close scrutiny from anticommunist politicians. Ethel and Julius Rosenberg were sent to the electric chair in June 1953 for spying for the Soviets. "It is indeed probable that if the full truth were known over here about the scale of this movement and the way it seems to permeate the Universities, the Civil Service and business, there would be a really serious revulsion against America," Hugh Gaitskell noted in 1952. "On the rational plane it condemns the main argument of the pro-Americans—that America is, after all, a free democratic country, while Russia is a cruel and ruthless dictatorship."[46] The traditional land of liberty now looked like a country in which nonconformism was tantamount to treason. Author Kingsley Martin suggested that McCarthyism "has the effect of rewarding mediocrity, cowardice, and sycophancy and silencing independence and creative talent." He also noted that "the effect of the witch hunt is to produce a general level of conformity, a new orthodoxy from which a man dissents at his economic peril."[47] Philosopher Bertrand Russell believed that an "Englishman going to America at the present time has the strange experience of a population subjected to a reign of terror and always obliged to think twice before giving utterance to any serious conviction."[48]

The Communist Party of Great Britain (CPGB) proved especially hostile to the United States. The CPGB comprised some 56,000 members at the end of the War and developed deep roots in the trade union movement. In the 1945 general election, the party won two seats in the Parliament with its 21 candidates garnering an average vote of 14.6 percent. The party also took over half a million votes in the following year's local council elections, as the number of communist councilors increased from 81 to 215.[49] During the Cold War, the communist party in Britain increased its attacks on American foreign policy, often on orders from the Soviet Union. Through economic power and military might, the US government, controlled by big business, was undermining the independence of nations and pursuing global domination. "Hitler's press and speeches were for several years devoted to the same theme. And it will also be remembered that the Germans propaganda barrage succeeded only because it was never resisted with firmness by the nations of Europe," noted *Daily Worker* journalist Derek Kartun. [50] "Imperialist America, leading the war camp, has conducted aggressive war in Korea, is threatening China, and rearming Western Germany," warned the Communist Party of Great Britain.

> It has war bases all over the world, and in the interests of a handful of exploiters tries to dictate to all nations and to crush popular struggles for freedom. It piles up atom bombs and colossal offensive armaments, and is openly preparing for a third world war. It is already dictating what policies the countries of Western Europe, including Britain, shall pursue in rearmament and foreign trade: it aims at the forcible suppression of colonial liberation movements and at organising an aggressive war against the U.S.S.R.

The communist party demanded that Britain break "once and for all with the American policy of aggression and world conquest."[51]

By the 1950s, the communist party reserved its greatest hostility for the growing cultural and military influence of America on Britain. Eschewing revolution in favor of the parliamentary road to socialism, the party sought to situate its policies in British traditions, celebrating native cultural customs and expressing hostility to every new cultural development that originated in the United States. "Go home, America! We don't want you here," wrote Derek Kartun of the *Daily Worker*.

> We can get along in our quiet way without Coca-Cola, American admirals, and American G I's. We want Britain for the British, not for the United States. We do not believe you are defending civilisation. We do not believe you are defending democracy. We do not even think you understand the meaning of the word. We think you are hell-bent for war. . . .We believe in an independent Britain, not a pawn to the United States."[52]

Between 1949 and 1955, the Communist Party of Great Britain mounted a campaign against American comics. In 1951, the communist party held a conference on "The American Threat to British Culture." At the conference, one speaker denounced the comics because they "stress cruelty [and] glorify power . . . violence and brutality." "[D]ecent people" must "stop the American vulgarization, this degradation, this perversion of our young people."[53]

Left-leaning intellectuals joined with conservatives in criticizing American culture and materialism. Marxist Raymond Williams, a professor at the University of Cambridge, resented the American influence on British youth and criticized "synthetic culture" emanating from the United States. "In Britain, we have to notice that much of this bad work is American in origin. At certain levels, we are culturally an American colony," Williams suggested. "But of course it is not the best American culture that we are getting."[54] Richard Hoggart, an English lecturer at Hull University, condemned the "shiny barbarism" associated with the homogeneous and inferior US-influenced culture such as pulp fiction, pop music and cinema, which were destroying the urban working-class culture.[55] Philosopher Bertrand Russell believed that Americans could not talk properly. Britons "have a certain beauty of diction," he felt, and they are "responsible for handing on an unimpaired tradition in diction and enunciation." Americans, however, simply want to "make their meaning clear" and their "vocabulary is small, and sounds which should be distinguished are blurred."[56] Francis Williams, advisor to the Labour Party and from 1951 to 1952 the governor of the BBC, revised accusations of American materialism prevalent since the colonial era.

> In American society the need to buy takes precedence over almost all other emotions—even that of sex, as much as Americans dwell on this in their literature. At once romantic and pathetic, the urge to buy and buy again is at the heart of the American dream. To buy and to waste.[57]

Intellectuals, whether of the left or the right, condemned American popular culture because of their nationalist and class-conscious support of British upper-class traditions. Conservative writers and left-wing academics enjoyed the same classical music, literature and arts and saw the import of American popular entertainment, and its appeal to the working classes, as a threat to the culture that they so cherished. Raymond Williams, Evelyn Waugh, Bertrand Russell and F. R. Leavis had their political differences but they all attended Cambridge University or Oxford University, the bastions of the British upper classes. Bertrand Russell, a son of the British aristocracy, had more in common with Evelyn Waugh than with the British working class. Many British left-wing intellectuals, disappointed by the tastes and often the politics of the British working class, gave vent to their feelings by expressing their disgust of American popular culture, which British workers so admired.

This cross-political opposition to American culture was evident in the attempts of Conservative and Labour governments to limit US influence on Britain. To counter Hollywood's economic and cultural dominance and stimulate the British film industry, for example, successive governments, whether of the left or the right, limited the number of American films shown in Britain. The Cinematograph Films Act of 1927, introduced by a Conservative-controlled Parliament, required British cinemas and distributors to show a quota of British films. The quota was initially set at 7.5 percent for exhibitors, which rose to 20 percent by the mid-1930s. In October 1948, the Labour government set a new quota requiring 45 percent of all films shown in Britain to be British. With the British film industry unable to meet the quota, the number was reduced to 40 percent and then to 30 percent in October 1950. In another attempt to limit the influence of Hollywood, in the summer of 1947 Clement Attlee's Labour government imposed a 75 percent import duty on all foreign films. Hollywood responded by boycotting the British market and in March 1948 the government rescinded the tax but imposed an annual limit on how much money could be repatriated. The remainder of the earnings of foreign films would be spent in Britain, helping to stimulate the British film industry.[58]

The BBC, founded in 1922 as the British Broadcasting Company and renamed the British Broadcasting Corporation in 1927, limited American influence in radio and television. Enshrined in the BBC Charter and championed by John Reith, BBC's first Director-General, the BBC sought to inform and intellectually elevate the listener by promoting high-brow rather than popular culture. The BBC espoused "a strong vein of anti-Americanism, rooted in a distaste for the United

States' supposedly vulgar and cultureless society and a suspicion of her growing challenge to British economic and political influence on the world stage," as suggested by author Stephen Barnard.[59] The BBC, which monopolized the airwaves, played modest amounts of the music emanating from across the Atlantic. Recognizing the need to appeal to different tastes and under competition from Radio Luxembourg, an English language commercial radio station operating from Continental Europe, the BBC launched three channels in 1945: the Home Service, which concentrated on news, the Light Programme, which focused on more popular entertainment, and the Third Programme, which played classical music. The Light Programme still played little music from America and chose to play British versions of American songs rather than the American originals. The BBC *Variety Programmes Policy Guide for Writers and Producers*, a booklet of guidelines issued by the BBC in 1948 to the producers and writers of its light entertainment programs, urged their staff to maintain the purity of British traditions. "American idiom and slang, for instance, frequently find their way quite inappropriately into scripts, and dance band singers for the most part elect to adopt pseudo American accents. The BBC believes that this spurious Americanisation of programmes—whether in the writing or in the interpretation—is unwelcome to the great majority of listeners ... [T]he BBC's primary job in light entertainment must be to purvey programmes in our own native idiom, dialects and accents. The 'Americanisation' of British scripts, acts and performances is therefore most actively discouraged."[60] *Saturday Skiffle Club*, first transmitted on the Light Programme in June 1957, broadcast pop music for a younger audience but BBC management was concerned about the high proportion of American songs performed on the show. "Too many American work songs," said one BBC executive, "Doesn't anybody know any British work songs?" The producers responded:

> A very great deal of thought and effort has been expended here to seek British material for these programmes ... in the four programmes to date, approximately one in three songs has been British. We had regarded this as something of an achievement—and are disappointed that this seems not to have been appreciated.[61]

Loathing of American popular culture was evident among those who resisted the introduction of commercial television into Britain. Although Britain was the first country to provide television broadcasts, the United States innovated in introducing paid advertising into television coverage. After the Conservative government published a White Paper in 1952 outlining its intention to end the BBC monopoly of television, the National Television Council (NTC) was formed by opponents of the idea, including economist William Beveridge, novelist E. M. Forster and philosopher Bertrand Russell. In their manifesto "Britain Unites against Commercial TV" they argued that commercial television would lower standards in Britain because of the need to produce low-brow entertainment to appeal to advertisers and to capture a mass-viewing audience. The BBC provided a public service while commercial television based on the American model was interested in profit and ratings. To support their view, those opposed to the introduction of commercial television pointed to the inferior and vulgar nature of American broadcasting, which they feared would be replicated in Britain. Conservative Party Home Secretary Sir David Maxwell Fyfe thought otherwise. "I am not impressed by analogies from the United States. We have our typical British way of resolving problems of taste," he stated in 1952. "We are a much more mature and sophisticated people."[62] To allay fears of Americanization, the newly launched network, Independent Television (ITV), restricted foreign, meaning American, imports to 14 percent of their coverage and the BBC followed suit.[63]

Pro-American Sentiment

In the end, those who overtly criticized American popular culture and Americans were a distinct minority consisting mostly of the Conservative right and middle-class intellectuals. Many of the Labour left disliked free-market capitalism found in the United States and right-wing politics in the country but not Americans. Left-wing MP Barbara Castle insisted that "we are not anti-American. We are anti-capitalist."[64] In foreign policy, the leadership of the Labour government around Prime Minister Clement Attlee and Foreign Secretary Ernest Bevin committed Britain to the alliance with the United States. Bevin played a leading role in the formation of NATO and the Labour government allowed American military bases to operate in Britain.[65] By 1949, even the Labour left found a clear distinction between the foreign policy of the two superpowers. In the House of Commons, only four Labour MPs voted with the Communists against the formation of NATO. "Whatever follies have been committed by American policy in Europe since 1945 (and they are manifold), the major purpose and the major result has been to provide aid without which recovery from the war would have been infinitely more arduous," stated Michael Foot, no supporter of American-style capitalism. "The major purpose of Soviet policy has been the complete subjection of as many countries as possible to the Soviet will."[66]

Conservatives were even more supportive of US foreign policy and American society than the Labour Party. Conservative Prime Ministers Winston Churchill and Harold Macmillan held the United States in high regard, partly because of the influence of their American mothers. Churchill cemented the war-time alliance with President Roosevelt and strongly supported the United States in the Cold War. When the Conservatives returned to power in 1951, they backed the alliance with the United States and firm action against the Soviet Union. Conservatives may have seen themselves as culturally superior to Americans but many Tories began to view American society as a thriving alternative to the socialism of the Labour government. Conservatives portrayed themselves as champions of individual liberty against the socialism of Labour and often equated Labour socialism with creeping communism. The *Daily Express* ran a series of columns entitled "Watch America" after Labour won the 1945 general election to highlight the economic success of American capitalism and the failure of Labour socialism.[67] In his book, *Return from Utopia*, published in 1950, Conservative MP Richard Law poured scorn on those who sought to use the power of government to create a utopian society.

He highlighted the failures of the Soviet system and of the Labour government in Britain while highlighting the successes of the United States.

Law noted

> That the expansionist economy of the United States has achieved greater results than the restrictionist and defensive outlook of Britain (and, indeed, of Europe as a whole) is beyond question. By any material test the standard of like of the American people in general is higher than that of any people in the world, at any time in history. Not only is the total of wealth greater. Its distribution is far wider . . . It can scarcely be denied that, judged by its results, the system of competitive free enterprise as it exists in America produces, by comparison with any other system, the greatest amount of wealth and the widest distribution of it.[68]

Both Conservative and Labour voters were supportive of America in the Cold War. Opinion polls showed that Labour voters supported the Marshall Plan and NATO in similar numbers to Conservative voters.[69] Many Labour voters wanted Britain to maintain its independence from the US. In 1949, 57 percent of Conservative voters thought the British government should form a close attachment to the United States while 49 percent of Liberals and 40 percent of Labour voters felt the same way. In 1952, during the midst of the Korean War, 31 percent of Conservative voters still believed that the United States and Britain were "natural allies and should always stick together," while 18 percent of Liberals and 16 percent of Labour voters felt the same way.[70] Still, the general public demonstrated far more support for the United States in the Cold War than they did for the Soviet Union. A Gallup poll from March 1952 found that 34 percent disapproved of the role the United States was playing in world affairs but 72 percent disapproved of the role of the Soviet Union.[71]

The BBC's opposition to American popular culture can also be overstated as far from wanting to exclude American influence, the Corporation often embraced it. The BBC broadcast American radio programs, established a North American Representative in New York in 1936 to stay in contact with innovation in American radio programming, and copied the format of American game shows. Most broadcasters believed "irrespective of nationality, we must think in terms of good broadcasting."[72] The BBC broadcast programs that offered sympathetic and positive views of the United States after the war. In 1946, the BBC added Alistair Cooke's weekly *American Letter*, later changed to *Letter from America*, to its schedule, which already included the current affairs program *American Commentary*. "There is and always will be a place in programmes for authentic American artistes and material," the BBC told its writers and producers in 1948.[73]

The main reason the BBC played limited amounts of American music was because of agreements the BBC entered into with record companies and the Musicians' Union. Record companies wanted a restriction on the amount of recorded music played on radio so that people would buy the record, not simply listen to it for free. In turn, the Musicians' Union wanted the BBC to employ British musicians to perform live on the radio rather than employ presenters to play records. The record companies and the Union established a series of "needle-time" agreements with the BBC at the end of the war, which restricted the amount of recorded material, much of it of American origin, which the BBC could broadcast. Only 22 hours per week of recorded music could be played on the radio and only one in three records could contain vocals.[74] The Musicians' Union also sought to protect their members by pressuring the government to limit the entry of foreign acts into Britain. Prodded by the Union, who feared that Americans acts were coming to Britain while there was no reciprocal demand for British acts in the United States, from 1935 the Ministry of Labour refused to issue work permits for US musicians and only allowed American singers into Britain as long as they accompanied themselves or British musicians backed them. The Musicians' Union lifted their ban in 1956 and Bill Haley and the Comets became one of the first recipients of the relaxed rules when they came to Britain in 1957.

Not only has the stance of the BBC to America often been misinterpreted but so too has the views of those who opposed the introduction of commercial television in the mid-1950s. Most opponents of commercial television were less concerned with the Americanization of British TV and more concerned that the commercial nature of ITV would lead to programs of lower quality. Television companies, they believed, would descend to the lowest common denominator of taste and quality to attract large audiences for the advertisers. "The worry was less about American programmes dominating British television than about the creation and effects of a commercialized television service," author Paul Rixon found in his study of American influence on British TV.[75]

There seemed to be no particular dislike of Americans in Britain, or at least no more than there was of other foreigners. In 1947, Fred Vanderschmidt, *Newsweek*'s London correspondent, may have suggested that "one out of three Englishmen were more or less antagonistic to anything that came from America" but of course, two-thirds were not.[76] A public opinion survey undertaken in the summer of 1948 found that 58 percent of Britons believed Americans to be progressive, 52 percent generous and 39 percent peace-loving, while 52 percent saw them as conceited and 37 percent as domineering. Subsequent polls found similar results.[77] The public seemed to have more complaints about the upper-class British influence on the BBC rather than the American influence. Harman Grisewood, assistant to the Director-General of the BBC, told former MP Harold Nicolson that he regretted "that the public should rather like American accents, and says that they never get letters of protest about it. What does arouse public rage is the upper-class or 'U' accent. They even complain that the News announcers all speak 'la-di-da.'"[78] The US Information Agency found that the majority of Britons, 57 percent in 1958 and 59 percent in 1960, had a "favorable opinion of the United States."[79]

Most Americans who lived in Britain suffered no overt prejudice. When American author Mary McCarthy suggested on the BBC Third Programme channel in 1954 that there was strong anti-American feeling in Britain, she provoked a strong backlash from Americans living in the country.[80] Frances Paulu, an American woman who had lived outside London for nearly a year with her husband and three children, wrote to *The Listener* in disgust: "Either we are extremely insensitive and thick-skinned or else we have not encountered any of the anti-American feeling which depresses Miss McCarthy. From our first days in England we have been impressed by the warm, friendly spirit with which the British have welcomed us." Paulu pointed out that many of the people an American author would have contact with in Britain would be "liberal, literate, cosmopolitan central Londoners," those most prone to prejudice against Americans. Even then, "they may be critical of American foreign policy.... disturbed about Senator McCarthy—though no more so than are Joseph N. Welch, Edward R. Murrow, or the *New York Times* editorial columns," she concluded.[81] John Walters, an American visitor to Britain, was pleasantly surprised at the welcome he received. "Here in the States I had read about the 'wave of anti-American feeling' in Britain. But I failed to detect any sign of such a wave. On the contrary I found oceans of goodwill for the United States," he concluded.[82] "We have some good friends here, and I have yet to meet anyone who shows a feeling of hatred towards us personally, as so often one reads in your periodicals," a US serviceman wrote to *Picture Post* in 1952.[83] A survey of 5,000 US servicemen stationed in Britain seemed to confirm this view as some 47 percent believed that the attitude of the British people toward the Americans was friendly and only 12 percent believed that it was hostile. Some 81 percent of the servicemen had been invited into a British home.[84]

The British working classes, the majority of the population, were much friendlier toward America and American culture than the intelligentsia of either the left or the right. The middle classes adopted jazz in the postwar years but rock 'n' roll was clearly the music of working-class youth. The working classes similarly loved Hollywood movies, even adopting the style of dress of the stars. In his study of 1930s' cinema, Jeffrey Richards found that "while a large proportion of the population at large went to the cinema occasionally, the enthusiasts were young, working-class, urban and more often female than male."[85] The working classes not only went to the cinema more than the upper classes, they were also more attracted to American films and in particular to gangster movies and Westerns. An "important class distinction emerges in the question of whether people went in the main to British or to American films. It emerges forcibly from a number of surveys that working-class audiences preferred the latter," concluded Jeffrey Richards.[86] Television and American television programs in particular were increasingly central to the leisure time of the working classes. By 1957, 45 percent of the British working class watched television for an average of four hours per night, while the population as a whole watched it for less than two hours.[87]

The Welsh and the Scottish, with their history of conflict with the dominating English, seemed to have a special liking for American culture. One study in 1937 found that Scottish audiences disliked British films because they were dominated by English themes and actors. A Scottish exhibitor suggested that these films "are more foreign to his audience than the products of Hollywood, over 6,000 miles away." More generally, working-class audiences complained "of 'old school tie' standards inherent in so many British films."[88] In Glasgow, singer Lulu, who "loved all things American," said of her mother: "She would never go and see an English film. They were too silly and slapstick, she said. American movies were polished and sophisticated. It was like a promised land... a place she dreamed about."[89] An 18-year-old Scottish railway employee pronounced: "I like going to the movies because I like glamour. I wish to be sincere so I will tell you now that I prefer American films to British. The average British film in my opinion is dull, uninteresting lacking the glamour which is essential to film."[90] In 1947,

Marcus Cunliffe from Lancashire, England, became a student at Yale University, and found that the English upper-class students condemned Americans for being too casual and not deferential enough. "On the other hand, the scholarship boys, the Scots and Celts, *novi homines* such as myself, felt liberated from the intricate discrimination of the mother country."[91] "Scots feel that they made a huge contribution to the early development of the U.S." Roderick McNeill, born in Edinburgh, Scotland in 1945, remarked "and we have retained a great fondness for" the United States.[92]

Younger people admired the United States more than their parents' generation. They listened and danced to American popular music, wore American-style clothes and devoured American movies and television programs. In 1946, 69 percent of 16–19 year olds went to the cinema at least once a week but only 11 percent of those over 60.[93] While every male on reaching the age of 18 years was required to undertake two years' National Service, and most young people labored in low-wage employment, the freedom and affluence that young people craved seemed to be found in the United States. Rock 'n' roll songs celebrated the myriad leisure pursuits and products available to US teenage consumers. American teenagers drove cars and met in places such as drive ins and diners, inhabited exclusively by young people. "To be an American, it seemed, was where it was at, and to be English absolutely wasn't. England was a miserable place for kids compared to how I imagined the States would be, and that wasn't just my opinion," recalled Ian McLagan, who was a teenager in 1950s' London.[94] At first, American Alan Lomax, collector of American folk music, found it odd that young working-class Britons would be drawn to American folk and blues music and especially to "Negro prison songs . . . . At first it seemed very strange to me to hear these songs, which I had recorded from convicts in the prisons of the South, coming out of the mouths of young men who had suffered, comparatively speaking, so little. But I soon realized that these young people *felt* themselves to be in a prison—composed of class-and-caste lines, the shrinking British Empire, the dull job, the lack of money—things like these. They were shouting at these prison walls, like so many Joshuas at the walls of Jericho."[95]

Even among the middle classes, a generational split emerged as many young people were drawn to the United States. "I grew up in a small village in west Dorset—or even because I grew up, etc.—I was ravenous for American comics, novels, music (rock 'n' roll and jazz), movies, TV, musicals and plays (which I read but never saw)," theatre director Richard Eyre, educated at elite private schools, revealed. "I loved the energy and the optimism—the lack of Englishness I suppose -and if in 1958, when I was 15, you had asked me what were my three wishes, all three would have been to emigrate to America."[96] Author Kingsley Amis noted that animosity toward the United States was declining particularly among younger middle-class people "who enjoy American products without a sense of guilt and without a sense of superiority."[97] "The social contempt for America has almost entirely vanished, certainly among the younger generation on the right in this country," Peregrine Worsthorne, assistant editor of the *Daily Telegraph*, argued in 1962. "The kind of ambitious young lower-middle class Tory . . . sees America as an attractive kind of society; because there is no doubt that in America, if you have what it takes to be successful, when you get to the top, you are, in the full sense accepted."[98] Students at Oxford University seemed to follow this trend. In 1957, the Oxford University Union Society voted 280 to 203 in favor of the motion: "This House will resist a spread of the American way of life to this country," but three years later the Union motion: "That this house holds America responsible for spreading vulgarity in Western society" proved too much for the students who packed the debating chamber and voted 485 to 309 against the proposal.[99]

In general, British women were more open and accepting of America and American culture than British men. During the war, young women found the GIs charming and confident, better dressed than British soldiers and generous with their supply of nylon stockings, chocolate, chewing gum and cigarettes. Mothers, with little money and enduring the hardships of rationing, marveled at the generosity the soldiers displayed to their children. "They brought with them colour, romance, warmth and a tremendous hospitality to our dark, shadowed island," recalled Jean Lancaster Rennie in Norwich. A 19-year-old nurse in Exeter suggested that the American soldiers "were so friendly and turned everything into fun." The men begrudged the GIs' attraction to local women. "They took all the girls," one British war veteran ruefully recalled. Eric Westman complained "since I was a young British serviceman and not an attractive young woman, my memories of GIs are pretty sour!" A Shropshire man in the Home Guard suggested that "the presence of troops at a 'do' meant competition for the village lads. The Americans were resented for their smart appearance, with uniforms of a superior cut and quality, for their money and endless supply of small luxuries."[100] So enamored were many British women with the GIs that 70,000 British women eventually became American war brides.

During the austere 1950s, the attraction lingered. British women still found themselves drawn to the American servicemen stationed in Britain. "Here are big-spending, interesting young men with luxurious cars, eager to show them a good time, free with their compliments, fascinating with their Hollywood accents," *Picture Post* commented in June 1952. "It is the movies come to life."[101] "I was at a luncheon given by some men's-wear specialists the other day and up jumps a well-known fashion-girl to say that British men would all look better in American-style clothes," *Daily Mirror* columnist Noel Whitcomb informed his readers. "Girls prefer their boyfriends to wear Yank fashions," the young woman announced, "with heavily draped jackets and long, easy lapels."[102] With traditional British areas of entertainment such as pubs and spectator sports dominated by men, young women gravitated to those areas that offered American amusements such as juke box filled coffee bars and milk bars, which offered a liberated space for girls and young women. More than anywhere, British women ruled the dance floors of Britain. In 1950, 20 percent of boys but 39 percent of girls said that dancing was their preferred way to spend a Saturday night.[103] Political scientist Pierangelo Isernia, who conducted a study on anti-Americanism in Europe during the Cold War, found that opinion polls invariably showed "Males are more likely to be anti-American than are females."[104]

Young British women envied the affluence and greater freedom girls in the United States seemingly enjoyed. Christine Paine born in 1948, in Poole, Dorset, saw her grandfather's sister immigrate to the United States. "From a fairly early age—I remember big parcels arriving from the USA approximately twice a year with clothes, toys, books for me, clothes and presents for my parents and grandparents. One year I got a transistor radio some time before they were generally affordable here." She enjoyed American films at Saturday Morning Pictures and loved the music of Elvis Presley, Bill Haley and Buddy Holly. As a teenager, she greatly admired the life of her counterparts in the United States. British schoolchildren wore restrictive school uniforms and most attended single sex schools while high school students in Hollywood films seemed to wear t-shirts and jeans. Dating was difficult for British teenagers as few owned a car and their cramped homes offered little privacy but in the States the car allowed teenagers to go anywhere they wanted and to indulge in romantic adventures.

> American music, films, TV were all pervading and I think most of us wanted to go to an American High School, go to the drive in, hang out in a diner. It was a time when Britain still had a lot of old fashioned attitudes towards young people and we saw American teenagers on film and on TV driving their own cars, seeming to have a much freer way of life than we did.[105]

British women of all ages saw Hollywood female stars as an alternative to traditional female role models. In the summer of 1943, a sample of 5,639 Britons found that 34 percent of women went to the cinema more than once a week while only 28 percent of men did so. Men visited the cinema on average 1.9 times per month, while women attended 2.3 times per month.[106] Women not only visited the cinema more than men, but they were more enthusiastic about the stars they saw on the silver screen. For young women, female figures in Hollywood films provided a wide range of role models of independent and glamorous women that were not found in the middle-class housewives and timid girls portrayed in British movies.[107] "I like films of the type of *A Tree Grows in Brooklyn*," stated a 24-year-old machine operator. "The people in this film were characters that one could believe in. They were real; the harassed, over-worked mother, the sensitive imaginative little girl, the happy-go-lucky father, with his Micawber-like optimism, and the gay lovable, warm-hearted 'Aunt Cissie.'"[108] American actresses like Jayne Mansfield, Jane Russell, Ava Gardner and Marilyn Monroe offered a sexual confidence unseen in British film stars. Joan Crawford, Bette Davis, and Barbara Stanwyck seemed to be assertive, strong-willed and confident.[109] Julie Walters loved actress Bette Davis because "she always played strong women who had to be reckoned with, who were not there simply to function as a fantasy to attract and please men."[110] Growing up in Liverpool, Cilla Black wanted her "life to be like Doris Day's."[111] Doris Day was so admired because she was down to earth, assertive but not too sexy and her girl-next-door looks were attainable for British girls. Cilla Black believed that she "lived in a world where the model of all that was good in life was in a Doris Day movie."[112]

America in the British Working-Class Imagination

While British intellectuals decried the materialism of America, the working class, whose homes were often less than opulent, gazed in frustrated jealous longing at

American luxury. In 1961, 46 percent of private dwellings in Britain had been built before 1920, 33 percent from 1920 to 1938, 3 percent from 1939 to 1947 and, despite the postwar housing boom, only 18 percent after 1947.[113] Many lived in two-bedroom terrace houses with no front or back garden. In the early 1950s, thousands still resided in prefabricated dwelling, or "prefabs," ostensibly built as temporary shelter after the war but often standing for 20 years or more. In 1951, over 37 percent of Britons still lived in dwellings with neither a bath nor a shower.[114] Most would bathe in a tin bath, filled with endless kettles of boiling water while some went to the public baths to pay for a bath with hot water. Many endured outside toilets. "The outside toilets were dismal, insanitary places and in the winter they were always freezing cold," one resident of the Gorbals in Glasgow remembered. "If it was very cold, tenement inhabitants used chanties, which they stored under their beds. These bedpans were then slopped out in the morning. For toilet paper, strips of the *Daily Record*, *Evening Times* or the *Glasgow Citizen* were used."[115] Heating the home was a constant problem. By 1964, only 8 percent of British households enjoyed the luxurious comfort of central heating.[116] People huddled in the living room to keep warm by the coal fire or the increasingly popular gas fire. Many sat with rugs on their laps and draft excluders lined the bottom of the door. The rest of the house was damp and perishing. Kitchens and living rooms with cold lino floors and bathrooms and toilets in particular were fridge like. "Climbing the stairs to go to bed at night was often likened to scaling the north face of the Eiger," remembered Julie Walters growing up in the West Midlands in the 1950s.[117] Only 22 percent of households owned telephones and only 38 percent refrigerators in 1965.[118]

Most knowledge of America came from movies, imported television programs and magazines in which America seemed to offer a comfortable standard of living for everyone, an attractive idea to those that had just gone through six years of war, rationing and postwar austerity. Most British people believed that Americans "live in fabulous houses, Penthouses, Ranches, Farms where everything is automatic or electric, and everybody has at least two cars, one of which is sure to be a Cadillac," one Englishman suggested in the summer of 1957. "In fact, America is a land of milk and honey, and the sidewalks are paved with gold." Hollywood films, according to one observer, gave the impression that America was a world of "luxurious penthouses, mink coats, motor yachts, expensive automobiles" where everyone has a "swimming pool in his back garden."[119] Paul Wood, born in the middle of a Nazi bombing raid on September 24, 1940, in Mitcham, Surrey, found that Hollywood films offered a positive view of the United States. "Very family orientated, homely country but far better off money wise, everyone owned a large car, and had fridges in their homes. They had more money than the UK working population."[120] Others gained their view from relatives in the States. "Mum's cousin visited us from San Francisco, she was born in Clonakilty," Mary Minnock, the daughter of Irish immigrants to Britain, remembered.

> She knew other family members who had settled in USA. She exemplified better opportunities, better lifestyle, and higher standard of living. Other cousins came on holiday to Cork from U.S.—I thought they were much more confident than "us" . . . .

> and, they could afford the holiday!!! They had more technology in their homes, especially in the kitchen, their homes were better heated and they had air conditioning. I don't think I understood what that was exactly, but like much else it seemed to have the WOW factor to me.[121]

Everyone agreed that what came from America was simply better than anything available in Britain. Newspapers were full of advertisements for "American-style" men's jackets and shirts and women's coats, dresses, sandals, swim wear, bags and bracelets. To entice women to buy hair curlers, advertisers informed them that they were "used by 25 million American women."[122] Retailers advertised houses for sale with "American style-kitchens."[123] Not just commercial advertisers but the British government seemed to believe that people wanted American rather than British styles. In 1952, the Ministry of Housing and Local Government issued a report that suggested that local authorities should build houses based on the American model to appeal particularly to the younger generation. "New kind of terrace house with an American—style inside, recommended today by the Ministry of Housing and Local Government, may revolutionise the traditional British idea of what a home should be," the *Daily Mirror* suggested. "As in the small homes that are the background of many Hollywood films, dividing walls are swept away and almost the whole of the ground floor is given over to 'living space.'"[124]

> Visiting the home of a young British working-class couple, particularly in a new housing development area, one is often struck by the Americanized looks of their home as reflected in the presence of a radio-phonograph, a television set, a refrigerator, of American-style illustrated women's magazines often carrying Hollywood columns, and in the tendency towards large sofa cushions and tasseled standard lamps rather than imitations of severe British upper-class furniture,

T. R. Fyvel, literary editor of the *Tribune,* noted in 1952.[125] "As a child growing up in post-war Britain, where sweets were rationed and the radio played a solemn diet of classical piano recitals, it is not hard to see why just the word 'America' had an almost mystical ring," Chris Welch, later a music journalist on *Melody Maker*, suggested. "Our heroes were all Americans, whether cowboys, movie stars, rock 'n' rollers or beboppers."[126]

The natural and built environment in Britain seemed colorless and uninspiring compared to the exciting images of the United States they saw on Hollywood movies. Blue skies, sunshine, beaches and palm trees contrasted sharply with the gray skies, coldness, dampness and what often seemed like the endless rain of austere Britain. The cities and towns of Britain were scarred with bomb sites, a legacy of World War II, and were the main play areas of local children. Because of all the coal fires, a dense unhealthy smog, a mixture of smoke and fog, settled over cities and blackened red brick buildings. In the so-called Great Smog that descended on London for five days in 1952, as many as 12,000 people may have died. It was only the Clean Air Act passed by Parliament in 1956, and the introduction of gas and electric fires, that reduced pollution levels.[127] "The most striking memory of all of these films was the shock of Technicolor in the dark theatre, which made the gray streets waiting outside in their drab monochrome even grimmer than they actually were," remembered Gordon Sumner growing up in Newcastle in the 1950s.[128] American movies and songs evoked the freedom of the open road, which contrasted with the narrow lanes of rural Britain or the crowded roads that linked British cities. In the cinema, the deserts of Arizona and Texas and the big open spaces of the West suggested escape and freedom from dense, overpopulated Britain with the cramped living of terrace houses, overcrowded tenements and the stifling conformity of a close-knit community. The built environment in America looked so modern with new suburbs, skyscrapers and shopping malls while Britain looked old. "Britain was ancient, it was falling to pieces. I mean it was awful. You have no idea, even by 1965, how miserable and grey Britain was. It was a ghastly place," recalled Patrick Uden.[129] "I was a Yankophile," Peter Noone, lead singer of the Herman's Hermits, declared. "You have to imagine that these poor English guys were living in miserable, provincial, rainy, dreary cities, and saw posters with James Dean standing in the boots and the jeans and the T-shirt, with the cigarettes rolled up in the sleeve."[130]

While Britain rested on restraint and deference, for young people the United States enjoyed an enticing rebellious aura. Hollywood films, whether Westerns or detective stories, centered on ordinary individuals fighting a corrupt system or an injustice. American actors Marlon Brando and James Dean personified the youthful disrespect for authority that seemed absent in British films. Those young people that listened to rock 'n' roll music defied their parents and other adults, who so often condemned the music. Because the BBC rarely played rock 'n' roll or other American music, the music enjoyed an outsider status. Rock 'n' roll was heard in fairgrounds and amusement arcades, on Radio Luxembourg, and on jukeboxes in teenage-filled coffee houses. The overt eroticism of rock 'n' roll was a great attraction and a revolt against a prudish Britain that frowned upon any open discussion of sexuality. English author Ray Gosling declared that Americans "were the first attraction that made me want to rebel—and then came rock 'n' roll. That sent me hell-bent to smash to smithereens everything my parents' generation had built." Gosling used America as a model in his rebellion against British society.

> We wanted a new world, where you weren't hidebound by class and etiquette and by having to follow your betters and where you could respond to basic human instincts and have some fun and be free like the Americans were. We wanted to kick the old world of afternoon tea and school dinners and having to sit upright into touch. And we did.[131]

Young Britons did not simply embrace the United States as a rebellion against conformity and deference, but they also saw it as an alternative to Britain's social inequality. Britain had achieved greater egalitarianism in the period after World War II but the nation remained class-ridden with a rigid social hierarchy. The unelected monarchy and the House of Lords still retained some political influence. Students from prestigious independent schools, such as Eton, Harrow and Winchester, and from the universities of Oxford and Cambridge, dominated politics, the civil service, the Armed Forces and the BBC. Upper-class accents permeated cinema newsreels, radio and television, the courts and Parliament. Accent and vocabulary was a signifier of social class as was the newspapers you read, the food you ate, the clothes you wore and the sport you followed. Even though the 1944 Education Act widened educational opportunities by providing free secondary education for all, scant changes in social mobility ensued. In 1955, only 5 percent of University entrants came from semi-skilled or unskilled parents. Eight years later, the report of the Committee on Higher Education, chaired by Lord Robbins, noted that still only 7 percent of undergraduates originated from the families of the semi-skilled or unskilled.[132]

In contrast to the elitism of British society, everyone seemed to be treated equally in America. The United States offered a vision, even if a mythical one, in which you could be talented and successful even if you came from an unfashionable region or from a working-class community. On film, ordinary Americans were courageous, confident, heroic individuals often challenging a controlling system, while British workers were deferential, who did what they were told to do and who knew their place. "Hollywood has evolved a whole class of films which has no parallel in England—films which tell stories, plain or coloured, of ordinary working people," an editorial in *World Film News* in 1936 suggested.

> A high proportion of the American productions, love stories or crook dramas, comedies, farces or melodramas, are played out with truck drivers and clerks, cops and garage hands, shop girls and paid help as protagonists. The English film . . . . totters only as far as Piccadilly or St. James, or country houses with 40 bedrooms, situated in what always looks like Hampshire. Butlers and parlourmaids are necessary evils, but heroes look like thousands a year and heroines like speech day at Roedean. Working people, when presented at all, are presented only as figures of fun by kind permission of Mr. Gordon Harker or Mr. Sydney Howard.[133]

"The number of British films that have ever made a genuine try at a story in a popular milieu, with working-class characters all through, can be counted on the fingers of one hand," observed film director Lindsay Anderson in 1957.[134] Singer Adam Faith believed that if he became an actor, the "kind of roles I'd have in the Britain of 1954 would at best be a dimwit corporal playing opposite the scathing, witty, debonair middle-class officer and gentleman (usually Kenneth More)."[135] "I have two ambitions which I hope one day will come true" a 16-year-old shorthand-typist and son of a butcher stated hopefully,

> the first is to go to America, which in my opinion is the greatest place on the map of the world. Where everybody is classed as one, which (if you don't mind me saying so), is not a policy generally carried out by all of the English people at the present day. Secondly I hope to become a Vocalist of great renown with some popular American band.[136]

American literature too exuded this vision of classlessness. Class distinctions were clearly drawn in Britain while American novels seemed to suggest an absence of snobbery and overt class distinctions in the United States. Because British detective novels focused on the upper classes often in rural country-house settings, British workers could more easily identify with the earthy language, ordinary characters and urban settings of US writers like Dashiell Hammett and Raymond Chandler. American writers "were talking the way we talked," an ex-docker remarked.[137] "My generation found their own lives often more accurately mirrored in American fiction than in British fiction," television presenter Melvyn Bragg reminisced about his upbringing in provincial Wigton, Cumbria, in the north of England.

> Of course, there was D.H. Lawrence behind us, and Kingsley Amis and the others to come, but for a time John Steinbeck and *Cannery Row* with its skiving, drinking, philosophical "boys" seemed much more relevant to the more entertaining human stories lived out in Wigton than anything being written over here.[138]

Maurice Micklewhite, who was born into a working-class family in south London in March 1933, admired the social leveling of American culture. After leaving school at the age of 16, Micklewhite was called up for National Service in 1952. He found that American literature and films portrayed working-class life and the experiences of a soldier in a more inclusive and realistic way than British books or movies. "British authors wrote about officers; in the library I discovered Norman Mailer's *The Naked and the Dead* and James Jones's *From Here to Eternity*," he remembered. "Here at last were stories about the experiences of soldiers I could identify with." More than books, movies and American movies in particular, provided Micklewhite with a refuge from postwar austerity. "The one blinding light in the middle of all this gloom was the cinema, where I could escape for a couple of hours to somewhere better—usually America" opined Micklewhite. "Movies opened the world to me. They offered a way to a new life. America fascinated me. I thought of it as a great paradise." British films reflected old-fashioned class interests while American films were more democratic. Micklewhite believed that British films showed working-class people as "monosyllabic, kowtowing, forelocks-touching oafs . . . . In American pictures, you had working-class heroes and young actors came from the working class. Even the ones from society families like Bogart looked and talked like they were from the working class." Watching numerous war films confirmed this view. "For young working-class boys like me, America was really exciting. British war films were always about officers; American films were about enlisted men." According to Micklewhite, British movies "seemed to be about the lives of the middle class and the aristocracy, whereas people in American films seemed to be more like me." Micklewhite changed his name to Michael Caine after seeing the Humphrey Bogart film *The Caine Mutiny*, became an actor, and went on to become an international film star.[139]

Certainly, British workers imagined the United States in negative ways, especially as a place with a penchant for violent crime. In the summer of 1957, Americans Doris and Edward Bernays in their visit to Britain found that Britons thought that in the United States "Gangsterism is rampant. Juvenile delinquency is widespread." Hollywood films, according to one cinema goer, gave the impression that America was a world of "dope addicts with monkeys on their backs, of gangsters, rackets and corruption."[140] Yet violence in the United States seemed glamorous with little graphic violence portrayed in the movies or on television.

Most Americans appeared unaffected by the violence in the West or the gangland murders that predominated on TV and in movies. In television series like *The Untouchables* and *The Fugitive*, the violence of organized crime and the domestic murders of suburban America seemed remote from the daily lives of ordinary Americans. American novelists like Dashiell Hammett and Raymond Chandler portrayed the corruption and violence in the United States as an aberration solved by smart detective work. Hollywood showed that crime would not pay as criminals were always caught, the divide between criminals and police was clear and police were the heroes of the films. The extent of the everyday violence of inner-city America remained hidden from British view. Guitarist and blues enthusiast Eric Clapton recalled that the television programs and movies he watched as a child and the blues records he listened to as a teenager created an exotic image of Chicago. "Needless to say, where I came from, we didn't get the full picture, the harsher aspects of it. It seemed incredibly romantic, gangster-ish and exciting.... It became the place I wanted to go to as a teenager."[141]

In addition to America's violent image, Britons noticed the discrimination suffered by African Americans. Many Britons first became aware of race relations in the United States when confronted with the injustice black soldiers faced from white GIs in Britain during World War II. A survey undertaken in 1943 found that Britons "expressed disapproval of the way these people are being treated, and many were shocked at the attitudes of American white to black troops in this country."[142] These negative views of American race relations continued after the war. In a survey undertaken in 1948–1949, 43 percent of Britons believed that the United States was "guilty of persecuting the Negro."[143] "Many otherwise normal English people," reported the *Newsweek* correspondent in England, "are quite convinced that... the American way of life consists of a mad orgy of iced drinks, profiteering, Negro lynching, and persecution of liberals."[144] Media reports of discrimination, such as the attempts to exclude black children from Little Rock Central High School in Arkansas in 1957, shocked many. What angered Alan Stepney, a teenager in London in the 1950s, "was the anti-coloureds attitude of (some) US military, many of whom were stationed in the UK in the 1950's, and the" events in "Little Rock, which we read about. We were used to having coloured people, although, of course, most were from the British Empire and so 'almost' British! We didn't have that prejudice and, generally, weren't happy about it and certainly wouldn't accept it here."[145] In the late 1950s, 66 percent of British respondents in a Europe-wide poll had a "bad" or "very bad" opinion of the way the United States treated African Americans.[146]

Even though there may have been some sympathy for the plight of African Americans, Britons still held rather negative views of them. The British vision of black America in the 1950s was partly determined by their views of Africans in the British Empire. Books, newsreels and magazines portrayed black Africans as backward and uncivilized people who needed the British to look after them. "Among the books I devoured as a child were plenty by Victorians such as Kipling, Conrad, Henty and Haggard, racists all, whose stories of European supremacy in the face of savagery operated, a century on, as the backdrop to public opinion," Val Wilmer, growing up in London in the 1950s, recalled.[147] Blacks were seldom on the television in the 1950s and when they were, they were inevitably scantily clad, living in mud huts with bones through their noses. The only view many whites in Britain had of African Americans was from Hollywood movies, which portrayed blacks as passive people who endured hardships submissively and who endeared themselves to white audiences as "a clown, a buffoon, an idiot and a superstitious fool." Invariably, blacks played "ignorant servants, lazy janitors, superstitious toilet-attendants, nit-wit maids, valets, shoe-shine boys, faithful retainers, tramps and no-accounts, and Uncle Tom roles of every description," suggested English author Peter Noble in 1948.[148] More realistic portrayals of African Americans emerged after Noble's book appeared in 1948 but even by 1962 author Edward Mapp in his extensive study of blacks in films could note that "there was no real abandonment of traditional Negro stereotypes in the American motion pictures released during the year."[149]

American Influence on Working Class

Almost inevitably, Britons were inspired by what they saw on screen and heard in the music and incorporated some of that attitude and behavior into their daily lives. The exciting music and raucous dancing of America encouraged Britons to shed their inhibitions and become more demonstrative and less reserved. The creativity and improvisation found in the Twist and other American dances replaced the physical rigidity of British dancing. Rock 'n' roll music further encouraged unrestrained behavior that was so different from British sensibilities of self-control. Musicians like Elvis Presley, Jerry Lee Lewis and Little Richard inspired exuberance and wilder behavior in young Britons who were tired of staying calm. America encouraged a decline of deference and self-restraint in Britain and an increased self-confidence in British working-class youth. A growing distaste of authority and formality evident in Britain by the late 1950s owed much to the increased income and education but also to American influences. America provided Britons with a model of irreverence, evident in the casual clothing of blue jeans and t-shirts, the informality of speech and the gum-chewing swagger seen in Hollywood movies.[150]

In addition to inspiring changes in behavior, America fueled consumerism in Britain. The availability of goods and the increased income to buy them were obviously important for the development of a consumer society in Britain, but so too was the inspiration provided by the enticing images emanating from America. "The constant reiteration of visions of 'the good life' in American feature films, in the form of lavish meals and lavish settings was an important fuel for the emergence of a fully-fledged mass consumer society in Britain in the 1950s," claimed Paul Swann in his study of American films in Britain.[151] Britons lusted after the expensive clothes, new cars, luxurious homes and consumer goods displayed on cinema and TV screens, on billboards and in glossy magazines. Hollywood movies revealed that luxury commodities could be affordable to ordinary people and not be restricted to the wealthy. "Hollywood showed them a new world where there was no food rationing and no shortage of nylons," historian Peter Clarke argues, "often an opulent lifestyle, yet not that of the status-bound upper classes in Britain, but one in which automobiles and refrigerators were as much of a common culture as smoking cigarettes."[152] Increased employment opportunities and incomes allowed women to buy the clothing, accessories and household gadgets that were an important part of the image of American life. "They have helped to teach the British wage-earner's wife and daughter that working-class life today need be neither proletarian nor humble," T. R. Fyvel, literary editor of the *Tribune*, noted in 1952. "They have helped to popularize notions of cleaner living and eating, or modern kitchen units, of labor-saving household devices," Fyvel believed. "The young British housewife's admiration for the brighter, cleaner, more classless American way of domestic life may often be unconscious, but it is usually plain enough."[153]

Imagining the United States led many Britons to not only desire consumer products, but also to become disgruntled with the gap between the promises of the "never had it so good" consumerism seen in American movies and on TV and the reality of their lives. In a survey of British cinema audiences undertaken at the end of the war by the movie magazine *Picturegoer*, one young man, the son of a welder, noted that he was dissatisfied with his home town because

> there are no drug stores on the corner of the street where you can take your girl friend and have some ice-cream or a milk-shake. In our town there are no sky-scrapers or really high buildings and there are not half as many buildings which are lit up as those on the films are such as Broadway.

"I certainly think that films make you dissatisfied with your own way of life," a 30-year-old housewife with two children exclaimed. "The average working girl never has in real life, such a lovely home or apartment, or the clothes and boy friends (plus car) that the screen girl is shown to have. Of course, there is another way of looking at it, which is that we go to films to see a more glamourous and luxurious way of life, a life we should like to live ourselves."[154] Little had changed six years later. A 19-year-old in the RAF believed that "This country's no good. It's finished. I'd like to go to America and have a car, and one of those flats you see on the flicks, with a refrigerator and a telephone, and all that. We're behind the times I tell you." A teenage bank clerk suggested that watching American films had made her disappointed with young British men. "[A]fter seeing the polished lover on the screen it is rather disillusioning to be kissed by a clumsy inexperienced boy," she wearily suggested.[155]

The exalted view of a prosperous United States not only led to dissatisfaction with their own situation, but it also prodded some working-class youth to try to move beyond their unfortunate circumstances, seeking change either by individual effort or collective action. Many who had once accepted slum housing and deprivation now found another world of possibilities. Adam Faith, for example, who became a famous singer, suggested that "the cinema sharpened the hunger I felt to get free of the Acton Vale flats" where he lived.[156] Others looked to emigration. In February 1957, 41 percent of the public said they would emigrate if they could, the highest figure since 1948.[157] Many acted on their desire. From 1950 to

1959, 195,709 residents of the United Kingdom immigrated to the United States, the highest number since the 1920s.[158] The mood of discontent was also evident on the shop floor. Increased expectations of higher standards of living played a part in fueling industrial militancy as did full employment, which strengthened the bargaining power of trade unions and their willingness to improve their working conditions. "The most striking trend is the rise in acquisitive instincts as expressed in shop-floor behavior," suggested Ferdynand Zweig in his study of factory workers in the late 1950s. "Money-mindedness plays an ever-increasing part in a man's attitude to his work." Some skilled workers took unskilled work if it paid more money and workers expressed a constant desire for overtime. "Ninety-five percent of all grievances, complaints and squabbles on the floor are about money. It's money, money all the time," both supervisors and shop stewards agreed.[159]

The victory of the Conservative Party in three successive general elections in 1951, 1955 and 1959 was partly a product of the desire by many for an American-style consumer society in Britain. The Labour and Conservative parties both wanted to maintain full employment and accepted the reality of the mixed economy and the welfare state, but the Conservative Party tapped into the feeling of discontent by promoting lower taxes, consumerism and a "property-owning democracy."[160] Viewing American society led many to reject the austerity of Labour and accept the Conservative promise to increase peoples' living standards while maintaining the security of the welfare state. "I fancy that in the last year or two, more and more people are beginning to turn to their own personal affairs and to concentrate on their own material advancement," Hugh Gaitskell stated after the Conservative election victory in 1951. "No doubt it has been stimulated by the end of post-war austerity, TV, new gadgets like refrigerators and washing machines, the glossy magazines with their special appeal to women, and even the flood of new cars on the home markets. Call it if you like a growing Americanization of outlook."[161] In power, the Conservative government promoted home ownership by halting the construction of council houses, maintained low taxes and abolished hire purchase restrictions, which helped initiate a consumer boom.

> Sir Oliver Poole, the Conservative Party Chairman in the late-1950s, used to drive every Saturday from his nearby country home to Watford to look at the crowds revelling in their new consumer goods, which they had not been able to afford before: cars, television sets, washing machines, refrigerators, and so on,

according to historian Vernon Bogdanor.[162] Evidently, Conservatives were happy with the consumer society that they and the United States had helped create.

By concentrating too much on the views of intellectuals of the left and the right, and by misconstruing legitimate criticisms of US foreign policy and of American society as "anti-American," historians and some political commentators of the time have been too quick to describe the 1950s as a decade of anti-Americanism. Certainly, as Hollywood movies and jazz music flooded into Europe after World War I, intellectuals expressed a deep anxiety about the influence of American popular culture, which they considered vulgar and immoral. After World War II, concerns about a US cultural invasion continued but was now joined by anxieties about Britain's subservience to the United States, economically, militarily and diplomatically. The left condemned US foreign policy and the inequalities of American society while the right still evoked the superiority of the British character and culture. Increasingly, however, Conservatives admired American society as an alternative to socialist Britain.

To those most alienated from English upper-class culture and constrained by societal norms, the working classes, young people, women and the Celtic peoples, American popular culture and the American way of life proved most enticing. The majority of Britons admired American notions of individual freedom, social equality and social mobility that challenged Britain's rigid class structure. They believed that the United States was a far more exciting, affluent and democratic place than the drab, austere and deferential country in which they lived. There was a certain prejudice against American people, but there was far more support in Britain for the US government and its foreign policy than there was for the Soviet Union. Most Britons admired both the American culture they encountered and the society across the Atlantic they imagined. Some wanted to migrate to the United States, others adopted the clothes, demeanor and lifestyle of Americans they saw on screen and others still became dissatisfied with their own lives and used either individual or collective effort to improve their position.

The decade of the 1950s was a period of growing affluence and security for young men and women in Britain. People enjoyed higher wages, greater employment opportunities, more comfortable homes, free schooling to university level and a safety net if they lost their job or became sick. Yet the pace of change was slow and the United States offered the opportunity, affluence and unbounded glamour and excitement that Britain could not match. Americanization liberated rather than subjugated the minds of young Britons like David Bowie who revolted against traditional values, and released their pent-up frustration by adopting and adapting American cultural forms. As we will see in the next chapter, this young generation, inspired by the United States that they imagined in the 1950s, came of age in the 1960s and helped to usher in a cultural renaissance that would change Britain forever.

3

The British Working Class and the United States, 1963–1979

The United States of America continued to deeply impact Great Britain in the 1960s and 1970s. The Swinging Sixties, the name given to the exhilarating decade in which Britain became the world center of popular culture, was profoundly shaped by the United States. The music of the Beatles, substantial elements of the counterculture, the clothes of the era and the iconic James Bond movies that suggested a new modern cool Britain would not have transpired without American input. The new music stars of the 1970s, like David Bowie, Rod Stewart and Elton John, took their musical inspiration from the United States while the discotheques of Britain moved to the sounds of African-American music. From Martin Luther King, Jr. to Neil Armstrong, from Kojak to Luke Skywalker, from Muhammad Ali to Farah Fawcett, young Britons found icons both real and fictional in the United States while the sons and daughters of the New Commonwealth immigrants were particularly inspired by the African-American role models and the civil rights movement that they saw across the Atlantic.

During this period, however, the British working-class, those previously the most enamored with American society, developed a more ambiguous view of the United States as both American and British society went through profound changes. The year 1963 was an historical turning point in British perceptions of the United States. Beatlemania ushered in an unprecedented global appreciation of British popular culture and set the tone for a more confident, prosperous and liberal society. At the same time, the assassination of the popular US president John F. Kennedy in November 1963 and the television coverage of the confrontations between civil rights activists and the police in Birmingham, Alabama, conjured up a bleak image of the United States to many Britons, an image validated by the depictions of urban crime and decay both in imported television programs and in Hollywood movies.

American Influence on Britain, 1963–1979

In the 1960s and 1970s, the United States became even more economically involved in Britain than it was in previous decades. The United States was the leading investor in the country; corporations committed more money to Britain than to any other country except Canada.[1] In 1960, US companies invested US$3,231 million in Britain, rising it to US$7,996 million in 1970 and to US$12,461 million in 1974.[2] US investment in the United Kingdom in 1968 was 15 times greater than that in 1939, with over 1,600 US firms employing more than half a million employees, producing about one-tenth of British manufacturing output.[3] American products streamed into Britain. A British man "shaves with a Gillette razor blade, eats Heinz beans for breakfast, drives to work in a Ford on Esso fuel, and runs his office with Remington typewriters and IBM computers, while his wife Hoovers the house and shops in Woolworth," *Encounter* reported in 1967.[4] Some worried about America's dominance of the British economy. In 1968, journalists James McMillan and Bernard Harris in their book, *The American Take-Over of Britain,* decried the country's economic reliance on the United States, which threatened the independence of Britain. "From the moment an English baby is weaned on American-owned baby food, until he is carted away in an American-owned funeral car he is, to that extent, American-orientated from the cradle to the grave," they complained.[5]

American-style political campaigning influenced British politicians like never before. The use of advertising agencies to create an appealing image for political candidates spread from the United States to Britain when Prime Minister Harold Macmillan hired an advertising agency to run the Conservative party's successful 1959 election campaign and American concepts of polling and marketing crept into British politics.[6] With its slickness and greater emphasis on presentation, Thomas J. Carbery, a lecturer at the University of Strathclyde, found that the Conservative Conference in Blackpool in the Autumn of 1963 "was reminiscent of a party convention in the United States."[7] Labour leader Harold Wilson partly modeled his party's triumphant 1964 general election campaign on John F. Kennedy's successful run for presidency in 1960, associating himself with the youthful and modernizing spirit of the president. Wilson copied Kennedy's use of sound bites for television coverage, the first British politician to make "it a priority to provide the media with brief, compelling phrases or sentences," noted author Martin Rosenbaum in his history of political campaigning in Britain since 1945.[8]

American political campaigning techniques may have influenced both political parties, but US social movements and their emphasis on identity politics inspired young people in Britain to a greater degree. Americans studying in London and British academics and students who spent time at American Universities transferred political ideas across the Atlantic. Dramatic confrontations involving blacks, students, gays and women in the United States filled British TV screens. As a result, the left in Britain began to voice many of the same issues and adopt the same tactics as found in the United States. Students' Free Speech Movement at the University of California, Berkeley, in 1964–1965 encouraged student revolt in Britain that began at the London School of Economics. The National Organization for Women (NOW), organized in the United States in 1966, and the first National Women's Liberation Conference held in Chicago, Illinois, in 1968, inspired the inaugural Women's Liberation Movement conference in Oxford in February 1970. The Gay Liberation Front formed in London in October 1970 found encouragement in the Gay Liberation Movement in the United States.[9]

Those looking for alternative lifestyles took inspiration from the counterculture of the West Coast. Hippies, who rejected materialism and the conventional working life and indulged in drug use and sexual promiscuity, appealed to those looking for an alternative to modern consumer capitalism. The Summer of Love of 1967, when thousands of young people converged on San Francisco's Haight-Ashbury district, gained much publicity in the press and television and helped the countercultural ideas to acquire adherents in Britain. Scott McKenzie's "San Francisco (Be Sure to Wear Flowers in Your Hair)," which celebrated the influx of young people into San Francisco and spread a positive and romanticized image of the flower power movement, reached number one in Britain in 1967. "The radical *style* that expressed its generational separateness was largely an American export," author H. L. Malchow claimed,

> the tie-dye t-shirts and jeans, the marijuana, rock music, and afro hairstyles, the Underground papers, comix, and posters, the natural foods, granny glasses, and sandals, all the wide range of hippy paraphernalia of the alternative society that brought San Francisco or the East Village via Portobello Road to Hornsey, Hull, Sussex, Essex, and the L.S.E.[10]

The blue denim jeans worn by hippies, and others, became the signature clothing of young people everywhere. Denim fabric, first made in the French town of Nimes hence the name "de Nimes," was imported into the United States in the nineteenth century where it was worn as working clothes especially by cowboys in the West. Hollywood cowboy movies brought blue denim jeans to the eyes of the world, while Marlon Brando, James Dean and Elvis Presley made them a symbol of rebellion. Denim jeans were imported into Britain in the 1950s and by the 1970s they had become standard clothing for the world's youth. Blue jeans helped to introduce a new casualness into British dressing and became a symbolic item of clothing that appealed to the young generation. Denim jeans were transformed "from clothing into a ubiquitous cultural statement all around the world, one of independence, rebellion, equality, freedom," remarked author Harold Evans.[11] The appeal endured. A poll of 3,000 Britons undertaken in 2012 voted denim jeans the best American export.[12]

Mods, often seen as a uniquely British youth cult, modeled much of their look on American style. They adopted the American college Ivy League look of slip-on Bass Weejun shoes (called loafers in Britain), button-down collar shirts and wrinkle-free Sta-Prest trousers. London stores such as David's on Charing Cross Road, Austin's on Shaftesbury Avenue and the Ivy Shop in Richmond became the main suppliers of Ivy League clothes imported from the United States. Movie stars like Steve McQueen, Paul Newman and Anthony Perkins further exposed the look to a wider public. The popular American television soap opera *Peyton Place* brought the Ivy League look into the living rooms of Britain. Ryan O' Neal's character Rodney Harrington in *Peyton Place* wore a G9 jacket made by British company Baracuta, with their tartan lining, side-buttoned pockets, elasticized waist and two-button collar. Ironically, *Peyton Place* made the jacket so famous that they became known as "Harrington" jackets.[13]

Imported American television programs continued their hold on the British public. "It is disheartening, looking back, to reflect that nearly all the programmes with which I was really smitten as a child came from America," remembered author Brian Viner.

> I liked *The Clangers* and *The Wombles*, but not as much as I liked *The Addams Family* and *The Beverly Hillbillies* . . . . Even the British-made dramas for children seemed to lack something of the pizazz of their American counterparts. *The Adventures of Black Beauty* and *Follyfoot* were no match for *The Life and Times of Grizzly Adams* and *The Man from Atlantis*, at least not for a boy.[14]

Terry Christian, growing up in Manchester in the 1960s, recalled

> we loved all things American . . . . We hated *Blue Peter* and well-spoken, upperclass kids in TV dramas and we loved *The Beverley Hillbillies*. We were born in England, but felt more akin to the Americans, who didn't seem to look down their upper and middle class noses at us or speak in accents that made us want to switch the TV off.[15]

In the 1970s, the catch phrase "Book 'em Danno" from the American detective series *Hawaii Five-0* could be heard on playgrounds across the United Kingdom while Lee Majors, star of *The Six Million Dollar Man*, and Farah Fawcett from *Charlie's Angels* married and became the golden couple of the 1970s. "America was an obsession for everyone who liked telly, since Americans were never off the telly, in cop shows, films, cartoons and sitcoms," remembered English comedian Alan Davies. "Everything they did was so much more informal, loose, their conversation an appealing mix of colloquialism and grammatical shortcuts that washed through stuffy old England," Davies continued. "All of it seemed cooler, less constrained and restrained."[16]

The American effort to put the first man on the moon riveted the whole of Britain. When Neil Armstrong became the first human to step on the Moon in the early hours of July 21, 1969, most British children were asleep in bed. Those that stayed awake, viewed the landing in black-and-white images seemingly shot in a blizzard that made them difficult to decipher. Yet the moon landing inspired millions of British youngsters.

> The moon landing is stuck in my mind and I remember watching the programmes which showed the astronauts actually stepping onto the moon landscape was amazing, there is also a picture on the front page of the *Daily Express* that I cut out and kept, I really was in awe of the whole moon race,

13-year-old Ray Kennedy, growing up in Scunthorpe, recollected. "Although I may have forgotten the names of the actual astronauts I would daydream about becoming an astronaut, instead of a jockey which was what I really wanted, but for a while being an astronaut and landing on Mars took over."[17] In Islington, London, Gary

Kemp, another British child obsessed with the moon landing, was "woken early to see black-and-white ghosts walk upon the moon. My father cried. We watched it over and over until the morning came and the magical moon faded from outside our window."[18] The space race triggered a fascination with outer space, evident in the space-related television programs, movies and music and the boom in toy astronauts and rockets. With 28.6 million viewers, the Apollo 13 splashdown of April 1970 was the most watched program on British television in the 1970s.[19] *The 100 Greatest TV Moments*, a Channel 4 program broadcast on September 11, 1999, voted Neil Armstrong's first steps on the moon the number one moment in television history.[20]

America still dominated the cinema screens of Britain. Between 1961 and 1971, American production companies bankrolled two-thirds of all films made in Britain, including iconic British films like *Tom Jones*, *A Hard Day's Night*, *Dr. Strangelove* and the James Bond series of movies. There was an influx of US productions into the United Kingdom to make use of the talented British technicians. Hollywood hits like *Star Wars, Superman* and *Indiana Jones and the Lost Crusade* were all made at Elstree and Pinewood studios in England.[21] In the 1970s, Hollywood blockbusters made with large budgets and spectacular special effects like *Towering Inferno* released in 1974, *Jaws* in 1975 and *Stars Wars* in 1977 dominated the box office. To increase the anticipation, and to make the film's opening a huge event, the film companies undertook unprecedented advertising campaigns in the weeks leading up to their release in the United Kingdom and started huge merchandising tie-ins consisting of toys, posters and stickers of characters featured in the film. "May 7th 1977 (*Star Wars* release date) changed my life!" exclaimed Patrick Mills aged eight at the time. "Ask anyone in the sciences who went to grad school in the 90s and this will be the same." Inspired by the movie, Mills went on to become a science professor.[22]

All the leading lights of the British music scene, which enjoyed unparalleled international success in the 1960s, were heavily influenced by the United States. Rock 'n' roll was, of course, a major influence on all of the bands of the so-called Beat Boom including the four members of the Beatles: John Lennon, Paul McCartney, George Harrison and Ringo Starr. "It was nothing but Elvis Presley, Elvis Presley, Elvis Presley," John Lennon's Aunt Mimi recalled after her nephew first heard Elvis. "In the end I said 'Elvis Presley's all very well, John, but I don't want him for breakfast, dinner and tea.'"[23] The others were just as besotted with Elvis Presley, Little Richard and Buddy Holly and formed a band to imitate the music of their heroes. "We're the receivers, we're just interpreting it as English kids," Lennon told an interviewer, suggesting that the Beatles copied American music. "Don't let anybody ever kid you it's original. It's all a rip off."[24] Other types of American music inspired the Beatles. John Lennon's first band, the Quarrymen, advertised themselves as country, Western and rock 'n' roll musicians and sported cowboy shirts with Western-style string ties. The country sound could also be found on the melodies written by Lennon and McCartney and in the guitar sound of George Harrison who idolized country guitarists Carl Perkins and Chet Atkins.

The early years of Ringo Starr, born Richard Starkey in Liverpool in July 1940, illustrates the Beatles fascination with all aspects of the United States. The young

Starkey loved American music and American Westerns that he saw in the movie theatre. Gene Autry, the "Yodelling Cowboy," and singer Johnnie Ray were early heroes but Elvis Presley was the main inspiration. "No one believes what an effect that had on my life," Starkey opined, "just this lad with sideboards and shaking his pelvis and being absolutely naughty."[25] He became so obsessed with the West that he wanted to immigrate to Texas. In 1958, Starkey and a friend obtained immigration forms and a jobs list in Houston, Texas.[26] He bought a drum kit and joined a skiffle group in 1957 and two years later Starkey joined a rock 'n' roll band called the Raving Texans, which became Rory Storm and the Hurricanes. In deference to his Westerns heroes, Rory's band adopted Western-sounding names. Johnny Byrne became Johnny Guitar, the name of a Joan Crawford Western movie; Charlie O' Brien assumed the name Ty Brien in deference to Ty Hardin, star of the *Bronco* TV series; Wally Eymond adopted the more American-sounding Lou Walters; and Ritchie Starkey became the cowboy-sounding Ringo Starr.[27] Ringo left Rory Storm and the Hurricanes to join the Beatles in the summer of 1962. In homage to their country and western influences, the Beatles covered "Act Naturally," a classic Buck Owens song, on their 1965 album *Help!* with Ringo on vocals. Starr's first solo album, *Sentimental Journey* released in 1970, was a collection of American show tunes and standards, a tribute to the music of his youth.

Paul McCartney was particularly taken with American songs from the pre rock 'n' roll era, first introduced to him by his father. Jim McCartney, born in Liverpool in July 1902, loved ragtime music and learned to play the trumpet and the piano. During World War I, McCartney played with the Masked Melody Makers and later Jim Mac's Band while holding down a job as a salesman at the local cotton exchange. In the 1950s, Jim entertained relatives at family gatherings by playing American jazz standards, show tunes and pop ballads on his piano.[28] "What would happen would be, us kids would arrive at the do, the carpets would get rolled back, all the women would sit around on chairs with their little drinks of rum-and-black, gin-and-it, Babycham and all that," Paul McCartney reminisced. "Someone would play the piano and it was normally my dad. They would play all these old songs: 'When the red, red robin . . . ,' 'Caroline Moon,' 'Bye Bye Blackbird.' They'd sing these all night, that was the party."[29] According to McCartney, "when I got into songwriting, I realized how well structured these songs were. I think I took a lot of my lessons from them."[30] "I do think they did have quite an influence, really, on us melodically . . . . It's in a lot of the songs we were trying to write, even though we were now living in the rock and roll era and influenced by it."[31]

The Beatles continued to be fans of contemporary American music. They played covers of Motown songs and their harmonies and lyrics were inspired by girl groups like the Shirelles and The Cookies. The Beatles covered a total of 12 songs by American artists on their first two albums. The Beatles first met Bob Dylan in 1964 and he prompted them to focus on writing more serious lyrics. Dylan's influence on the Beatles' lyrics is particularly evident on John Lennon's songs like "I'm A Loser," "You've Got to Hide Your Love Away" and "Help," which showed evidence of more personal and introspective use of words. "Anyone who is one of the best in his field—as Dylan is—is bound to influence people." The song "A Hard Day's Night" was in a Dylan vein until he "Beatle-ified it," Lennon stated in 1965.[32] The song writing and studio sophistication of the Beach Boys *Pet Sounds* album released in 1966 also inspired the Beatles when they made *Sgt. Pepper's Lonely Hearts Club Band* the following year.[33]

America had a similar impact on the Rolling Stones, the other leading British band of the 1960s. Keith Richards, born in 1943 in Dartford, Kent, wore a cowboy outfit as a child and spent endless hours fantasizing about Roy Rogers. "I asked Keith what he wanted to do when he grew up. He said he wanted to be like Roy Rogers and play guitar," Mick Jagger remembered. "It seemed America had all the things England had only *lots* more," recalled Richards. "I loved the movies. Just *lookin'* at American westerns, the panoramas and the countryside were fantastic. You don't come across mountains like *that* where *I* lived. It all seemed so *exotic*. The wildest countryside I ever saw were the marshes across the River Thames." Richards subsequently visited the local library to read up on American culture and history. "Keith knows more about America than he does about his own country," his mother revealed.[34] Keith Richards described first hearing Elvis Presley's "Heartbreak Hotel" on Radio Luxembourg as an "explosion." "That was the stunner. I'd never heard it before, or anything like it. I'd never heard of Elvis before. It was almost as if I'd been waiting for it to happen. When I woke up the next day I was a different guy."[35] As rock 'n' roll lost its way in the late 1950s, the future members of the Rolling Stones became obsessed with blues music. The Rolling Stones, named after a Muddy Waters song, made their first live appearance at the Marquee Club in London on July 12, 1962. They played a louder and brasher version of the blues with the plaintive voices of African Americans replaced by the more assertive singing of Mick Jagger. "The Stones were never very influenced by English music," Mick Jagger suggested. "You've some early folk influences, and there are some Elizabethan pastiches and stuff, but most of our influences were American. I would say the Stones were always an American band with a tiny bit of Englishness."[36] Little wonder that when Keith Richards arrived in the United States for the Rolling Stones first American tour in 1964 he felt like he had "died and gone to heaven."[37]

Other leading lights of the 1960s' British music scene were inspired by the varied sounds coming from the United States. "We had wanted to be a blues band. Our inspiration and heart was there," Ray Davies of the quintessential London band, the Kinks, rather surprisingly recalled.

> But I realised early on—and I'm going to be crucified for saying this—that white guys don't play the blues too well. I adapted what I knew about the blues into my music. "You Really Got Me" is my idea of a blues song, but it became very English because I discovered what lyrics are.[38]

Ray's brother Dave Davies of the Kinks agreed. "Emotionally, we hooked up with the blues. A black bass player I once knew in LA coined the term 'white negroes' to describe The Kinks."[39] The Who's Pete Townshend and John Entwistle first played in a Dixieland jazz band called The Confederates. Roger Daltrey joined a rock 'n' roll band called the Detours while drummer Keith Moon performed in a surf band. Once they formed the Who, the four Londoners played rock 'n' roll numbers but also became influenced by the soul sounds of James Brown and Booker T. & the MG's.[40]

Not only did America influence British musicians, but all types of music emanating from the United States remained extremely popular in Britain. The bestselling album of the 1960s was *The Sound of Music* soundtrack released in 1965 with music and lyrics written by Americans Richard Rodgers and Oscar Hammerstein II. The soundtrack to *West Side Story*, composed by Leonard Bernstein and Stephen Sondheim, was close behind. Bob Dylan, Simon and Garfunkel, the Beach Boys and Jimi Hendrix played a major role in influencing the lyrics, musical styles and production techniques of British bands. In the 1970s, the Jackson 5 and the Osmonds became rivals for the teeny bop market while David Cassidy rose to fame as fictional teenager Keith Partridge, part of a musical group in *The Partridge Family* TV series, and then pursued a solo career that put his poster on the bedroom walls of girls across the country. Bread and the Eagles seduced Britain with songs about outlaws, deserts, hot summer nights and highways sung to a Californian sound marrying country, folk and rock. Five of the top ten selling singles in Britain in the 1970s were by American artists and six of the ten top selling albums of the 1970s were American.[41]

The Sex Pistols, the pioneering punk band in Britain, were highly influenced by the minimalist sound of some US acts. The term "punk" was originally an American word that began to be used to describe the bands that came out of New York in the mid-1970s. In 1973, Malcolm McClaren, co-owner of the boutique "Sex" in London's Kings Road, travelled to New York City and befriended the New York Dolls. He became their manager and returned to London to recruit his own British version of the Dolls. The band he founded, the Sex Pistols, with guitarist Steve Jones, drummer Paul Cook, Glen Matlock on bass guitar and John Lydon renamed Johnny Rotten on vocals, played their first gig at St. Martin's College in November, 1975. They performed cover versions of songs by American bands The Monkees, The Stooges, Jonathan Richman and the Modern Lovers and Chuck Berry.[42] Malcolm McLaren encouraged his charges to adopt Television guitarist Richard Hell's abrasive attitude, his spiky hair and ripped clothes.[43] The Sex Pistols signed with EMI and released their first single, "Anarchy in the U.K," in November, 1976.

American musicians inspired other punk bands. Siouxsie, lead singer of the band Siouxsie and the Banshees, "mirrored herself on all those pop stars, Nico and Patti Smith," a friend of the band revealed, while lead guitarist Severin acquired his name from the lyrics of the Velvet Underground's song "Venus in Furs" and "modeled himself on John Cale [and] Lou Reed."[44] When Mick Jones, later of the Clash, started his first band London SS he placed an advert in the music paper *Melody Maker* asking for musicians inspired by the Stooges, MC5 and the New York Dolls to contact him. The Patti Smith Group played their UK debut gig at the Roundhouse in London on May 16, 1976, to an audience that included Joe Strummer, Mick Jones and Paul Simonon, future members of the Clash, Viv Albertine, who later joined the Slits, and John Lydon of the Sex Pistols.[45] Members of the Sex Pistols, the Clash and the Damned all went to see the Ramones when they played their first British concerts in London in July 1976.[46]

White American rock music may have conquered the charts, but the sounds of black America became a vital part of British youth culture in the clubs and discotheques of urban Britain. In the 1950s, cafes and cinemas were the major meeting place for young people, but in the 1960s and 1970s they were overtaken by the discotheque. Soul music, pioneered by Ray Charles and James Brown, with its roots in gospel and rhythm and blues music and its emphasis on impassioned vocals and a mesmerizing beat, developed into the soundtrack of discos across the country. By the mid-1960s, DJs at the Scene and Flamingo in London, the Twisted Wheel in Manchester, the Club-A-Go-Go in Newcastle and the Sink in Liverpool played imported American records to a Mod audience, who reveled in the exclusivity of the music.[47] The TV programs *Ready Steady Go,* which began broadcasting in August 1963, and *Top of the Pops,* which was first aired in January 1964, and the new pirate radio stations launched in 1964 helped to gain the music a wider audience.

The commercial sound of the Detroit label Tamla Motown became a regular feature on the British singles chart thanks to a milkman's son from South London. In the mid-1950s, teenager Dave Godin was enjoying a treat in an ice cream parlor in London's Bexleyheath when Ruth Brown's "Mama He Treats Your Daughter Mean" came on the jukebox. The emotion of the music was unlike anything Godin had heard before. "I can only describe it as one of those rare 'magical moments' that a person experiences every once in awhile, a bit like falling in love. That moment truly affected the rest of my life," he revealed.[48] He built a network of like-minded soul music enthusiasts by contacting those who sent letters on the topic of black music to the music paper *Record Mirror* and went on to form the Tamla-Motown Appreciation Society in 1963. After Godin wrote to Berry Gordy, the founder of Motown records, Gordy invited the young Englishman to Detroit where he met all the leading Motown artists and became the company's consultant in Britain. Godin encouraged DJs to play the music and established a distribution deal for the Tamla Motown label through EMI. In 1967 he founded Soul City, the first specialist soul music record shop in the country, which began in Deptford High Street, London, and later moved to Monmouth Street in Covent Garden. Godin continued to promote the music by writing for the music journal *Blues & Soul.* Forever a purist, Godin had little time for those white artists who imitated black music. At Dartford Grammar School he met Mick Jagger and introduced him to many of the sounds of black America, "I'm ashamed to say. It's ironic that as a result of meeting me he's where he is today," Godin both boasted and lamented.[49]

By the 1970s, soul music had become ubiquitous in the discos of Britain. Artists like James Brown and Sly and the Family Stone had moved soul music into the more dance-orientated funk music, which emphasized the bass and drums. Funk music was uplifting, and discos offered the hedonism of late nights and freedom of dark subterranean spaces where men and women could come together to enjoy a shared experience of sheer joy. The "US is not grasping the importance of the discotheque," *Billboard* magazine bemoaned in 1974. "Its use had not been properly developed. England is ten years ahead—there are hundreds in London and the provinces."[50] DJs played soul and funk music imported from the United States in discotheques but also in pubs and American-style bars decorated with flashing lights, ritzy furnishings, plush carpets, dimly lit black interiors, mirrored walls and fake palm plants. Here, the music conjured up images of neon-lit streets and American nights full of sensual pleasures. With the traditional music press ignoring soul and funk music, magazines and newspapers devoted to the music began to appear including *Blues & Soul* in 1966, *Black Music* in December 1973 and *Black Echoes* in 1976.[51] British funk bands began to form including Hi Tension, Light of the World and Level 42, but the disco remained the focus of the scene, not the live music venue.

Funk music inspired the Soul Boy and Soul Girl youth culture, which emerged in the mid-1970s in the South of England. The Soul Boy and Soul Girl scene combined American and British styles. They listened to American imports of soul and funk music, copied the sartorial elegance of Bryan Ferry and David Bowie and wore the old American clothing available in vintage shops. Inspired by the look of Bowie and Ferry, white Soul Boys and Girls wore wedge haircuts, straight hair at the back and sides and long fringes at the front. Boys sported plastic sandals, or similar flat shoes that were easy to dance in, white socks, capped sleeve t-shirts, American-style bowling and Hawaiian shirts, cowboy scarves, mohair jumpers, dungarees, 1940s-style pleated or pegged trousers narrowing at the ankle with turn ups, and American jeans worn with brightly colored belts. Girls wore deck shoes or ballet pumps, which were more suited for dancing in than high-heeled shoes, and 1950s' style full skirts worn with footless tights. Many drove American cars such as the 69 Mustang Convertible or the more common Ford Capri.[52] "Here was the true working-class youth movement," suggests Soul Boy Gary Kemp, "dressed to the nines in all its aspirational glory, every hard-earned penny spent on clothes, haircuts and American soul imports; a detail-obsessed, dancing Narcissus."[53] Here too was the first British youth culture that included both black and white youngsters. Young black Britons saw soul music as their music, sung by African Americans who, unlike blues musicians, seemed to live a life of glamour and provided an image of upward mobility. By the early to mid-1980s, the scene was beginning to wane, but the Soul Boy and Soul Girl look of the 1970s evolved into the New Romantics and the casual cultures that emerged in the 1980s.

In the mid-1970s, funk music developed into the more commercial disco sound, which relied on strings and a softer tone. Disco may have started in obscurity but it soon entered the mainstream. Three of the top ten selling singles of the 1970s in the United Kingdom were by commercial disco acts, two by Boney M and one by Village People.[54] All the major British pop stars including Elton John, Rod Stewart, the Rolling Stones and David Bowie adopted the disco sound. Disco was often criticized as shallow but not only did it outsell punk music, the darling of the media, it was also far more influential, inspiring hip hop, house and techno music. The film *Saturday Night Fever*, released in Britain in 1978, and starring John Travolta with the soundtrack supplied by the Bee Gees and other disco acts, touched off a media frenzy and the phenomenon of male dancers, either humorously or seriously, trying to dance like Travolta at weddings and discos across the country.

While modern funk and disco music dominated the south of England, so-called northern soul music ruled the dance halls of northern Britain. When Motown-style soul music with its fast stomping beat began to be superseded by funk music, DJs in the north began to import obscure Motown-sounding soul records that had been made in the 1960s to satisfy the demands of their crowd. Music that had died out in London discos still thrived at clubs like the Twisted Wheel in Manchester, The Golden Torch in Stoke on Trent, the Catacombs in Wolverhampton and the Mecca in Blackpool and was played in the pubs, working men's clubs and youth clubs in the towns of the north and midlands of England. Recognizing the regional adherence to the fast upbeat soul music, Dave Godin coined the phrase "northern soul" in *Blues and Soul* magazine in June 1970.[55]

Northern soul grew increasingly popular. "I got bookings everywhere, the phone never stopped ringing," northern soul DJ Kev Roberts recalled.[56] Stuart Maconie "heard soul music wherever you went in Wigan .... In Wigan, we were raised on soul. You didn't even realize it was soul. It was just that music, the one you heard in every pub, at every youth club ... All social gatherings were soundtracked by Northern Soul."[57] "One thing's for certain," wrote Roger St Pierre in the *New Musical Express* in the early 1970s, "if a cult of such epidemic proportions was happening in London, rather than far-off Blackpool, Keighley, Warrington and Manchester, the pop press would be full of it and the record industry would be rushing out the records like peas in a pod."[58] Yet the attraction for many was that the music was not well known. "We were the keepers of a faith that had been heretically ignored and could be hedonistic and righteous at the same time! And the records we treasured were by singers with fabulously exotic names," Neil Rushton stated, "that made the whole experience even more glamorous compared to the pop charts rubbish being fed us by the mainstream."[59] Some of these previously obscure soul records made the British charts in the mid-1970s and when some of these African-American singers, many unknown in the United States, arrived in Britain, they were shocked at the ecstatic reception they received. Unlike the Mods or the southern Soul Boys, northern soul was more concerned with the music and the dancing rather than with the style of dress. Northern soul dance floors were dominated by acrobatic and athletic dancers wearing clothes that allowed for energetic and sweat-induced dancing. Men wore baggy trousers with high waistbands and vests or tank tops and women sported long loose-fitting skirts and skimpy tops.

At the height of the music's popularity in the mid-1970s, the most famous northern soul venue was the Wigan Casino located in a small industrial town sandwiched between Liverpool and Manchester. On September 22, 1973, the Wigan Casino staged its first northern soul all-nighter, which lasted from 12:30 a.m. to 8 o'clock in the morning. "The entrance to the Casino was really tatty, zero money spent on maintenance. It was almost a dump," recalled Wigan regular Ian Dewhirst. There were record stalls placed around the club with dealers selling obscure seven-inch imported singles, some at exorbitant prices, and up to 2000 dancers performed high kicks, splits, acrobatic spins and back-drops on the heaving dance floor. Rather than alcohol, which was unavailable at all-nighters, some dancers used amphetamines to maintain their energy through the night. Many brought sports bags containing a towel and change of clothes to replace their sweat-drenched attire in the morning. "If it was a really busy night, there would be steam coming out of the entrance," Dewhirst recalled.

> As soon as you walked in, this whole thing hits you. You're aware there's a really fast record playing, clouds of condensation hits you in the face, you hear the handclaps; it's almost like a drug. At its height, it was a real buzz. You know some clubs get it right. The right club at the right time with the right DJ; all the ingredients are right. And that's how it was with Wigan.[60]

The club became tremendously popular attracting over 100,000 members. In 1977, *Billboard* voted the Wigan Casino the best disco in the world.[61]

Northern soul almost inevitably declined in popularity in the late 1970s. The finite number of old, obscure, Motown-sounding records inevitably dried up and the quality of the newly unearthed material became increasingly lame. Wigan Casino closed in December 1981. Devotees of the music still gathered for northern soul nights but the modern form of American soul music, disco, made its ubiquitous way into northern Britain.

Black Britons

The sons and daughters of black immigrants to Britain took a particular liking to the United States. People of African descent had lived in Britain since Roman times but the black population dramatically increased as the British government invited New Commonwealth residents, mostly from the Caribbean and South Asia, to rebuild the war-ravaged infrastructure and to staff the growing health and transportation services. In 1951, the combined South Asian and West Indian population in Britain was less than 80,000 but by 1961 the figure climbed to 500,000 and in 1971 to 1,500,000 or 3 percent of the whole population.[62] Although only a small proportion of the overall population, their visibility was heightened by their concentration in London and the larger towns and cities of the north and the midlands.

Animosity toward black immigrants and their British-born children put into shade any prejudice Americans endured. Whites complained that immigrants were taking their jobs, sponging on welfare, driving down house prices or bringing crime to Britain. Many whites worried that Commonwealth immigration would change the culture and social fabric of Britain that they wanted to preserve. In the summer of 1958, whites attacked Afro-Caribbean's in the streets and in their homes in Notting Hill, West London, and in the Chase district of Nottingham in an outbreak of violence lasting for days. "Paki bashing," the unprovoked attacked on Asians in the streets, marred the late 1960s. Some Asians faced harassment as they brought paper shops and other small businesses in white areas and suffered abuse when they worked in Indian restaurants. A study of racial discrimination in Britain undertaken in 1967 found that in "employment, housing and the provision of services—there is racial discrimination varying in extent from the massive to the substantial." Blacks faced unfriendliness, cold hostility and personal abuse. "You see it every day," said one immigrant. "People say things 'You should be sent back home on a banana boat.' People's attitudes. Rude, unfriendly names like 'black bastards,' 'niggers,' and swearing." Another said, "Because I am black people say all sorts of things like 'go back to the zoo.' They don't believe we were born by human beings."[63] The so-called jokes about "Paki's" and "coons" were common on television, in the stage acts of comedians and in the workplace. Black footballers like Cyrille Regis, Laurie Cunningham and Brendan Batson, who all played for West Bromich Albion, endured monkey chants from opposing fans who also threw bananas onto the pitch.[64] Openly racist political parties such as the National Front (NF), founded in 1967, campaigned for the compulsory repatriation of all black people.

Little wonder that many young blacks born in Britain could identify neither with the homeland of their parents nor with the land of their birth. Many never felt accepted in Britain because of the constant talk of repatriation in the British media and because of the discrimination they faced from white Britons. Writing in the early 1970s, Chris Mullard, born in Hampshire, England, in 1946 of a Jamaican father and white English mother, described himself as "a black who cannot forget he is black... a black born and bred in the United Kingdom, who still feels an outcast."[65] Professional boxer Errol Christie, born in Coventry in 1963 to Jamaican parents, became one of the first black men to box for the England team. "For the first time, I found myself draped in the Union Jack, an icon also being paraded up and down Britain's high streets by National Front thugs. In truth, this left me with mixed emotions."[66]

Unable to fully identify with British cultural traditions or to find role models at home, a new generation of blacks looked to the United States for political and cultural inspiration. Black Britons recognized a shared African identity and history with black Americans and they found encouragement in the triumphs of African Americans. "Although being Black in Britain meant that you constantly had to be on guard for unsolicited attacks or abuse, we had a continuous supply of inspiration from our Black American cousins," jazz singer Terri Quaye recalled.

> 1962 was like a rescue mission. The Harlem Globetrotters took England by storm—I thought I would have lost my voice cheering—and still more was to come in the most wonderful sight and sound of the Duke Ellington Orchestra. By the end of 1962 I'm sure I'd grown four inches taller![67]

The civil rights movement offered heroes and triumphs that were seemingly unavailable in Britain. "It's often said that the Vietnam War was the first major conflict to be played out nightly on TV," suggested Mike Phillips,

> It wasn't so for us. For us, it was the Civil Rights struggle and the subsequent battle between the Black Power activists and the American government. During those years we got to know their names and faces better than the next door neighbours... These were great days, when we could watch black giants walking the earth.[68]

The words of Martin Luther King Jr. and his leadership in the civil rights movement inspired many blacks in Britain. King appeared on the popular *Face to Face* interview program on BBC television on October 29, 1961, and his visit to Britain in December 1964, en route to receive the Nobel Peace Prize in Stockholm, gained extensive publicity.[69] King urged those immigrant leaders he met in London to organize against racial discrimination. Subsequently, black activists formed the Campaign Against Racial Discrimination (CARD) in January 1965 to combat racism in Britain.[70]

A new slogan, Black Power, first brought to prominence by Stokely Carmichael head of the Student Nonviolent Coordinating Committee (SNCC) at a civil rights march in Mississippi in June 1966, caught the mood of alienated African Americans and became the rallying cry for some young blacks in Britain. Using headline-grabbing rhetoric, and inspired by the writings of Malcolm X, advocates of Black Power suggested that African Americans should jettison nonviolence and defend themselves against racist attacks. Instead of trying to assimilate into white culture, nationalists suggested blacks should take pride in their own culture and in the achievements of the black race.[71] In October 1966, Bobby Seale and Huey P. Newton created the Black Panther Party for Self-Defense in Oakland, California, to oppose police brutality. Wearing black berets and leather jackets, marching in military formation and openly carrying guns, some members became involved in deadly gun battles with police. The party attracted young urban blacks and soon had chapters across the United States. Influenced by anti-imperialist struggles in Asia and Africa, and revolutions in Cuba and China, the Black Panthers came to espouse a Marxist perspective.[72]

The ideas of Black Power travelled across the Atlantic, finding a receptive audience among first and second-generation black youth. After Malcolm X visited Britain in December 1964 and February 1965, local activists led by a young Trinidadian Michael de Freitas, who renamed himself Michael X, formed the Racial Adjustment Action Society (RAAS) in 1965.[73] Stokely Carmichael's visit to Britain in the summer of 1967 led to the formation of the Universal Coloured People's Association, which adopted the Black Power ideology. In the summer of 1968, activists established a small branch of the British Black Panther Party, the first Black Panther party to form independently outside the United States.[74]

Black Power provided a model of political action for a minority in Britain but for most it afforded a cultural identity. Black youths let their hair grow into an Afro style, wore African-style cloths and adopted African-based names. "In the UK, the whole Black Panther Party ethos seemed quite alluring," recalled Don Letts, who was born in London in January 1956 to Jamaican parents. "Black people were not taking any shit and at the same time looking really cool with their leather jackets, Afro's and shades. The mixture of soul music and militant right-on politics was a powerful combination."[75] It was not only their chic style that appealed to Letts.

> From reading *Seize the Time* and studying the politics of the Black Panther Party, I gleaned little bits that definitely helped me get through my day; it was empowering and made me feel less isolated. Also James Brown's "Say it loud, I am black and I am proud," simplistic as it is now, was almost a mind-blowing concept. Before that, it was "Don't say I am black" as if it made you a second rate citizen.[76]

Pauline Vickers, born in the London suburb of Romford in October 1953 to a white mother and Nigerian father, was more interested in events in the United States than in Britain because she found there the black role models unseen in her homeland. She watched the Motown girl groups on *Ready Steady Go*, studied Motown and Stax record covers and identified with the lyrics of "Respect" sung by Aretha Franklin. The "majority of black people I saw on the evening news were being savagely beaten or hosed down against a wall by uniformed men .... Even though they were on another continent, separated by thousands of miles of ocean, these were 'my people' who were maligned, spat on and ridiculed."[77] Marsha Hunt, a 19-year-old actress starring in the London musical *Hair*, encouraged Pauline to comb out her hair into an Afro and, much to the consternation of the white couple who adopted her, she painted "Say it Loud, I'm Black and I'm Proud" on a poster in her bedroom. She was drawn to the militancy of the Black Panthers, running to the library to read the works of Malcolm X, Stokely Carmichael and Eldridge Cleaver. In recognition of the new identity, Pauline Vickers changed her name to Pauline Black. She became the lead singer of the Selector, a ska revivalist band formed in 1979, which espoused strong antiracist politics.[78]

Some of the sons and daughters of South Asian immigrants identified with Black Power symbolism too. Hanif Kureishi, born in London of a Pakistani father, never felt at home in England or in Pakistan.

> You walk down the street and people say to you all the time—where are you from? Yeah, but where are you really from? You sound like us, but you're not one of us, are you? Being attacked, being beaten up, being spat on—it happened the whole time. [I had a] girlfriend who said—you can't come round tonight, if my dad sees a fucking Paki sitting at the dining room table he'll do his fucking nut.

When Kureishi visited Pakistan, it was clear that he was not one of them. "One man said to me 'We are Pakistanis, but you will always be a Paki.'"[79] Kureishi remembered how emboldened he felt when he first saw pictures of the Black Panthers in the late 1960s. "I tore down my pictures of the Rolling Stones and Cream and replaced them with the Panthers. I found it all exhilarating. These people were proud and they were fighting. To my knowledge, no one in England was fighting." The Black Power salutes of athletes Tommie Smith and John Carlos at the 1968 Mexico Olympics thrilled him further. He read the works of African-American authors James Baldwin and Richard Wright and went on to become a playwright with much of his work focusing on race and racial identity.[80]

Britain Is More Affluent and Liberal

For all of the admiration of the United States, fewer working-class Britons looked to the United States for their dreams and aspirations. In the 1960s, as consumer products became commonplace in virtually every home in Britain, the United States portrayed in movies and on television no longer looked as prosperous or as enticing as it did in the 1950s. The 1960s saw Britain transformed into a modern landscape, as high-rise flats, concrete-and-glass office buildings and new motorways spread across the country. By the 1970s, central heating, double-glazing, wall-to-wall carpeting and electric blankets made the cold damp winters much more bearable. In 1951, only 14 percent of households owned a car but by the end of the 1970s, 67 percent owned one.[81] By the early 1970s, more than half the population owned their own home, almost twice as many as two decades earlier, 69 percent a fridge and more than 90 percent a television. Unsurprisingly, Britons in general were more contented than ever before. A major survey undertaken in 1977 found that 82 percent were satisfied with life in Britain, compared with 68 percent in France and 59 percent in Italy.[82] "By almost any indicator—statistical, political or the observation of unclouded eyes—Britain is a solid, healthy society, bursting with creative vigour," Bernard Nossiter, *The Washington Post* correspondent in Britain, found in 1978. "It is a country more at peace with itself than its own daily papers reflect."[83] In 2004, a report published by the New Economics Foundation named 1976 as the best ever year to be alive in Britain based on low crime rates, minimal pollution levels, economic equality and substantial public sector investment.[84]

The allure of the United States declined not just because of increased prosperity but also because Britain became much more liberal, modern and freer in the 1960s. National Service ended in November 1960 and young men no longer had to endure a two-year stint in the Armed Forces. The birth control pill was introduced into Britain in 1961, reducing the risk of pregnancy and helping to increase the rates of sex outside marriage. Thirty-five percent of women who married in the late 1950s reported that they had had sex before marriage. In the early 1970s, the figure climbed to 74 percent.[85] Successive governments passed legislation that liberalized British life. The Betting and Gambling Act of 1960 legalized gambling, turning bingo and horse race betting into popular working-class pursuits. By the end of the 1960s, there were 16,000 betting shops in Britain and in 1974, 1,820 bingo halls.[86] The Labour government abolished capital punishment for murder in 1965 and in 1967 decriminalized abortion and homosexuality for those over the age of 21. The Divorce Act of 1969 made it easier to divorce as breakdown became a ground for ending a marriage.[87] In November 1965, theater critic Kenneth Tynan probably became the first person to use the word "fuck" on television when he appeared on a late night BBC show. By the 1970s, British films like *Get Carter* (1971) and *Clockwork Orange* (1971) showed explicit violence and nudity on screen for the first time while Jackie Collins and Harold Robbins produced sexually explicit novels that became best sellers, unthinkable 10 years earlier. In 1970, *Oh! Calcutta!* displayed full-frontal nudity on stage for the first time and on November 17, 1970, 20-year-old German model Stephanie Rahn became the first woman to pose topless in a national newspaper when she appeared on page 3 of the *Sun* newspaper.

In the 1960s, Britain was not only more affluent and more liberal but also more confident than ever before as a cultural renaissance led by the Beatles heralded an era of unparalleled British dominance of popular culture. The Beatles released their first single, "Love Me Do," in Britain in October 1962. Their catchy songs, exotic appearance, undoubted intelligence and cheeky humor unleashed Beatlemania the following year. The Beatles finally broke through in the United States when their single "I Want to Hold Your Hand" reached number 1 on

February 1, 1964.[88] The Beatles arrived in New York City, the center of the music industry, on February 7. Approximately 73 million people, 40 percent of the population and the largest television audience of the time, watched the Beatles' first television appearance on *The Ed Sullivan Show* on Sunday, February 9, 1964. On March 31, 1964, the Beatles captured the top five single positions on the *Billboard* chart. Until they broke up in 1970, the Beatles pushed the boundaries of popular music, wrote songs that have become pop standards all around the world and reflected and inspired some of the cultural and social changes of the 1960s. Their willingness to experiment, to move into different genres of music and to write songs that had cross-generational appeal set them apart from the other bands of the time.[89]

The Beatles' success paved the way for other British artists to dominate the international scene. In 1964–1965, British acts held the Number 1 spot for 56 weeks in the United States. In 1963, only three British singles cracked the American top 40 but in 1964, 65 made the charts, and in 1965, 68.[90] From 1956 to 1959, some 62 percent of British top ten hits were American. This figure fell to 20 percent by 1964.[91] To illustrate the changing perception of British music, the record producer Tony Visconti left the United States in April 1967 at the age of 23 to work in "the Mecca of modern pop music. No one did it better than the Brits and no Brits did it better than the Beatles." Visconti believed that "It seemed like nothing was happening in New York City while everything was happening over in England."[92] The Byrds, America's answer to the Beatles, toured Britain for the first time in the summer of 1965 and added their voices to the chorus of adulation. "In the States, Britain is still regarded as the Mecca of pop," guitarist David Crosby revealed. "This is our first tour of Britain, and we're very excited about it."[93] British artists were still inspired by the United States but, unlike many British performers from the 1950s, they were no longer copying American styles but were developing an identity that was something new and distinct from the American. The Beatles, the Rolling Stones, the Who, the Kinks, the Small Faces and David Bowie sang in British accents and about British places and events. Many British bands played American music but combined it with British folk and music hall traditions to create a new sound that would gain worldwide success. Elton John, David Bowie and Rod Stewart became regular installments on the international pop charts in the 1970s. Other British rock musicians embraced new styles and set trends that others followed. Led Zeppelin and Black Sabbath pioneered heavy metal, Pink Floyd, King Crimson, Yes and Genesis developed Progressive Rock, and David Bowie introduced Glam Rock to the world.

Not just in music but in all areas of popular entertainment, Britain set the trend. "London, the most exciting city in the world," the *Daily Telegraph*'s weekend magazine of April 16, 1965 announced, a year before the famous *Time* magazine article of April 15, 1966, which used the term "London: The Swinging City"[94] Carnaby Street, Mary Quant, Vidal Sassoon and Twiggy turned London into a fashion capital. British film stars regularly won Oscars. *Dr No* released in 1962, *From Russia with Love* in 1963 and *Goldfinger* in 1964 made James Bond an internationally known symbol of modern Britain. To top it all, England won the World Cup for the first time in 1966. "We went mental at the final whistle. We were chanting. 'Ee, ay, adiyo, we won the cup' for hours and hours," remembered Tony Cook who was 13 and who went to the game with his 16-year-old brother. "I couldn't convey to anyone how wonderful it was to have been there—the emotion of it all. It was the most wonderful moment in the history of the universe."[95] From January 1963 to June 1964, Charles Hamblett and Jane Deverson interviewed a number of young people and found them less than enamored with the United States. "Today, young Britain no longer relies on Hollywood and Madison Avenue for its movies, its music, or its instant-Zen," the authors concluded. "It idolizes Cilla, Dusty, Kathy, Susan, and the big beat boys for their Englishness, and Gor-blimey Americanisms are old-hat."[96]

Changed View of the United States

Young British visitors to the United States in the 1960s observed that the country was more conservative and less appealing than they had previously imagined. In the summer of 1964, the Rolling Stones embarked on their first US tour and ventured into the Deep South where they were met by groups holding biblical quotations that condemned the ungodly long hair. "America," bass player Bill Wyman decided, "was going to be just as prejudiced as Britain. The Land of the Free?"[97] In July 1967, Pete Townshend toured America with the Who and found another America than the one he had found and admired in New York.

> San Francisco was full of pharmaceutical gurus and New York was arguably the capital of the world, but some places in between felt reactionary in the extreme. In the South we were banned from swimming pools without bathing caps because our hair was too long, and nearly beaten up by men who took offence at what they saw as our obvious homosexuality.[98]

On her first trip to America in 1966, model Twiggy even found the people in sophisticated New York City to be conservative. "I look like an alien," she noted. "Bambi meets ET. Those butter-wouldn't-melt-in-their-handbags American girls lining the sidewalk can't have been much older than me, but with their gloves and matching court shoes we were from different planets."[99]

The modern civil rights movement that erupted in the South in the 1950s exposed the racial intolerance of the United States to a British audience. Most working-class Britons in the early 1950s had little knowledge or understanding of the African-American experience and the problems they faced in the United States. Tony Carricker, an art school student, recalled: "We knew there were blacks in America but we had no idea what it really meant. We didn't even know much at that time about the racial divide and all that Jim Crow stuff that was still going on."[100] Now the issue could not be ignored as sit ins and demonstrations to protest racial discrimination were shown on British television and reported in the press. Press coverage was overwhelmingly sympathetic to the plight of African Americans and supportive of Martin Luther King's nonviolent strategy of civil disobedience.[101] The *Daily Mirror* front page headline of September 16, 1963, "Race Hate Blast Kills Girls in Church" after a bomb exploded in a Baptist Church in Birmingham, Alabama, was typical of the coverage.[102] Even the conservative *Daily Express* led with front page headings like "The Night of Terror: Negroes Weep as Mobs Attack" after a white crowd attacked a Baptist church in Montgomery, Alabama, in May 1961.[103] "I wish I'd been born coloured," singer Dusty Springfield revealed after she had returned from a tour of the United States. "When it comes to singing and feeling, I just want to be one of them and not me. Then again, I see how some of them are treated and I think, 'Thank God I'm white.'"[104] In March 1964, 68 percent of Britons held the view that the treatment of blacks in the United States was bad or very bad and 44 percent of Britons stated that the racial problems in the United States had lowered their opinion of the country.[105]

Muhammad Ali, one of the most admired sports figures in Britain among both blacks and whites, helped expose racial discrimination in the United States. Ali, or Cassius Clay as he was originally called, first came to Britain to fight Englishman Henry Cooper at London's Wembley Stadium on June 18, 1963. Britons warmed to the brash American and liked Clay's fast-talking humor and undoubted charm displayed in his verbal sparring with BBC boxing commentator Harry Carpenter. When he returned as world heavyweight boxing champion to fight Henry Cooper at Arsenal's Highbury Stadium in London in May 1966, Clay had joined the Nation of Islam and changed his name to Muhammad Ali. At the end of 1965, respondents in a Gallup poll chose racing driver Jim Clark sports personality of the year with Ali coming in second. In 1966, the year in which the England football team won the World Cup, England captain Bobby Moore and star player Bobby Charlton were chosen as sports personalities of the year followed by Ali in third place ahead of English manager Alf Ramsey and England player Nobby Stiles who were fourth and fifth.[106]

Ali's popularity as a man of honor and integrity increased further in Britain after boxing authorities stripped Ali of his world heavyweight title in April 1967 for refusing to serve in Vietnam. Once he returned to the ring, some three and a half years later in October 1970, Ali's fights became major occasions in Britain. Many who had no interest in boxing got up in the middle of the night to listen to his fights on the radio, cheering on his every punch. In 1974, Ali was the overwhelming choice as sports personality of the year in a Gallup poll.[107] In 1973, 1974 and 1978 Ali won the BBC Overseas Personality of the Year Award for an unprecedented three times. "I am taking away memories of the most wonderful reception I have experienced anywhere in the world," Ali stated in July 1977 after he visited the north east of England for a series of charity functions. "I never thought it possible for my family to be made so welcome by so many white people. I expect this kind of reception in Africa. It's commonplace there; but to receive a reception like this in a European country!"[108] Ali wrote a letter of thanks to "the people of Great Britain (who) stood with me during the difficult days of my exile from boxing."[109] Ali's popularity endured. In December 1999, the British public voted Ali BBC Sportsman of the Century, winning more votes than the other four candidates combined.[110]

Black Britons particularly loved Ali. He used his appearances on television programs like the Michael Parkinson Show to condemn the way blacks were treated in the United States and around the world. "As a young black boy growing up in

Small Heath, Birmingham, Ali was a symbol of hope," stated Wilfred Emmanuel-Jones, born in Clarendon, Jamaica in November 1957, who moved with his parents to England in 1961.

> He showed no fear and was his own man. In 1970s Britain I spent most of that time feeling like an outsider. Nothing but failure was expected of young black boys living in the inner cities. I didn't see much of a future for me and many a time I felt it was a curse to be born "coloured" (the term used to describe us back then). When Ali exploded on to the scene he opened my eyes to a world of possibilities. He was confident, talented, charming, funny and, more importantly, unafraid. I was brought up in the Pentecostal church and its approach was that, as believers, we had to endure humiliation, discrimination and injustice; for this endurance was the price to be paid to gain entry to the kingdom of heaven. For the first time in my life I saw a black man who answered back, who did things on his own terms. I can remember watching his fights on the television in a state of anguish, for every victory meant that people like me could keep our hopes alive and that some day we too could become somebody.[111]

Gary Younge, born in Hertfordshire in 1969 to Barbadian parents, loved the music of the Jackson 5 and urged on the Harlem Globetrotters on TV but Muhammad Ali held a special place in his heart. He named his pet rabbit "Muhammad" and wore a "Float like a butterfly, sting like a bee" t-shirt in honor of the great man.[112] Errol Christie's "role model was Muhammad Ali. To us, he was a living god—a black man with unbeatable fists, a clever mind, a mouth he didn't fear to use, strong opinions and a refusal to be cowed by the Establishment." Inspired by Ali, Christie later became European boxing champion.[113]

The television show *Roots,* which traced the history of African Americans, exposed the inequities of US race relations to the British public like never before. The 12-part miniseries, based on a book by Alex Haley, attracted a mass audience when it was shown on British television in 1977 and repeated in 1978. *Roots* tells the harrowing story of Haley's ancestor, the African Kunta Kinte, and his descendants. Britons were horrified to see Kinte abducted from his homeland, forced to endure the horrors of the Middle Passage and condemned to suffer the daily tortures of slavery in the American South. The series follows his siblings as they endured violence, racism and segregation. The series gripped the nation night after night and became a talking point at home, at work and at school the following day.[114] Blacks were horrified by the cruelties endured by the slaves but inspired by their bravery. Twelve-year-old Ian Roberts, born in London to Grenadian parents, watched *Roots* with his family and was brought to tears by the sight of the slave master whipping Kunta Kinte until the African proclaimed that his new name was Toby, the one assigned to him by his master. The distraught Ian told his mother that he was going to trace their family tree and assume an African name. Roberts later adopted the name Kwame Kwei-Armah.[115]

The assassination of President John F. Kennedy in November 1963 dramatically altered many people's views of the United States. Kennedy, elected at the age of 43 in 1960, was particularly well-liked because he represented youthfulness and modernity in contrast to the old staid politicians like Harold MacMillan, the British prime minister of the early 1960s. His assassination on November 22,

1963, shocked the nation. BBC and ITV halted regular programming and even *That Was the Week That Was*, the satirical show that lampooned politicians, aired a special tribute to the president.[116] "Growing up I would suggest the American with the biggest influence on Britain would most definitely have been President Kennedy," Ray Kennedy from Scunthorpe remembered. "I believe everyone knows where they were when he was assassinated and who was supposed to have done it. I was at home and my mother was in front of the fire warming her backside when it came on the TV."[117] Peter O'Neill, born in London of Irish parents, heard the news on his newly acquired television.

He remembered,

> I remember my mum and dad in a state of shock and knew something very serious had occurred over in America. Also, I recall seeing the tragic scene unravel and feeling that it was such a cowardly act something in total contrast to the heroic Americans in my comics and depicted on the television screen. JFK was highly regarded and dearly loved particularly as his family came from County Wexford not far from where dad was born and brought up. Even today you will find his photograph in most of the households of County Wexford. My aunt has his picture in her front room and she lives in County Waterford.[118]

Christine Paine, fifteen years old at the time of the assassination, found that her views of the United States became more negative. "The assassination of Kennedy had a deep effect on many of my generation, we couldn't understand how or why this could happen. It was probably the first negative side of America many of us had really understood."[119]

Riots that blighted major US cities gained huge coverage in the British media adding to the view of a violent America and raising concerns that racial conflict could come to Britain. On August 11, 1964, the Watts district in Los Angeles erupted into violence after a confrontation between a white police officer and a black youth. Within six days, 34 people were killed, more than 800 were hospitalized, over 4,000 were arrested and US$45 million worth of property was damaged.[120] The following year the country experienced 11 riots that lasted two days or more and 25 such riots in 1967. Between July 12 and 17, 1967, 26 died and over a thousand were injured in Newark, New Jersey, and just over a week later 43 were killed in Detroit and more than 2,000 injured in the worst rioting of the decade.[121] Further violence erupted again in most major cities after Martin Luther King was assassinated on April 4, 1968. Shortly after returning from a trip to the United States where he had witnessed the riots that broke out after King's assassination, the right-wing English politician Enoch Powell made his so-called "Rivers of Blood" speech in which he suggested that there would be violence in the streets unless Commonwealth immigration was halted. With the riots fresh in people's minds, Gallup found in May 1968 that 74 percent of respondents supported Powell's views.[122] In the 1970s, Powell continued his crusade against black immigration and suggested that continued immigration "carries a threat of division, violence and bloodshed of American dimensions."[123] "I think it should be stopped before we have all this that's on in America, black and white fighting," Alan, a caretaker in Blackburn, believed. "Too many immigrants," Tim, another young man from Blackburn, suggested. "There ought to be some sort of control.

Stop 'em altogether. If you let so many of them all live together, you'll get the same problem you've got in America."[124]

Newspapers and the police introduced the term "mugging" into Britain to bring publicity to the level of violence on the British streets but the furor also had the effect of drawing attention to the high level of street crime in the United States. In February 1969, for example, a *Sunday Express* reporter detailed how she was robbed on a New York City street, an everyday occurrence in America it seemed. She suggested "to the harried police forces of Washington and New York, incidents [of robbery] . . . are now almost as routine as parking offences." The term "mugging," previously used in the United States to describe urban street assaults, began to be adopted by the British media. "As crimes of violence escalate, a word common in the United States enters the British headlines: Mugging," the *Daily Mirror* of August 17, 1972, reported. "To our Police, it's a frightening new strain of crime."[125] The *Daily Express* suggested that mugging is "an American import that must not be accepted here." The *Sun* told the British public to "stop thinking of the police as 'fuzz' and 'pigs' " because "it will be too late to scream for their help when we are afraid, as New Yorkers are, to walk down our own streets in broad daylight." In October 1972, John Maxwell Hill, Chief Inspector of Constabulary for England and Wales, feared "a New York situation arising in this country."[126]

The murder rate in the United States, which increased rapidly in the 1970s, gained enormous attention in the British media. "America's different," suggested Tim from Blackburn in the early 1970s,

> I mean, cops have guns there for a start. You can't walk the streets at night. I know a lad who works in Detroit, and he daren't go out in Detroit at night. He comes home from work, and that's it, he stops at home. They have 200 murders a year in Detroit alone. That's more than the whole country.[127]

Newspapers consistently printed the sensational. "For newly-wed Christina Cunningham, 29, from Yorkshire, life was starting anew in Space Age Houston, Texas. Now, three months later, she is just another statistic of American violence—raped and stabbed to death by an intruder" the *Daily Express* of October 1977 reported.[128] Even the US capital gained notoriety. "America's capital has become a city under siege by thugs. A city of dreadful day and even more dreadful night. And as the autumn leaves fall and the nights draw in, it becomes increasingly perilous for the honest citizen to go for a stroll or to walk the dog," the *Daily Mirror* reporter Donald Ludlow, who had lived in Washington DC for 20 years and who had himself become a victim of street crime, suggested. "Perhaps American may have to find a new capital, somewhere clean and fresh where conflict between the races can be wiped from the slate."[129]

As the United States celebrated its bicentennial in 1976, the British view of the United States had become darker as American movies exposed the underbelly of urban life. Films from the 1950s had centered on gangsters or murder mysteries but movies in the late 1960s and early 1970s exposed the seediness and everyday violence of the street with a casual indifference to violence and with its impact displayed in gory detail. "To me America is synonymous with violence,"

Pat Kimber, a housewife from Carshalton, Surrey, opined. "I went to the cinema the other night to see *Bullitt*, a good film but the violence was terrible. Americans seem to accept violence as part of their everyday life."[130] Movies such as *Midnight Cowboy, Taxi Driver, The French Connection, Dog Day Afternoon, Dirty Harry, The Taking of Pelham 123* and *Serpico* all depicted the United States as a land of violence, drugs, police corruption and moral decay. The divide between criminals and police blurred and often lawbreakers were the heroes of the film or the film was told from their perspective. "I'd always seen America as this benign fabulous source of everything stylish," one Briton believed, "now I saw the other side of it, starting with *Serpico*."[131] Nothing compared to the impact of *Death Wish*, a film that saw Charles Bronson, whose wife is senselessly murdered and whose daughter is brutally raped, seeking out and killing muggers and rapists. The story of the vigilante had more of an impact in Britain than most films as it portrayed an everyday American simply snapping under pressure. Directed by British director Michael Winner and released in 1974, the film set off a whole series of television and newspaper stories about muggings and gun culture in the United States. "In New York, where the chances of getting mugged during an evening stroll are about the same as getting wet during a thunderstorm, it has been received with wild cries of enthusiasm," *Daily Express* film critic Ian Christie suggested. "As a fable for our time its works very well indeed," Christie concluded.[132]

Brian O'Sullivan, born and raised in North London, blamed American movies for darkening his view of the United States. As a child in the 1960s, O'Sullivan watched imported television programs and Hollywood movies. "My earliest views were shaped by western heroes and war movies; I saw Americans as adventurous and a force for good." He imagined the United States as the land of "rugged individualism," where there was a "triumph of good over bad." By the 1970s, however, he watched movies like *Catch-22*; *Five Easy Pieces*; *A Man Called Horse*; *Soldier Blue; Patton*; *Dirty Harry*; *French Connection*; *Klute*; *The Godfather* and *Serpico* and now experienced a "growing uneasiness with the traditional view of America, but still retaining elements of nostalgia. Changing images of women and Native Americans. Increasing focus on urban crime. Dangerous cities plagued by slums, drugs and criminals, including mentally unstable criminals." The fictional portrayals of the United States, together with the negative media reports, produced an altogether different view of the country he admired as a boy. "In my twenties, having not visited America yet, my views were shaped by images of urban decay and crime," O'Sullivan concluded.[133]

Imported detective series like *Kojak* and *Starsky and Hutch*, which replaced American Westerns and spy shows on British television in the 1970s, added to the violent image of the United States. *Kojak*, starring Telly Savalas as Lieutenant Theo Kojak of the New York Police Department, became a major hit in Britain. The shiny bald head, the constant sucking of lollypops because he had given up smoking, and his catch phrase "who loves ya, baby" turned Savalas into a major star in Britain. He even had a number one pop hit for nine consecutive weeks in Britain with the dreadful "If." *Starsky and Hutch,* which starred Paul Michael Glaser and David Soul as two detectives from the fictional Bay City in California, became equally popular. Each episode saw the detectives become involved in high-speed car chases in their Red Ford Torino with a white stripe down the side. This series introduced Britain to David Soul who became a huge pin up for teenage girls. Like Savalas, Soul also had a hit single, the equally dreadful "Don't Give up on us." "Everyone loved the show," noted Derek Tait from Plymouth. "I even got my mum to knit me a Starsky jumper. There were several people in the area that added white stripes to their red Fords so it would look more like Dave Starsky's car."[134] Both series featured pimps, drug pushers and murderers and included armed police engaging in violent confrontations with criminals. Roderick McNeill, a police officer from Edinburgh, Scotland, and then an avid *Starsky and Hutch* fan, "thought that violet crime was prevalent there but that the Americans at least met this crime wave with effective law enforcement and sensible sentencing policies."[135] Journalist Brian Viner noted that

> the fact that America needed so many crime busters and that they were all so damned busy, with dreadful murders to solve every week, was grist to the mill of those who considered it the most dangerous country on earth. I have another old friend, Roger, whose grandmother was incredulous when she heard that he was planning a trip to New York City. "Haven't you seen *Kojak*?" she spluttered.[136]

Violent events in New York City and their extensive coverage in the British media confirmed to many that urban America was out of control. The power blackout in New York City on July 13 and 14, 1977, which led to looting, robberies and rioting, received extensive exposure in Britain, much of it gleefully exaggerating the events. "The information served up by their *Times* and on TV (by BBC) was downright frightening," American Warren Meislin, who was staying in London when the blackout occurred, remembered.

> Some of the less responsible British dailies had huge headlines stating the city may "NEVER RECOVER." And the family I was staying with was especially smug about such an event (the blackout and looting) never occurring in England.... To the BBC's credit, their reporter first pointed out how New Yorkers were helping out and coping, but most of the report focused on the vandalism and chaos that was reigning citywide.... It wasn't till I arrived home a month later that I found out (in those pre-Internet days) that the city had not burned completely to the ground and that those on the upper East and West sides (of Manhattan where my sister, her husband and my cousin all resided) coped as New Yorkers always manage to in grave situations.[137]

Inez H. Robertson from New York was so outraged at the coverage the Blackout received in Britain that she wrote an indignant letter to the *Daily Express.*

> The reports of the recent New York blackout in British newspapers were very exaggerated. I'm not saying the experience was a picnic, but no one was hurt and the only trouble was the looting. The weather was great and most people were sunning themselves on the beach. The mood of everyone was pleasant, funny, and very refreshing.[138]

A study of the foreign press coverage of the United States published in the late 1970s summed up the mood. "To some extent, the British press seems to reflect the European media's favorite cliché: the horrors and dangers of life in New York City."[139]

American foreign policy and in particular the Vietnam War, which often led the news headlines in Britain in the late 1960s and early 1970s, prodded many to condemn the United States for hypocrisy for bringing its military might to bear on a poor peasant country. America's involvement in Vietnam had progressed from a small cadre of "military advisors" in the mid-1950s to a full-fledged land force within ten years. The conflict, which dragged on until 1973, ultimately took the lives of 58,000 Americans and more than three million Vietnamese. The United States dropped more bombs on Vietnam than had fallen during the whole of World War II. The Vietnam War penetrated the living rooms of Britain as television ownership increased and news programs beamed live coverage from the battlefield. Media coverage was generally supportive of America in the early years of the war but as tall, heavily armed US soldiers set fire to the huts of small peasants, and napalm bombs rained down on villages, television exposed the immorality of the war.[140] "In the '1960s' (as the period between 1963 and 1973 is usually labeled), the American image in the European and Third World press was, as a rule, extremely poor," a survey of foreign press coverage of the United States found. "Whether in sorrow or in anger, many publications subjected American society to a devastating critique with emphasis on racial problems and the war in Vietnam. In some quarters, this constituted in practice something of a reverse reaction to the high reputation the United States has enjoyed since World War II."[141]

As the Vietnam War gained more news coverage, public skepticism about US involvement in the war increased. Recognizing the unpopular nature of the conflict, British Prime Minister Harold Wilson refused President Lyndon Johnson's request to send troops to Vietnam. Opinion polls showed most Britons were turning against the war. In September 1964, a Gallup poll found that 41 percent of Britons approved "of the [recent] American armed action in Vietnam" while 33 percent disapproved. By December 1966, only 30 percent of Britons approved of "American armed action in Vietnam" while 51 percent disapproved. In April 1965, 32 percent believed the United States should "pull out its forces," rising to 41 percent in August 1966.[142] The British Campaign for Peace in Vietnam (BCPV) was founded in May 1965 by trade union organizations, Communists, Labour party activists and Christian groups calling for US troop withdrawal from Vietnam.[143] By October 1969, 54 percent of respondents believed that the United States should "begin to withdraw its troops" from Vietnam.[144] Still, despite opposition to the Vietnam War, the British confidence in US foreign policy remained strong, suggesting opposition to the war did not translate into a wider abandonment of its ally in the Cold War. In May 1965, 64 percent of Britons had confidence in US foreign policy, in April 1968, 64 percent still had confidence in US foreign policy and in June 1972, as the war drew to a close, the figure still reached 57 percent.[145]

In 1973, as the war in Vietnam came to an end, the Watergate scandal exposed the corruption within the US political system. Over a period of months, newspapers led by the *Washington Post* exposed President Richard Nixon's role in covering up a break-in that took place at the Democratic National Committee headquarters at the Watergate office complex in Washington DC in 1972. The British media paid enormous attention to the scandal until Nixon resigned from office in August 1974. "I didn't even begin to understand Watergate, and I don't recall my parents ever trying to explain it to me," Brian Viner remembered, "but the names—Nixon, Haldeman, Ehrlichman, Dean—were somehow singed into my consciousness."[146] The David Frost interview with President Nixon shown on television in 1977 gained a huge television audience and reopened the debate about the Watergate scandal.

The Central Intelligence Agency (CIA), which gained much coverage in the British media because of Philip Agee's *Inside the Company: CIA Diary* published in 1975, became a byword for illegal and immoral actions. Agee was a former CIA agent who exposed the Agency's unsavory methods to achieve their ends, particularly in Latin America. Agee left the CIA in 1969 and moved to London in the early 1970s, where he published *Inside the Company*. In his book, Agee revealed the identities of dozens of CIA agents, which led the US government to seek his deportation. Agee's case was taken up by MPs, journalists and human rights activists as he fought expulsion. The government eventually deported Agee from the United Kingdom in June, 1977.[147]

Some on the Labour left feared that the United States government and the CIA were actively undermining the Labour government. William Colby, the Director General of the CIA, admitted to a Congressional committee in Washington that the Agency had helped opponents to undermine President Salvador Allende's government in Chile before it was overthrown in a military coup in September 1973. "There were rumours that this week that the CIA had been responsible for a collision in the Thames which sunk a shipload of buses from Leyland going to Cuba," Tony Benn, cabinet member in the 1974–1979 Labour government, wrote in February 1975 after Labour had formed a government.

> I noticed today that Ivan Yates, an *Observer* correspondent and a contemporary of mine from Oxford, has died in a street accident, only a week after David Wilson, also an *Observer* correspondent and the son of Sir Duncan Wilson, the former Ambassador to the Soviet Union, died in a similar accident in London. I record it here only because later we may discover more than we now know: the Americans denied for years that they had done anything to destroy Allende in Chile and yet they have now had to admit under cross examination in Washington that they did spend a lot of money de-stabilizing the Government, supporting the lorry drivers' strike and finally bringing Allende down.

Benn continued to be suspicious of the actions of the US government. "Kissinger must have toyed with the idea of de-stabilizing the British Government," Benn wrote on February 28, 1975. "I am putting all these thoughts down because, improbable though they may seem, at some stage one might be able to look back and make sense out of what they really mean." On December 24, 1976, Benn told journalist Mark Arnold-Foster: "The only anxiety I have is that the Americans might destabilize us." After Arnold-Foster denied that this would happen because of close links between the United States and Britain, Benn replied: "I think you are right but the CIA activities have certainly done a great deal of damage in shaking people's confidence."[148]

Even though punk rock music was clearly influenced by American music, punk was the first youth subculture in Britain to be overtly critical of the United States. "For a relatively young nation, the USA is remarkably slow when it comes to tapping talent—even though sucking the cents out of every available European culture is the national pastime," wrote punk rockers Julie Burchill and Tony Parsons. "American bands are old and cold and still coming to terms with the fact that the sixties ran out on them."[149] The two also criticized the materialism of the United States: "*In $ They Trust . . .* in a nation of failed Henry Fords where even health must be bought, you can take the Yankee out of Wall Street but you can't take Wall Street out of the Yankee." American teenagers are privileged and supine.

> American kids get everything on a plate, especially their recreation. After a decade of munching trash-food from foil plates while staring at their interminable Technicolor television brain candy, pre-teen kids at Aerosmith, Kiss and Queen concerts are equipped for nothing more strenuous (especially after washing down the bare essentials of Quaalude-depressants with cheap wine) than being able to focus on the stage.[150]

Journalist Paul Morley suggested that American musicians ignore "the existence of everyday problems and values that have pushed the U.S. into the bland and self-deluding state that it's in today."[151] The Clash's song "I'm So Bored With the USA" from their self-titled debut album released in 1977 expressed an anger against US support for military dictatorships, its political corruption and the growing dominance of US culture in the United Kingdom. A letter to the *New Musical Express* the bible of punk rock, put it more succinctly: "Yanks are wankers."[152]

While first- and second-generation black Britons admired the Black Power movement and African-American icons like Muhammad Ali in the 1960s, by the mid-1970s Jamaica competed with the United States for their attention. A new soundtrack from Jamaica opened up a new world for many inner city blacks in Britain. When it first reached the shores of Britain, ska and reggae music was seen as novelty music but now Bob Marley and other reggae musicians commented on more serious issues using sophisticated studio techniques. They sang about Jamaica, which most blacks had some knowledge of, and racial oppression, which black Britons, who faced discrimination and higher levels of unemployment than their white counterparts, could recognize.[153] Disco music appealed to those blacks who were upwardly mobile and at peace in an increasingly multiracial Britain, while reggae attracted the more dissatisfied section of black youths. Seeking an identity that was neither British nor traditionally West Indian, many identified with Rastafarian beliefs that blacks were living in Babylon, the immoral Western world. "Just listening to the music and emulating the black American blueprint was not working for me," Don Letts claimed.

> OK, I had attended Black Panther meetings proudly wearing my Angela Davis badge, but that movement just wasn't totally relevant to the Black British experience. It didn't exactly translate to my life, which was something of a dilemma for

me. I wanted to empower myself. Luckily around the same time I began to discover Rastafari through reggae... It seemed a whole lot more attractive and a whole lot more relevant to my situation in Britain where I was feeling alienated, downtrodden and oppressed. I was experiencing the end result of racism, being pulled up every fucking day on the streets. Reggae was more militant and seemed more identifiable to me than the Black Power struggles that were going on in America.[154]

Jon Denton, entering his teenage years in the late 1960s, summed up the prevailing view of the United States. As a child, he watched "every western ever made and countless world war two films with the likes of John Wayne leading the charge, not to mention Disney, Tom and Jerry and most of the 'U' rated American cops, robbers and gangsters." These programs conveyed a "fantasy world of colour, where everything was longer, taller, wider and much, much, better than anything in our little grey world, there were no negatives because it wasn't real... was it?" Denton's view of the United States altered in the 1970s.

The America of the 70's seemed all too real in comparison to the 60's; Agent Orange, napalm The Ho Chi Min trail, and B 52 bombers featured all too heavily on our news. America was the news! Harlem seemed to represent Drug Central within a city called Crime Central. *Shaft*, *Dirty Harry*, *The Green Berets*, and Charles Bronson's *Death Wish* seemed to provide some hope from America's violent attackers.

A contradictory view of the United States emerged.

America had turned into a crime ridden hell-hole at home whilst waging total war against an elusive and rag tag Vietcong population, and with no obvious means of escape. On the positive side America produced some fabulous popular music during the 70's, with their superb stable of singer song writers and super groups. America was also our insurance policy, our big brother, who provided us all with a secure buffer against those pesky Red's in the USSR, The People's Republic and their respective satellites.[155]

For all of the misgivings of Jon Denton, there is no doubt that the explosion of cultural creativity and rise in identity politics that defined 1960s' Britain was partly inspired by events across the Atlantic. Young Britons looked to American music to forge a new sound that dominated popular music not only in Britain but around the world. From the Ivy League look to denim jeans, the British street was dominated by American clothing. Through the identity politics that swept across the Atlantic in the wake of the civil rights movement, the United States inspired a large segment of the population to seek rights denied to them because of their sexual orientation, gender or race.

Despite their continued admiration for American popular culture, Britons expressed more ambivalent feelings about the country that filled the newspapers, television and movie screens. American racial problems, urban crime and political corruption concerned many as did American foreign policy. The British working classes were less envious of the United States than they were in the 1950s as Britain became more prosperous and freer in the 1960s. Free college education for their children, free health care and retirement security were available to all while home ownership, a car, annual holidays and an array of consumer goods were attainable for most. Britain produced its own distinctive brand of music, fashion and television that provided Britons with enormous self-confidence and their own home-grown heroes. In the midst of this cultural renaissance, however, a new generation of conservatives grew increasingly weary with the changes brought to postwar Britain and looked to the United States as a model of economic freedom. Energized by the United States, the Conservative Party gained political power in 1979 and started to remake the British economy on the US model, fundamentally changing British society in the process and igniting further opposition to the United States.

4

The United States and the Politics of Thatcherism, 1979–1990

In May 1979, Margaret Thatcher became the first woman in British history to be elected prime minister. When she resigned in November 1990 she was the longest serving prime minister of the twentieth century having won three consecutive general elections. Many saw Thatcher's Conservative government as the savior of Britain, freeing the nation from trade union power, regenerating individual responsibility and ushering in a new enterprise culture. Others, however, opposed the Conservative's free-market philosophy, decrying the inequality and social conflict their policies engendered and arguing that Thatcher was unconcerned with the plight of the disadvantaged. But virtually all her supporters and critics agree that Thatcher's 11 years at 10 Downing Street left an indelible mark on British society.

Ever since the ideology of "Thatcherism" was first introduced by cultural theorist Stuart Hall in an article in *Marxism Today* in January 1979, the nature and roots of Margaret Thatcher's ideas, policies and values have divided political scientists and more recently historians. Hall saw Thatcherism as a movement of the "radical right," which gained substantial popular support and constituted something new in British politics. Subsequently, some argued that Thatcher's policies were a decisive break with the traditions of the Conservative party and others that her ideas date back to nineteenth-century liberalism.[1] Others have suggested that Thatcher's politics were rooted in the upheavals of the 1970s and developed pragmatically and cautiously in the 1980s.[2] Scholars have focused on her early parental influences, her time at Oxford University in the 1940s or the failure of Edward Heath's Conservative government of the early 1970s as the defining events that shaped Thatcher's thinking. A recent study has even suggested that Thatcher was a defender of the postwar consensus against the "progressive consensus" of the 1960s, seeking to restore the order and harmony of the immediate postwar years.[3]

When and why did Margaret Thatcher develop her conservative politics? A until now overlooked answer to the question is that the ideology Thatcher espoused was rooted in her vision of the United States of America. Too few biographers and commentators have taken seriously the influence of the United States on the evolution of Thatcher's beliefs. Those that have examined American influences on the prime minister focus on University of Chicago economist Milton Friedman and his theory of monetarism but, as this chapter makes clear, Friedman had less impact on her thinking than the positive view of the United States that Thatcher developed in her formative years. Long before the Chicago school and monetarism became standard points of reference in conservative circles, Thatcher's imagined view of the United States played a key role in shaping her ideas.

Because Prime Minister Thatcher tried to make Britain more like America and cemented a close relationship with President Ronald Reagan based on shared free-market politics and strident anticommunism, the 1980s saw a sustained period of hostility to the foreign policy of the U.S. government and criticism of American society. The policies of Thatcher and Reagan provoked enormous opposition from the left in Britain but the antipathy to the politics of the two governments spread beyond the confines of left-wing activism to embrace larger stretches of the population who feared that Britain would become a target in the Cold War and that the inequalities, urban decay and harsh business practices of American society were coming to Britain.

The Conservative View of the United States

Margaret Thatcher's affection for the United States began as a child growing up in interwar England. She was born Margaret Hilda Roberts in Grantham, a small provincial market town in Lincolnshire some 100 miles north of London, on October 13, 1925. The young Margaret Roberts lived with her parents, Alfred and Beatrice Roberts, and her older sister, Muriel, above a grocery shop the family owned. Coming from a provincial and relatively modest background, she showed no traces of the aversion to American popular culture found among conservatives of the time. She loved the American songs she heard on the family radio and on the gramophone player of family friends. Margaret Roberts particularly loved the music and lyrics of Jerome Kern and Cole Porter. The song she loved the most was "Smoke Gets in Your Eyes," a song made famous by American film actress Irene Dunne. The wistful Margaret was drawn to the strong melodies and simple messages of love and domestic bliss sung with soothing intimacy by suave-sounding men and elegant women. The songs suggested romance and sophistication that was a world away from the quiet and simple Lincolnshire town in which she lived.[4]

More than the wonderful music she heard on the radio, Hollywood movies exuded a magical appeal to the teenage Margaret Roberts. Margaret's access to dancing was curtailed by her Methodist father who forbade her to engage in such unseemly behavior. On "Saturday nights some of the girls at my school would go to dances or parties. It sounded very nice. But my sister and I didn't go dancing," she regretted mournfully.[5] The cinema was one of the few pleasures her parents allowed the young Margaret to indulge in as an adolescent. It was the "coming of the cinema to Grantham which really brightened up my life," she later remarked. "Until the 1930s, there was no way that a young girl living in a small English provincial town could have had access to this extraordinary range of talent, dramatic form, human emotion, sex appeal, spectacle and style," the adult Margaret Thatcher recalled.[6] In an interview published in March, 1987, Thatcher enthusiastically reminisced about the films she saw as a youth at the local cinema in Grantham and further afield in Nottingham, comparing the movie stars to the pop music heroes of contemporary teenagers.

> Ginger Rogers, Fred Astaire—fantastic! And these great musical films; there was Jean MacDonald, Nelson Eddy, and Ann Siegler, Webster Booth, . . . Jean Arthur in *The Plainsman*, all the Western things and there was Carmen Miranda in *South of the Border*,' but the point I'm making is that those stars meant as much to us, because it was a life that was away beyond anything we ever imagined and we thought it was very glamorous.[7]

The America Thatcher imagined in the darkened cinema offered to her an alternative vision of how her life could be. Thatcher found the female characters particularly inspirational and followed their fortunes by devotedly reading movie magazines such as *Picturegoer*.

> We looked at them avidly because it was a kind of escapism from the lives that we led and it was something that women were lovely and they seemed to lead very exciting lives while we led humdrum lives and sometimes very difficult lives.[8]

"I was entranced with the romantic world of Hollywood," Thatcher reminisced. "Grantham was a small town, but on my visits to the cinema I roamed to the most fabulous realms of the imagination. It gave me the determination to roam in reality one day."[9] Hollywood films and movie magazines opened her mind to a world of opulence so different from the simple life Thatcher's parents imposed on her in the small town of Grantham. On the screen, America was a land of huge luxuriously furnished houses, big cars and good-looking men, women and children. More than wealth, Hollywood films suggested values that Thatcher could identify with and principles she would always associate with America. The Westerns she loved featured rugged individuals overcoming obstacles in the pursuit of justice. Hollywood propounded a vision of America in which the individual triumphed and you could be successful even if you came from a small town or from a modest background. With a young family and busy career, Thatcher exhibited less interest in music and film as an adult but the magical view of the United States she gained in her childhood never left her.

The young Margaret Thatcher's positive view of the United States, which began with music and film, was confirmed by war-time and Cold War experiences. There were a large number of American airmen and soldiers stationed in local RAF airbases near Grantham during the war, bringing excitement to what was usually a dull town. The young Thatcher was impressed by their friendliness and generosity when she met GIs on the streets and when they came into her family shop. She appreciated American sacrifices during the war, which contrasted with her distrust for the other nations of Europe whom, she believed, weakly succumbed to Nazism. "She was antipathetic to Germany," Charles Powell, advisor to Thatcher, revealed. "It stems from a girl brought up at an impressionable age coinciding with the rise of Nazism and the Second World War."[10] Grantham housed a major munitions factory and was surrounded by airfields, which made it a constant target for German bombers. Thatcher remembered crawling under the table in her house during German bombing raids, which killed more than 70 people in the town.[11] She was grateful for the aid the United States supplied to Britain through a postwar loan and the Marshall Plan. Thatcher saw the United States as the bastion of democracy fighting against the communist Soviet Union, and she enthusiastically supported America's defense of Europe through NATO during the Cold War. "Not one of my generation can forget," Thatcher declared to the US Congress in February 1985, "that America has been the principal architect of a peace in Europe which has lasted forty years... The debt the free peoples of Europe owe to this nation, generous with its bounty, willing to share its strength, seeking to protect the weak, is incalculable."[12]

Thatcher's first visit to the United States, some eight years after becoming a Member of Parliament, cemented her positive view of the country. In early 1967, the United States Embassy in London selected her to participate in the International Visitor Program for British politicians and business leaders. She spent about six weeks visiting various US cities and meeting political figures. She dropped in on the International Monetary Fund in Washington DC and the NASA center in Houston. She returned again for a four-week visit two years later under the auspices of the English Speaking Union. "The excitement which I felt has never really subsided," Thatcher declared. "At each stopover I was met and accommodated by friendly, open, generous people who took me into their homes and lives and showed me their cities and townships with evident pride."[13] Thatcher paid two further visits to the United States after she became leader of the opposition in 1975 and made many subsequent trips to the United States as prime minister. "I always feel ten years younger—despite the jet-lag—when I set foot on American soil: there is something so positive, generous, and open about the people—and everything actually works. I also feel, though, that I have in a sense a share of America."[14]

The Tory leaders' affection for the United States stemmed partly from a political culture that she assumed Britain and the United States shared. Thatcher believed that "the ties of blood, language, culture and values which bound Britain and America were the only firm basis for U.S. policy in the West."[15] In June 1987, Thatcher went as far as to claim that "I tend to regard the United States as Europe on the other side of the Atlantic, which of course is really very much what it is."[16] She saw the United States as embodying the same political ideals she espoused. "I passed my childhood in a part of England not far from the home of George Washington's family," Thatcher told an American audience in January 1981.

> And, above all, my own political convictions are founded in that love of freedom, that rejection of tyranny and repression, which inspired the Pilgrim Fathers and those who followed them to America. To any European who loves liberty, America has a very special significance. Nowhere else has freedom been pursued with so much singleness of purpose, and amid such opportunities.[17]

Thatcher liked to sprinkle her speeches with quotes from the founding fathers of the United States, but out of all the American presidents Abraham Lincoln seemed to appeal to her the most. Her favorite quote, "you cannot strengthen the weak by weakening the strong," which she, and many others, wrongly attributed to Lincoln, littered her speeches since the 1950s and she allegedly kept a scrap of paper containing these words in her handbag.[18] "Who do you see as your historical counterpart?" an interviewer asked her in 1989.

She replied,

> You go back to the person who really had to fight for what he believed in and – I couldn't begin to compare myself with him – it was Abraham Lincoln.

Like Lincoln, Thatcher saw herself rising from humble beginnings, speaking with a moral voice and fighting and winning a struggle that changed the fortunes of the nation. She read his writings and speeches and found them eloquent and inspirational, just like the words of Winston Churchill, another hero of hers.[19]

Her negative opinion of postwar Britain strengthened Thatcher's admiration for the United States of America. She increasingly saw America with its free-market economy, low taxes and minimal government as an alternative model to the state socialism, high taxes and comprehensive welfare system introduced into Britain by the Labour Party. As trade unions in Britain grew in influence and militancy, Thatcher admired the less adversarial style of industrial relations found in the United States. Mostly, however, she looked on enviously at America's minimal welfare state and free-market economy. "From the American side the contribution which I would stress most is that of the enterprise culture, which rewards initiative, encourages people to set up their own business and to be self-reliant, to provide for their own families rather than look to the State to do so."[20] While socialism had established strong roots in Europe, she found no such socialist tradition across the Atlantic. Thatcher noted that the United States has "free enterprise built into her constitution. She has no socialist party and no danger of ever having one. She is the land of free enterprise, she is the land of freedom, she is the country of last resort and of safe haven for money."[21] In 1985, Thatcher told an American interviewer that the United States had a strong tradition of enterprise and self-reliance and that the Constitution is "one of the best-drafted documents I have ever seen."[22]

Ultimately she saw the United States rather than Britain as having the type of economy she wanted in her homeland.

> There are significant differences between the American and European version of capitalism. The American traditionally emphasizes the need for limited government, light regulations, low taxes and maximum labour-market flexibility. Its success has been shown above all in the ability to create new jobs, in which it is consistently more successful than Europe.[23]

The meritocratic nature of American society and the absence of a hereditary upper class appealed to Thatcher's sensibilities. "I would also single out respect for hard work and success rather than for rank or birth as a major and beneficial influence from the United States," Thatcher declared.[24] Coming from a modest background, Thatcher had little affinity with the aristocracy and the One Nation paternalistic landowners who had dominated the Conservative party. Thatcher supported the traditions associated with the Monarchy and the House of Lords but disliked the heads of the more liberal state-subsidized institutions like the BBC, the universities and the Church of England. Instead she admired the successful entrepreneurs and the small business owners, like her parents, whom she believed would gain more respect and enjoy greater prosperity in the United States because of its enterprise and lack of class prejudices. She disliked the sneering attitude of British elites to self-made men and women and admired the more open acceptance and celebration of wealth she found in the United States.

As Britain faced economic and industrial problems under both Conservative and Labour governments in the 1960s and especially in the 1970s, the number of Conservatives who joined Thatcher in voicing a more favorable opinion of the United States increased. Journalist Andrew Neil, born in Scotland in 1949, worked for the Conservative Party as a research assistant and then joined *The Economist* as a correspondent in 1973. Neil became American correspondent for *The Economist* from 1979 to 1982 and was based in New York and Washington DC. He fell in love with the United States, especially with the greater economic opportunities, the emphasis on merit rather than birth and the optimistic "can do" attitude he found there. Neil was inspired by the free-market economy and the more libertarian ideas he discovered across the Atlantic, which contrasted so sharply with the government control that he believed had held Britain back. When he returned to Britain, Neil became editor of *The Sunday Times* in 1983 and the paper remained a major supporter of Thatcher's government until he left the post in 1994.[25]

Journalist Paul Dacre, formerly a student radical, had his political views changed by visiting the United States. He joined the *Daily Express* after he graduated from college in the early 1970s and journeyed to the United States in 1976 to cover that year's American presidential election. Dacre left behind a sagging economy and found that ordinary Americans were financially better off than the average Briton.[26] Leaving behind a Britain "ossified by an us-and-them, gaffers-versus-workers mentality," Dacre was overjoyed to find less class conflict and a much a smaller amount of government-funded housing, trade union militancy and nationalized industry in the United States. Dacre became deputy news editor and assistant editor of the conservative-supporting *Daily Mail* in the 1980s. "Mrs Thatcher, in what was a terribly painful process . . . empowered the individual and restored aspiration and self-reliance in this country," he suggested.[27]

Thatcher and other Conservatives were not uncritical of the United States and voiced concern at the increasing social problems evident in 1960s and 1970s America. While extolling the free-market economy found in the United States, rising crime, racial divisions and student unrest all provoked dismay. The American counterculture and its critique of traditions of authority held little appeal to

Thatcher. She especially disliked the comprehensive form of public education found in the United States, preferring instead the stratified grammar school system solidified in the 1944 Education Act. In May 1970, Thatcher told the Westminster Catholic Parents Association that because of its social problems and low "educational standards" the United States was not the perfect model for Britain.[28] In the same month she informed the National Association of Head Teachers Conference that the United States had "colossal problems" in spite of the comprehensive system of education and the high educational expenditures.[29]

Thatcher expressed no dissent on economic policy while part of the Conservative government of 1970 to 1974 but after the party's defeat at the 1974 general election, she increasingly believed that the country needed to move in a different direction and turned to American sources to develop her policies. "I had always been an instinctive Conservative, but I had failed to develop these instincts either into a coherent framework of ideas or into a set of practical policies for government," Thatcher later remarked.[30] Now Thatcher and her allies articulated a series of policies heavily influenced by ideas springing from the United States. The New Right in the United States and conservatism in Britain forged close links as political and economic ideas moved back and forth across the Atlantic. The American Enterprise Institute, the Heritage Foundation and the Hoover Institute worked closely with conservatives in Britain.[31] Austrian-born economist Friedrich von Hayek, one of the few who championed free-market capitalism in the immediate postwar years, spent time in both the United States and Great Britain promoting his ideas. Hayek's *The Road to Serfdom,* first published in Britain in 1944, rather dramatically argued that socialism leads to the end of freedom.[32] It was as an undergraduate at Oxford University between 1943 and 1947 that she first read *The Road to Serfdom,* which inspired Thatcher's thinking on the evils of socialism.[33] At one of his many public talks in the United Kingdom, journalist William Rees-Mogg remembered Thatcher "listening to Friedrich von Hayek like a schoolgirl, her face glowing with attention."[34]

In the years after she became leader of the Conservative Party, Margaret Thatcher and other Conservatives seized upon the theories of the American economist Milton Friedman. Friedman, born in New York in 1912, worked as an economist for the federal government and after World War II taught at the University of Chicago helping to foster the "Chicago School" of economics, known for theories associated with free-market libertarianism. A market economy is self-regulating and should be freed of government intervention as much as possible, Friedman argued. Often termed a neoliberal or neoclassical economist because of his adherence to Adam Smith and earlier classical economists, Friedman was even more dismissive than classical economists of the governments' role in the economy and in providing welfare. Most famously, Friedman disagreed with Keynesian orthodoxy, which suggested that government spending would increase employment, by arguing that there was a natural rate of unemployment and that government spending would not lower unemployment but increase inflation. Controlling inflation rather than maintaining full employment should became the object of government economic policy and control of the money supply the most important instrument of economic policy to achieve these ends. Friedman suggested that "inflation is always and everywhere a monetary phenomenon" and that inflation is caused by "too much money chasing too few goods." Therefore, to control inflation, Friedman called for governments to decrease the money supply by printing and spending less money. Friedman and the Chicago school, dissenting voices against the prevailing economic orthodoxy, did not invent monetarism but they popularized these ideas and made them accessible through televisions programs, interviews, books and magazine articles. Friedman won the Nobel Prize for economics in 1976 for ideas that in effect called for an end to Keynesian policies that had guided Western governments, including Britain, for the preceding 30 years.[35]

Milton Friedman visited Britain frequently and his ideas were widely disseminated in conservative circles in the 1970s. Friedman taught at the University of Cambridge in the 1950s and became a regular speaker at the Institute of Economic Affairs (IEA), a major think tank for free-market ideas founded in 1955. Thatcher began attending IEA meetings and reading their publications in the 1960s and was probably first introduced to Friedman's ideas there. Friedman met Thatcher for the first time in 1978, at a dinner arranged by the director of the IEA, Ralph Harris. Harris remembered that Thatcher scrupulously took notes when Friedman talked and asked numerous questions.[36] Friedman's views also seriously influenced Keith Joseph, one of Thatcher's closest advisers who later served as Thatcher's Minister of Trade. When the Conservatives lost power in 1974, Joseph founded the Centre for Policy Studies (CPS) a Conservative think tank to champion free-market ideas. Thatcher joined the Centre as Deputy Chairman and Friedman became a frequent speaker at its meetings.[37] Others acted as transatlantic bridges to spread Friedman's ideas. Canadian economist Harry Johnson, who held professorships at the University of Chicago and the London School of Economics in the late 1960s, propagated monetarist ideas in Britain. British monetarist Alan Walters was a visiting professor of economics at the University of Chicago in 1959, Professor at the London School of Economics (LSE) from 1968 to 1976 and then worked at The Johns Hopkins University in Maryland before becoming Thatcher's main economic adviser between 1981 and 1983.[38] Newspapers like the *Daily Telegraph* and journalists like Samuel Brittan at *The Financial Times* and Peter Jay and William Rees-Mogg at *The Times* brought monetarist ideas to their Conservative readers and to the leading lights in the City of London.[39]

Alongside monetarism, public choice theory, which originated among American economists, proved important in cementing Thatcher's opposition to government control of the economy. Public choice theorists used such neoclassical models of economic theory that emphasized self-interest and the benefits of competition to examine the nature and efficiency of government. Anthony Downs' *An Economic Theory of Democracy* (1957) and James M. Buchanan and Gordon Tullock's *The Calculus of Consent: Logical Foundations of Constitutional Democracy* (1962) argued that politicians and government officials were not benevolent servants of the people but self-interested individuals building power bases for their own personal gain. Therefore, public choice theory questioned the benefits of government action and the efficiency of government in providing services.

Conservatives used these theories to call for provisions previously provided by the government to be turned over to private enterprise and for greater competition in the public sector to improve government performance. James Buchanan visited Britain in the 1960s and Gordon Tullock in the 1970s. Both spoke at the IEA and the IEA published some of their work, bringing their ideas to the notice of Margaret Thatcher.[40]

After Margaret Thatcher's Conservative Party won the general election in May 1979, the new government implemented policies partly influenced by Friedman and the Chicago school. Friedman's belief that the government would be able to identify and limit the money supply, however, proved overly optimistic as the growth of credit made it more difficult to measure and to control the amount of money in circulation. Inflation increased to 22 percent in 1983 and unemployment, which had stood at 1.3 million in 1979, rose to more than three million in 1983.[41] The Conservative government relied on tax cuts, especially for the wealthy, to improve economic growth, deregulated the business and financial sector, reduced government welfare payments and introduced legislation that curtailed union influence. Thatcher believed that "equality—being an unnatural condition which can only be enforced by the state—is usually the enemy of liberty."[42] After their reelection in 1983, Thatcher's government privatized state-owned industries and sold off stocks and shares to the general public hoping to create a popular share-owning capitalism based on the US model. The government introduced elements of the free market into the NHS by making doctors and hospitals compete for funding within an "internal market" and began contracting out cleaning and other services in the NHS to the highest bidder. At the local level, Conservatives outsourced services to private contractors, modeled on the practice found in US states. Under Thatcher, economic policy in the United States and the United Kingdom converged and what transpired was an Anglo-American model of capitalism based on a free-market orientation that differed from the social democratic model of continental Europe. Now the British economy would be built on private rather than state investment, less government regulation of business, low public spending and taxation, fewer public services, a low-wage insecure workforce and greater inequalities in wealth.[43]

British Conservatives looked to the United States for inspiration in social policy far more than any previous administration. The Thatcher government, in particular, wanted to introduce some of the innovations in welfare reform found in the United States. American states had introduced workfare programs that forced the unemployed to accept work offers or at least attend a training course to continue receiving benefits. More than 20 US states operated a form of workfare by 1986.[44] Conservative Ministers and civil servants made fact-finding missions to the United States and in June 1986 Thatcher told the House of Commons "We are looking into the way in which workfare operates in the United States." Subsequently, "The Thatcher government looked to American state, local and federal programmes in developing the British welfare-to-work system," noted author David P. Dolowitz in his book on British welfare reform. The government incrementally and experimentally introduced community work programs, youth training schemes, job clubs that helped the unemployed with job applications and interviews, and legislation that withdrew benefits if welfare recipients could not prove they were actively seeking work or willing to accept job offers, all derived from the US experience.[45]

When it came to educational reform, the Thatcher government again looked to the United States as a model of efficiency and excellence. College enrollment in Britain was spectacularly low compared to its main economic competitors. The Conservative government wanted to expand college enrollment but at minimal cost to the government and they looked to incorporate some ideas from the US market-driven mass-based higher education system into the government-controlled British model. The Higher Education Reform Act of 1991 and the Further and Higher Education Reform Act of 1992 adopted some US-style market initiatives including providing universities with a degree of financial independence from the state, introducing competition between colleges for government funding and replacing government-funded student grants with student loans.[46]

When Republican Ronald Reagan was elected US president in November 1980, Thatcher found a natural ally across the Atlantic. Reagan was born into a humble and provincial background in small-town Illinois in February 1911. He enjoyed a career as an actor in Hollywood and then entered politics. At first a Democrat, he supported right-wing Republican Barry Goldwater in the 1964 presidential election and was elected governor of California in 1966 serving two terms. He campaigned for the Republican presidential nomination in 1976 but lost to Gerald Ford but had better luck in 1980 and went on to beat incumbent Jimmy Carter in the presidential election. Reagan exuded an optimistic and a reassuring demeanor and enjoyed film-star good looks. Thatcher first met Reagan in April 1975, shortly after she became leader of the Conservative party, when the former actor and Governor of California visited London and called on her at the House of Commons. She later claimed to have known of Reagan from his movies *Kings Row, The Voice of the Turtle* and *The Hasty Heart* and was pleased to meet in person a real life Hollywood star.[47] The meeting scheduled for 45 minutes lasted more than an hour and a half. With Thatcher's love of old Hollywood movies and her warmness toward Americans, the two bonded even though they had different styles and temperaments. Thatcher exuded a preaching tone while Reagan was polite, charming and genial with a depreciating sense of humor that Thatcher lacked. But the different personalities complemented each other and they became firm friends.[48] "I liked her immediately," Reagan recalled, "she was warm, feminine, gracious, and intelligent—and it was evident from our first words that we were soul mates when it came to reducing government and expanding economic freedom."[49] In turn, Thatcher was "immediately won over by his charm, sense of humor and directness."[50]

Reagan and Thatcher shared a common view of the world, based on a commitment to free-market capitalism and fervent anticommunism. Thatcher believed that Britain should remain a staunch ally of the United States, the main bulwark against the Soviet Union, and that Reagan was an American leader who would stand up to the Soviets. "Ronald Reagan's election was of immediate and fundamental importance, because it demonstrated that the United States, the greatest force for liberty that the world has known, was about to reassert a self-confident leadership in world affairs," Thatcher suggested.[51] Both leaders wanted to control public spending on welfare but not on defense. Reaganomics, or supply-side economics, put great emphasis on lowering taxes, believing that tax cuts for the wealthy would encourage them to invest their new-found riches. This, in turn, would lead to economic growth, which would eventually trickle down to the wider population, and lead to more tax revenue for the government. "In this present crisis, government is not the solution to our problem; government is the problem," Reagan announced in his inaugural address on January 20, 1981. "Many of the policies you are following are the policies we are following," Thatcher told a joint session of the US Congress on February 20, 1985.

> You have brought inflation down. So have we. You have declared war on regulations and controls. So have we. Our Civil Service is now smaller than at any time since the War. And controls on pay, prices, dividends, foreign exchange—all are gone. You have encouraged small business—so often the source of tomorrow's jobs. So have we. But above all, we are carrying out the largest programme of denationalisation in our history.[52]

Notwithstanding the admiration that Thatcher showed toward Reagan and the United States, the closeness of the relationship between the two leaders is often overstated. Thatcher championed "Victorian" values of minimal government, hard work, thrift and self-reliance but not the social conservatism proposed by Reagan. While Reagan publically extolled his Christian faith and anti-abortion stance, Thatcher avoided public pronouncements on religion and voted in Parliament to legalize homosexuality and abortion. Much to the annoyance of the British government, it took a great deal of persuasion before the White House would publicly come out in support of the British in the Falklands War in April 1982. The US invasion of the Caribbean island of Grenada in October 1983 caused Thatcher to erupt in fury as Reagan omitted to inform Thatcher of his plans to attack a member of the Commonwealth with the Queen as its Head of State. The Cold War also led to disagreements. The Reagan and Thatcher governments fell out in 1982 over the proposed US sanctions against the Soviet Union that threatened the building of a gas pipeline from Siberia to Western Europe. Reagan's offer to give up nuclear weapons in negotiations with Soviet leader Mikhail Gorbachev in Reykjavik in October 1986 provoked outrage in Downing Street. Still, their personal relationship, and the relations between the two governments, remained strong despite these disagreements.[53]

For all the links between the Conservative Party in Britain and the New Right in the United States, Thatcher's ideas owed less to Friedman than is often thought. The concept of monetarism, controlling the money supply to reduce inflation, was accepted before Friedman popularized the idea—by those who would not call themselves Thatcherites. John Maynard Keynes often spoke about the importance of controlling the money supply and the previous Labour government had adopted monetarist policies even though they thought that it should not be the only method used to control inflation. Monetarism was a new name for the well-established quantity theory of money stated Nigel Lawson in August 1980.

Friedman had not invented the theory; it had been used by political parties of all persuasions in the industrial world since the nineteenth century.[54] In a radio interview in August 1982, Thatcher went even further by suggesting that monetarist policy was "as old as money."[55]

Friedman's importance to Thatcher lay not so much in the economic theory of monetarism, but in his contribution to reawakening free-market principles in conservative circles and in providing intellectual justification to the ideas that the image of America had previously inspired in her. Friedman and the American New Right publicized free-market reforms and added to the revival of classical liberal economics, which coincided with Thatcher's thinking on economic ideas. Thatcher often discussed conservative philosophy with other students while at Oxford University in the 1940s. She was conversant with the "invisible hand" of Adam Smith and the natural rights of John Locke, which emphasized the free market, free trade and limited government long before the rise of the New Right in the United States.[56] The significance of the United States to Margaret Thatcher lay in the alternative vision it provided to her in the days when socialism seemed triumphant. Thatcher saw the United States as a successful model of free-market liberalism that Britain could have become if Labour had not gained power in 1945. She wanted to return British society and the British economy to the pre-1945 of her youth, believing the postwar Labour reforms were an aberration and a departure from the limited government and free-market economy Thatcher cherished. She often spoke of this need to recreate Britain and to restore the incentives, eradicated by socialism, which would allow Britons to once again seek prosperity.[57]

In the absence of free-market liberalism in Britain, Thatcher held up the United States as the model society she wanted Britain to emulate. "For many years, our vitality in Britain was blunted by excessive reliance on the State," Thatcher told a joint session of the US Congress in February 1985. "Our industries were nationalised controlled and subsidised in a way that yours never were. We are having to recover the spirit of enterprise which you never lost."[58] Nigel Lawson, Chancellor of the Exchequer in Thatcher's government, made the connection between Thatcher's vision of pre-socialist Britain and the United States explicit.

> A subsequent formulation of the Government's supply-side policy objective which I was to use frequently and which was also much used by Margaret was the recreation of the "enterprise culture" in the UK. The model in this case was the United States—although that country had in turn derived it from the vigorous enterprise culture of Victorian England and Scotland, and developed it further.[59]

Opposition to US Foreign Policy

Margaret Thatcher may have welcomed Ronald Reagan's victory in the November 1980 presidential election but Reagan's reputation as a right-wing Republican and staunch anticommunist worried many of those on the left. "It looks as if Reagan has beaten Carter in the American presidential election, and it is a dark day for the western world," left-wing Labour MP Tony Benn wrote in his diary.[60]

"It seems as it everyone's worst nightmare came true," the *Socialist Review*, journal of the Trotskyist Socialist Workers Party declared. "Ronald Reagan is the next president of the United States."[61] President Reagan proceeded to take a more aggressive stance toward the Soviet Union than previous American administrations, which led to concerns about a war between the two superpowers and a possible nuclear holocaust. In June 1982, Reagan told the British parliament that he intended to "leave Marxism-Leninism on the ash heap of history" and described the Soviets as the "focus of evil in the modern world" in a speech in March 1983. Later the same month, Reagan announced research into a missile shield for the United States, the Strategic Defense Initiative, commonly known as Star Wars. If installed, Star Wars would allow the United States to launch a nuclear attack on the Soviets without being annihilated in return.[62]

A new wave of resentment against the United States' foreign policy, such as to be unseen since the late 1960s, swept Britain as people feared that Reagan and Thatcher made the country a target for the Soviet Union. In the late 1970s, the Soviets began deploying SS-20 missiles targeted at Western Europe, an upgrade on previous intermediate-range nuclear missiles. NATO responded by deploying American missiles to Western Europe including Britain. President Jimmy Carter and British Prime Minister James Callaghan had originally agreed to the deployment of ground-launching cruise nuclear missiles in Britain; Thatcher quickly implemented the agreement when she entered Downing Street. In June 1980, the Conservative government announced that they would install 160 American-owned and American-controlled cruise missiles at RAF airbases in Greenham Common in Berkshire and Molesworth in Cambridgeshire. With the prospect of Britain becoming a battleground in a nuclear war between the United States and the Soviets, fear of nuclear annihilation, reminiscent of the 1950s, returned to haunt Britain. "Certainly, the threat of nuclear war felt very real," remembered Tom Bromley, a teenager in York. "I vividly remember reading Raymond Briggs' *When The Wind Blows*," a novel about a nuclear attack on Britain by the Soviet Union, "and feeling terrified enough to hold my duvet tighter that night (because that would really have helped)."[63]

Some pacifists turned to direct action to stop the stationing of American missiles on British soil. In September 1981, a group of protesters established a women-only peace camp outside the perimeter fence at Greenham Common RAF base aiming to stop the deployment of the missiles. The women tried to sabotage the building of missile silos by cutting holes in the perimeter fence and staging sit-ins in the construction area. On December 12, 1982, 30,000 women linked arms in a human chain around the perimeter fence. In April 1983, 70,000 people forged a human chain linking Aldermaston nuclear research center and Greenham Common, a distance of some 14 miles. In spite of the protests, the missiles began to arrive at Greenham Common in November 1983.[64]

The anger against US foreign policy that developed in Britain embraced a larger section of the population in the 1980s than it did during the Campaign for Nuclear Disarmament (CND) marches of the late 1950s or during the Vietnam protests of the 1960s. Nuclear power accidents such as the Three Mile Island incident in Pennsylvania on March 28, 1979, and the far more serious Chernobyl disaster in

Ukraine in April 1986, heightened fears about the dangers of nuclear power in general. Stephen Foster from Stoke arrived in Norwich in 1989 and noticed that "one in every three cars displayed a Greenpeace or a 'Nuclear Power—Nein Danke!' bumper sticker."[65] The siting of American cruise missiles in Britain added to the anxiety. The CND membership had fallen to little more than 2,000 in 1979 but rose to 9,000 in 1980 and to 100,000 in 1984.[66] The Labour Party adopted a policy of unilateral nuclear disarmament at its 1982 conference. In October 1981, a quarter of a million demonstrated in London against the deployment of cruise missiles and in October 1983, just before the proposed arrival of the first cruise missile, 400,000 demonstrated in Hyde Park against their deployment.[67] Many joined a political protest for the first time in their lives. The mother of teenager Louise Wener from Essex "sniffed disapprovingly whenever the Greenham Common women came on the news" and never joined in any political debates at home. In 1983, however, both mother and daughter went on a CND march in London. "Kids with ordinary net-curtain-washing housewife mothers find themselves unexpectedly yanked away from their stereos and dragged up to London to join the march."[68] Opinion polls in 1983 at the height of the campaign found a majority of the population against deployment of the missiles and some 94 percent wanted a "dual key," which would prevent the United States from launching the missile without British consent.[69] Most Britons opposed American nuclear weapons being stationed on British soil but believed Britain should maintain its own nuclear arsenal. In December 1986, a Harris survey showed that only 24 percent of respondents believed Britain should dispose of its nuclear weapons while 70 percent opposed the idea. In contrast, 51 percent believed that Britain should remove American nuclear bases and only 41 percent that it should retain them.[70]

Not only did nuclear proliferation and Cold War tensions worry many on the left, so too did Ronald Reagan's aggressive stance in Central America. In Nicaragua, a revolution brought the left-wing Sandinista National Liberation Front to power in 1979, but the United States opposed the regime on the grounds that the Sandinistas supported communism and had links with the Soviet Union. The Sandinistas, named after Augusto César Sandino, who led the resistance against the US occupation of Nicaragua in the 1930s, found itself under attack from US-backed opponents, the Contras, stationed in Honduras. In El Salvador, the United States backed a military government, added by vicious right-wing vigilantes, who fought against a left-wing guerilla group, the Farabundo Marti National Liberation Front (FMLN). Reagan's military support for opponents of the Sandinistas led to the formation of the British Nicaragua Solidarity Campaign. To show their solidarity, the punk band the Clash released an album entitled *Sandinista!* in December 1980 containing the song "Washington Bullets," an indictment of US foreign policy. Sandinista and FMLN T shirts become a common piece of clothing on the campuses and streets of 1980s Britain while some young idealistic and adventurist Britons joined "coffee brigades" to harvest coffee in Sandinista-controlled Nicaragua.

The anti-apartheid movement, a particularly significant political movement in 1980s' Britain, poured further condemnation on both Prime Minister Thatcher and President Reagan for their unwillingness to take action against the white racist

South African government. South Africa operated an apartheid regime, denying blacks the right to vote and imprisoning the African National Congress (ANC) leader Nelson Mandela. Both Thatcher and Reagan verbally opposed apartheid but were reluctant to take action against the South African government, worried about the procommunist elements in the ANC and their "terrorist" activities. While the world imposed economic sanctions against South Africa, the two leaders opposed them proposing "constructive engagement" with the South African government instead. In 1984, Thatcher welcomed South African president P. W. Botha to Britain, drawing worldwide condemnation.[71] Reagan vetoed a bill from the United States Congress to impose sanctions on South Africa. "Reagan has outdone Thatcher in trying to clothe economic expediency in moral respectability, calling sanctions against South Africa 'repugnant,'" comedian Michael Palin disgustingly wrote in July 1986.[72] Journalist Gavin Martin, writing in the music weekly *New Musical Express*, now the bastion of left-wing journalism, went a little further by suggesting that "Many innocent people will die. Their blood will be on all our hands."[73]

The Anti Apartheid Movement (AAM) became the center of British opposition to the white South African government. In 1965, the total membership of the AAM was approximately 2,500 and stayed around this number until the mid-1980s when membership increased to 7,500 in 1985–1986, to 18,000 in 1987–1988 and peaked at nearly 20,000 in 1989.[74] Membership did not reflect the depth of support. Over 120,000 people attended an anti-apartheid rally in November 1985 and 250,000 gathered in Hyde Park on June 28, 1986, calling for sanctions against South Africa. This figure was matched at the Nelson Mandela Freedom Rally held in Hyde Park on July 17, 1988. Many supported AAM's call for a boycott of South African goods. "Apartheid was at its peak, all matters white South African were boycotted by everybody, even by people who didn't have any principles whatsoever," noted Stephen Foster from Stoke, who spent the decade living and working in London.[75] Tom Bromley, a teenager in York, led "a personal campaign against Cape fruit, which pissed my dad off no end as he really liked his grapes."[76] On June 11, 1988, Artists Against Apartheid organized a star-studded concert at Wembley Stadium celebrating Nelson Mandela's 70th birthday and calling for his release from prison. BBC television screened the entire event. A Gallup poll taken after the concert showed that 70 percent of those polled supported the call for Mandela's release.[77]

While left-wing elements opposed US foreign policy in Central America and South Africa, a wider section of the population condemned Reagan's foreign policy initiatives that directly involved Britain. The US invasion of Grenada in October 1983 caused much dismay in Britain as Reagan neglected to inform the British government of his plans to attack a member of the British Commonwealth. Further resentment was expressed over the US bombing of Libya in April 1986. After the United States suspected that Libya was involved in terrorist activities, Thatcher gave the United States permission to bomb Tripoli with American planes flying from Lakenheath and Upper Heyford RAF bases in England. In a MORI poll conducted after the Grenada invasion, some 52 percent opposed the incursion and only 32 percent approved. After the Libyan raid, 25 percent believed Thatcher was right to give the United States permission to use British bases while 71 percent thought she was wrong. In March 1981, 22 percent of Gallup poll respondents believed that the British relationship with the United States was too close. In March 1984, this figure had risen to 34 percent and to 47 percent after the Libyan bombing in April 1986.[78]

In the 1980s, British distrust of the United States government and their foreign policy was greater than ever. Some who had previously admired the United States now relentlessly condemned American foreign policy. Author Jan Morris, who first came to America in the 1950s and "loved the country from the start," now despised the actions of the US government. "Something snapped in me, and I faced up to a conviction I had been trying to stifle for years: the reluctant and terrible conviction that the greatest threat to the peace of humanity is the United States." She could "no longer stomach America's insidious meddling across the face of the world. I live a life of perpetual travel, and wherever I go I find myself more and more repelled by the apparently insatiable American urge to interfere in other people's business."[79] After Reagan had bombed Tripoli, Monty Python comedian Michael Palin wrote almost in disbelief in his diary "that 90 percent of Americans are behind him. My feelings of revulsion against this dark side of America—the clumsy, ugly face of power without intelligence, the world bully—have quite put me off going over there next week."[80] Denis Healey, Shadow Foreign Secretary during the 1980s, suggested that the invasion of Grenada and other foreign policy developments have "led some people in Britain, as much on the far right as the far left of politics, to wonder whether de Gaulle was not right after all—that it is not possible for the American elephant to live in the European farmyard."[81] Confidence in US foreign policy was lower in the 1980s than it was even in the worst years of the Vietnam War. Opinion polls showed that British approval of the US role in world affairs declined compared to that for the role of the Soviet Union. In August 1983, 30 percent of Britons approved of American foreign policy, while only 8 percent approved of the Soviet's role in world affairs. In October 1985, the United States approval lead over the Soviet Union fell slightly to 18 percentage points, by March 1986 it had declined to 12 percent, and by April the countries were virtually even, with less than a quarter of Britons approving their roles.[82]

Reagan's foreign policy even divided the Conservative Party. Some Conservatives were outraged that Thatcher would dare to criticize Reagan over the US invasion of Grenada. On December 7, 1983, author Kingsley Amis wrote to historian Robert Conquest:

> what the hell got into Mrs T over Grenada? Proving she wasn't Ronnie's poodle? Threats from the cabinet? Womanly pique? What have you heard?.... Need hardly tell you that I've met nobody who doesn't solidly support the US action, even in the Garrick, as you know Tory but no hotbed of pro-Americanism.[83]

The *Daily Express*, an ardent supporter of Thatcher, believed that Britain should have supported the invasion with military assistance if necessary. "Our government, instead of displaying resolution, has determined to play chicken," the paper concluded.[84] "The Grenada affair has shattered my confidence in Mrs. Thatcher as an intuitive politician," Paul Johnson, an ardent supporter of Thatcher, announced.

> I would have expected her to endorse Reagan's attitude publicly and to give it every assistance—diplomatic, military and moral—in our power. It is painful to hear her adopt the sanctimonious humbug of her progressive opponents and to see her slip so easily into the anti-American posture of the far left.[85]

Other conservatives were less supportive of Thatcher and US foreign policy. Right-winger Enoch Powell accused the government of turning Britain into "something horribly resembling a satellite of the U.S." The so-called wets or moderates within the Conservative Party, such as Kenneth Clarke, Michael Heseltine and Chris Patten, opposed some of Reagan's policies and the nation's subservient relationship to Reagan and the United States. Peter Carrington and Ian Gilmour worried at the stridency of Reagan's foreign policy while other "wets" believed that Britain should develop closer ties with Europe rather than with the United States.[86]

Cultural nationalism was a strong component not only of right-wing but also of left-wing criticisms of the United States as many worried about Britain's declining status evident by Thatcher's subservience to the United States. Reagan's invasion of Grenada, the stationing of American nuclear weapons on British soil, and America's use of British bases to bomb Libya, convinced many that the United States could now do as it wished with Britain. The leadership of the Labour Party sought to show that they valued the Atlantic Alliance, but others proved less reticent to criticize Britain's dependence on the United States. "I am, just now, what you class 'anti-American,'" wrote historian and CND activist E. P. Thompson. Mrs Thatcher is "the betrayer of our national integrity and our national honor," suggested Cambridge-educated Thompson.[87] Journalist Gavin Martin writing in the *New Musical Express* suggested after the bombing of Libya that "Margaret Thatcher sacrificing any vestige of British national honor left after the Falklands—inspires feelings of shame and disgust."[88] Tony Benn referred to Britain as an American "colony." Denis Healey described Thatcher as "President Reagan's obedient poodle . . . It is time you got off your knees and joined other allies of the United States who are deeply concerned about present trends in American policy," he concluded.[89] "Why kid ourselves about 'Great' Britain any longer when we could, if we wanted, become the 51st state of the Union?" a lead article in left-of-center *The Guardian* ironically suggested. "Or, if not that at first, an 'outlying area under US jurisdiction territory,' like Guam or Wake Island or Johnston Atoll? The endless litany of alleged independence can't be worth the candle when Britain's rulers so manifestly draw their residual vestiges of inspiration from across the Atlantic."[90]

Much of the opposition to the policies of the US government focused on the personality of Ronald Reagan. Dubbed the "Great Communicator" in the United States, many Americans liked Reagan's optimism, his personal charm, and his down-to-earth and nonabrasive manners but in Britain many believed him to be simple-minded and reckless who would be willing to use nuclear weapons against the Soviet Union. Many symbolically identified Reagan as a cowboy, a lone individual operating outside conventional society and conventional restraints, fighting against what he saw as wrongdoers who should be brought to justice. "Because he was such a ridiculous person to be the most powerful man in the world it was difficult to take him seriously," opined Labour supporter John O' Farrell. "Perhaps all the jokes were a defence mechanism against the horrific reality that this rather simple bigot had his shaky singer over the nuclear button. Jimmy Carter, as president of the United States, had obviously automatically been a bad guy, but Ronald Reagan was just not on the scale."[91] Steve Bell, the cartoonist for *The Guardian* newspaper, made a career out of drawing grotesque caricatures of Reagan, portrayed him as an aggressive extremist obsessed with communism.[92] *New Musical Express* called him "The Great Rondini (the Bard of Bullshit, the De Niro of Doubletalk)." He'd proved those wrong who "said the world's most powerful nation couldn't be administered on a regime of green jellybeans, weekly facelifts and afternoon naps!"[93] *Spitting Image*, shown on ITV from 1984 to 1996, satirized current events by featuring puppet caricatures of famous people with Ronald Reagan playing a starring role. The show portrayed Reagan as a childish buffoon often seen in bed with his wife Nancy reading comics. Next to his bed were red buttons labeled "Nurse" and "Nuke." Thatcher swooned over Reagan who she called "Ronnie." A regular feature on the show was Reagan starring in the thriller "The President's Brain Is Missing." Opinion polls confirmed the negative views of Reagan. By June 1982, only 31 percent of Britons believed Reagan was a good president and by November 1982 the number had slipped even further to 23 percent.[94] In December 1987, a MORI poll found that 39 percent put more trust in Soviet leader Mikhail Gorbachev as against 19 percent for Reagan to reduce tensions in the Cold War.[95]

The 1980s produced some of the most political music ever by British artists, much of it critical of the unpopular Ronald Reagan and US foreign policy. Heaven 17 worried about the extreme politics of Reagan on their debut single "(We Don't Need This) Fascist Groove Thang" in early 1981. The punk band the Damned released "Bad Time For Bonzo" in October 1982, a mocking reference to Reagan's 1951 film *Bedtime for Bonzo*. Frankie Goes to Hollywood reached number one in May 1984 with the single "Two Tribes," which described Reagan as a cowboy and alluded to his religious extremism. The Fun Boy Three had a major hit in 1981 with "The Lunatics (Have Taken Over the Asylum)" in which they sang of cynics and cowboys and worried about a crazy man pressing the nuclear button.[96] Most innovatively, Stiff records in London put out an album in December 1980 entitled *The Wit and Wisdom of Ronald Reagan*—both sides of the album were silent.

In the 1980s, television series and movies reflected a concern about the collaboration between the Thatcher and Reagan governments, its detrimental impact on British society and the danger of stationing American nuclear weapons on British soil. In the television series *Edge of Darkness* (1985), an antinuclear activist Emma craven, is found dead. Her father, a British police detective, discovers that her death is covered up by the British government and CIA agents active in Britain who are colluding with American business in hiding the dangers of nuclear power. Similarly, the political thriller *Defense of the Realm* (1985) centered on a high-level cover up after a near-nuclear disaster. In the movie, a young man gets killed on an

American airbase by an aircraft that's landing with a nuclear bomb on board. Both films suggest that British politicians and the secret service were willing to break the law to appease the United States and protect the nuclear power industry.[97]

Some authors combined fear of the Reagan government with traditional stereotypes of individual Americans. *A Very British Coup*, a 1982 novel by Labour Party left-winger Chris Mullin, centered on the establishment's reaction to the election of a left-wing Labour government led by Prime Minister Harry Perkins. The Perkins government promised to remove US military bases from Britain and disarm Britain's nuclear weapons. The US government joins with Conservative politicians, civil servants, business leaders and the media to destabilize the left-wing government. The United States uses its influence on the IMF to impose stringent conditions on a loan, undertake covert operations from the American Embassy in England and pressure American-owned multinationals to transfer money out of Britain. The US president is a cigar-smoking gum-chewing man with a "considerable frame" while Secretary of State, Marcus J. Morgan, was "a corporation lawyer, very fat and very rich . . . whose knowledge of the geography was largely gleaned from a *Time-Life* Atlas and the currency markets." When the president met his chief of staffs, military advisers and cabinet members, they were "all big men with heavy jowls and large bellies." In the end, Perkins is forced to resign and the new government bows to internal and external pressure and reverses the previous government's radical positions.[98]

American Society in the British Imagination

While Prime Minister Thatcher held positive views about the enterprise culture, the minimal welfare state and the free-market economy found in the United States, many others drew more negative conclusions about the country that they read about in the newspapers and saw on the television news. The gun violence in America, for example, appalled many. In October 1985, Jon Connell in the *Sunday Times* suggested that the United States

> tolerates a level of violence in its inner cities that would make constant headlines in Britain. Staggeringly, more than one in every three blacks who die between the ages of 15 and 24 is murdered (in almost every case by another black). The 6,000 black Americans who lost their lives in black-on-black violence in 1981, rivals the number of black servicemen killed during the 12 years of the Vietnam conflict.[99]

"Gun shows, travelling supermarkets of weaponry now numbering about 1,000 a year, traffic openly in everything from 'stunguns' to napalm kits," *The Sunday Times* incredulously reported in November 1985. "At a summer show in Dallas, a 50-calibre machinegun was displayed with the sign, 'Reach out and touch someone,' T-shirts bore the messages, 'Gun control is being able to hit your target' and 'Join the marines, travel to exotic distant lands, meet exciting, unusual people—and kill them.'"[100] In May 1990, Peter Pringle of the *Independent* was equally horrified when he met 10-year-old Tim Foster from Texas.

> Tim and 200 others at the Third Annual Hill Country Machine Gun Shoot at Helotes, a little town near San Antonio, took turns to fire 100 different automatic weapons—from an Uzi sub-machine gun to a Thomson.45 calibre—the kind that Eliot Ness used when he fought Al Capone,

an amazed Pringle reported. "Tim had his picture taken for the newspapers firing an M16, the weapon of the Vietnam GI. They came to the shoot-out in cars with bumper stickers declaring: 'The More People I Meet The More Bullets I Need' and 'Freedom Wasn't Won With A Registered Gun.'"[101]

In addition to urban violence, newspapers exposed the crack cocaine epidemic in inner city America. Cocaine, the *Daily Express* informed its readers, "has now become the all-American drug, as much part of the U.S. scene as hot dogs and Mom's apple pie."[102] "Widespread concern at the epidemic of cocaine abuse, spurred by the availability of a highly addictive distillate called 'crack,' has been highlighted by startling recent statistics," *The Times* reported in July 1986.

> These show that one in six has tried cocaine while at school; the drug now has four to five million regular users; the plague is costing America about 25 billion dollars (16 billion pounds) a year; and more than half of all crime in the United States is now related to drugs.[103]

In August 1986, journalist W. J. Weatherby, writing in the *Guardian,* decried the changes drugs had brought to New York City.

> When I came the first time . . . . you could play chess in the Village until dawn, buying no more than one cup of coffee without being harassed to buy more as you would be today, and then go home without any fear of being mugged. I knew of one solitary person who had been mugged years ago, but it didn't become an everyday fear until drugs became mass market.[104]

Those who visited the United States could not fail to notice the inequalities and urban decay. "I first visited America in 1980, and went on a tour of Los Angeles, the Grand Canyon, Las Vegas and San Francisco. In 1982 I went to Florida and in 1988 I went to New York and Boston," remembered Mike Lyons, an office worker from London.

> Therefore, I did see some of the reality of living in America. During my visits I saw some poor places in Los Angeles in particular, there was a huge gap between the rich and poor and watching the TV news in hotel rooms, there were many reports of gun crime and gang land killings. This was a far more violent place to live in, compared to England. It was not just the popular culture that informed my views of America, it was going there myself, to see what some places were like. If you had a good job, it paid well, you could live in a nice mostly sunny in places, such as Los Angeles and Florida. You could have a good quality of life, if you were able to afford, the wonderful consumer goods that were available. If you do well in America, you can live the "American Dream," if you do not do well you will face a life of poverty and insecurity in a land of plenty.[105]

Gareth Rowlands, a student from Wales, decried "the disparities in the country" and believed that it was now clear "for the first time that the biggest piece of propaganda the culture mills produced was the myth of the classless society."[106]

The drugs and the violence of the urban ghettoes became a dominant story from America in the 1980s, but so too did the seemingly American disease of AIDS (Acquired Immune Deficiency Syndrome). In April 1983, a BBC documentary entitled "Killer in the Village" introduced AIDS to the British public, setting off a series of sensational newspaper articles that focused on the sexual promiscuity of gay men. AIDS may have become known in the public mind as the gay disease but, with so few cases in Britain, it also became closely associated with urban America. In August 1985, under the headline "Aids: The American Nightmare," *The Times* reported that in the United States "the myth, the mystery and the increasingly terrifying paranoia, grows."[107] A two-part series entitled "The dying pains of freedom" published in *The Times* in 1987 reported on the AIDS epidemic in San Francisco. "Top US health officials predict 270,000 American cases by 1991 compared with 29,000 now," the second article reported.

> Aids has hit hard in the world of the arts in New York, a city where at least 500,000 people are believed to be carrying the virus. The pall of despair is almost tangible in Greenwich Village, where business has slumped in restaurants and shops and funeral cars and young mourners can be seen daily in the streets.[108]

Imported television soap operas such as *Dallas* and *Dynasty* provided escape routes from the relentlessly depressing news emanating from inner city America. *Dallas,* set among the Ewings, a wealthy Texas family in the oil and cattle-ranching industries, and *Dynasty,* which revolved around the Carringtons, an affluent family in the oil business living in Denver, Colorado, featured glamorous costumes, lavish sets and sweeping outdoor scenery. *Dallas* became a national obsession in Britain. "They were very wealthy, very glamorous and it all seemed very exciting," exclaimed teenager Helen Bushby. "Not like life on the Wirral," she added.[109] "The most dramatic story on BBC television's showpiece nine o'clock news Monday night was not the insurrection in South Korea, the manhunt for the murderer of a retired vicar in southern England or the prison escape of a legendary London gang leader," reported an incredulous *Washington Post* in May 1980.

> Instead it was the shooting of a Texas oilman who has become Britain's most popular television villain—J. R. Ewing of *Dallas*. Staid BBC news televised a replay of the brutal, unsolved crime in the Ewings' penthouse offices in downtown Dallas that about 25 million Britons had watched "live" just minutes earlier.

The BBC audience for the "Who Shot JR?" episode amounted to nearly half the country's population. Discussion of the shooting dominated morning newspapers, radio shows and work conversations. "Dallas Fever!" proclaimed the front page headline on Britain's largest selling newspaper, the *Sun.*[110] *Dallas* and *Dynasty* inspired many women to wear shoulder pads and sport blow-dried and lacquered hair. "Newcastle at night was full of allusions to Linda Evans and Joan Collins.

Blonde perms or streaks, highly glamorous glittery clothes referred to the camp ostentation of *Dynasty*," Hilary Fawcett remembered.[111]

Critics poured scorn on the shows and on the audiences who watched them but many female viewers enjoyed the programs because they featured strong-minded independent female characters. Many of the stories centered on the women characters who were portrayed as assertive people enjoying successful careers. "There was a less one-dimensional image of women portrayed in *Dallas* and *Dynasty*," Mary Lyons, who worked in accounts in Brighton in the 1980s, noted, "some shown as doing the same demanding jobs as men or in charge of men, which was reflecting the changing face of the workplace in the UK as well as the US."[112] Many career women found role models in other American TV programs. "Women and black people became more empowered in programmes such as *Charlie's Angels* and *Shaft*," legal executive Patricia McManus from London believed.

> Women's roles were developed and, in some cases, the previously male dominating roles had been reversed. Women were shown to have jobs and careers, previously considered to be only for men i.e. detectives as in *Cagney and Lacey* and lawyers as in *LA Law*, which may have encouraged a lot of women to pursue their own careers.[113]

Little wonder that a survey found that women liked American television programs more than men as 43.4 percent of males thought there were too many American programs on British TV but only 37.8 percent of women had the same opinion. Similarly, 27 percent of men disliked or strongly disliked current American programs on British television but only19.1 percent of women held similarly negative opinions.[114]

Programs like *Dallas* may have provided positive female role models but they, along with movies like *Wall Street*, helped to strengthen the image of an America dominated by a materialistic and ruthless business ethos. The characters in *Dallas*, especially that of J. R. Ewing, exhibited self-interest, duplicitous behavior and unprecedented ruthlessness in the pursuit of money as they warred with other members of their equally self-interested family. Hollywood movies showed similar behavior and ideas. "Greed, for lack of a better word, is good. Greed is right. Greed works," announced the Wall Street financier Gordon Gekko played by Michael Douglas in the 1987 film *Wall Street*. "Male characters such as JR Ewing and Gekko from *Wall Street* depicted a nastier and more unscrupulous image of business and inter-personal relations. And so too for female characters such as Joan Collins in *Dynasty*," observed Mary Lyons. "Money seemed to be all-important."[115] Peter O'Neill from London found that American TV and movies were showing "a country obsessed with wealth and money. Programmes and films were full of beautiful people and the happy ending was marrying into money."[116]

Opposition to the Import of American Society

Hostility toward the United States in 1980s Britain was not simply confined to opposition to their foreign policy but encompassed a fear that Thatcher's government was introducing the less savory aspects of American society into Britain.

Like America, the British economy was now increasingly built on private enterprise rather than on the public sector and British society featured greater income inequality and a smaller and less extensive welfare state. Thatcher rejoiced in the fact that Britain was becoming more American, but her opponents, mostly on the left but some on the right, found little to rejoice about. While worries about Americanization in the 1950s were mostly concerned with the import of American popular culture into Britain, in the 1980s fears of Americanization were more concerned with the import of American society and American social problems into Britain.

The number of Britons who opposed Thatcher's adoption of an American-style free-market economy in Britain was substantial. Opinion polls suggest that public disillusionment with trade union militancy and an overgenerous welfare state declined as the Conservative government passed legislation that weakened the trade union movement and reduced unemployment benefits. Whilst Thatcher cut public spending and taxes, majorities favored increased spending on health and education and showed a willingness to pay higher taxes to finance the expenditure. Throughout the 1980s, the British Social Attitudes survey consistently found that most in Britain believed that the government not the private sector should provide health care (97.7 percent in 1985 and 97.9 percent in 1986), should afford a descent standard of living for the elderly (96.6 percent in 1985 and 97.9 percent in 1986) and should reduce income disparities between the rich and the poor (69.4 percent in 1985 and 72.3 percent in 1986).[117] Even though Thatcher's Conservative Party won three consecutive general elections, the Tories never gained a majority of votes cast. In the 1979 general election the Conservatives won 44 percent of the votes cast, in 1983 42.4 percent of the votes and in 1987 only 42 percent.

Opinion polls confirmed that only a minority of Britons wanted the country to model itself on America. A MORI poll published in March 1986 found that some two-thirds of those polled declared that they liked Americans and would love to take a vacation in the United States and half stated that they would not mind working for a US company. Most British people, however, resented the extent of American influence on British society and the economy. Three in five would not want to live in America if they had to live somewhere other than Britain. A Gallup poll from 1984 found that only 24 percent agreed that "we would be better off if we were more like the Americans in many respects." When the same question was asked by Gallup in 1942, nearly twice as many Britons, 41 percent, felt that Britain should emulate the United States. In 1942, 52 percent of Britons believed that Americans "are a more democratic people than we are" while only 36 percent felt the same way in 1984.[118]

Britons were more troubled than people in other countries with the failings of American society because they saw the problems afflicting urban America coming to Britain. Steven K. Smith and Douglas A. Wertman in their analysis of opinion polls in Western Europe in the 1980s found that British views of how well Americans looked after their sick and needy declined over the decade. "Among the four largest countries . . . the biggest change in attitudes was in Britain, where opinion of U.S. performance declined substantially." The decline was, of course, a reaction to the cuts in social programs undertaken by Reagan's administration, but the views in France, Italy and West Germany, failed to regress as much as they did in Britain even though the people in these countries had similar access to information about the United States as the British did. Britain, however, was more sensitive to the changes in American society because it had a Conservative government that enjoyed a closer relationship with the United States and enacted right-wing policies that made Britain look increasingly like the United States. The British view of the policies of the Reagan administration was in essence a reflection of how Britons perceived Thatcher's policies. Significantly, when asked if the United States provides "a desirable model for other countries," the authors found the British along with Spain "were least likely to see the USA as a good model." Between 1982 and 1987, "the largest change by far was once again in Britain, where a 40 per cent margin of good (52 per cent) over poor (12 percent) dropped to only a 5 percent margin (31–26 per cent)," the authors stated.[119]

Many expressed concern that Thatcher's policies were bringing America's social problems into the country. Riots on the streets of London and Liverpool in the 1980s could only conjure up images of race riots and violence in America. "It's getting to be more like America all the time," a police officer worried after the latest round of violence in Brixton, London.[120] *The Guardian* reported that an expert on homelessness was "a witness to the American nightmare, the growing number of homeless: no longer just single men and women, but broken families living on the streets; single mothers and the elderly trapped in houses unsuitable for their needs; and abandoned properties decaying in the inner cities." The expert, the newspaper told its readers, "is convinced that the nightmare is coming here."[121] Journalist Peter Jenkins in *The Independent* complained about the "Americanisation, particularly of urban society, with its attendant growth of social violence, physical dilapidation and ostentatious degradation of the poor."[122] In May 1987, David Steel, leader of the Liberal Party, decried the influence of a "trans-Atlantic intellectual Right" that wanted to dismantle the welfare system and impose social values that were foreign to British traditions. Steel warned of "the Americanisation of Britain, complete with sharper inequalities, greater levels of private corruption and of civil violence, and the acceptance of an alienated underclass of unemployed and unemployables."[123] "America today is too often a mirror of Europe tomorrow," *The Independent* editorial apprehensively stated in 1989. "One year the mirror may reflect credit cards and crazy litigiousness; the next, a big jump in drug abuse, riots in destitute inner cities, the proliferation of guns, or Aids .... If Europe continues to evolve towards a more heartlessly commercial society, it will doubtless experience more of the polarisation which so sharply differentiates those who make it in the United States from those who fail."[124]

Others thought American business ideas were becoming dominant in the British economy and in the workplace. "How much further do we want the Americanisation of Britain to go?" asked journalist Christopher Huhne. Rather than depend on public services, such as the NHS or public transport, people are encouraged to use private insurance and cars, he suggested.

> In this sense, it seems to me that the British economy is incontrovertibly becoming more American. There is less willingness to ask whether something which is

> profitable is also worthwhile. The cost of private choices is often a diminution of public welfare, as any Londoner who has tried to get around their city knows.... Don't please, get me wrong about America. It is one of my favourite foreign places. It is just that I want to keep it foreign.[125]

"The 1980's was when I really felt that Britain was becoming 'Americanised,'" Mary Lyons believed.

> There was a Special Relationship between Thatcher and Reagan and "greed is good" reflected both of their attitudes to their countries. Working longer hours was exported from America and Mrs Thatcher took on the power of the unions in order to make Britain's workplaces like that of America.... I think the fashion for power-dressing reflected the image now expected of the British and American worker: the long haired scruffiness of the Seventies was replaced by neat and tidy, smart and business-like attire for the 80's office worker.[126]

The British film *Local Hero* released in 1983 reflected this anxiety about the impact of uncaring American business practices on Britain. The movie starred Burt Lancaster as the boss of an American oil company seeking to build a refinery on the site of a fishing village on the north coast of Scotland. The company representative, the Porsche-driving "Mac" McIntyre, is sent to Scotland to buy the village and he falls in love with the place and the simple life of the people living there. Lancaster's character is the stereotypical eccentric American, who is not surprisingly the patient of a psychiatrist and a hardnosed businessman with greedy, callous intentions. The whole film is built around the fear of heartless American businesses seeking to destroy untouched landscape and the simple way of life of those living in Britain.[127]

The more moderate wing of the Conservative Party, the wets, expressed concern about the American takeover of British business enterprises. When the American corporation Sikorsky attempted to buy the British-owned aerospace company Westland Helicopters in 1985, an outcry ensued. Thatcher believed that the owners of the company should sell it to anyone they wished while Minister of Defense Michael Heseltine and other wets opposed the sale believing that Britain was better protected by having European rather than American control of one of their defense suppliers. The Westland Helicopter Company finally approved a rescue bid by the American corporation and Michael Heseltine resigned his position in January 1986. Similar opposition was voiced to the prime minister's plans to sell off a section of the last remaining British-owned car firm, the state-owned British Leyland, to Americans. The Ford Motor Company wanted to buy the Austin Rover division and General Motors the truck and Land Rover division. After opposition in her own party, the prime minister was eventually forced to back down. Former prime minister Edward Heath believed that the public did not want to see "our country and our industries handed over more and more to the American firms." The British people seemed to agree. A poll undertaken in February 1986 showed that only 19 percent of respondents believed that a US takeover of British Leyland should have been allowed while 77 percent believed the company should have remained in British hands.[128] Recent years have seen "a steady shift, during which the British have in fact become more like the Americans," noted American journalist Rushmore M. Kidder in 1986.

> Under Prime Minister Margaret Thatcher, in particular, the nation has moved strongly toward private enterprise and deregulation. Some of the latest issues here—the debate over whether to sell the Westland helicopter firm and parts of the British Leyland auto industry to US buyers, the question of allowing stores to open on Sunday—all hint at the magnetic pull of Americanism.[129]

While conservatives expressed nationalistic concerns about US corporate takeovers in Britain, others voiced alarm about ruthless business practices and greed that were seeping into Britain from the United States via Thatcher's policies. Richard Compton Miller, the gossip columnist on the *Daily Express*, regretted that the American emphasis on money meant that old elites no longer enjoyed the same social status in Thatcher's Britain. "Mrs Thatcher's Britain is all about money. Money can buy you anything, it can buy you in anywhere nowadays. Old families, old money doesn't matter, because the heroes people want to read about now have made their own." Financial success is all important and flaunting it is a necessity. "We have become just like America."[130] Television presenter Melvyn Bragg railed against this "alien" American mentality of greed.

> [W]hen in the 1980s we were lectured through the movies and through the new triumphalist commentators that "greed was good" and "greed is everything," it was time to say "that's not us." Greed replaced public service as the ethos. The very words "public service" became a despised aside. It was in that time that the traditions and virtues of Britain, coming out of its dark, post-imperial night of the soul, reasserted themselves.[131]

Bernard Nossiter, *The Washington Post* correspondent in Britain, suggested in 1978 that Britain was uniquely different from America in that the British valued leisure over work and money. A decade later he suggested that Britain was now as materialistic as America.

> The hustle of yuppies in the City of London is Wall Street, only less regulated; the roaring speculative boom in southeast house prices, fueled by big tax cuts for the rich, matches those around New York, Boston and Washington; VCR's, autos, vacations on the Continent are critical ingredients of middle- and working-class life.[132]

Nasty animosity toward American influence often held sway over reasoned criticisms. "On previous visits we have seen 'Yanks go home' written up on walls, we have heard mutters of 'damned Americans' from people in stores, we have listened to grumbles about how crowded everything is because so many Americans come over to England," Patricia Lockhart from California complained.[133] Punk rock band Crass turned their ire on imported American popular culture with the song "Smash the Mac" released in1986. "We've been occupied, culture smashed and betrayed... E.T go home. Mickey Mouse fuck off," they not too subtly sang. Another punk band, the Exploited, was even more direct. "There really is nothing nice about USA," they sang on "Fuck The USA" from their album *Troops of*

Tomorrow released in 1982. In the spring of 1984, a young English football fan nonchalantly told an American journalist that "All Americans are wankers," a casual utterance that would be often repeated throughout the decade.[134]

Television comedians joined in the invective. The BBC television comedy series *A Bit of Fry and Laurie* included a number of sketches that mocked Americans and made none too subtle criticisms of the American influence on Britain. In one sketch broadcast in March 1990, two boys knock on the front door on Halloween and after Hugh Laurie and Stephen Fry open the door the boys bellow "Trick or Treat?" In response, Laurie exclaims, "Trick or Treat? This is England not America" and proceeds to grab the two boys and take them away for a roughing up. In another sketch broadcast in January 1989, Hugh Laurie sits at a piano wearing a Bruce Springsteen-style head band, flannel shirt and jeans and sings a Billy Joel-style sentimental dirge: "America, America, America, America, America, America" followed by "the States, the States, the States, the States, the States, the States." Stephen Fry enters from stage right in a suit, shirt and tie, smugly shrugs to the audience, and punches the unsuspecting Laurie off the stool and on to the floor.[135]

Fearful of American society, Britons now wanted closer links with social democratic Europe. A Gallup poll in 1969 found that 34 percent of the British people believed that America was most important to Britain's future, 34 percent thought the Commonwealth, but only 21 percent Europe. When the same question was asked in 1986, Europe now scored 39 percent, America 29 percent and the Commonwealth only 26 percent.[136] The British Social Attitudes survey found that in 1984, 52.9 percent wanted closer links with Western Europe while 21 percent wanted closer links with the United States. By 1987 the figures were 57.1 and 18.4 percent, respectively.[137] A MORI poll from the mid-1980s found that Britons ranked the United States as their fourth most admired country behind the social democratic heartlands of Switzerland, Sweden and West Germany.[138]

Praise for Europe and condemnation of American foreign policy and American society in the 1980s was far more visible among left-wingers than among Conservatives who had previously been America's most vociferous critics. Conservatives traditionally saw Americans as uncultured and the United States as a place that needed to become more like Britain but, Margaret Thatcher, who took inspiration from an imagined America she first conjured up from the music and movies of her youth, believed Britain should become more like America and Britons more like Americans. Thatcher and her Conservative supporters embraced the United States as a paradigm of economic liberty and sought to remake the British economy using the United States as a model. By the end of her reign, Thatcher had remade the British economy to look more like the American one than it had at any time since World War II and in the process changed the social and political landscape.

Thatcher was more inspired by an imagined view of the United States than by any American political movement or any particular person. The stance of Ronald Reagan and the economic theories of Milton Friedman coincided with rather than changed the ideas of Thatcher. Indeed, Thatcher's philosophy had less to do with American politicians or economists and more to do with British traditions of neoclassical economics and liberalism, which she found, ironically, embodied in the United States. The United States acted as a model of a free-market economy and an enterprise culture, which Thatcher found missing in Britain. It could be said that Margaret Thatcher owed more to Hollywood movies than to Milton Friedman for ideological inspiration.

When Republican Ronald Reagan was elected president of the United States in November 1980, Margaret Thatcher and the Republican president rejoined the special relationship between the two governments that had withered under previous administrations. Sharing a worldview of aggressive anticommunism and a devotion to free-market principles, the two kindred spirits dominated the world stage. Many, not just those on the left, feared President Reagan because of his nuclear brinkmanship and foreign policy adventures. Others criticized Thatcher for introducing an American-style economy and its related social problems into Britain. Opposition to US foreign policy and dislike of certain aspects of American society led to an almost automatic hostility to American cultural imports and prejudice against individual Americans.

Opposition to US foreign policy subsided by the end of the decade. In December 1987, the United States and the Soviet Union signed the Intermediate-range Nuclear Forces (INF) Treaty and agreed to remove all ground-based medium-range nuclear missiles from Europe, including the American cruise missiles deployed in Britain. In 1990, the Sandinistas in Nicaragua stepped down after losing the presidential election to the US-backed Violeta Chamorro. The South African government released Nelson Mandela from prison in February 1990 and in April 1994 he was elected president of South Africa, ending the country's apartheid system. Reagan, an extremely unpopular figure in Britain, was replaced by the more distant and less polarizing figure of George H. Bush in January 1989. By the end of the year, Eastern Europe was in revolt and within two years the Cold War ended with the collapse of communism in the Soviet Union. The conclusion of the Cold War, however, ushered in more fear of the United States as it seemed that the United States became economically and politically more dominant than ever and that America was taking over every facet of British life.

5

Culture Wars: American Global Supremacy and British Nationalism, 1990–2001

In September 2000, journalist Julie Burchill announced that

> the U.S. has done, is doing and will do more damage to this planet and its people than Nazi Germany, fascist Japan and [the British comedian] David Baddiel put together. In the face of this, the rest of the world seems somehow to have reverted to the state of impressionable native—and instead of waving shiny beads in our faces, the Americans now wave shiny Starbucks, Seinfeld and Britney Spears instead.... America is greatly responsible for turning the earth into an open sewer—culturally, morally and physically.

American "energy is the energy of the vandal, psychotic or manic depressive, fuelling acts of barbarism and destruction from My Lai to Eminem." Burchill further believed that

> any Briton who emigrates to America is a pathetic, traitorous little sneak, a disgrace to the human race that is currently suffering under the studded cowboy boot of Uncle Sam, and as such deserves to be stripped of their British citizenship—which could then be given to some nice, appreciative refugee—and never allowed back on this sceptred isle again.

Soon, she concluded, "there will be a mighty day of reckoning, when the free world will break loose of the American yoke, and all the Great Satan's whores and quislings will dangle from the nearest lamp-posts."[1]

Burchill's views maybe intended as humor and to provoke a reaction, but they illustrate a deep seated British hostility toward Americans and US influence abroad, which was apparent in the years before the events of September 11, 2001, or the invasion of Iraq in March 2003. Many commentators who find American foreign policy culpable for provoking hostility around the world claim that antagonism toward the United States had receded once President Ronald Reagan had left office in early 1989 and only reappeared after the election of George W. Bush in November 2000. "The Cold War framework of European anti-Americanism ceased to exist, and the resentment felt in Europe toward American civilization consequently began to subside," author Jesper Gulddal proposed. "Being against the United States was all of a sudden less of a cultural and ideological necessity than it had been for a very long time."[2] "The decade of the 1990s had been, for the most part, a quiet time: history had 'ended,' and foreigners marveled at America's achievements—its technological feats, soaring prosperity, and commercial products," believed authors Andrew Kohut and Bruce Stokes. "The first hints that the world was becoming troubled by America came soon after the election of George W. Bush."[3]

The reality was rather different. A new wave of anger against the United States erupted in Britain in the 1990s but this was no longer directed at US foreign policy or at a particularly unpopular leader such as Ronald Reagan. The Cold War had ended, the Soviet Union had collapsed, the nuclear issue had receded into the background and Bill Clinton, elected president in 1992, had proved to be a less polarizing figure than President Reagan. Still intellectuals of the left and right resented the growing American influence on the country. The role of the United States as the only remaining superpower, US-led globalization and the continued imitation of American political and social policies by Margaret Thatcher's successor John Major and, even more worryingly for the left, the leader of the Labour Party, Tony Blair, awakened nationalist opposition to all things American.

American Influence on Britain

American influence on Britain increased dramatically in the last decade of the twentieth century as people from the United States of America entered Great Britain in unprecedented numbers. Since the 1960s, more Americans had migrated to Britain than New Commonwealth immigrants and by 2001, 155,030 people born in the United States were living in Britain, up 8 percent from 1991.[4] Britain was the most popular destination for American students. In 2001–2002, 30,143 Americans studied in Britain, 18.7 percent of all Americans studying abroad, with Spain the second most favored destination attracting only 17,176 American students or 10.7 percent of the total.[5] Americans journeyed to Britain in their thousands to work in the City of London and to take up prominent positions in business and the arts. Barbara Cassani from Boston assumed leadership of the new British Airways budget airline Go Fly and New Yorker Michael Kaiser became head of the Royal Opera House. During the 2001 Last Night of the Proms, the festival designed to celebrate British music, the BBC Symphony Orchestra was led by newly appointed conductor Californian Leonard Slatkin.[6] Ruby Wax from Illinois undertook outrageous interviews with celebrities and political figures in her own prime time BBC series *Ruby Wax Meets* while Virginian Katie Puckrik hosted *The Word* a popular late night youth program.

The introduction of satellite and cable television in Britain dramatically increased the number of American programs on British television. The first

British satellite company Sky television started broadcasting on February 5, 1989. Suffering massive losses, Sky Television merged with rival British Satellite Broadcasting in November 1990 to form British Sky Broadcasting. Soon satellite television started transmitting hundreds of channels into Britain including the American channels Cable News Network (CNN) and Music Television (MTV). The "bulk of all programming available on satellite and on cable was American movies, American series and scores of entire American niche channels," noted Jeremy Tunstall in his study of British television.[7] Terrestrial television followed suit. In the 1990s, domestic TV programs dominated peak time on the BBC and ITV but American programs ruled the schedules of Channel 4, launched in 1982, and Channel 5, which started broadcasting in 1997. By the 1990s, 75 percent of the airtime in Britain was filled with American programs.[8] *Beverly Hills 90210,* set around wealthy high school students in Los Angeles, and *Baywatch,* which followed the fortunes of California lifeguards, fulfilled Britons' desire for blue skies, sunshine and attractive young bodies, while the casts of *Friends, Frasier* and *ER* became household names. Imagery of the West, skyscrapers, suburbs and Hollywood pervaded British TV adverts even when selling non-American products.[9] Yahya Kamalipour, who visited Oxford from the United States in 1996, found that

> the cultural influence and presence of American products could visibly be experienced everywhere. For instance, not only a high percentage of programs on the Independent Television (ITV) network were American, but Oprah Winfrey's poster—advertising her talk show—was plastered on the shelter of nearly every bus stop throughout Oxford and other cities.[10]

American visitors to Britain expressed shock at how many British television programs imitated American ones. "Hollywood is the template, with imitations of *Gladiators* and Oprah (in the person of Crystal Rose) joining *Brighton Belles* (a licensed version of *Golden Girls*) and the goofily Amerocentric youth magazine show *The Word,*" observed American political theorist Benjamin Barber.[11] "Comedian Sean Hughes's popular British comedy, *It's Sean's Show,* is a direct rip-off of *It's Garry Shandling's Show,*" American authors Steven Daly and Nathaniel Wice discovered. "With *The Last Resort,* Jonathan Ross installed himself as Britain's premier talk-show host by lifting wholesale David Letterman's meta-talk-show format, complete with corny cityscape backdrop, pedestrian-harassing outside broadcasts and Elvis Costello's former pianist as the Paul Shaffer rock-biz burnout band leader," the authors noted.

> Elsewhere, *291 Club* attempts to translate the roiling fervor of the *Saturday Night at the Apollo* variety show to East London's Hackney Empire . . . some years ago the Labour M.P. Robert Kilroy-Silk briefly charmed U.K. housewives by adopting Donahue's silver-haired smoothie act for his own talk show . . . . American popular culture is not merely fashionable in Britain, it's close to hegemonic

suggested Daly and Wice. "It's been a remarkable turnaround, almost as if the end of the cold war has relieved the British of any pretense that they're not complete Americanophiles at heart."[12]

The growth in computer ownership and the launch of the Internet added to the US influence on Britain. In the 1950s, the US defense department developed the Internet, which allowed communication between computers. Computers had been used for decades but the personal computer revolution started in the United States in the mid-1970s when a young entrepreneur, Ed Roberts, used the newly devised microchip to assemble the Altair 8800 computer, the prototype of the desktop machine. "The era of personal computing in every home . . . has arrived," the magazine *Popular Electronics* announced. In the 1990s, the development of the World Wide Web by British-born scientist Tim Berners-Lee, allowed users to view web pages containing text and images. Anyone with a telephone line and a modem could connect to the Internet on their home computers and communicate with users across the world. In October 1994, 3.8 million computers were connected to the Internet, which rose to 19.6 million in July 1997.[13] In 1997, 34 percent of households in the United Kingdom owned computers while many others used computers at school, at work, in local libraries and in the Internet cafes that now became a fixture of the British high street.[14]

The United States was the undoubted leader in the development of computer technology and online services. Intel's personal-computer chip powered the computer, Dell and Apple manufactured cutting-edge desktop and laptop computers and Microsoft Windows dominated the operating system market. Amazon, which launched online in 1995 as a bookseller but branched out to become a purveyor of a wide range of products, pioneered online shopping. The American company eBay, which started as AuctionWeb in September 1995, sold US$7.2 million worth of goods by the end of 1996. By the end of 2000, the value of goods sold on eBay reached US$5.4 billion with 22 million users.[15] Google, started in 1998 by Larry Page and Sergey Brin, became such a ubiquitous search engine that Google has entered the English language as a verb meaning to search for information online.

In addition to pioneering the use of computer technology, the United States dominated the cinema screens of Britain as attendances once again started to increase. Cinema attendances fell from the peak of 1635 million admissions in 1946 to a postwar low of 54 million admissions in 1984 but increased to 97.37 million in 1990 and to 139.75 million in 1999.[16] American multiplex cinemas, multiple screen facilities with comfortable seating and a wider choice of food and drink, were partly responsible for attracting people back into the cinemas. The first multiplex opened in Milton Keynes in 1985 by American company AMC. By 1990, there were 41 in the country and by 1999, 177. Single-screen cinemas were converted into multiscreen operations to compete with new multiplex cinemas. There were a total of 1,685 screens in the United Kingdom in 1990, which rose to 2,758 in 1999.[17] American blockbusters dominated the plush new movie theatres. *Jurassic Park* released in 1993, *Independence Day* in 1996, *Men in Black* in 1997, *Titanic* in 1998 and *Star Wars Episode I: The Phantom Menace* released in 1999 became major box office hits in Britain. By the mid-1990s, 93 percent of the films shown in Britain were American made.[18] "Hollywood tops the scale," notes author Geoff Brown in his study of British cinema in the 1990s. "Hollywood also comes second, third and fourth. Britain delivers a few big pleasures. The rest of the world scarcely features. So perhaps our film culture, if we have one, is basically American, not home-grown at all? The point is worth considering."[19]

Compared to the 1980s, the British film industry enjoyed somewhat of a renaissance, but here too the American influence was apparent. A typically British film, such as *Shakespeare in Love* (1998), which won best picture at the Academy Awards "was produced and distributed by American companies, co-written by an American, starred and co-starred an American, and many of the 314 screens in Britain, which hosted its release in 1999, had been built by Americans," commented author Eddie Dyja.[20] The British set comedy *The Full Monty* (1997) "was entirely financed and distributed by one of the U.S. majors, Twentieth Century-Fox," author Geoff Brown stated. "The praise went to Britain, but all the film's profits went to America," Brown depressingly concluded.[21] Moreover, since US companies controlled international distribution networks, and financed many British films, the United States enjoyed considerable influence over the type of British films that were made.[22] Hollywood wanted British filmmakers to make movies that appealed to international, mostly American, audiences. Hence, British films like *Four Weddings and a Funeral* (1994), *Notting Hill* (1999) and *Sliding Doors* (1998), among others, starred American actors like Andie MacDowell, Julia Roberts and Gwyneth Paltrow in scenic British locations.[23]

The lifestyles of Hollywood actors and actresses fascinated the British public. Magazines such as *OK* Magazine launched in 1993, *Now* in 1996 and *Heat* in 1999 provided a hefty coverage of American celebrities. Sunday newspaper supplements and tabloid papers bowed to public demand for news about the private lives of Hollywood stars. Europe's first Planet Hollywood restaurant franchise opened on May 17, 1993, in London's Leicester Square with the backing of Hollywood stalwarts Sylvester Stallone, Bruce Willis and Arnold Schwarzenegger. The opening of the glorified burger bar, which sold itself on the ability to view Hollywood memorabilia and to dine with the stars, attracted over 10,000 people in the pouring rain.[24]

African-American music continued to have a major influence on British music and culture in the 1990s. Hip hop music and the culture that surrounded it emerged from New York City in the early 1970s. The Sugarhill Gang's "Rapper's Delight," one of the first rap records, reached number 3 on the UK charts in 1979. Gangsta rap, a subgenre of hip hop that depicted black urban life in America, gained a large following in Britain. Californian rappers N.W.A. (Niggaz with Attitude) whose debut album *Straight Outta Compton* (1988) included provocative songs such as "F*** Tha Police," gained the genre considerable notoriety. Some of the songs were autobiographical and some fantasy but the lyrics often documented the activities of gangs and drug dealers in inner city America, with rappers using profane language to brag about their violent behavior, sexual promiscuity and conspicuous consumption. Subsequently, the focus shifted from the West to the East Coast as New York rappers Tupac Shakur and Biggie Smalls, better known as the Notorious B.I.G., became major stars before they were shot dead in 1996 and 1997, respectively. By the end of the decade, Eminem a white rapper from Detroit dominated headlines worldwide, joining Jay Z and 50 Cent in selling millions of albums, while British artists such as Wiley, Roots Manuva, Dizzee Rascal, So Solid Crew and The Streets forged the sound of UK Garage and Grime from American hip hop influences.[25]

In the 1990s, many black and white youngsters became fascinated with the black urban experience they saw portrayed in expensively made rap music videos and in Hollywood movies. *Boyz "n" the Hood* (1991), *New Jack City* (1991) and *Menace II Society* (1993) starred well-known gangsta rappers and depicted the violence of inner city life, conflict with police, gang culture and the drug trade. Many British youths living in inner city housing estates, which began to resemble the projects of the United States, identified with what they saw on screen. Others found the "ghetto" portrayed in the songs and on screen to be a location of adventure, so different from their unexciting existence, and copied the look of inner city American youth. Youngsters walked the streets of Britain wearing trainers, hooded jackets, baseball caps and baggy jeans, often worn fashionably low. "There can rarely have been a time when British popular culture was more saturated with things American," claimed Steven Daly and Nathaniel Wice in 1993. "Today the most visible football regalia on London streets is not that of [English football clubs] Arsenal, Chelsea or Tottenham Hotspur—it's the silver and black of the L.A. Raiders, as trademarked by California's gangsta rappers."[26]

American slang terms and words permeated the language of the young and not so young. According to journalist Cosmo Landesman

> young Britons may not speak much French or German, but they are fluent in black American. Kids in Harlesden talk like kids in Harlem with their shouts of "wicked" and "bad." The other day, an eight-year-old Asian demanded I give him "high five" and parted with the cry of "Later, dude."[27]

Writers in the film magazine *Empire* used words like "yeah," "geddit," "go figure," and "cur-*reeee*py!" to review the latest movies.[28] Author Anna Quindlen, a visitor to London in the mid-1990s, expressed surprise at the influence of American tourists, rap music and American sitcoms on the English language. "While once we were warned to ask for the bill, not the check, and to order a sweet, not dessert, almost no wait staff in a London restaurant looks twice if you ask the American way."[29]

Rap music may have been the dominant sound of the street, but music from Chicago and Detroit became the principal sound of British dance clubs. House music, named after the Warehouse nightclub operating in Chicago from 1977 to 1983, evolved from DJs mixing disco music to some making their own records using drum machines, pounding pianos, gospel tinged vocals and inspirational lyrics. The more psychedelic and minimalist examples of house music became known as "acid house." Detroit techno music, another important ingredient in British dance culture, used more computer technology and fewer vocals and was less influenced by old-style soul music than was the music emanating from Chicago. Soon British dance clubs played the music from Chicago and Detroit and it broke into the British charts.[30] "Love Can't Turn Around" by Farley "Jackmaster" Funk went to number 9 in the summer of 1986 and then Steve "Silk" Hurley's "Jack

Your Body" reached number one in January 1987. When he first visited Britain, Chicago house DJ Chip E was astounded at the popularity of the music in Britain compared to the United States. "At home house was played in underground clubs and on the radio sometimes, but when we came over here they were playing it on TV, on *Top of the Pops*," the weekly music show on BBC television, which claimed a weekly audience in the millions.[31] By the 1990s, house and techno music became the sound of young Britain as many of the major house and techno DJs hosted shows on BBC Radio 1 and charged exorbitant fees for personal appearances, TV commercials featured house music and monthly magazines appeared devoted to the phenomenon.[32]

Music emanating from white America also gained a substantial audience in Britain in the 1990s. American grunge music popularized by the Seattle band Nirvana, moved out of the underground rock circuit and gained mainstream success with the release of *Nevermind* in 1991. Led by the charismatic singer and song writer Kurt Cobain, young white Britons identified with Nirvana's songs of alienation and dissatisfaction and copied their taste for plaid shirts, torn denim jeans and long hair. Other American alternative rock bands such as Pearl Jam, Alice in Chains, Soundgarden, Husker Du, Sonic Youth, the Pixies, Mudhoney, Afghan Whigs and Pavement gained a wider audience because of the success of Nirvana.[33] A new slick country and western sound from Nashville, with a lyrical emphasis on conservative values and sentimental emotions, also became hugely popular in Great Britain. Garth Brooks from Tulsa, Oklahoma, exemplified the commercial success of country music. Brooks, with his trademark cowboy hat and blue jeans, embarked on a 1994 UK tour, selling out huge venues such as Birmingham's National Exhibition Centre and London's Wembley Arena, and returned in 1996 for another sold-out tour. In recognition of the music's status, in 1994 Country 1035, an Independent Local Radio station based in London, started broadcasting country music 24 hours a day, 7 days a week.

Young people, as always, generally admired the music and culture of the United States but in the 1990s many older people too embraced American popular culture. Parents, having grown up with American entertainment, continued their liking for music, movies and clothes emanating from the United States. Blue jeans were now worn by those over 30 as well as younger people. Pop concerts attracted people even as they married and had children of their own and the older generation became a major part of the record market. In the 1980s, record companies boosted record sales by reissuing original vinyl albums on to the new Compact Disc (CD) format and in the 1990s gained more income by remastering the same records. The CD arrived in shops in 1982. By 1990, 24 percent of households owned a CD player, 45 percent in 1993, and 67 percent in 1997.[34]

Even American team sports, long invisible in Britain, made their major breakthrough in the country during the 1990s. The newly created Channel 4 television channel broadcast American football and in 1986 viewing figures peaked at 4 million for the National Football League (NFL) Super Bowl game between the Chicago Bears and the New England Patriots. Some were inspired to play the sport and others wanted to experience a live game. By 1986, 237 teams in Britain played American football.[35] NFL Europe, which included the London Monarchs team, was established in 1991 and lasted until 2007. As the popularity of the sport grew, the NFL introduced the American Bowl series in 1986 in which NFL teams played preseason games outside of the United States for the first time. A total of nine American Bowl games took place between 1986 and 1997 in the United Kingdom and Ireland involving 14 NFL Franchises. In total, eight games were played at Wembley Stadium in front of sellout crowds of 80,000 on each occasion.[36] In October 2007, the Giants beat the Dolphins at Wembley Stadium in the first regular season NFL game to be played outside North America. "In England, where football (soccer) and cricket once dominated weekend sports broadcasting, viewers can now watch the NFL Game of the Week," American political theorist Benjamin Barber noted with surprise in 1995.[37]

Britons fell in love with American food and drink as American chains transformed the British high street. Kentucky Fried Chicken became the first US fast food chain to cross the Atlantic when it opened for business in 1965. McDonald's, which launched its first restaurant in Britain in Woolwich, southeast London, in 1974, opened their 100th restaurant in 1983, their 400th in 1991, and their 1000th in 2000.[38] At least "Europeans everywhere scorned American coffee and beer," author Richard Pells confidently wrote in 1997.[39] Yet, within a year, Starbucks had opened their first outlet in the United Kingdom, in Manchester, England, and by April 2009 there were 727 Starbucks coffee shops in the country.[40] Contrary to Pells's wishful thinking, young people drinking bottles of Budweiser beer became a common sight in British pubs.

The look of British towns was greatly influenced by modern concepts of consumerism and convenience springing from the United States. Stores and restaurants opened for longer, copying American practices. John Major's Conservative government passed the Sunday Trading Act of 1994, which permitted large shops, such as department stores and supermarkets, to open for up to six hours on Sunday between 10 am and 6 pm. Previously, the streets of Britain were virtually deserted on Sundays as only small family-run shops and chemists could remain open. Now Sunday seemed like any other day of the week. The Metro Centre, a shopping center opened in Gateshead in 1986, was the first of many American-style shopping malls to open in Britain. "British planners, in the light of a general cultural imitation of American trends, are adopting stateside practices such as the 'doughnut effect,' where town centres become abandoned by shoppers for malls on the outer ring," Mike Storry and Peter Childs insisted in 1997. "A largely consumer culture has been imported across the Atlantic and modern buildings reflect this: shopping malls, multiplex cinemas, theme parks, out-of-town supermarkets, Disney stores and fast-food restaurants, some of them drive-ins." The British high street in the 1990s had many of the same shops that appeared on an American main street.

> Most cities and towns in Britain can be expected to have a number of fast-food outlets such as Burger King, a range of clothes shops like The Gap, a Safeway or similar shopping centre away from the town, a Super Bowl, Laserquest or ten-screen cinema complex, leisure centres with computerized workout gyms, and hoardings that advertise the American Dream along with their cigarettes,

Storry and Childs concluded.[41] The growth of chain stores and self-service supermarkets continued to change the look of the high street by undermining the profitability of specialized face-to-face neighborhood shops. In 1961, there were about 150,000 independent food retailers in Britain; by 1999 this was down to 25,000.[42] Britain was no longer a nation of shopkeepers.

Clinton and the Rise of New Labour

Even the Labour Party, which returned to power in May 1997 after 18 years in opposition, became highly influenced by America, and particularly the electoral strategies, political positions and economic policies of President Bill Clinton and the Democratic Party. The Labour Party lost four general elections in a row between 1979 and 1992 with their fortunes reaching a low point in 1983 when the party suffered its worst electoral defeat for 65 years, getting less than 28 percent of the vote. The 1983 election manifesto, which called for unilateral nuclear disarmament, renationalization of key industries privatized by the Conservative Party and withdrawal from the European Economic Community (EEC), was termed "the longest suicide note in history" by Gerald Kaufman, a member of Labour's shadow cabinet. The Democrats in the United States had faced similar problems, losing three consecutive presidential elections from 1980 to 1988. In 1984 Republican Ronald Reagan won 49 of the 50 states in a landslide victory over Democrat Walter Mondale. However, while Labour lost the general election in April 1992, the Democratic candidate Bill Clinton defeated incumbent George H. Bush later that year, returning the Democrats to power after 12 years out of the White House.

The victory of Bill Clinton and the Democrats grabbed the attention of the so-called "modernizers" in the Labour Party led by Tony Blair and Gordon Brown. Tony Blair, born in Edinburgh, Scotland on May 6, 1953, came from a relatively affluent middle-class family. Blair spent most of his childhood in Durham, England, where his father lectured in law at Durham University. He attended Fettes, a prestigious public boarding school in Edinburgh, between 1966 and 1971, and then studied law at Oxford University. Blair showed no interest in student politics while at Oxford but he joined the Labour Party in the mid-1970s and became active in the party after he met Labour activist Cherie Booth, whom he married in March 1980. Gordon Brown, the other leading modernizer in the Labour Party, had a longer association with Labour than Blair. Brown, born on February 20, 1951, in Kirkcaldy, Scotland, studied at the University of Edinburgh where he earned a PhD in History specializing in the history of the Labour movement. He joined the Labour Party in 1969 and developed a firm commitment to trade unionism. Brown appeared introspective and intellectual while Blair exuded a more confident manner, building personal relationships easily, persuading through charm as well as intellect and exhibiting a relaxed style in front of the camera and microphone. "In Tony Blair you have the candidate that every Tory mother would love their daughter to bring home as son-in-law," commented one journalist in the early 1980s.[43] Both men entered parliament in the 1983 general election, as Labour's fortunes were at their lowest ebb. Blair was elected MP from Sedgefield in northeast England while Brown became Labour MP for Dunfermline East in Scotland. Soon they rose through the ranks with Brown becoming Shadow Chancellor of the Exchequer following the 1992 election defeat and Blair taking up the position of Shadow Home Secretary.[44]

Blair and Brown had much less affection for the United States than did Margret Thatcher. Like many of their generation who came of age in the 1960s and 1970s, Blair and Brown held a skeptical view of the United States. They saw the violence of the civil rights movement and the Vietnam War explode on their television screens and witnessed the urban violence displayed on countless television series and movies. "I came to love America," Tony Blair later declared.

> Frankly, I didn't start that way! Not that I disliked it; but I hadn't visited America, and didn't know many Americans at school or university. My first trip was in 1985, at the age of thirty-two. I was a junior Opposition Treasury spokesman. My view of America had been formed from countless movies and TV shows and the odd interaction with American tourists. I had a touch of that British raised eyebrow at our American cousins.[45]

Continental Europe provided a stronger attraction for the two modernizers. Blair spoke French fluently and visited continental Europe on a regular basis while both men read widely on European history and literature. Many Britons living in postwar austerity admired prosperous America but Blair's and Brown's generation enjoyed greater affluence and had their own cultural heroes in Britain. Like many teenage boys in the late 1960s and early 1970s, Blair loved rock music, particularly British bands such as the Beatles, the Rolling Stones, Free, King Crimson and Led Zeppelin. At Oxford University he sang and played guitar in a rock band called Ugly Rumours.[46] The ever-studious Brown had little interest in the popular culture of either America or Britain, preferring the more sedate sounds of classical music.[47]

Although previously unimpressed with the United States, the rise of Bill Clinton and the Democratic Party grabbed the attention of both Blair and Brown. They watched closely the victory of Clinton in 1992, the same year Labour lost their fourth consecutive election. Clinton had won back the "Reagan Democrats" and the modernizers sought similar success with those who had deserted Labour for Thatcher in the 1980s. Blair and Brown wanted to appeal to the working class that had bought their council homes and taken part in the "share-owning democracy" initiated by Thatcher, and to the middle class that had been put off by Labour's association with higher taxes. In January 1993, Blair and Brown visited the United States where Jonathan Powell, diplomat in the British embassy in Washington DC and later Downing Street Chief of Staff under Tony Blair, introduced the two Labour politicians to many leading members of Clinton's election team who spoke to them about strategy and campaigning techniques.[48] Elaine Kamarck, from the public policy think tank the Progressive Policy Institute (PPI), observed that Blair "took out a small notebook and asked us some questions about how we had begun in 1989 and we talked him all the way through it. He took furious notes about everything we said." Labour and the Democrats remained closely linked with many of those who worked for Clinton finding themselves in senior positions in the Labour Party's election campaigns. Stanley Greenberg, a leading Democrat strategist, left the White House in the Spring of 1995 to work for Tony Blair, and Sidney Blumenthal, advisor to Clinton, liaised between the White House and Labour.[49]

Tony Blair and the other modernizers may have instinctively believed that they needed to appeal to middle-class voters but Clinton's campaign helped them to see how it could be done. Previously, Labour focused on issues such as economic equality and ignored topics like crime and defense. The main policy implication of Clinton's victory for the Labour Party was that the Party must appropriate tough stances on traditional Tory issues such as crime, taxes, defense and welfare. They must stress personal responsibility and emphasize a pro-business stance and fiscal responsibility in order to reassure aspirational working class and middle-class voters.[50] When Blair returned home from his trip to the United States in early 1993, he adopted tougher positions on the issue of crime. Speaking as Shadow Home Secretary, Blair put renewed emphasis on morals, personal responsibility and family values in controlling crime and downplayed the role of economic deprivation espoused by many Labour activists. "It is important to show that we identify with the victims of crime," Blair said in January 1993. "We should be giving our young people rights and opportunities and chances but we should also be demanding responsibilities."[51] Three days after Blair returned from the United States in January 1993, he told a television interviewer that he would be "tough on crime, tough on the causes of crime."[52] In November 1993, Blair visited New York City to meet Republican Mayor Rudy Giuliani and observe the "zero tolerance" law enforcement methods that had reduced crime in the city. He was impressed with the tough practices the police used to uphold the law and enthusiastically endorsed these tactics in his speeches.[53] When in government, crime policies and slogans used in the United States were introduced into Britain. Blair announced "zero tolerance on crime," appointed a "drugs czar" to oversee the government's anti-drugs policies and spoke of "three strikes and you're out" to indicate mandatory sentencing.[54]

After the sudden death of Labour leader John Smith in May 1994, the party elected Tony Blair leader. Clinton's victory encouraged Blair to make a special effort to repackage the party's identity and ditch Labour's image as a party of the industrial working class. "Some of the problems that the Democrats had, particularly that they seemed trapped with a declining base of support, are not dissimilar to the problems that Labour has faced here," Blair argued. "The Clinton campaign reached out to a broader section of the population and we've got to do that too."[55] As Clinton had distanced himself from the traditional liberal left in the United States, Blair broke with the trade union movement and socialism. Blair wanted to weaken the links with trade unions whose membership was declining and whose popularity was low among the middle classes and he became an avid supporter of one member one vote in the party, a policy Labour adopted in 1993 to lessen union influence in the party. Labour appeased the City and business, who were concerned about the Labour Party raising taxes, with promises that increased spending would be financed by economic growth, not higher taxation. At a Special Conference in

April 1995, the Labour Party revoked Clause 4 of its Constitution, which stated that the party sought "To secure for the workers by hand or by brain the full fruits of their industry and the most equitable distribution thereof that may be possible upon the basis of the common ownership of the means of production, distribution and exchange." Even though no one seriously thought that the Labour Party was advocating socialism, the removal of Clause 4 made a symbolic break with Labour's left-wing past.[56]

In addition to adopting new policies that distanced Labour from socialism, Blair copied Clinton's public relations techniques. In honor of the New Democrats and to indicate a break with the Labour policies of the past, during Blair's first speech to the Labour Party conference as leader in October 1994, the banner "New Labour, New Britain" was emblazoned behind him. Blair adopted the use of symbolic gestures, slogans and style from Clinton's campaign to present his policies in a voter-friendly language. He adopted phrases like "Time for a Change" and "Partnership between Government and People" directly from Clinton's campaign. In December 1995, the party set up a new "war room" at Millbank Tower near Westminster in London, modeled on Clinton's campaign headquarters. Labour made greater use of opinion polls and focus groups to shape policy, a strategy that they learned from Clinton and the White House. Like Clinton, Blair prioritized management of the media, introducing the American term "spin doctor" into British politics. Blair employed Alastair Campbell, a former journalist with the Labour-supporting tabloid, the *Daily Mirror*, as his press secretary after he became the leader of the Labour Party. Campbell leaked stories to his favored journalists, harangued others to write stories to his liking and vetted the speeches of Labour leaders so that they stayed on message and adhered to a common line.[57]

Labour won a landslide victory in the May 1, 1997, general election, winning more seats than they did in the historic triumph of 1945. Blair, symbolized a young, dynamic and modern Britain that could be identified as different from the stale John Major years, but he never challenged the basic tenet of Thatcherism that private ownership and market forces was preferable to government control. Labour MP Claire Short believed that "neither Blair nor New Labour had any significant guiding principles, philosophy or values," but in fact Blair was committed to the free market and to neoliberal globalization.[58] New Labour increased investment in the public services, especially in their second term in office but extended market forces to the National Health Service and other government-run industries and left untouched the anti–trade union laws, the privatization of industries, and the lower income tax rates for the wealthy introduced by Margaret Thatcher's Conservative government. In June 2002, Peter Mandelson declared that economically "in the urgent need to remove rigidities and incorporate flexibility in capital, product and labour markets, we are all 'Thatcherite' now."[59] Little wonder that when the Tory candidate for Eastleigh met Margaret Thatcher at a party in November 2002 and asked her what she believed to be her greatest achievement, she allegedly replied "New Labour."[60]

After the election victory of May 1997, Prime Minister Blair appointed Gordon Brown as Chancellor of the Exchequer, a position he would hold for ten years. Trying to replicate the unprecedented successes of the American economy under

Clinton, many of the economic policies initiated by Gordon Brown came directly from the United States. Brown granted the Bank of England independence based on the Federal Reserve Bank model. The New Deal program introduced by Labour in 1998 sought to reduce unemployment by providing training and work experience to the unemployed, a system based on the American workfare approach to unemployment. One commentator stated in the *Sunday Times* that "it would be hard to think of a more American feature of the highly Americanised Blair government than its much trusted new deal on welfare to work."[61] Brown further emulated Clinton's policies of encouraging the unemployed to take poorly paid jobs by cutting taxes on low earners through the use of tax credits. The Working Families Tax Credit introduced by Labour in October 1999 was modeled on Clinton's Earned Income Tax Credit. The government launched Sure Start in 1998, aiming to provide early education, childcare and family support, similar to the Head Start program in the United States. The Labour government introduced a national minimum wage on April 1, 1999, based on the one in operation in the United States. Brown spent government money on promoting small business start-ups in poor areas copying Bill Clinton's Business Improvement Districts.[62]

The Premiership of John Major saw a decline in the special-relationship between Britain and the United States, but Clinton and Blair cemented the political ties between the two countries again. John Major actively supported George Bush in the 1992 presidential election, which soured relations between the two heads of government once Bill Clinton became president. This would change with the rise of New Labour. Blair briefly met Clinton in June 1994 when the American president attended a reception at Downing Street. Blair and Clinton had a formal meeting in November 1995, when Clinton, en route to Ireland, stopped in London to meet with Queen Elizabeth II and John Major and to address Parliament. Blair, then the leader of the opposition, and Clinton had a personal meeting at the residence of the US ambassador in London.[63] Blair developed a close relationship with Clinton. Both had studied at Oxford University, shared a left-of-center politics and enjoyed intellectual conversation. "We were political soulmates," declared Blair. "We shared pretty much the same analysis of the weakness of progressive politics. We were both quintessential modernizers."[64] They grew closer when Blair became prime minister and they conversed over war in the Balkans, sanctions against Iraq and the Northern Ireland peace negotiations. Clinton and Blair were in constant contact by telephone. "It was acknowledged in both capitals that they spent more time talking to each other than either did with any other world leader," author James Naughtie revealed.[65]

British Attitudes toward America at the End of the Cold War

Unlike during the 1980s, US foreign policy did not arouse hostility in 1990s Britain. The Persian Gulf War of 1991 brought much opposition, particularly from left-wing activists, but this dissipated once the conflict ended. In December 1998, President Bill Clinton ordered the bombing of Iraq in "Operation Desert Fox" and three months later American and other NATO warplanes bombarded Kosovo, but neither brought the same revulsion as Reagan's foreign policy adventures. As the United States became a reluctant participant in the war in the Balkans, support for US intervention rather than opposition ensued. The British, more than any other nation, consistently believed that the United States should exercise leadership in the world. In 1993, 65 percent of Britons believed that it was "very desirable" or "somewhat desirable" that the United States exert strong leadership in world affairs. Five years later the figure had increased to 77 percent. In France, the figures were 37 and 53 percent, in Germany 70 and 64 percent, and in Italy 47 and 65 percent.[66]

Rather than turning their ire on US foreign policy, British intellectuals decried the growing cultural influence of the United States on Britain, and particularly on the working class, and the relative weakness of Britain compared to the United States. As the world's only remaining superpower, the United States faced envy and resentment, which increased further as the United States spread its influence into, what seemed to be, a pliant Britain in awe of the giant across the Atlantic. At the end of the Cold War, the United States enjoyed uncontested global supremacy and its political, economic and cultural influence was spreading into the former Soviet Bloc and across the world. It did not help that a triumphalist tone emerged from Washington with President George H. Bush suggesting the emergence of a New World Order and conservative academics like Francis Fukuyama championing the triumph of liberal capitalism and the so-called "end of history."[67] In a November 2000 United States Information Agency poll, 76 percent of Britons had a very favorable or somewhat favorable view of American movies, music and TV. However, 62 percent of Britons regarded US popular culture as a threat to indigenous culture while only 36 percent viewed it as no threat at all.[68]

Condemnation of US influence was couched in defensive nationalistic terms with critics suggesting that the powerful United States was subjugating or seducing a weak and pliant Britain. "Now, just as their airmen are heading home from UK bases after 'winning' the Cold War, battalions more of our U.S. cousins are arriving, taking over historic institutions, businesses and neighbourhoods. There are 200,000 U.S. citizens living in the UK, twice the number of ten years ago, despite a sharp drop in military personnel. Counter-colonisation is in progress." Richard Reeves wrote in the *Observer* in January 2000.

> Can we stem the invasion? And do we really want to? Perhaps we rather like economic success, people who talk to strangers and good coffee after all. One American director of the UK branch of a US company captured the fears or hopes of many. "Everybody says it is not like America yet," he said. "But it will be. It will be."[69]

In 1999, Peter Hall, former director of the National Theatre, suggested:

> Every day, I see our culture creeping into internationalism. And this means Americanism. This is not always a bad thing, but it is a sad thing—particularly when we have so much creative energy of our own. We shall soon have one hundred television channels to choose from, and most of them will be American.[70]

Many of the Tory intellectuals who supported Thatcher's pro-American policies "share many of these fears about Americanisation," author Stephen Haseler wrote. "They often claim to be worried about the loss of 'Englishness;' and they find the American concern with 'abstract principles' such as freedom, democracy and liberty distasteful, preferring instead what they call 'tradition.'"[71]

The resentment directed towards the United States was part of a general rise in nationalistic sentiment in 1990s Britain. Skepticism toward European integration and worries over immigration added impetus to nationalism but so too did Americanization, which was seen by many as a threat to Britain's cultural identity. The British Nationalist Party (BNP), founded in 1982, called for the repatriation of illegal immigrants, voluntary financially aided repatriation for existing legally settled immigrants, withdrawal of the United Kingdom from the European Union (EU) and a British foreign policy less subservient to the United States. The BNP, which won a series of local elections, appealed to those who considered immigration to be a threat to their jobs, claimed that black people received preferential treatment from the government and believed that non-white people destroyed British cultural traditions. A less racist branch of nationalism, the United Kingdom Independence Party (UKIP), formed in 1993, focused on British withdrawal from the EU but, ironically, the party gained three seats in the 1999 elections to the European Parliament.[72]

A rise in nationalistic sentiment came not just from British right-wing parties but also from the Scottish and Welsh desire for self-rule. Many Scottish and Welsh people felt that parliament in London paid little regard to their interests. The Scottish National Party (SNP) formed in the 1930s was committed to achieving independence for Scotland. Plaid Cymru, founded in the 1920s, promoted cultural renewal and gained strong support in Welsh-speaking parts of the country. The devolution elections of 1979 found 52 percent in Scotland in favor of a regional assembly and only 20 percent in Wales supporting a Welsh assembly. Both enjoyed increased support in the 1980s because of the economic blight that gripped both Scotland and Wales. Tony Blair's New Labour responded to the nationalistic sentiment by establishing national assemblies in Scotland and Wales. In Scotland, 74.9 percent voted in favor of a Scottish assembly in the 1997 referendum while 50.3 percent voted for a Welsh assembly. In response to Scottish and Welsh nationalism, English nationalism became more visible, evident in the discussions of Englishness, unseen since the days of George Orwell, and the visible presence of the Cross of St. George rather than the traditional Union Jack. Jeremy Paxman's *The English: A Portrait of a People* published in 1998 and the *Sun* newspaper's "100 Reasons Why It's Great to Be English" four-page supplement released on St George's Day 1999, showed the growth of English nationalism; albeit from differing intellectual positions. A survey in 1999 found that those identifying themselves as English, rather than British, doubled in the previous two years.[73]

This rising nationalism and thirst for a Britain free of American influence was reflected in the culture of nostalgia that swept the nation. Membership of the National Trust rose to over 2.5 million in 1997–1998 and 11.7 million people visited the 251 National Trust sites. *Best of British* magazine was launched in 1994 under the motto of "celebrating everything British—past and present." Soon the magazine gained a readership of nearly 100,000 readers each month. [74] A number of British television programs and films appeared with historical themes, beautiful locations, and a literary bent; often referred to as costume dramas or heritage films. BBC television produced a number of popular literary adaptions such as *Pride and Prejudice*, *Martin Chuzzlewit* and *Vanity Fair*[75]. *Shakespeare in Love* (1999) won the best film award at the Academy Awards, *Sense and Sensibility* (1995) won best screenplay award, *Elizabeth* (1998) was nominated for seven Oscars including Best Picture, and Cate Blanchett won the Best Actress Oscar for her starring role as the English Queen. *Howards End*, a 1992 film directed by James Ivory and produced by Ismail Merchant, who made a career out of depicting British nostalgia, received nine Academy Award nominations while their following film, *The Remains of the Day*, released in 1993, was nominated for eight.[76] The return of James Bond movies *Golden Eye* (1995), *Tomorrow Never Dies* (1997) and *The World Is Not Enough* (1999) brought back nostalgic memories of the swinging 1960s.

The heightened nationalism and nostalgia for the past was evident in the anger that greeted the most innocuous American imports. "There can be no clearer symbolic illustration of the source of Labour's business model for education than the surreal news that the government intends to import school buses from the United States (you know, the yellow ones with flashing lights)," Michael Prowse writing in the *Financial Times* claimed.

> "If they are good enough for American children," says John Prescott, the deputy prime minister, "why shouldn't our children have them?" I'm all for safe transport, but that doesn't mean British children must have the very same buses as their American counterparts. This compulsion to emulate the U.S. is nothing short of pathological.[77]

Daily Express reporter Zoe Dare Hall expressed outrage at being told to "Have a Nice Day" after buying a coffee. Already "we get canteen staff in baseball caps, dress-down days and terms like 'downsizing.' It's the next phase in our Americanisation, along with soul-searching chat shows and self-help psychobabble."[78]

British newspapers blamed America for all of the problems that inflicted British society. The growth of gun violence and gangs in Britain were attributed to the influence of hip hop music. The high earnings of football players were blamed on British clubs' imitating the sporting culture of the United States. Increasing compensation for British boardrooms was accredited to American influences.[79] Some blamed the United States for the boorish behavior of the Royal Family. "American architecture, slang, pop music, film and sport are pervasive in London. Even the city's iconography seems to be utterly Americanised, from the logos on baseball caps worn by people who will never play the game to the neon signs of burger joints," Stephen Amidon depressingly noted in the *The Sunday Times*. "Most notably, we now have a coterie of young royals who seem to have learned their manners and attitudes from *Dynasty* instead of their dynastic forebears."[80] "First it was burgers and movies. Now Uncle Sam has a finger in everything British," regretted journalist Richard Reeves in *The Observer*. "The outposts of U.S. culture-huge bookshops, coffee shop chains, long working hours, fast talking, high divorce rates, 'dress down' Fridays are everywhere."[81] "What bothers me about life now is the gradual Americanisation of Britain," film critic Barry Norman moaned. "In the Sixties people were judged by what they did and what they were. Now they're judged by what they earn and what they own."[82] After the outpouring of emotion at the death of Princess Diana in August 1997, the British media griped about the "Americanization" of British emotions.

Those who were disillusioned with the increasingly right-wing policies of New Labour, made the strongest connections between America's influence on Blair and his right-wing drift. Author Joe Rogaly believed that Tony Blair had "designed and built New Labour, using blueprints faxed from Little Rock."[83] Some political commentators talked of "Blair's American Revolution." "Everyone knows how Blair borrowed the Clinton campaign style, but few appreciate the extent to which New Labour is transforming Britain along American lines," insisted Iain Macwhirter writing in *The Scotsman*. "It amounts almost to a cultural revolution."[84] Many traditionalists simply could not envisage learning anything from the United States and were skeptical of American razzmatazz. Members of the Shadow Cabinet including John Prescott and Clare Short were particularly opposed to any attempt to "Clintononize" the party.[85]

In the 1990s, the left united in opposition to American-backed globalization. Many on the left in Britain were despondent over the rightward drift of the Labour Party and the demise of the utopian dream of communism; they harbored resentment against the triumphalist capitalism of the United States. Environmentalists, anarchists and the main party of the radical left, the Trotskyist Socialist Workers Party (SWP), demonstrated against globalization, a term that became common currency in the 1980s and especially in the 1990s to describe the increasingly integrated world economy and the global dominance of large, mostly American-owned, corporations. The SWP and anarchists complained that transnational corporations were encouraging governments in poorer countries to compete for their business by reducing wages, banning unions and lowering environment and labor standards. The Labour left complained about the loss of high-paying jobs in the West as businesses switched operations to take advantage of cheap labor and tax incentives elsewhere. Most activists equated globalization with Americanization and saw the United States as the leader and main beneficiary of this new world order. As the richest country in the world, the United States promoted free trade, which its strong corporations could dominate and in 1973 the United States became the first major nation to abolish capital controls allowing US corporations to expand abroad. The fall of the Soviet Union in 1991 convinced many on the left in Britain and the rest of the world that the United States as the only remaining superpower would now seek uncontested dominance of the world. At the end of the Cold War, the International Monetary Fund (IMF) and the World Bank, both dominated by US economists and policy makers, promoted free-market initiatives in the developing world, specifically the lowering of taxes, deregulation, privatization, cuts in public expenditures and the opening of economies to American trade. Successful

American-owned multinational companies, such as Nike, Gap, Starbucks and McDonald's, who increased profits by employing low-paid, often child, labor working in terrible conditions in the developing world, became the public face of globalization.[86]

There were a number of protests in Britain and across the globe against the American symbols of globalization. The establishment of the World Trade Organization (WTO) in 1995, which promoted free trade by providing legally binding rules for international commerce and trade policy, led to the founding of an anti-globalization movement. The Global Street Party, which took place at the same time as the 24th G8 Summit in Birmingham, England, in May 1998, and the Carnival against Capital in June 1999, an international day of protest timed to coincide with the 25th G8 Summit in Cologne, Germany, saw major protests in the banking area of London. More protests broke out in other countries. In December 1999, thousands of protestors took to the streets to disrupt the World Trade Organization Ministerial Conference in Seattle, Washington. Symbolizing their identification of globalization with US corporate dominance, protestors smashed the shop windows of American-based corporations such as Starbucks, McDonald's and Old Navy. Violent confrontations between the police and protesters at the 27th G8 Summit in Genoa, Italy, in July 2001 resulted in the death of a protestor.

McDonald's, more than any other company, became the visible symbol of globalization and America's expanding global influence. McDonald's, who opened their first restaurant in Des Plaines, Illinois, on April 15, 1955, opened their 400th restaurant in Britain in 1991.[87] In September 1986, *The Economist* magazine launched the Big Mac Index as a humorous way of measuring the purchasing power parity (PPP) between two currencies; this was indeed an indication of the growing global influence of McDonald's. Because of its ubiquitous presence on the high street, McDonald's became a despised emblem of American-led globalization. In April 1985, activists organized the first international day of action against McDonald's, complaining that the company destroyed rainforests, sold unhealthy food, treated animals inhumanely and exploited their workforce.

Opposition to McDonald's culminated in a court case dubbed McLibel that gained world-wide attention. In October 1986, London Greenpeace, one of the main organizations behind the campaign against McDonald's, distributed a leaflet entitled "What's Wrong with McDonald's" during a World Day of Action Against McDonald's. As a result of the leaflet, in September 1990 McDonald's sued two activists, Helen Steel and Dave Morris, for libel. McDonald's might have thought they could silence opposition by such actions, but the result was the opposite: the court case captured international headlines and became a public relations disaster for McDonald's. Steel and Morris defended themselves aided by the McLibel Support Campaign (MSC), which raised money and provided publicity for the defendants. The trial, which began in March 1994, lasted nearly three years, the longest trial in English history. The judge found the defendants liable on several points raised by the plaintiff but, for certain allegations made by the defendants, such as the plaintiff endangered the health of its customers by misleading advertisements and paid unreasonably low wages, the judge decided against McDonald's.[88]

Most Britons supported globalization in theory but worried that it undermined the British way of life and fostered insecurity. Britons liked the increased cultural connectedness, travel and communications of globalization but believed that in practice American multinational corporations were gaining at the expense of the British public. According to a US State Department poll in the fall of 2000, 65 percent of the British respondents "judged globalization to be primarily positive."[89] A MORI survey from September 2001, however, found that only 13 percent of Britons believed that globalization enhanced everyone's quality of life. Over 40 percent thought that the protestors in Seattle and Genoa were raising genuine concerns about the impact of globalization. Around 90 percent believed that the government should protect the environment and working conditions from the policies of multinational corporations.[90]

Anger against US influence and British weakness manifested itself in prejudice against individual Americans. Marc Carnegie, London correspondent for *The American Spectator*, found that

> it's impossible to spend more than a few days here without the English telling you, either in the press or in person, how horrible America and the Americans really are. It's not only that we're overpaid, oversexed, and over here—that was the postwar judgment, after all, when our popularity rating was still relatively high. Now we're loud, tacky, uncultured, stupid, arrogant, sloppy, and revoltingly sentimental.

On one occasion a man confronted him in a pub, screaming "I hate Americans. You've got no history, you've got no culture . . . and you've got no class" before he fell drunkenly onto the bar.[91] "Wussy boys are a new breed of anti-macho American men in touch with their feelings and proud of it," the editorial in the *Sunday Express* of October 8, 2000, pronounced. "About time, too, most of us must feel. The American stereotype of the arrogant and loud-mouthed male has been all too real for too long."[92] Obesity in America became a subject of ridicule in 1990s Britain as newspapers employed condescending headlines like "Hefty folk weigh in with a bigger say," "Anti-fat pill gives hope to 58 million obese Americans" and "World health: Americans eat themselves to death."[93]

Documentaries and travel shows joined in the laughter as they depicted America as the land of the weird and the wacky. In 1992, Jonathan Ross journeyed to the United States to make *Americana* a three-part series, which explored American culture with the episodes entitled "Fat," "Dumb" and "Rich." Americans are shown gouging on fast food, loving their guns and spending their money on useless commodities. Ross sneers at the eccentric people and shallow culture he encounters on his road trip to the Precious Moments Chapel, part of a theme park run by a giftware company, to a stripper museum and to the Tupperware Hall of Fame. "The Greeks may have cornered the market in ancient philosophy and the diligent Japanese the future of technology but for the things that really matter like large men stuffing inflated balls through metal hoops the world takes its cue from America," Ross began one episode.

> The most immediately impressive thing about America is not its size nor its wealth nor its exceedingly pleasant weather. No what's most striking about America is how

> dumb it is; incredibly, unbelievably, wonderfully dumb ... I don't want to make Americans out to be drooling idiots forever seeking cheap transitory frills, but much of the evidence points this way.[94]

The British felt better about themselves by laughing at American stereotypes and by shaking their heads at the inadequacies of American society including the level of violence in the United States. As the number of media outlets expanded in the 1990s, violence in the United States dominated headlines. The Los Angeles riots of April 1992 drew live television coverage. Even though the American football star O. J. Simpson was little known in the United Kingdom, the O. J. Simpson murder trial was screened live on Sky Television in 1995. The Columbine High Schools shooting by two students that left 13 dead in 1999 led to extensive media coverage on guns in America and on the alienation of American teenagers. After a string of attacks on British tourists in Florida, Columbus Travel Insurance produced posters on the London Underground advertising their services with the words: "We won't let the American Dream turn into a nightmare," and urged travelers to take out insurance to avoid their US holiday turning "into a nightmare of medical bills and muggings."[95]

Publicity given to serial killers, a term first used in the 1980s, added to the image of the United States as an extremely violent society. Serial killers like Charles Manson, John Wayne Gacy, Jeffrey Dahner and Dennis Nilsen gained tremendous media coverage in Britain. Big box office hits in Britain such as *The Silence of the Lambs* (1990), *Natural Born Killers* (1990) and *Basic Instinct* (1992) revolved around serial killers. "Suddenly, America seems awash with serial killers," *The Guardian* suggested in August 1991. "The latest claim, by the former US Marine Donald Leroy Evans that he has committed 60 unsolved murders, most of them while on parole from prison, has caught the imagination of a country still flocking to *Silence of the Lambs*."[96] In January 1993, ITV screened a documentary on serial killers that included an interview with multiple-killer Dennis Nilsen and the same channel's *Storyline* series presented a feature on Henry Lee Lucas who had been in custody in Texas for a decade having confessed to 300 murders.[97]

The representation of America as an exceptionally unsafe country did not, however, match the statistics. More people were shot and killed in the United States than in Britain, but crime especially burglaries and robberies were more prevalent in Britain than in the United States in the 1990s. In 1981, there were 106 residential burglaries per 1,000 households in the United States, compared with only 41 per 1,000 households in England and Wales. Ten years later, however, the US rate had decreased to 65 per 1,000 households, while the English level had increased to 68.[98] The US Department of Justice in 1998 found that rapes were more prevalent in the United States than in Britain but the rates for assault, burglary and motor vehicle theft were all lower in America than in England and Wales. In June 2000, the CBS News program compared crime statistics between the United States and England and Wales and found that people were more likely to be burgled, twice as likely to be robbed and two-and-a-half times more likely to be assaulted in England and Wales than in America.[99]

Not only did many Britons feel better about their own country by condemning the violence in the United States, but they also expressed anger at the barbarity of the American justice system. Outrage reached beyond intellectual circles in 1997 when a 19-year-old British au pair Louise Woodward stood trial in Massachusetts for the killing of an 8-month-old boy left in her care. The Sky News cable channel provided nonstop live coverage of the court proceedings and saw its ratings jump 500 percent. Seeing Woodward in shackles "was a particularly horrifying image" for Britain, observed Judie Newman, head of the British Association for American studies. The eventual murder conviction of Woodward unleashed a wave of resentment against America. "In the twinkling of a verdict, Britain's normally ironic affection toward America has turned into something nasty," reported the *Toronto Star*.

> Long-forgotten wounds—"Remember the American Revolution?"—are being uncovered again. Americans, or at least their judges and juries, are being sneered at with open disgust. "Barbaric" is how one Londoner summed up the U.S. justice system last week. And this was no tabloid editor but a law teacher at one of England's most respected schools.

Hillary Clinton had to enter the US embassy through a side door to avoid angry "pro- Louise" protesters during her visit to London. Inside, embassy staffers fielded about 2,000 angry calls. "There's a great deal of anti-Americanism," revealed a member of staff. Over 100,000 phone callers participated in a Sky poll, with 93 percent expressing the view that Woodward did not receive a fair trial. "Free her," read a huge headline in the *Sun*, which announced it was launching a campaign to keep Woodward out of a "hellhole American prison." In "the civilized world," said attorney Stephen Jakobi, he could not think of a trial as unfair as Woodward's. "I'm looking at Morocco for possible comparison," he suggested. "A gruesome case in Russia? Bulgaria? . . . . Broadly speaking," he opined "it confirms the notion that Americans are really rather barbaric people and really ought to come back into the empire."[100] Marc Carnegie, London correspondent for *The American Spectator*, outlined the depth of outrage.

> People on talk radio were ready to bomb Massachusetts. There were calls to demolish the American Bar Association's memorial at Runnymede. One pub landlord dumped all his American booze in the trash, and took burgers off his menu. A transportation company at Manchester airport banned Americans from its fleet of English-made autos. And a woman in Woodward's home town was assaulted, because she wasn't wearing one of those yellow ribbons.[101]

All aspects of American society faced condemnation and ridicule. Writer Susan Marling suggested in 1993 that Britons often characterized the United States "as home of the serial killer, the therapy junky, the cabbage-patch doll collector, the fornicating evangelist, the Miami matron, the brain-dead redneck, the weirdo."[102] "[T]he U.S. is crass, poorly educated, obsessed with money, riven by race, plagued by extremism and filled with people who either eat too much or exercise to the point of fanaticism," Jonathan Freedland evoked the view of America held by middle-class intellectuals.

> They lack irony, kill each other for a nickel, invade small countries, know nothing of the world and require a credit card before they will treat the sick. Their children are either on crack, having children of their own, or sitting goggle-eyed in front of 100-channel TV with *Beavis and Butthead* on every station. America is the land of Bible-quoting fundamentalists, lame-suited game-show hosts and gun-toting maniacs. Culturally it is a desert: theme parks substitute for history and dumbed-down slang serves for language.[103]

"I hate America's grotesque commercialism (no TV programme seems to last longer than a few sentences before some egregious ad breaks in offering vast pizzas or exercise machines too late, fatso)," journalist Ann Leslie wrote in the *Daily Mail* in November 2000.

> I'm repulsed by its hordes of grotesquely obese people (a small side-order in any restaurant would feed an Ethiopian village for a day). Outside of New York and Washington, I'm astonished by its provincialism ("foreign news" very often means nothing more than something which happens in another American state), repelled by its cultural arrogance, its belief that "feelings" have more validity than reason (seen a Jerry Springer show lately?) and astonished by the sheer inefficiency of the most technologically advanced nation in the world.[104]

Those who offered favorable opinions about aspects of the United States faced vitriol. When Jonathan Freedland, *The Guardian's* US correspondent, published *Bring Home the Revolution* in 1998, arguing that Britain could learn from American democracy, the liberal press burst into outrage. "Freedland's book is such a mish-mash of irrelevant statistics, doubtful statements and outdated fact," Angus Wolfe Murray wrote in *The Scotsman*. "His embrace of the American way is as blind and uncompromising as those idealistic young men who went to Russia in the Thirties and came back starry-eyed about communism."[105] Writing in *The Observer*, Peter Conrad said

> I agree with every directive on Freedland's "road map to the future"; I wish, all the same, that his grand design hadn't been predicted on an enviously idealised account of the United States, where he spent four years as a *Guardian* correspondent. America encourages its citizens to dream, and promises that their lives will be a wish-fulfilment of fantasies, binges of instant gratification. It can afford to make such generous predictions because it releases people into an empty continent, awaiting exploitation,

Conrad continued:

> Its optimism depends on geographical largesse, and will never transfer to our own overcrowded terrain. Nor has the US been able to keep its promise of bliss and bounty, except for the very few. The dream is more often a disillusioned nightmare, and these days Americans pursue happiness by suing each other if they slip over on

> the snow or are scalded by a cup of coffee: the law is traduced, turned into a means of getting rich quickly.[106]

Television presenter and author Melvyn Bragg, once enthralled by American society, now expressed his utter disillusionment with the country. Born in October 1939, in Wigton, Cumbria, Bragg, like most British youth, loved American music, movies and literature. "We imitated the accent, we chewed the gum, we smoked like they smoked," Melvyn Bragg recalled. "The American invasion was under way."[107] In the 1980s, however, Bragg became active in attempts to halt creeping Americanization. In 1983, Bragg took a leading role in a campaign to stop McDonald's opening an outlet in a Grade II listed building in the middle-class bastion of Hampstead High Street in North London. He was joined by other local residents, including actor Tom Conti, writer Margaret Drabble and Glenda Jackson, MP for Hampstead and Highgate. Why were they concerned about MacDonald's?—journalist Cosmo Landesman asked in December 1993. "Because it is a symbol of creeping and crass Americanisation. Ronald McDonald has become the [President of the European Commission] Jacques Delors of the chattering classes a bogeyman out to undermine the British way of life."[108] The branch finally opened in 1993 after a ten-year struggle with anti-McDonald's campaigners.

Melvyn Bragg underlined his distaste for American culture and society when he presented a two-part documentary entitled *Bragg on America* on ITV in early 1997. Bragg begins by taking a journey from his home in Cumbria to New York where he meets British exiles David Hockney, Alan Parker, Martin Amis and Jackie Collins. After visiting New York, Bragg travels to California. There he is appalled by the consumerism and materialism of the United States. Hollywood movies, "brilliant and thrilling though some of them are," he admitted,

> have shown a society whose values are violent, infantile and nihilistic. There is nothing there to nourish the dreams of a Coleridge looking for a paradise on earth or a working man in Wigton looking for a new better beginning. It seems increasingly a foreign place well worth knowing and trading with and enjoying, but no longer either the dream that draws us there or the spell that comes back to bind us. Perhaps in a quiet way, it is time for us to make our own Declaration of Independence.[109]

Britpop

Britpop, a term coined by journalist Stuart Maconie to describe a musical movement of the 1990s, embodied a nationalist reaction to the growing American influence in Britain. The scene began as a rejection of American grunge music and then developed into a movement representing a general dislike of American culture. "Nirvana were out there, and people were very interested in American music, and there should be some sort of manifesto for the return of Britishness," Justine Frischmann, lead singer of Elastica, declared. "We didn't think Nirvana said anything to us about our lives. I wasn't remotely interested."[110] Britpop bands gained inspiration from the British invasion bands of the 1960s, when British music had its imperial moment and ruled the waves. British groups such as Elastica, Pulp, Oasis, Blur, Sleeper and Supergrass referenced British songwriters such as Ray Davies of the Kinks in interviews, sang in decidedly British accents and sported sixties-style haircuts and clothes. Previously, the flying of the Union Jack was virtually taboo, particularly among rock stars, but now Noel Gallagher of Oasis played a guitar with the Union Jack on it and members of the Spice Girls wore clothing adorned with the flag.

The English group Suede, probably the first Britpop band, set the tone in its criticism of the United States. Suede, influenced by David Bowie and the Smiths, released their first single in May 1992. "It pisses me off immensely that America has kidnapped British music, and I find the idea of British bands singing in American accents horrifying," Brett Anderson, lead singer of Suede, told the music paper *NME* in 1992. "All great British pop artists from The Beatles to The Fall have celebrated Britain in some way. Whereas to me, America is exemplified by some dullard like Bruce Springsteen," Anderson claimed. "Let's face it, The Beatles were a huge one-nil. I'm not anti-American but I've never been impressed by it. I'm not remotely attracted by New York. I mean, all the streets are laid out in a grid. Doesn't that say everything? In Britain, it takes this convoluted, arcane knowledge to get from one bus-stop to the next. That claustrophobic, stifled Englishness is conducive to great art. Compare an American cop show to a Mike Leigh film or an Alan Ayckbourn play."[111] In April 1993, Anderson appeared on the cover of *Select* magazine with the Union Jack as a backdrop and under the headline "Yanks go Home!" Evoking Britain's finest hour, the issue contained features on similar bands, St Etienne, Denim, Pulp and the Auteurs under the subheading "Battle for Britain."[112]

Blur, the most celebrated Britpop group, forged an identity around a backlash against grunge and a general animosity towards the United States. Blur were formed in London in 1988 and released their debut album *Leisure* in 1991. They found themselves on a near-three-month tour of the United States in September 1991 and pining for home. In thrall to grunge music, the American public proved unimpressed with Blur. Small crowds turned up for in-store appearances and interviewers seemed to know little about their music or assumed that they were from Manchester. The group became increasingly disgruntled with their treatment and annoyed with American culture and Americans. "Quite acceptable Americanisms become absolutely painful: everything turns into this bullshit blizzard. We became quite embittered," bass player Alex James recalled.[113] "We crossed the Canadian border and it felt like someone had flicked a switch that made everything all right again."[114] When Blur returned to Britain they began to write songs with a romanticized if sardonic view of Britain and to wear Doc Marten boots, Fred Perry shirts and the trappings of quintessential British Mods. Mike Smith, a friend of the band, believed that they were on a crusading mission to create an alternative to American music. Their manifesto was to claim "we are not going to take this shit, we are ambitious, and we are proud to be British and fuck America, fuck all your music."[115] Blur released their second album *Modern Life Is Rubbish* in May 1993, a record they originally titled *Blur vs America*. It featured songs about traditional British activities and celebrated British culture under attack from Americanization. In March 1997, *Vanity Fair* published a special edition on "Cool Britannia" with Liam Gallagher, lead singer of Oasis, on the cover and features on fashion designer Alexander McQueen, artist Damien Hirst and Graham Coxon of Blur. By then, the movement had peaked. Lacking the musical inventiveness or, ironically, the willingness to incorporate music and ideas from abroad, the music descended into turgid retreads of past glories.

Britpop nationalism influenced older rock stars including English singer David Bowie who voiced dismay at the culture of the country he once loved. In 1985, Bowie released the song "This Is Not America (sha la la la la)," which was written for the film *The Falcon and the Snowman* and suggested disillusionment with the country that so fascinated him in his youth. The lyrics seem to refer to a dying dream, and suggest that this is not the America that Bowie grew up with and had placed so much of his hopes and aspirations upon. As Britpop raged around him, Bowie appeared in a Union Jack jacket on the cover of his album *Earthling* in 1997. A single from the album entitled "I'm Afraid of Americans," suggested an aversion to American cultural influence in the world. The video to accompany the song was set in New York City and featured Bowie chased by an American stalker, and as Bowie flees he is confronted by incessant and random acts of violence.

European Influences and British Traditions

Those who opposed American influence on Britain and Britain's subservience to the power of the United States exaggerated the impact of the United States on Britain and particularly the influence of Bill Clinton's policies on Tony Blair's thinking. In fact, modernizers including Tony Blair and Gordon Brown were convinced that Labour had to distance themselves from unions and to attract the middle-class vote long before Clinton's election victory in 1992. Indeed, most of the major changes in Labour policies occurred before Tony Blair became leader in 1994. Under the leadership of Neil Kinnock, chosen leader after the 1983 defeat, the Labour Party had already reversed its commitment to unilateral nuclear disarmament, renationalization of privatized industries, withdrawal from the European Economic Community and repeal of Thatcher's anti–trade union legislation. Labour passed the one member one vote rule, which curtailed trade union influence in the Labour Party, at the 1993 conference, almost a year before Blair assumed leadership of the party.[116] Presentation of message and marketing techniques were considered important by the Labour Party even before 1992 and were already valued by Blair prior to Clinton's victory. The Shadow Communications Agency (SCA), a group of volunteers from the world of advertising and marketing, established by Peter Mandelson in 1985, guided Labour's electoral campaigns in 1987 and 1992. The SCA symbolically replaced Labour's traditional red flag logo with a red rose in 1986 and made extensive use of focus groups, slick political advertising and management of the media. All these methods were simply intensified and prioritized in the run-up to the 1997 general election.[117] Indeed, Kinnock's 1987 general election campaign centered on presidential-style campaigning and focused on his personality as much as policies, a strategy that became synonymous with Blair in the 1997 campaign and later when in government.[118]

Policy influences on Blair and the other modernizers also came from places other than the United States but it was the American influence that gained all the negative publicity. Blair had more of an international outlook than Thatcher. He lived in Australia for three years as a child, where his father was a lecturer in law at the University of Adelaide. Blair's mother was an immigrant from Ireland where he holidayed each summer, he visited both France and Italy before he entered politics and he spoke fluent French. When elected to Parliament, Blair was influenced by developments in New Zealand and Australia as well as the United States. New Zealand's Labour government elected in 1984 granted independence to their central bank in 1989 which was an important model for Labour's decision to grant independence to the Bank of England.[119] The young Tony Blair had a deep "interest in Australia," Australian Geoff Gallop, who became close friends with Tony Blair at Oxford University and went on to become premier of Western Australia, recalled. "He didn't like the continuing stuffiness of British class society and spoke of his admiration for what he saw as the robustness, classlessness and productivity of Australian life."[120] Tony Blair and other Labour modernizers admired the Australian Labour Party and the governments of Bob Hawke in the 1980s and Paul Keating in the 1990s. Blair and Brown visited Australia in the early 1990s and learned from Hawke and Keating about how to modernize the Labour Party and how to govern when they took power in the United Kingdom. Australian Labour governments introduced welfare-to-work measures and maintained a tight monetary policy long before the British Labour Party came to power in 1997.[121]

In most other areas of life, intellectuals exaggerated American influence on the country as British traditions held sway. Home-grown product still dominated British television screens. In 1997, only 22 percent of the households owned satellite dishes and most Britons watched regular television channels that imported far fewer American programs.[122] These channels, which now included Channel 5 launched in 1997 as a commercial rival to ITV and BBC 1, broadcast American programs mostly outside of prime time. Football and cricket were far more popular than American sports in Britain; the viewership for the NFL consisted of a niche audience. Even on satellite broadcasting, American channels adapted their programming to reflect British tastes. In the 1990s, CNN and MTV established outlets in Europe that focused on European news and music and used British presenters. All of the most watched television programs of the 1990s were British and British stars dominated the music charts.[123] Only four of the top ten bestselling singles of the 1990s were from the United States and Madonna was the only American artist on the list of top ten bestselling albums of the 1990s. British chain stores like British Home Stores, Boots and Marks and Spencer were still a fixture on the high streets. McDonald's and other fast food retail chains built outlets that blended in with local architecture and faced increasing competition from greasy spoon cafes and traditional British foods, which had come back into fashion in response to American fast foods.

It was clear that the major story of the 1990s was less the American influence on Britain, and more the growing influence of Europe and the rest of the world on British life. Britain first joined the European Economic Community (EEC) in January 1973. While the Conservatives wanted to keep aloof from Europe, the election of Tony Blair and New Labour meant that Britain began to play a greater role in the European Union created in 1993 out of the EEC. After the May 1997 general election victory, Labour ended its opt-out from the Treaty on European Union (TEU), or the Maastricht Treaty, named after the Dutch city in which it was signed in February 1992 by the members of the European Community. The Treaty established the European Union and led to the creation of the single European currency, the Euro, which Britain declined to join. Since Britain joined the EU, British sovereignty has been tempered by Brussels and Strasbourg much more than by Washington DC. English and Scottish law was often subordinated to European law and the European Parliament made crucial decisions that affected all aspects of Britain's economy and society. The Blair government signed the EU Social Charter, which guaranteed certain social and economic rights, and incorporated the European Convention on Human Rights into British law through the Human Rights Act of 1998.[124]

Renewed waves of emigration and immigration cemented connections with Europe. Immigration from Eastern Europe came to Britain after the expansion of the European Union, and the reduction of residence restrictions in 1992 allowed those from the erstwhile Soviet Bloc to enter Britain. The percentage of British tourists traveling to the United States was relatively small compared to those going to Europe. In 1991, only 7 percent of British travelers abroad went to Canada and the United States while 74 percent traveled to EEC countries, 9 percent to non-EEC Western European countries and 9 percent to the rest of the world.[125] In May 1994, the Channel Tunnel opened between London and Paris creating the first link between Britain and France since the Ice Age and allowing trains to travel between the two cities in three hours. The Chunnel brought more than tourists to Britain. In the 1990s, baby boomer Britons who enjoyed a strong sterling and high house prices moved to the Spanish coast and to the French and Italian countryside to enjoy their retirement, many buying summer houses, others making a permanent move. In 1995, there were probably over 300,000 Britons living in Spain.[126] Cheap airline travel encouraged Britons to travel to continental Europe in greater numbers, many of them to follow their football teams. Extended television coverage of European teams inspired many Britons to take weekend trips to see the major clubs in Europe, not just to games involving British teams. The publication of *The Football Grounds of Europe* by Simon Inglis, in 1990 and *European Football: The Rough Guide* by Peterjon Cresswell and Simon Evans, in 1997, highlighted a desire by Britons to visit European stadiums.

Dance music, for long the preserve of African-American artists in Britain, became less American influenced. Kraftwerk, a German band who played futuristic and hypnotic music on electronic instruments, toured Britain in 1975, inspiring a whole host of young people, and spawning British synthesizer bands of the 1980s like Depeche Mode, Ultravox, Soft Cell, Heaven 17 and the Human League, who in turn influenced Detroit techno music. The dance music scene in Britain was also influenced by Ibiza, the Spanish island in the Mediterranean, a major holiday destination for British youth. DJs traveled to Ibiza and returned inspired by the clubs and the Balearic Beat of electric dance music played on the island in the 1980s. With the emphasis on the beat and with little singing on many of the tracks, acid house opened up an opportunity for European groups to succeed in Britain. For the first time, European bands, not just American or British ones, swept the British charts and most of the top DJs were European. The futuristic sound of electronic music made American rock music sound dated and laid the basis for the most innovative music of the next 20 years.[127]

The British diet and drinking habits were completely changed by European influences and by immigrants from elsewhere. British people drank cappuccino rather than tea, ate croissants instead of traditional bacon and eggs and drank Polish lager rather than British ale. Wine consumption increased by 450 percent from 1970 to 1995. More people, especially the young, drank European-style lager rather than British Bitter. Hofmeister, Carling Black Label and Oranjeboom used extensive advertising to increase their sales.[128] British television programs featured celebrity chefs such as Gordon Ramsey, Jamie Oliver and Nigella Lawson who made dishes from traditional British recipes and from a multicultural mix of influences including Europe. Olive oil and garlic became mainstays of cooking in a British kitchen while European-style outdoor cafes and restaurants became a fixture of British streets. “You could, in 1960, eat Italian or Indian, but you'd have to make a special expedition to Soho,” suggested author Hunter Davies in the late 1990s.

> Now, such restaurants are in every High Street. In ordinary homes everywhere it is now commonplace to have Chinese or Thai takeaways, heat up a frozen pizza, eat naan bread or pitta bread and consider pasta, in all its forms, as part of the staple British diet. In 1960, spaghetti still came in tins, often in hoops, and any raw, uncooked pasta was looked upon as terribly exotic.[129]

In 1950 there were only six Indian restaurants in Britain but by 1994 there were 7,500.[130] Chicken Tikka Masala overtook fish and chips as Britain's favorite dish and curry and chips became a staple of British fish and chip shops.[131]

British football became more European influenced. The English Premier League (EPL), which began in 1992 with enormous financial backing from Sky Television, attracted players and managers from all over the world. German World Cup winner Jürgen Klinsmann joined Tottenham, Dutch star Ruud Gullit signed for Chelsea while his compatriot Dennis Bergkamp joined Arsenal, and Italian Gianluca Vialli became a Chelsea player. Arsene Wenger from France became manager of Arsenal and Ruud Gullit manager of Chelsea. New or recently rebuilt all-seater stadiums and international stars brought crowds back to grounds after attendances had been dwindling for decades. English clubs with their glamorous foreign stars gained a huge international audience. Soon the EPL became the most popular league in the world watched in 600 million homes across the globe in 2008 and with the star players featuring in TV commercials and their private lives filling the pages of tabloid papers.[132] The Europeanization of British football was also apparent at the national level. Sven Goran Eriksson from Sweden became the first non-English manager of the England football team in 2001 followed by Italian Fabio Capello who became manager of England in 2007. German Berti Vogts became the first foreigner to coach Scotland in 2002.

Tony Blair and New Labour were more open to the Europeanization of British society than Margaret Thatcher and the Conservatives and less influenced by the United States than their opponents often suggested. From an early age, Margaret Thatcher liked the whole idea of America while Tony Blair simply admired the Anglo-American economy constructed by Thatcher's Conservative government and the methods Clinton's New Democrats used to present revisionist policies. New Labour supported the Anglo-American economic model and free-market ideology introduced into Britain by Thatcher, making it almost inevitable that New Labour would examine economic and social policies enacted in the United States. Political similarities with Bill Clinton's Democrats further encouraged Blair to adopt policies first developed in the United States. While Thatcher was inspired by an imagined view of the United States rather than the concrete policies of any particular government or person, Blair had no such affinity with the United States but admired the political strategies and policies of Bill Clinton.

There is little doubt that in the 1990s the United States influenced Britain to a considerable degree. American was now the only superpower and its corporations profoundly changed British television, clothes, movies and music. Tony Blair and the Labour government elected in 1997 reinforced this Americanization of British life as they exhibited a fascination with US politics and US kind of solutions to economic and social problems. This increased cultural and political influence led to a new upsurge of animosity toward America and Americans, most vociferously by the left, who blamed them for the inequalities nurtured by globalization, and by middle-class intellectuals who decried the Americanization of British society. They highlighted the unsavory aspects of American society such as the gun violence, the harsh justice system and the high obesity levels, which, they believed, made the United States inferior to Britain. Critics of the United States downplayed the growing influence of the rest of the world on Britain in order to emphasize the American influence on British society. The new decade would bring an even greater upsurge of animosity to the US government, American society and Americans and a subsequent decline in American influence on British society.

6

September 11 and After: From Hostility to Indifference, 2001–2013

In the afternoon of September 11, 2001, as a stunned television audience watched hijacked airplanes crash into the World Trade Centre in New York City and the Twin Towers collapse into a heap of rubble, a wave of sympathy for the United States swept across Britain. Almost immediately, people began to lay flowers, candles, notes and flags at the US Embassy in Grosvenor Square, London, in memory of the 3,000 people murdered in New York, the Washington DC area and Pennsylvania. Two days after the attack, Queen Elizabeth II ordered the playing of the "Star-Spangled Banner" at the changing of the guard outside Buckingham Palace. Prime Minister Tony Blair announced that Britain would stand "shoulder to shoulder" with the United States as he flew to Washington DC to sit in the visitors' gallery next to First Lady Laura Bush while President George W. Bush spoke to a joint session of Congress on September 20. A month later, the royalty of British rock music including Paul McCartney, the Rolling Stones, the Who, Eric Clapton, Elton John and David Bowie starred at a benefit concert for the victims of the atrocity, staged at Madison Square Garden in New York City. The relationship between the two countries seemed warmer and closer than ever before.

As the Bush administration responded militarily to the attacks in the months after September 11, solidarity declined as broad sections of British society began to express an intense dislike of the American government, people and society. This hostility had its roots in the past and was similar to previous outbreaks of resentment against America. The main reason for the animosity was the foreign policy of the US government, like it was during the years of Ronald Reagan's presidency. It reflected longstanding concerns about US cultural influence on Britain and the nature of American society, and it revived prejudices against American people that had existed since the colonial period. Tony Blair's willingness to support the Bush administration's military actions following September 11, however, produced an unprecedented, broad-based, intense hostility to the United States. Nevertheless, by the end of the decade, the latest wave of resentment against America had subsided. In its place, an indifference to the United States developed, denoting neither disapproval nor admiration but a resignation that Britons no longer cared as much about the United States as they had in previous decades.

Opposition to President Bush and US Foreign Policy

The election of George W. Bush as president of the United States in a close and controversial contest in November 2000 was immediately greeted with dismay in Britain. George Walker Bush, the son of the 41st president of the United States, George H. Bush, was born in Connecticut in 1946 and attended Yale University and Harvard Business School. After episodes of alcohol abuse, Bush became a born-again Christian in 1985 and quit drinking. He became Republican governor of Texas in 1994 on a right-wing pro-business and socially conservative platform. As a non-drinking, evangelical Christian, opposed to abortion and gun control, Bush was out of step with the views of most Britons. Bush developed a Texas drawl and constantly had problems pronouncing words; his mispronunciations came to be known as "Bushisms." To his supporters this made him a down-to-earth, straight-talking American who disliked the sophistication of the eastern elites but, to the British, Bush was an inarticulate simple-minded Texan, who knew or cared little about the world beyond the borders of the United States or even of the Lone Star State. Apprehension of the British people soon turned to anger. Wishing to pursue a unilateralist foreign policy, Bush and his cabinet were unwilling to enter into international agreements. In March 2001, the US government announced that it would not implement the Kyoto Climate Protocol, adopted at the third session of the United Nations Framework Convention on Climate Change (UNFCCC) in Kyoto, Japan, in December, 1997. The refusal to sign the Kyoto agreement, designed to reduce carbon dioxide emissions into the atmosphere, proved that the United States did not care about the environmental impact of American industry. Bush offered unconditional support for Israel and its right-wing prime minister Ariel Sharon when they met in the White House in March 2001, even when the rest of the world sought a Palestinian state. Hardly surprisingly, in August 2001 George Bush's approval ratings in Britain trailed the previous president Bill Clinton's by 49 percent.[1]

George Bush's popularity declined even further because of the US government's response to the events of September 11 and its so-called "War on Terror." Bush spoke of the world in terms of good versus evil with the United States representing good and opponents of the United States: Al-Qaeda, Iran, Iraq and North Korea, constituting an "Axis of Evil." Bush and his cabinet wanted to aggressively use its economic and military strength to promote American-style governments and economies in other countries and objected to having US policy constrained by international treaties, obligations or allies. After the United States invaded Afghanistan in October 2001 to root out Al-Qaeda and overthrow the Islamic fundamentalist Taliban regime, the Bush Administration established the Guantanamo Bay detention facility in Cuba to hold detainees from the war, an idea that troubled many because of its disregard for human rights. In May 2002, Bush refused to sign the Treaty of Rome, which established an International Criminal Court based in The Hague to try suspected war criminals. The following month, the US government withdrew from the Anti-Ballistic Missile Treaty, an agreement signed by the United States and the Soviet Union in 1972, which limited missile development. Ignoring the protests of the rest of the world and bypassing the United Nations, the Bush administration proceeded to invade Iraq in March 2003, claiming that the Saddam Hussein regime enjoyed close ties with Al-Qaeda and amassed a stash of weapons of mass destruction, which the regime or Al-Qaeda could use against the United States and its allies.

Left-wing intellectuals, as always, proved to be the most vociferous critics of the United States government. Almost immediately, they blamed US foreign policy for provoking the September 11 attack. Rather than sympathy, Philip Lader, former US ambassador to Britain, appeared on BBCs *Question Time* 48 hours after the attack, and faced jeers and slow-hand clapping from some sections of the audience who relentlessly condemned US foreign policy. Mary Beard, lecturer in classics at Cambridge University, suggested in the *London Review of Books* "that, however tactfully you dress it up, the United States had it coming. That is, of course, what many people openly or privately think. World bullies, even if their heart is in the right place, will in the end pay the price."[2] Compassion for the victims of the attack was in short supply. An editorial in the *New Statesman* urged readers to look at images of

> Americans running in terror from the New York explosions and then ask yourself how often in the past (particularly in Vietnam and more recently in Iraq) you have seen people running in terror from American firepower. American bond traders, you may say, are as innocent and as undeserving of terror as Vietnamese or Iraqi peasants. Well, yes and no. Yes, because such large-scale carnage is beyond justification, since it can never distinguish between the innocent and the guilty. No, because Americans, unlike Iraqis and many others in poor countries, at least have the privileges of democracy and freedom that allow them to vote and speak in favour of a different order. If the United States often seems a greedy and overweening power, that is partly because its people have willed it. They preferred George Bush to Al Gore and both to Ralph Nader.[3]

Little did it matter that the vast majority of Americans did not vote for George Bush and that more people voted for the defeated challenger Al Gore than for the eventual winner.

Like Ronald Reagan before him, George Bush endured much personal abuse because of his image as a dim-witted but overconfident American. "Having an imbecile for a president is a little embarrassing for the military-industrial complex that governs the United States," journalist and left-wing activist Paul Foot opined. Paul Marsden, a Labour MP who defected to the Liberal Democrats in December 2001 because of his opposition to the war in Afghanistan, believed that "President Bush struggles to find Islamic states on a world map."[4] Antiwar demonstrators held up posters of George Bush sporting an Adolf Hitler-style moustache and American flags with the stars rearranged into the shape of a swastika. The

"Madness of George Dubya" a play satirizing Bush became a big hit in London in 2003. The play portrayed President George Bush as a pajama-wearing simpleton clutching his teddy bear as he cowers in a bunker while his military advisors make preparations for the war in Iraq. *The Guardian* theatre correspondent, Michael Billington, reported that the play "had a packed house at this north London fringe theatre cheering it to the echo."[5]

In the 1980s, opposition to the foreign policies of the American government was most apparent among leftists, but in the twenty-first century it embraced conservatives too. Patrick O'Flynn, political editor of the conservative *Daily Express* and "a pro-America, pro-war-on-terror" advocate, suggested that

> the President gives the impression of simply not understanding the unique responsibility of being the most powerful man in the world; the need to treat others with respect, to seek to take other nations with America when it makes the case for military expeditions; to understand that might is not always right.[6]

"For America to brush away its recent disgraces, the electorate will have to bin this administration," former Conservative MP Michael Portillo wrote in the lead up to the 2004 presidential election. "I never expected to say this to my American friends: vote Democrat."[7] Adrian Wooldridge, a British journalist working in Washington DC, visited a

> Conservative haunt in London's clubland in the tense weeks before the invasion of Iraq. As a visitor from Washington, D.C., I would normally have expected a few warm inquiries about the health of Britain's closest ally; instead, I was subjected to a vigorous inquisition from the assembled Tories. A retired Foreign Office panjandrum denounced the Bush administration for its crass ignorance of the Arab world. A curmudgeonly barrister proclaimed his intention to march for peace. A senior banker complained that he can't visit New York these days without being shocked by the money-grubbing vulgarity of the place. The only person present who didn't regard George W. Bush as a warmongering simpleton was an American émigré who had worked for Richard Perle in the Pentagon back in the 1980s,
>
> . . .
>
> British Tories have come independently to exactly the same views as [Michael] Moore.[8]

As George Bush spoke about spreading democracy abroad, the rest of the world paid particular attention to the type of American democracy that would be exported. Britons condemned America's gun culture, the influence of money on American politics, inadequate health care and public displays of Christianity. "To Europeans, religion is the strangest and most disturbing feature of American exceptionalism," an *Economist* editorial noted. "They worry that fundamentalists are hijacking the country. They find it extraordinary that three times as many Americans believe in the virgin birth as in evolution."[9] In 2003, artist and illustrator Paul Davis from London asked people on the street what they thought of Americans. He encountered hostility to individual Americans and particularly to their religious beliefs. One suggested that "Americans are a bunch of terrifying Christian fundamentalists" and another stated that "It's the God thing that's so annoying."[10]

In March 2008, a poll entitled "Anglo-Saxon Attitudes" undertaken in the United States and Britain unearthed the fundamental differences over religion and the role of government that had developed between the two peoples. The poll found that

> the differences between the two countries look more striking than the similarities. But the difference in views is so wide that even British Conservatives are a great deal more secular than American Democrats are.... In their fundamental attitudes—regarding religion, society, the role of the state—Britons are more similar to their western European neighbours (and Canadians) than they are to the United States.

The poll found that 39 percent of Britons and 80 percent of Americans believed in God. Only 10 percent of Britons trusted the Bible story of creation while 40 percent of Americans put their faith in creationism; 13 percent of Britons believed homosexuality was a sin but 40 percent of Americans thought it was. In Britain, 21 percent thought that abortion should be illegal or only allowed when the life of the mother is threatened while 48 percent of Americans held the same views. When someone loses their job, 38 percent of Britons believed that the government should have prime responsibility for looking after them until they find a job while only 17 percent held the same view in America. On the role of the government, 36 percent of Britons deemed that the government should have less of a role in the provision of services such as health and education while 48 percent of Americans thought this way.[11] Unsurprisingly, another poll conducted in the spring of 2010, found that only 15 percent of Britons believed that the United States was the nation that most shared Britain's values. The top choice was Australia at 28 percent followed by Canada at 19 percent.[12]

The voice of opposition to the influence of US popular culture on Britain was raised like never before. "My anti-Americanism has become almost uncontrollable," wrote English novelist Margaret Drabble in May 2003, two months after the invasion of Iraq, in an article in the *Daily Telegraph* entitled "I Loathe America and What It Has Done to the Rest of the World."

> It has possessed me like a disease. It rises in my throat like an acid reflux, that fashionable American sickness. I now loathe the United States and what it has done to Iraq and the rest of the helpless world... I have tried to control my anti-Americanism, remembering the many Americans that I know and respect, but I can't keep it down any longer. I detest Disneyfication, I detest Coca-Cola, I detest burgers, I detest sentimental and violent Hollywood movies that tell lies about history.[13]

Some decried the extent of American influence.

> "I feel uneasy at my current resistance to American culture, which grows with every Seabiscuit that I'm fed," theatre director Richard Eyre revealed. "Like a member of the Academie Francaise, I find myself flinching when I hear people talking about 'taking

a rain check' or 'ballpark figures' or 'getting to first base' or 'striking out'—terms taken from baseball, a game not even played by amateurs in this country."[14]

The policies of George Bush reignited a widespread resurgence of prejudices against American people. "Anybody who has visited Britain and Europe, or followed the public conversation there during the past five months, will have been struck, even shocked, by the depth of anti-American feeling among large segments of the population," author Salman Rushdie declared in February 2002.

> Western anti-Americanism is an altogether more petulant phenomenon than its Islamic counterpart and far more personalized. Muslim countries don't like America's power, its "arrogance," its success; but in the non-American West, the main objection seems to be to American people. Night after night, I have found myself listening to Londoners' diatribes against the sheer weirdness of the American citizenry. The attacks on America are routinely discounted. (Americans only care about their own dead). American patriotism, obesity, emotionality, self-centeredness: these are the crucial issues.[15]

Writing in the *New Statesman,* Mark Thomas suggested that "Britain's anti-Americanism is blamed on jealousy. This must mean we want the highest obesity rate in the world and a leader who can't string two sentences together."[16] British television and movies included crude stereotypes of Americans. The Lardburgers, a fictional American couple, featured on a British morning television show entitled *The Big Breakfast*, starred Jeff and Stacey Lardburger as extremely fat, terribly dressed, gun-loving, crude and ignorant Americans.[17] In 2005, 64 percent of Britons thought Americans were greedy, 53 percent thought them violent, 39 percent believed they were immoral and 35 percent considered them rude.[18] Journalist and author Francis Beckett attended a standup comedy show in London just after the start of the Iraq War. "One comedian began his set: 'I hate Americans.' The clapping and cheering went on for several minutes," Beckett depressingly noted.[19]

The reelection of George Bush in November 2004 led to disbelief in Britain and anger at those who elected him. The failure to find weapons of mass destruction in Iraq, the publication of photos of the ill treatment of suspects at Abu Ghraib prison in April 2004, and the quagmire that developed after the invasion, produced intensely negative opinions about the Bush administration, which many thought would lead to the defeat of George Bush. In 2002, 69 percent of the British supported the US "war on terror" but in 2005 the figure had fallen to 51 percent.[20] "How can 59,054,087 people be so DUMB?" the headline in the *Daily Mirror* asked on November 4, 2004 when it became clear that Bush had indeed been reelected. "Mr Bush opposes abortion and gay marriage, doesn't give a stuff about the environment, is against gun control and believes troops should stay in Iraq for as long as it takes," the tabloid claimed, hoping to shock its readers by outlining Bush's radical agenda.[21] "Is this the first time we've had a seven-year-old as President of the Free World?" author Michael Faber asked. "Or, as my friend Brian Eno suggests, is it more a case of a president assuming a seven-year-old boy's intelligence on the part of his electorate?"[22]

In a poll conducted between November 2004 and January 2005, 64 percent of Britons viewed President Bush's re-election as negative for world peace and security.[23]

Americans living in Britain faced a backlash because of the policies of their government. Christian Cox, a US citizen residing in London, was shocked at how people verbally abused her and she suggested that the level of mistreatment felt like a form of racism. Cox, a 29-year-old former model who had lived in London for a year and was setting up her own business, revealed that she had been called, among other things, "terrorist," "scum," and "low life," and she felt that she was constantly being held to account for the actions of President Bush and for US foreign policy. She had traveled widely in other parts of Europe, Mexico, Canada and Australia but this was the first time she had faced such hostility. Cox had heard insults aimed at Americans in other countries but not the pure hatred she had experienced in England. No supporter of Bush or US foreign policy, Cox found that as soon as she opened her mouth people would explode in anger, directing at her their built up frustration with the US. To avoid confrontation, she lowered her voice in public.[24] Journalist Walt Rodgers revealed that an American acquaintance of his was approached by a man in London who said "Take your tanks and bombers and go back to America." Then the Londoner punched him repeatedly.[25]

Carol Gould, who was born in Philadelphia in 1953 and had lived in Britain since 1976, found the invective she suffered in London to be unbearable. A Bush supporter working in British television, she faced personal abuse from those she met at parties and also from people she encountered on buses, in pubs, in shops, in taxis and at the Proms, where she had to put her American flag away because of the hostility. "Readers must understand that visceral anti-Americanism in various sections of society goes back to before the days of Abu Ghraib, Guantanamo, or the Iraq War. It has been a feature of my life in Britain over 30 years. It has now reached epic proportions," Gould revealed. "In recent years, I have been on the receiving end of more verbal attacks than I can count." Understandably, she was bitter toward her adopted homeland. "The English are not known for public displays of fury (except, perhaps, at soccer matches), but there is something about an American accent that brings out their pent-up rage." Gould found "an atmosphere of anger and hostility that, for the first time in my lifetime, makes me fearful for my safety in my beloved country, Great Britain . . . What I find so frightening is that, increasingly, many Americans cannot conduct business or even take a taxi ride in London, Bournemouth, or Edinburgh without a scathing tirade about the scurrilous Yanks." Gould relocated to the United States in 2008.[26]

The experiences of Gould were uncommon, as many Americans living in Britain faced neither abuse nor prejudice. Kay Konop an American who had lived in the UK since 1988, claimed that she had been accepted by the British and had enjoyed hospitality rather than abuse. While fellow country woman Christian Cox faced persistent name calling, Konop found the British to be friendly and tolerant. Konop suggested that the British are at their worst under the influence of alcohol and the best way for Ms. Cox to avoid unruly or insulting behavior was to steer clear of the pubs![27] Edie Friedman an American who had lived in Britain for over 30 years, also faced few problems. "As a regular user of public transport and with constant exposure to people of many different backgrounds, I have never met the visceral hatred of Americans she describes." Others agreed.

> As American expats who have lived in London for just over four years, we have found our neighbours to be welcoming and gracious people. The truest measure of actual sentiments can be measured by the substantial majority of the British people who wish to see George Bush defeated. That is the ultimate expression of kindness towards the American people,

Ronald Garner from London believed.

> I am a Texan and have had the great pleasure of holidaying in Britain for many years. London is one of my favourite cities in the world. No one has ever been anything but kind. The people smile when they hear my accent, start conversations with me and give me friendly advice. It is a great disservice to both our countries to write of "American bashing,"

declared Patricia Redford Kidd from Valley Spring, Texas.[28]

In fact, many Britons displayed a strong aversion to other nationalities, not just Americans.

> As an American who has also spent most of my adult life here, I realised long before 9/11 that everyone here didn't love us. This "island race" does have antagonistic feelings verging on the xenophobic. Anyone who has heard the British praise France if it only wasn't for the French, or claim all Italians are sex-mad cowards, knows they distrust everyone equally and, so, shouldn't be surprised that we aren't exempt just because we are so sure we're God's gift,

pronounced Rick Bryant living in Exeter, Devon.[29] Another American who lived in England insisted that other ethnic groups faced more hostility than Americans. "I was called a 'colonial' in London once, and told to go back to America; my Indian-British friend, in contrast, was spat on and called a 'Paki.' It's narrow-mindedness that is the problem—in England as anywhere else in the world." He had differing experiences to Carol Gould who faced so much hostility in London.

> I've been to the same kinds of events and places that Gould has—including cafes on Edgware Road—and not had the same kind of experiences, to put it mildly. I merrily waved my U.S. flag at the Last Night of the Proms in 2006 with no problem or hostility whatsoever.[30]

The racist British National Party (BNP) certainly joined in the anti-American sentiment but most of their ire was focused on Muslims and non-white immigrants. The party concentrated its attack on the Islamic religion and condemned the Labour government for its immigration policies that allowed Muslims into the country and for letting Muslim extremists openly express their incendiary political positions. The BNP made large gains in the 2006 local elections where the party more than doubled its number of councilors.

Americans visiting and living in Britain may have escaped abuse on the streets but they could not escape the derision of some Britons, such as English comedian Sacha Baron Cohen, who made a career out of mocking Americans. He first came to prominence as the hip hop influenced character Ali G, who interviewed unsuspecting guests in the United States. He followed this up with the film *Borat* (2006), which starred Cohen as a journalist from Kazakhstan traveling through the United States. Cohen visits rural America where he provokes situations that expose Americans as stereotypically racist, sexist and ignorant. He attends a redneck rodeo in Virginia where the crowd cheers at Borat's gung-ho speech about the war in Iraq, stops at a Confederate-memorabilia store run by an elderly couple and visits a religious camp meeting. Cohen makes an all-white dinner party in Alabama rather uncomfortable by bringing along a scantily clad black woman and incites frat boys to make crude remarks about women and blacks.[31] In his next film *Bruno* (2009), Cohen repeats the formula but this time as a gay Austrian fashion reporter Brüno, who travels to the United States where he meets parents of child models, Christian fundamentalists and various celebrities. By this time, the joke had run its course and the film was a box office disaster.

Jerry Springer, an outrageous American television talk show host, allowed the British to laugh at crazy Americans. Making its US television debut in 1991, *The Jerry Springer Show* hosted by the former mayor of Cincinnati became a huge hit in the united Kingdom when the program was taken up by satellite and cable channel Living and broadcast by ITV in the early hours of the morning. Fights, obscene language, outrageous stories and shameless guests turned the show into a sensation. Newspapers devoted many column inches to the show with headlines such as "Triumph of trash TV" and "King of Trash TV Hits the Big Time."[32] Springer, who was born in London and moved with his family to the United States at the age of five, returned to Britain in 1999, when the popularity of repeated episodes of his US show persuaded him to record several episodes of the program with a British audience. He also hosted a late night talk show for ITV and spurred a number of British imitations of *The Jerry Springer Show* format including *Vanessa* and *Tricia*. A musical, "Jerry Springer—The Opera," became a hit at the Edinburgh Fringe in 2002 and subsequently played in London's West End before embarking on a successful UK Tour in 2006.

The takeover of major English football clubs by American owners, particularly the giants of the northwest Manchester United and Liverpool, provoked resentment against American influence. When the press revealed that Malcolm Glazer, owner of the Tampa Bay Buccaneers of the National Football League, wanted to buy Manchester United in 2005, supporters expressed outrage. His effigy was hung outside United's ground, Old Trafford, violent demonstrations occurred on a regular basis and opponents of the Glazer's takeover established an alternative club, United F.C. American businessmen Tom Hicks and George Gillett faced similar protests when they bought Liverpool in 2007. Liverpool protesters set up a Facebook page entitled "Thanks but NO YANKS" and in June 2010 a group of Liverpool supporters burned US flags in a series of protests against the two American owners.[33]

Opposition to Blair

Even though President George Bush and US foreign policy attracted sharp criticism, Prime Minister Tony Blair remained a staunch ally of the Republican administration. Blair first met President Bush at Camp David in February 2001. This was followed by more than 30 meetings between the two men in the United States. Bush believed the prime minister to be "candid, friendly and engaging."[34] Initially, Blair found that Bush had "a great sense of humour, was self-effacing and self-deprecatory in an attractive way, but the fact remained he was conservative and I was progressive."[35] Blair was ready to speak at the Trades Union Congress in Brighton on the afternoon of September 11, 2001, when he first heard of the attacks in New York City and immediately informed the conference of the events and issued his condolences to the American people adding that the "democracies of this world, are going to have to come together to fight" terrorism. The first phone call Bush made to a world leader after the events of September 11 was to Tony Blair. Blair told him that he would stand with the United States "one hundred percent" in opposing terrorism. "There was no equivocation in his voice. The conversation helped cement the closest friendship I would form with any foreign leader. As the years passed and the wartime decisions grew tougher, some of our allies wavered. Tony Blair never did." The British prime minister "grew into my closest partner and best friend on the world stage."[36] Blair, in turn, "had come to like and admire George. I was asked recently which of the political leaders I had met had most integrity. I listed George near the top."[37]

Blair's support for the Bush administration was more than verbal. He dispatched British troops to help the United States overthrow the Taliban regime in Afghanistan and offered intelligence to the United States to back up their assertion that Iraqi dictator Saddam Hussein stockpiled weapons of mass destruction and actively aided Al-Qaeda. At the instigation of the United States and with the support of the British government, in November 2002 the United Nations Security Council passed Resolution 1441, which called for Iraq to cooperate with UN weapon inspectors to verify that it was not in possession of weapons of mass destruction. While other nations opposed the war, Blair joined with Bush in toppling the Saddam Hussein government in March 2003. Even when the weapons were not found and the war turned into a military quagmire, Blair continued to justify the invasion. In recognition of his services to the Bush administration, in July 2003 Tony Blair became the first British prime minister since Winston Churchill to be awarded the Congressional Gold Medal for being "a staunch and steadfast ally of the United States."

The motivations of Tony Blair were varied. A devout Christian, Blair often spoken of his moral opposition to dictatorships and had previously shown a willingness to use military force to back up his convictions. In December 1998, Blair ordered British warplanes to join the American bombing of Iraq in "Operation Desert Fox," even though the attacks had no approval from the United Nations. Three months later, British warplanes joined American and other NATO warplanes in the bombing of Kosovo. In May 2000, Blair dispatched troops to Sierra Leone to back the government in a civil war. Blair believed it was the responsibility of the major powers to project the citizens of oppressive regimes "i.e. that a government could not be free grossly to oppress and brutalize its citizens."[38] Blair's Christian beliefs and desire to stop dictators and spread Western-style democracy coincided with the views of George Bush. Additionally, Blair believed that he, as the British prime minister, had special influence over the United States and could reign in the military excesses of the Bush administration, persuade them to focus on a multinational approach to international issues, and influence the United States to find a solution to the Israel–Palestine conflict.[39] In the words of a senior advisor to Blair, the strategy toward the United States even before September 11 was to "hug them close."[40] Labour minister Clair Short believed that "a hubristic pleasure in being the only world leader who could deal as an equal with the president of the United States, led Tony Blair to make an error that deeply damaged his premiership and will blight his reputation for ever more."[41]

Blair further wanted to establish himself as a major player on the world stage and enjoyed the glamour and prestige associated with standing next to the most powerful man in the world. After developing a close relationship with President Clinton and seeing the command and influence he wielded, Blair sought a greater role for himself in the international arena as a presidential-style leader. His status as an international figure depended on Britain maintaining the special relationship with the United States and remaining America's most loyal ally. He believed that Britons wanted their prime minister to play a leading role on the world stage.[42] "I always reckoned that even the ones who didn't like me (quite a few) or didn't agree with me (a large proportion) still admired the fact I counted, was a big player, was a world and not just a national leader," Blair suggested. "The British, whatever they say, prefer their prime ministers to stand tall internationally . . . Our leaders should stand out, and it not cut a dash, at least make an impact."[43] The bloody events of September 11 offered him this chance.

The British public indeed opposed the policies of the United States government, but Tony Blair's support for George Bush and the wars in Afghanistan and Iraq ignited the most anger in Britain. Many simply opposed Blair's unqualified support for the unpopular policies of the American president and did not want to see British troops killed or injured in Afghanistan or Iraq. Others feared Britain would become a target for Islamic fundamentalists because of its support for the United States, a fear that seemed to be confirmed with the July 7, 2005, bombings in London undertaken by young Muslim extremists that killed 52 civilians and injured more than 700.[44] Many of those opposed to the Iraq war believed that Blair was deceiving the country about the danger posed by Iraqi president Saddam Hussein. On February 15, 2003, Britain saw the largest demonstration in the history of Britain as two million people rallied in Hyde Park, London, against the impending war in Iraq, many holding placards with the letters in Blair's name rearranged to spell "Bliar." On February 26, 2003, 122 Labour MPs voted against the government in a resolution saying the case for war was unproven. On March 18, 139 Labour MPs voted against the war. Leader of the House Robin Cook resigned from the cabinet in March 2003 over Tony Blair's decision to go to war in Iraq because he "cannot support a war without international agreement or domestic support."[45] Cook was followed by Clare Short, Secretary of State for International Development, who resigned from the cabinet in May 2003 in protest at the government's refusal to seek a United Nations mandate for the war.

Blair was condemned in Britain because he was perceived as a weak leader slavishly following orders from Washington DC and humiliating Britain. "If one thing really needles me," Steve Williams, a hospital porter from Liverpool, complained "it's not what those corksuckers do; it's that Britain has become America's tart. We just lie down and get screwed." Steve's father Edwin added: "The difference between Britain and a business girl is that Anytime Annie gets paid for it, but we're paying to get screwed."[46] Many suggested that Margaret Thatcher would have been less compliant than Blair to American demands. "Thatcher was (is) a sociopath, following her convictions without regard for the effects they had on others," one angry Briton suggested in October, 2006, "but if Bush had tried to get her on board for Iraq the whole thing would have been done the British way or not at all."[47] Samuel Preston, lead singer of English rock band The Ordinary Boys, was more succinct "It's a total farce—we all want him out. Tony Blair is such a brown-noser, all the cliches are true. He's just George Bush's fluffer."[48]

Some people who grew up admiring the United States for its positive role in World War II and the Cold War now voiced resentment against Bush's military adventures and Britain's rush to support US foreign policy. "As I have friends in Pittsburgh I realise the government is not the people," 73-year-old Paul Wood from Mitcham Surrey stated.

> But I'm rather ashamed of the U.S. attitude around the world and we in the UK follow on as sheep. We are told the U.S. is our ally, I think only when it suits the U.S. Bully boys of the world sums up my attitude. Always poking their noses in others affairs and making the situation far worse. Causing the deaths of Americas and UK younger generations in the forces. Or don't do as we do but do as you're told. I believe the U.S. morals are at rock bottom and has dragged the UK down with them.[49]

Surprisingly few British musicians commented on the Iraq War in song, but those that did were unsparingly critical of Tony Blair. Billy Bragg, a constant left-wing critic of US foreign policy and New Labour, reworked an old Leadbelly song ("The Bourgeoisie Blues") as the "Bush War Blues," which he released in 2006. The song aimed, as the title suggests, at President George Bush, condemned Blair for his subservience to the Bush administration, describing the prime minister as Bush's lap dog.[50] Some artists not known for their political militancy also criticized the Iraq War with special condemnation reserved for Tony Blair's role in the affair. In the summer of 2002, George Michael released the single "Shoot the Dog," which made the Top 20 in Britain. Michael sang about a pliant little puppy who adored its master. To reinforce the point, the animated video that accompanied the song depicted Bush as a stupid child and Blair as his poodle.[51] The Pet Shop Boys' released "I'm with Stupid" as a single in 2006 and the song reached the Top 10 in the United Kingdom. The lyrics were built around a letter sent from Tony Blair to George Bush with Bush as "stupid" and Blair as an ingratiating lover.[52]

Certainly, many expressed a strong dislike of Blair because of his domestic policies, not just because of his subservience to George Bush. "Bliar is hated over more than Iraq," one Briton wrote in August 2010.

> His "New Labour" abandoned roots in traditional industries and the working class, nuzzled up too closely with Thatcherism (such a move wasn't politically necessary, the cons were in disarray by 1997 and had nearly been defeated by Kinnock-led party in, what, 1992), and generally became too showy with spin doctors and the like. By 1998, he was deeply unpopular in the area of North London where I lived (Wood Green)—well, at least by everyone I met at the post office and the GP's.

Another wrote in 2010:

> The Iraq War was not only severely misguided, but it also confirmed what many thought of Blair—that he was an American product: superficial and brash. I don't mean to convey that as my opinion of Americans—that's not the way I think—but as how he was seen. Still is. When he returned to drum up support for labour at the last election, the talk was of his tan and how American he looked.

In October 20, 2006, one Briton suggested that "since 2001" Tony Blair

> confused his own job with that of U.S. Secretary of State, flying around the world poking his nose into other people's problems whilst ignoring his own country's. The man is an embarrassment to the office of Prime Minister . . . . If I had my way, I'd have him publicly shackled in Trafalgar Square before being flown in a covert plane to The Hague, where he would face justice for his part in war crimes in the Middle East.[53]

A survey undertaken by *The Daily Telegraph* in 2006 revealed the depth of opposition to the United States. "There has probably never been a time when America was held in such low esteem on this side of the Atlantic," the article entitled "Britain falls out of love with America" noted. "A majority of Britons think American culture and the actions of the present American administration are making the world a worse place to live in, and almost no one believes America is now, if it ever was, a beacon to the world." The survey found that 49 per cent of Britons liked Americans as people "a little" and 32 percent "a lot" and 54 per cent were positive about the United States in general. Only 22 per cent believed that the Bush administration made the world a better place while 65 per cent thought they made it a worse place in which to live. Nearly three quarters of Britons, 72 per cent, believed American society to be "unequal" in terms of class and race, was dominated by big business and preoccupied with money. Large majorities of Britons looked down on Americans as "vulgar" (65 per cent) and "uncultured" (56 per cent) and "ignorant of the outside world" (73 per cent). "Still," the article concluded

> some individual Americans and U.S. institutions do strike a chord on this side of the pond. . . . [R]espondents take a positive view of such diverse American phenomena as Microsoft, Steven Spielberg, Tom Hanks, the Disney theme parks and television

> comedies such as *Friends* and *The Simpsons*. They take a much dimmer view—or so they say—of 4x4 recreation vehicles, McDonald's, the two Hilton sisters Paris and Nicky and, unsurprisingly, Michael Jackson.

The last question asked: "If you could, would you like to go and live in the United States?" Only 19 per cent replied that they would but 67 per cent said that they would not.[54]

Decline of Hostility

Many commentators thought that the latest wave of hostility to the American government and American society heralded a sustained period of animosity. "Any trip to Europe confirms what the surveys have been finding: The aversion to American is becoming greater, louder, more determined," Andrei S. Markovits noted in his 2007 publication *Uncouth Nation: Why Europe Dislikes America*.[55] Julia Sweig's *Friendly Fire: Losing Friends and Making Enemies in the Anti-American Century* published in 2006 suggested with deep foreboding that if the twentieth century was the American century, as publisher Henry Luce famously suggested, the twenty-first could be the anti-American century. Five years after the Twin Towers collapsed in New York City, Sweig suggested that "Anti-Americanism is going global, stretching from within America's own borders, across continents, classes, ideologies, religions, gender and generations."[56] Pessimistically, in 2009 Giacomo Chiozza examined the poll data and found

> a dim view of the American people overshadowed all other considerations in the formation of a negative view of the United States. This finding suggests that a change of U.S. executive will not be sufficient per se to alter popular attitudes towards the United States. For that to occur, views of the American people will have to improve as well.[57]

European anti-Americanism is "more likely to wax than to wane in the coming years," suggested Jesper Gulddal in his study of anti-Americanism in European literature published in 2011.[58]

Yet, those who saw this new wave of anger towards the US as something permanent or qualitatively new because it embraced all sections of British society from left to right and from young to old were shown to be mistaken as the latest wave of resentment against America quickly receded. Indeed there was less evidence of animosity toward the US government, American society and the American people in Britain after 2008 than there was even before the events of September 2001.

This latest round of hostile sentiment subsided with the removal from office of George Bush and the drawdown of the Iraq War. The election of Democrat Barack Obama in November 2008 was greeted with enthusiasm in Britain and the rest of the world. Born in Hawaii in August 1961 to a Kenyan father and white American mother, he subsequently lived in Indonesia before attending Harvard Law School and settling in Chicago where he worked as a community organizer. Obama made a rapid rise from election to the Illinois Senate in 1998, the US Senate in 2004 and then to president in 2008. Unlike his predecessor, Obama seemed articulate, intelligent and worldly. President Obama made an effort to exhibit a less aggressive and more multilateralist approach to US foreign policy. The election of the first African-American president seemed to confirm the possibilities of the United States. "The U.S. is not perfect, but I think that there is an overriding sense that you can make it if you try," Phillip Dick, a 50-year-old from Yorkshire, for example, believed. "The U.S. is the most diverse nation on earth and these days offer equality of opportunity to people irrespective of creed, colour, race or background."[59] A series of surveys undertaken by market research company GfK Roper to measure the global image of 50 countries, confirmed this positive view. In the spring of 2008, the survey found that the United States was the seventh most admired country in the world. In 2009, after the election of Obama, the United States became the most admired country, a position it maintained in the following two years.[60] The deployment of more troops to Iraq and political deals made with opponents to the occupation, all but ended the insurgency in Iraq. The United States stationed 165,000 soldiers in Iraq in 2007 which declined to less than 50,000 by 2010.[61] In December 2011, President Barack Obama removed the last troops from Iraq, bringing the war to an end.

Political changes in Britain helped to alleviate opposition to the American government too. Tony Blair resigned as prime minister in June 2007 and Gordon Brown became his successor. In April 2009, the United Kingdom ended combat operations in Iraq. Labour lost the 2010 general election and the Conservatives and Liberal Democrats formed a coalition government with Tory David Cameron as prime minister. The unpopularity of the Labour Party's close relationship with the United States meant that Cameron and the Conservatives kept their distance from their ally. "The perception that the British Government was a subservient 'poodle' to the U.S. Administration leading up to the period of the invasion of Iraq and its aftermath is widespread both among the British public and overseas," stated a report from the House of Commons Foreign Affairs Committee in March 2010. "This perception, whatever its relation to reality, is deeply damaging to the reputation and interests of the U.K." The committee recommended that the phrase "special relationship" be jettisoned. "The overuse of the phrase by some politicians and many in the media serves simultaneously to devalue its meaning and to raise unrealistic expectations about the benefits the relationship can deliver to the U.K."[62] Foreign Secretary William Hague promised that Britain would have "a solid but not slavish" relationship with the United States and Cameron's coalition partner, Liberal Democrat leader Nick Clegg, called for a reversal of "the default Atlanticism that has governed British foreign policy."[63]

At the same time, President Obama distanced himself from Britain and avoided developing a close relationship with either Gordon Brown or, initially at least, with David Cameron. Brought up in Hawaii, Obama had none of the Anglophilia of the eastern elites and, with a Kenyan father who had lived through the colonial struggle against Britain, he had little affection for Britain. During the 1950s, Britain had ruthlessly suppressed Kenya's Mau Mau rebellion, torturing many including, the president claimed, his own grandfather. George Bush had installed in the Oval Office a bust of Winston Churchill, prime minister during the early years of the

Kenyan uprising, but as soon as Obama entered the White House he returned it to the British Embassy.[64] Cameron and Obama only held the first formal meeting in July 2010 in the United States, a meeting decidedly less warm than the previous ones between Bush and Blair. Still, by the time of Cameron's next visit to the United States in March 2012, the relationship between the two men had become closer. Cameron spoke glowingly of Obama's "strength, moral authority and wisdom." Nile Gardiner, foreign policy adviser to defeated Republican challenger Mitt Romney, described the prime minister's words and actions in Washington as a "sad exercise in hero-worship before an extremely liberal White House . . . David Cameron's wholehearted support for Barack Obama has significantly harmed the image of the British Conservative Party among U.S. conservatives."[65]

However, tensions between a Conservative-controlled government in London and a Democrat-controlled White House in Washington DC remained. U S Secretary of State Hillary Clinton backed Argentina's calls for a negotiated settlement of the Falklands sovereignty question and Obama declared that America was "neutral" over the sovereignty of the islands. The Assistant Secretary of State, Philip Crowley, called the islands by the Argentinian name, the "Malvinas," further upsetting many in Britain. President Obama's aggressive criticism of BP, Britain's biggest company, in the wake of the oil spill off the coast of Florida in the summer of 2010 led to a furious backlash against the Obama administration in the conservative sections of the British press, with a growing perception across the Atlantic that the American president was anti-British.[66] "The special relationship is over," journalist Alex Singleton wrote in the *Telegraph* in March, 2010.

> We gave America years of unwavering support after September 11. And now we see how Barack Obama's administration repays us . . . . I'm normally pro-American, but Mr Obama's seeming support for Argentinian aggressors, who have no legitimate claim over the Falklands, is gratuitously offensive. So from today, I'm boycotting America as a tourist destination. This summer, I'll be going to France, not California. Let me be clear: I'm not normally in favour of boycotts, and I love the American people. I holiday in their country regularly, and hate the tedious snobby sneers against the United States. But the American people chose to elect an idiot who seems hell bent on insulting their allies, and something must be done to stop Obama's reckless foreign policy, before he does the dirty on his allies on every issue.[67]

Some on the left still feared the United States. "The phrase 'coca-colonisation' is a cliché but quite strongly describes my fears of the U.S. as a world power," Nik Skeat born in Leigh, Lancashire, in 1965, revealed.

> I feel the U.S. to be the biggest threat to world peace today, not just because of their military might, but also because of their insidious and all-pervasive media stranglehold on the world. A similar situation is slowly developing in this country, but thankfully we don't have Fox . . . .! The U.S. has become a huge influence in my world view, though sadly not in a positive way. The nation seems to emphasise all that is wrong in the world—greed, power, imperialism. Conversely, the American citizens I have met have been, on the whole, decent people who are perhaps a little too god fearing for my own taste.[68]

As long as the United States remains the bastion of free-market capitalism, and the world's most powerful nation, criticism from the left will endure.

For all of the tensions between the United States and the British government, and the ire of *Telegraph* journalists and left-wing critics, the decline of animosity to the American government and society among the general population became evident rather quickly. The Great Recession of 2008, a financial crisis and economic downturn, which originated in the United States and brought economic chaos to Britain, ignited little revulsion against the American people or government. The 1990s saw an anti-globalization movement that blamed the United States for the economic inequalities in the world but no such movement reemerged in the first decade of the twenty-first century even after the 2008 economic crisis.[69] Those, whether of the left or right, who looked for the causes of the crisis, blamed the policies of Gordon Brown and previous British governments and the practices of British banks and building societies, not the United States.[70] Merryn Somerset Webb, writing in the *Evening Standard* on January 8, 2008, expressed the prevailing view: "don't blame the states for the state we're in."[71]

A series of opinion polls confirmed that since 2008 the British view of the United States had become more positive. In 2007, a majority of Britons (57 percent), according to a BBC World Service poll, saw US influence on the world as mainly negative, while just 33 percent believed US influence was mainly positive. In 2010, the figures were 20 percent mainly negative and 52 percent positive.[72] The Pew Research Center found that in 2008, during Bush's presidency, 53 percent of Britons had a positive view of the United States, which rose to 69 percent in 2009 and fell slightly again to 60 percent in 2012.[73] In Spring 2012, Pew found that 72 percent of Britons had a favorable opinion of Americans.[74]

Decline of US Influence on Britain

Political changes on both sides of the Atlantic were not the only reason for the decline in resentment against the United States in Britain; so too was the apparent deterioration in US economic and cultural influence. American political leaders denied that the United States was weaker. "Anyone who tells you that America is in decline or that our influence has waned," said President Obama in his 2012 State of the Union address, "doesn't know what they're talking about." Most commentators who declared that American decline was a myth could point to the continued military and economic strength of the United States. The United States still enjoyed military dominance in the post–Cold War era, especially in the wake of September 11, 2001, and deployed thousands of troops in hundreds of military bases across the globe. Economically, the United States remained the largest economy in the world and the largest investor in the United Kingdom.

For all of its strengths, however, American influence on Britain and the rest of the world, economically, culturally and politically, began to diminish at the beginning of the twenty-first century. The United States may have unleashed globalization but it became clear that globalization was not Americanization and that other countries had benefitted more than the United States from globalization.[75]

In 2008, a US National Intelligence Council report, *Global Trends 2025*, noted that "the transfer of global wealth and economic power now under way, roughly from West to East" was "without precedent in modern history," and was the primary factor in the decline of the "United States' relative strength—even in the military realm." Because of the Iraq War, the United States was more reticent to engage in military action abroad. Many American corporations had been unable to succeed in the increasingly competitive world economy. Corporations from other countries took advantage of free trade and globalization by selling goods made by cheaper labor. In 1969, there were just over 7,200 transnational companies in the world, with 60 percent of them headquartered in the United States. By 2000, there were 63,000 but fewer than 30 percent now had their headquarters in the United States.[76] Many iconic American companies had been bought by emerging-market investors and companies. Chinese company Lenovo purchased IBM's PC business for US$1.75 billion in 2005. Chinese Dalian Wanda Group bought AMC Entertainment, America's second largest cinema chain, for US$2.6 billion in 2012. 3G Capital Management, a Brazilian private equity firm, secured a majority stake in Burger King in 2010 and in H. J. Heinz in 2013. In 2008, Belgian-Brazilian brewer InBev acquired Anheuser-Busch, maker of Budweiser beer, while the other major American beer company, Miller, was owned by a South African company based in London.[77]

China and India were not America's equal, and both remained very poor countries compared to the United States, but they had made major economic strides. Foreign companies established factories in China to take advantage of the cheaper labor costs while India became an outsourcing destination for white-collar work. While employment in the manufacturing sector fell from 17.2 million in 2000 to 11.5 million in 2010 in the United States, China saw its manufacturing workforce rise from 95 million to 130 million in the same period.[78] In 2012, China became the world's largest trading nation for the first time. Combined US exports and imports totaled US$3.82 trillion, while China's amounted to US$3.87 trillion.[79] In the third quarter of 2012, the Chinese company Lenovo became the world's biggest seller of personal computers, beating American giants HP and Dell.[80] The United States may not necessarily be in decline but, as journalist Fareed Zakaria suggested in his book *The Post-American World* (2008), China, India and others were catching up with the United States economically.[81]

The Great Recession of 2008 added to America's economic problems. The collapse of the housing market in the United States in 2007 triggered the worst economic crisis since the Great Depression of the 1930s. Banks began to close as their income dried up. The collapse of Lehman Brothers, the fourth largest investment bank in the United States, precipitated the Stock Market crash of September 2008. The US Stock Market peaked in October 2007, when the Dow Jones Industrial Average index exceeded 14,000 points and plummeted to a trough of around 6,600 in March 2009. To restore solvency, the US government bailed out some of the largest banks and investors, including the leading insurance company AIG, the Citigroup bank, and the two largest mortgage companies Fannie Mae and Freddie Mac, by offering credit to the tune of billions of dollars. Millions saw their savings and pensions wiped out while the unavailability of credit for companies brought job losses and bankruptcies.[82] These bailouts together with the wars in Afghanistan and Iraq and tax cuts undertaken by the Bush administration led to an exploding federal debt, which the United States served by borrowing heavily from China.

Deteriorating infrastructure and a decline in innovation added to the country's economic problems. In September 2012, the World Economic Forum published its global competitiveness report. With the rankings based on criteria such as infrastructure, education and public services, Switzerland came in first place followed by Singapore and Finland. The United States experienced a dramatic decline with its rankings falling four years in a row to reach a low of seventh.[83] America may also be losing its dominance in the sciences and research. The United States was spending less on research and development as a percentage of GDP and was falling behind countries like Israel and Finland that spend far more.[84] In 2011, the United States still dominated international patent filings. However, Patent Cooperation Treaty (PCT) applications (an international agreement for filing patent applications) from China more than trebled from 5,455 to 16,406 between 2007 and 2011, Japan's rose from 27,743 to 38,888, Germany's grew from 17,821 to 18,568 while the United States' saw a decline from 54,042 to 48,596.[85]

A decaying infrastructure, a growing disparity of wealth, manufacturing jobs moving abroad, unemployment rising to over 8 percent in 2010 and falling real wages since the 1970s meant that America in the twentieth-first century looked a far different place than it had looked to Britons in the 1950s. In 2008, 44 percent of Britons believed that the United States was the world's leading economic power. By spring 2012, the figure had fallen to 28 percent. In 2008, 29 percent of Britons thought that China was the world's leading economic power but by spring 2012, the number had risen to 58 percent.[86]

For years, the supremacy of the United States inspired both adulation and resentment but, because of this perceived decline in power and prestige, the US government and American society was no longer as greatly admired or as greatly disliked in Britain as it was in earlier decades. In previous years, the United States evoked a depth of emotion, whether positive or negative, that was simply not found in the second decade of the twenty-first century. "The world is moving from anger to indifference, from anti-Americanism to post-Americanism," journalist Fareed Zakaria declared.[87] "Europe can't even be bothered to hate America anymore," observed Howard Fineman *Newsweek*'s Washington Correspondent.

> And when you read about America in European newspapers, what you are likely to find is a tone bordering on pity. The United States is depicted as a fraying empire of obesity, ignorance, debt, gridlock, stagnation, and mindless war. Sure, the iPad is cool, but it is evidence of what America was, not what it will be again. The stories are not angry, accusatory, or even ideological. It's worse: they are condescendingly elegiac . . . America is no longer admired, imitated, or feared. We remain—for now—a safe haven for dollars (of which there are too many in the world). But we increasingly are seen less as a model or as an empire than as a cautionary tale of national neglect and decline.[88]

Politicians and much of the press hailed the 'special relationship' but many ordinary people believed the relationship to be of less importance. Interest in the

United States had declined and the faltering giant across the Atlantic was no longer as relevant to their lives.[89] While Britons in the 1950s marveled at American glamour, wealth and inventiveness, now they pitied its decay. "Every time I come back to the United States, the airports, the roads, the public spaces look to me more tattered, battered, old-fashioned," journalist Timothy Garton Ash suggested. "Modernity is no longer self-evidently here. After a long sojourn in the west, it may be moving back to Asia. There are still fantastic examples of technological, commercial and design innovation in the US—think iPad—but they are islands of modernity in a torpid sea."[90]

The United States was no longer the favored destination for British immigrants, which reflected the relative economic decline of the United States. A Pew survey undertaken in 2005 found that Britons no longer saw the United States as the land of opportunity as most, 31 percent, chose Australia as the place they would recommend young people to emigrate to.[91] In May 2010, a survey of 1,029 Britons discovered that an astonishing three-quarters of those polled wanted to emigrate. The survey found Australia to be the most favored destination, with a third of those polled saying they had considered moving down under.[92] In November 2012, another survey revealed that an even more astonishing 88 percent of Britons were dissatisfied with life in Britain and would consider moving abroad. The most favored destinations were the English-speaking nations, which had a similar culture and close ties with the United Kingdom, with Australia taking 15 percent of the vote and the United States 13 percent. Spain, which is the Britons' most popular holiday destination, finished above the United States in second place with 14 percent of the vote.[93]

If the United States had experienced a decline in economic power, it had equally seen a decline in cultural influence. American movies remained a major part of British entertainment but Hollywood was no longer a predominantly American concern and offered less of a window into American society. Since the late 1980s, Hollywood became a global entity with studios owned by French, Japanese, Canadian and Australian companies.[94] Hollywood films were no longer geared to the tastes of an American audience but to an international one. American films employed international directors, actors, writers and production staff and were filmed in studios and locations around the world using the history and literature of foreign countries as the basis of their stories. The hugely successful *The Lord of the Rings* trilogy: *The Fellowship of the Ring* (2001), *The Two Towers* (2002) and *The Return of the King* (2003), were based on the stories of Englishman J. R. R. Tolkien, directed by New Zealander Peter Jackson and filmed in New Zealand. Harry Potter was based on a series of British books, filmed in Britain and starred mostly British actors.[95] The Bourne series of movies: *The Bourne Identity* (2002), *The Bourne Supremacy* (2004), and *The Bourne Ultimatum* (2007), and Big Academy Award winners of recent years including *Slumdog Millionaire* (2008), *The King's Speech* (2010) and *The Artist* (2011)—all used exotic foreign locations. Woody Allen, who made films in the 1970s and 1980s that lovingly portrayed New York City, the city of his birth, set his more recent films in London, Barcelona, Paris and Rome. "The typical 'Hollywood' blockbuster in this era was something like

Fox's *X-Men* (2000), based on a comic book," author William Marling suggested in 2006.

> It starred an Australian (Hugh Jackman), a couple of Brits (Ian McKellen, Patrick Stewart), and some exotic Americans (Halle Berry, Rebecca Romijn-Stamos). It was filmed in Canada. Seven production companies were involved, four of them American. There were eleven distributors, nine of them subsidiaries of Australia's Fox empire that dealt with the French, Spanish, Japanese, German Italian, and Portuguese markets. Fifteen US special-effects companies were employed, but they outsourced work to Taiwan, Spain, Mexico, and the Philippines.[96]

Hollywood celebrities had also been upstaged by stars from other countries. Australian singer Kylie Minogue was voted Britain's Best Loved Celebrity in a poll in 2007. The Irish television presenter Terry Wogan came in second. The other celebrities on the list, Bruce Forsyth, Michael Parkinson and Dawn French, were all British.[97] Football players from around the world had become more popular than Hollywood stars. Argentinian Lionel Messi starring for Barcelona in Spain and Christiano Ronaldo from Portugal playing for Spanish side Real Madrid were household names in Britain. International football games and British soap operas gained higher television ratings than any American import.[98]

Further evidence of a waning US cultural influence was found in music. The twenty-first century saw the decline of white American guitar-based rock music that had emerged so dramatically in the 1950s. Like the other great American genres of music, blues and jazz before them, rock music had had its heyday. In the 1960s and 1970s, rock music became an art form with musicians producing some of the most innovative and enduring albums in any field of music. Since the 1990s, few new bands and no new genres of rock emerged to compete with established musicians of the 1960s and 1970s. The United Kingdom's top 100 best-selling songs of 2010 featured only three rock acts, the lowest level in half a century. One of the three was "Don't Stop Believin'," a 30-year-old track from the veteran rock act Journey.[99] In November 1952, when the *New Musical Express* published the first singles chart in the United Kingdom, 10 of the 15 singles in the chart were by American acts while five were British. Sixty years later, on November 17, 2012, the top 15 singles chart consisted of only two American acts, nine British ones and artists from Sweden, Korea, Barbados and Albania.[100] Young people who wanted to listen to innovative rock music and older people who wanted to relive their youth, turned to established classic rock bands. To meet the demand produced by the dearth of new talent, icons of the 1960s and 1970s reformed and played their classic songs in concerts that celebrated nostalgia. Without any new material in years or with weakly selling albums, the so-called heritage artists performed in sold-out arenas to fans who wanted to see them before they retired or died. The three highest grossing tours of 2012 were Madonna, Bruce Springsteen and the E Street Band and Roger Waters, formerly of Pink Floyd. The fourth was "Michael Jackson the Immortal World Tour," a production by Cirque Du Soleil of the music of Michael Jackson, who had died in June 2009.[101]

While rock music faded, electronic dance music became the dominant music of the early twenty-first century. Tracing its evolution back to the European rave music of the 1980s and 1990s, electronic dance music utilized drum machines, synthesizers and samples rather than electric guitars and incorporated influences from all over the world. The music travelled around the globe by the Internet, by social media like Facebook, Twitter and YouTube, and by DJs playing at festivals and on global tours. "Social media is connecting people globally, and making the old barriers between styles of music irrelevant," Flux Pavilion, a British producer, noted. "Anyone, anywhere in the world can make a tune in their bedroom and get it to thousands of people right away," Pavilion stated.[102] American artists such as Black Eyed Peas, Nicki Minaj, Jennifer Lopez and Lady Gaga were more inspired by electronic dance music than by American rock music. Matthew Adell, chief executive of the digital music store Beatport, suggested that the dance music industry, not just the music, has now gone global. "It's becoming less localized, it's becoming more mobile, and it's becoming more global in terms of people accepting art and commerce and communication from other parts of the planet."[103]

The increasing non-American influence on Britain was also evident in football. At the beginning of the 2012–2013 season, five of the 20 Premier League football clubs were completely in the hand of foreign, non-American, owners: Chelsea by a Russian oil billionaire, Fulham by an Egyptian businessman, Queens Park Rangers by a Malaysian entrepreneur, Southampton by a German-Swiss family and Manchester City by the Abu Dhabi United Group. In addition, a Russian company owned 51 percent of Reading and both Swansea City and West Ham United were part owned by foreign investors. Seven clubs were owned by UK nationals and five by Americans.[104] The Manchester City team that won the English Premier League title on May 13, 2012, included only three English players in their starting lineup but three from Argentina, two from France, a Spaniard, a Belgian and a player from the Ivory Coast. The three substitutes that came on to the pitch during the game came from Bosnia, Holland and Italy and the manager of the triumphant team was Italian.[105]

The eating and drinking establishments of Britain reflected this global influence. The traditional English pub was in decline, replaced by gastropubs, gentle places that sell Thai food and coffee as much as beer. Those drinking at home were no longer buying traditional British ale. In November 2005, the best selling beer in the United Kingdom was Carling, a Canadian beer, followed by Foster's Lager from Australia, Belgium's Stella Artois and Denmark's Carlsberg.[106] "Britons have cut back on many of the essentials of life in the recession, but one thing they won't scrimp on is pricey imported lager," *The Times* reported in May 2012. The total beer market in Britain was down 4 percent in the previous year, but imported beers such as Stella and Heineken saw their sales grow by 7 percent. More expensive European lagers, such as Peroni, Pilsner Urquell and Kozel, saw theirs increase by more than 10 percent at the same time.[107] Traditional fish and chip and pie and mash shops have been replaced by food establishments selling food from all over the world. On the eve of World War II, there were 30,000 fish and chip shops in Britain but by the end of the twentieth century this was down to 8,500. In the

1940s, London had 130 pie and mash shops but only a handful remained by the end of the century.[108] The trend was not confined to London. In November 2010, one student observed that

> even here in Edinburgh you cannot escape the multiculturalism as you walk down the street: Latin Bars, Authentic Italian Restaurants, Chinese Supermarkets, Carribbean Jewellery Street Stalls, Indian fashion stores. In my school, we were taught the Standard French/German, but also optionally taught Polish, Mandarin or Spanish because of its use in modern multicultural society.[109]

This worldwide influence was also evident in the economic investment in Britain. None of the ten largest takeovers of UK companies between 2000 and 2009 was by American companies. The largest was Spain's Telefonica purchase of UK mobile phone company O2 for £18bn in 2005.[110] In December 2006, *The Times of India* announced that India had become the second biggest investor in London after the United States. "London attracts over half of all Indian investment into Europe and provides Indian businesses with a gateway to the continent," Michael Charlton, chief executive of Think London, an organization that seeks to attract business investment in the capital, revealed. Indian company Tata Group bought steelmaker Corus for 4.3 billion pounds in 2006, Tetley Tea for 270 million pounds in 2000, Tyco Global Network for 69 million pounds in 2004 and Incat International, a British software company, for 53 million pounds in 2005. Apeejay International took over the tea company Typhoo for 80 million pounds in 2005.[111] By 2012, the Chinese had acquired a number of well-known British companies and services including Weetabix, Thames Water, Britain's biggest water company, Northumbria Water, Felixstowe port, Birmingham City Football Club and MG Rover cars.[112]

While the 1990s was dominated by stories of American cultural and economic dominance of Britain, the twenty-first century saw increased concern about the influence of the rest of the world on Britain. "Just for a moment, imagine being a tourist in search of the full British experience. Where would you start?" Alex Brummer, author of *Britain for Sale: British Companies in Foreign Hands,* asked.

> Well, you might take a sight-seeing trip around London on a red double-decker bus. You'd possibly visit a quintessentially British store, such as Boots the chemist, Selfridges or Harrods, before having a proper English tea at the Savoy, Fortnum & Mason or the Dorchester. You'd almost certainly go home, via a British airport, thinking you'd seen a slice of the real Britain. But, in one sense at least, you'd be totally wrong. That bus you boarded at Trafalgar Square is run by a German company. Boots fell to the Italians in 2007. Selfridges, Fortnum & Mason and the Savoy are owned by Canadians; Harrods has been bought by a firm based in Qatar; the Dorchester by one based in Brunei. As for our airports, most of them are now run by a Spanish firm,

Brummer irately reported. In 2012, foreign companies controlled 39 per cent of UK patents, far more than the percentage of foreign-owned patents in the United States (11.8 percent), Japan (3.7 percent) or even the European Union as a whole

(13.7 percent). "It won't be long before we're all working for foreign companies," Brummer depressingly concluded.[113]

Of course, America still influenced Britain. Trick or treating, fancy dress and pumpkins at Halloween became the latest American traditions imported into Britain. "Once a strange little footnote in the calendar when you might indulge in a ghost story or bob for apples Halloween is now a vast juggernaut of a national festival and a celebration of all things murderous, frightening and unpleasant," Flic Everett of the *Daily Express* insisted.[114] Many British schools started to organize American-style proms and school reunions, seen on American movies and TV programs. Because of the rise in popularity of 'prom' parties in UK schools, menswear retailer Moss Bros saw a double-digit rise in sales in 2011.[115] Many welcomed the influence of US culture on Britain. Television presenter Dawn Porter, who had lived and worked on both sides of the Atlantic, thought they were a good thing. "Baby showers, wedding rehearsals and Halloween parties are commonplace in America and I've definitely seen an increase in these among my family and friends since I've been back living in the UK," she noted in July 2012.[116] "I agree with Vanessa Feltz about the delights of high school proms," Isabelle North of Milton Keynes, Buckinghamshire, suggested.

> Like her, when I left school it was all very low key with no parties or any kind of celebration. In fact, it could have been the last day of any ordinary term. When my own son left school a couple of years ago, he and his pals had a real ball with all the usual prom trimmings like a stretch limo, tail suits and girls in fantastic evening dresses. The photos taken that night are a lasting reminder for him of his friends and the end of his schooldays and the whole affair was worth every penny.[117]

British politicians still looked to the United States for inspiration. Conservative leader Duncan Smith, leader of the Conservative Party from September 2001 to October 2003, wanted to mimic the "compassionate conservatism" of George W. Bush. At Smith's urging, in 2002 the Conservative Party Conference held debates on "helping the vulnerable" and "public services first."[118] In the British general election of May 2010, Conservative candidate David Cameron invoked President Kennedy's 1961 inauguration speech when he presented the Conservative manifesto, declaring: "As a great American President once said: 'Ask not what your country can do for you—ask what you can do for your country.'"[119] In the campaign, Cameron used words like "Change" and phrases like "Yes we can" previously popularized by US president Barack Obama. Both Labour and the Conservatives were so impressed by President Obama's victorious campaign that they hired some of his advisors.[120]

The United States Became More Knowable

Not only was the United States economically and culturally weakened during the opening decade of the twenty-first century, it also become more knowable and less mythical in the British imagination. In the immediate prewar years, few travelled across the Atlantic and most British views of the United States derived from

Hollywood movies. In the first decade of the new century, however, more people than ever traveled across the Atlantic. According to the 2000 US Census, 824,239 residents of the United States had been born in the United Kingdom. From 2000 to 2009, 171, 979 inhabitants of the United Kingdom obtained permanent resident status in the United States. With the growing ease of transatlantic travel, many Britons journeyed back and forth across the Atlantic for business and for leisure. In 2008, 5,480,917 Britons visited the United States.[121] In 1993, 6,205 UK students entered the United States, which rose to 16,502 in 2002.[122] By 2002, 40 percent of Britons had visited the United States.[123] The 2011 census showed that 177,000 people born in the United States were living in England and Wales, up from 144,000 in 2001.[124] In 2011, 16,185 Americans studied in the United Kingdom, the largest number of American students in any country.[125] In 2012, 2,840,000 Americans visited Britain.[126]

Not only travel but also innovations in computer technology had opened a wider window into the United States than was available in previous decades. In 2010, 77 percent of British homes owned a home computer, up from 72 per cent in 2008.[127] The growth of web-enabled cell phones and tablets like the iPad allowed even more people to have access to the Internet. The development of Web 2.0 technologies such as blogs, wikis and social networking sites promoted the sharing of information, interactivity and collaboration around the world. Web 1.0 consisted of websites with provider-generated content suitable for browsing and reading while Web 2.0 introduced user-generated material, which allowed mass participation in the production of content. Facebook, launched in 2004 for users to share information online, including photographs and videos, grew to dominate social networking. By October 2012, Facebook had a billion users, half the world's Internet population.[128] YouTube, which let people upload and share videos on the Internet, became one of the most popular areas of the web as movies, television programs and music videos vied with amateur films for global attention. Twitter, a microblogging service launched in 2006, enabled its users to send and read posts of up to 140 characters. By May 2012, Twitter had 10 million active users in the United Kingdom and 140 million worldwide.[129] The web cam, Skype and web conferencing software permitted people to view each other across the globe and conduct personal and business communication. Massive Open Online Courses (MOOCs) offered by companions like Coursera, Udacity, and edX joined nearly 5 million students across the world as they communicated on Facebook, Skype, Twitter and online discussion boards.[130]

Before the Internet, Britons depended on a few elite British newspapers or television news programs for information about the United States, now they enjoyed access to a greater variety of online sources for news. Much of the information can be derived directly from the United States: American newspapers, news outlets and websites. Blogs meant that news and opinion was no longer concentrated in the hands of a few big media companies. The views of an amateur blogger in Chicago were as easily accessible as the opinions of journalists at *The Times* or *The Guardian* newspapers in Britain. People in Britain and the United States communicate with similar interests in online chat rooms and on blogs. Teenagers in London discuss music with peers in California and New York and football enthusiasts in

Chicago communicate with other football lovers in Manchester. Americans leave comments on British blogs or newspaper articles while Britons do the same on US outlets. The downloading of American books, magazines, films and music offers similarly increased access to the United States. People in small towns or in rural areas, who previously had limited access to physical stores with their small inventory, now had a boundless supply of media available at their fingertips and a far greater access to America.

The global connectedness of Britain and America has led more Britons to develop views of the United States based on personal experience rather than Hollywood myths. Some, such as former Railway mechanic Ray Johnston, born in Birkenhead near Liverpool in 1944, found his positive view of the United States confirmed by visits across the Atlantic. Johnston had a long-held admiration for the United States.

> Why? Because no matter where there might be problem, earthquakes, starvation, flood or any other sort of disaster the USA and the UK are usually first there with aid. Let me add that in World War 2 the UK and the rest of Europe would have been lost without the USA intervention and never let anyone tell you differently.

Visits to the United States added to this positive view.

> Two years ago we went over to the eastern seaboard on a cruise: New York, Boston, Rhode Island and many other stops. It was wonderful. The people were so friendly, just as I recalled on my first trip there in '68. In '68 I thought how nice people were and in 2011 I discovered that not only were they so nice but they were even better in every way. I loved it![131]

Patricia McManus from North London also gained positive views from contact with Americans.

> When I was very young, I thought America was a very scary place but somewhat intriguing. I wasn't sure if I would ever want to visit America, nevertheless I was very curious. In 1979, I accepted a job working for American lawyers to The First National Bank of Boston based in London. Working for these lawyers helped re-shape my views on America. They were really lovely people to work for and were very generous, kind and fun employers. Naturally, they liked to talk about America, their homes and families. They impressed me with their patriotism and how, to them, America was the best country in the world. They also shared some of their experiences in the Vietnam War with us and expressed how it was a struggle for them to cope with normal life afterwards, but for them fighting for America was an honour. They persuaded me that America was definitely a place to visit; they were, of course, right![132]

Others have had their negative views of American society confirmed by personal experience. "In the last 20 years I have visited various parts of America," noted accountant Brian O'Sullivan from London.

> The impression I have formed is that it is a country of huge inequality and it is also still quite insular. Culturally it continues to be highly creative. My own views have

> been further shaped by working for an American bank in London for five years. There seemed to be a constant dilemma between so-called work/life balance and the demands of the job. There was an expectation of being on-call most of the time, including holidays and weekends. Junior employees were worked very hard with the promises of promotion and bonuses, which was not always fulfilled. The rewards escalated by seniority, but there was little job security. This experience reinforced by views that America has a quite divisive and money driven culture.[133]

Some Britons changed their views of the United States and of Americans because they travelled to the United States. Mike Penny, born in Nelson in the northwest of England in 1943, first visited the United States in 1978 and had subsequently been a regular visitor to the country and a keen admirer of American music and film.

> It is certainly the case that my view of the States has changed with familiarity. I went there with a certain European snobbishness in the 1970s, I now recognise it as a country of interest and achievement and love going. Whether the USA has contributed to any change in my attitudes I doubt but changes in my attitudes have probably influenced my view of the USA.[134]

Others had their opinions changed because of the Americans they met. "I had a very negative attitude to America and most things American up until I met my first real-life American, my now wife!" Gareth Rowlands born in Glanamman, Wales in 1962, revealed.

> If anyone had told me I'd end up coming to the U.S. and making my life here, I'd have laughed in their face. It was only being exposed to "ordinary" Americans that I realized that the stereotypes we were fed from my childhood onwards were simply that: both the good and the bad failed to truly represent the amazing diversity, genuineness and childishness of "real" America.[135]

The interconnections between the two countries together with the political changes in the United States may have lessened some of the prejudices against America and Americans. Sarah Wollaston, Conservative MP for Totnes, believed that Britons now

> really do feel like the Americans are family. It's not just that Main Street USA beams into our living rooms every evening; many of us have deeper links. One of my closest friends is American and her children have grown up with dual nationality in Britain. My nieces are U.S. citizens having been brought up in the States.[136]

Online communications may also have altered preconceptions. "I'm 25, and the new generation of Brits are MUCH more friendly than our older generation," a young Briton observed in June, 2012.

> We have much better access to information and connection with our friends overseas where as our parents didn't. So . . . . we understand that the Stereotypical Image of an

> American is actually not real, and most Americans I have met have been friendly, great fun to get drunk with and sing all the way home with.[137]

The United States still evokes a variety of opinions, often simultaneously, within the same person. "Because of the Vietnam War I became a peace and anti-nuclear protestor and these ideas still prevail," Liz Fiorani from Kent stated. "I became involved in supporting actions in Latin America through the church because of American interference in the politics of these countries including Cuba." But she had "at the moment no real hostility, a degree of admiration on the election of Obama. Some despair at the ingrained anti-socialist mindset of middle America, yet a degree of admiration for their self-reliance in hard times," she concluded.[138] "I admire some things, am appalled by others and indifferent about a lot too," Mike Penny declared. "If I had to choose one word" to describe my view of America,

> it would be interesting. And in the process I would also want to point out that the interest owes a lot to heterogeneity and difference. This is a complex society with regional, class and ethnic complexities that produce cultures rather than culture. It is also a wealthy country which has helped produce and sustain not simply commercial and business success but also an interesting intelligentsia and a veneer of high culture and academic success which stands comparison with anywhere in the world. All of this sits alongside degrees of disadvantage and inequality, manifest discrimination and levels of crime and violence which raise hackles.[139]

Peter O'Neill, from York, expressed the same ambiguity toward the United States.

> I am often bemused by the blatant in-equalities in American society. A country that sends its young men and women off to foreign shores defending the rights of oppressed peoples but will allow its own citizens to die because of lack of medical care. Why there is so much objection to Obama's medical reforms is a mystery to the world not just me. The hallmark of a civilized society is how it protects the vulnerable in its midst. The perception is that America is not quite there yet. Also, this hate obsession and paranoia with anything associated with socialism holds it back in accepting social change. After saying this I am still protective of America and believe it has been a land of opportunity for millions of people. It is not perfect but what nation is. I think America leads the world in research and technology with some of its universities world leaders of innovation. America pricked my imagination with its Apollo programme and since the 60s I have had a keen interest in space the 'final frontier'.[140]

For all of the misgivings of O'Neill and others, it is clear that the United States was more appealing to most Britons under the Obama administration than it was during the years of the George W. Bush presidency. The military and diplomatic response of President George W. Bush and Prime Minister Tony Blair to the terrorist attacks of September 11, 2001, unleashed an unprecedented wave of hostility toward the foreign policy of the Bush administration, which amplified existing animosity toward US cultural influence on Britain and prejudices against American people. This resentment against the United States declined rather quickly as George Bush and Tony Blair left office and the War in Iraq drew to a close. In place of hostility, British people showed greater indifference to the United States than they had at any time since World War II. It is not that the US was no longer liked or admired in the United Kingdom, but that people cared less than previously about what was coming from the United States. America did not have the same cultural or economic impact in the twenty-first century as it did in the 1950s. On the one hand, the United States exacted less economic, political and cultural sway on Britain and in turn Britain, more than ever, had become a site of international, not just American, influences. On the other hand, immigration, international travel, a global media and computer-generated communications made the United States less of a mythical land and Americans less of a mythical people. Prejudice against Americans still existed in 2013, as it did against other nations, and many British people disliked or admired aspects of American society, popular culture, or US foreign policy, but America no longer took up so much space in the British imagination.

Conclusion

Since the end of World War II, ideas and innovations emanating from the United States of America have shaped the lives of Britons to an unprecedented extent. The strength of the US economy, the American government's support for free trade and the quality of US corporate products and sales strategies were the driving force behind the export of American commodities and culture across the Atlantic. Innovations in technology such as cinema, radio, record players, television, transistor radios, video recorders, compact disc players and eventually computers transmitted American culture into Britain. In turn, a receptive British public, enjoying higher living standards and exhibiting a fascination with the giant across the Atlantic, drove up the demand for American products.

The British may have been inundated with American imports, but they did not adopt everything uncritically and wholeheartedly from America. Many British institutions and traditions have endured. The stability of the Royal Family and the continuity of the British parliamentary system are remarkable. Traditional British sports of football, rugby and cricket and the state-sponsored BBC and NHS have survived and prospered despite the barrage of American influences. A myriad of local customs and national traditions have remained virtually intact, including driving on the left-hand side of the road and drinking tea, the celebration of Guy Fawkes Night and Hogmanay and the rich pub culture found throughout the British Isles. British comedy from *The Goon Show* to *Monty Python,* from *Blackadder* to *The Office* has been little affected by the United States. The British have taken inspiration from the United States but have also adopted political ideas from Europe and religious practices from Asia. South Asian and Caribbean immigrants, the European Union and the forces of globalization brought changes to popular culture, political ideals and business practices in Britain. Britons adopted some aspects of American culture and blended it with indigenous traditions and innovations from elsewhere. Teddy Boys wore Edwardian jackets, Mods adopted Italian scooters and cloths and the dance scene of the 1980s and 1990s embraced Eurodisco sounds. Modern Britain betrays a strong American influence but the addition of these other global forces has produced a Britain in the twenty-first century that is far more than a replica of the United States of America.

For all of the British traditions that endure, however, it is clear that American influence on Britain has been extensive and transformative. American musicians, poets, playwrights, scientists, politicians, artists and architects have left their mark on British society. Immediately before and after World War II, Britons welcomed Hollywood movies, jazz music and new energetic dances originating across the Atlantic. In the 1950s, American rock 'n' roll music, clothes, food, imported TV programs and literature influenced the life styles and values of the young in Britain while American methods of production and consumption changed the British workplace, the home and the high street. A British thoroughfare, once full of locally owned butchers, fishmongers, newsagents, fish and chip shops, bookshops, greengrocers and pubs was, by the 1990s, populated with American-style supermarkets, fast-food chains, and American clothing outlets. American ideas of identity politics influenced political movements in Britain in the 1960s and 1970s while British politicians eagerly embraced American economic ideas and social policy in the 1980s and 1990s. The British parliamentary system may have lasted but the major political parties have adopted policies and ideas of presentation from the United States. The state-sponsored BBC and NHS had to embrace ideas imported from the United States while in April 2011 Arsenal became the fifth of the 20 English Premier League football clubs, along with Manchester United, Liverpool, Aston Villa and Sunderland, to be owned by American businessmen.[1] In the twenty-first century, the innovations of Bill Gates, Steve Jobs and other computer entrepreneurs transformed communications and connected Britain to the world like never before.

Britons created their own mythical image of US society, but they did not share a single vision of the United States. British people constructed their images of the United States with the help of journalists, novelists, musicians and filmmakers but their view of the US was guided by their social backgrounds and their existing beliefs. Class, generational cohort and political persuasion, and to a lesser extent ethnicity, race and gender, generated differing interpretations of America. Because of economic austerity and the cultural conservatism of postwar Britain, young people, in particular, expressed discontent with traditional British social and cultural values and looked to the United States for inspiration. Women enjoyed the benefits of American modernity and saw positive role models on TV and in movies while the sons and daughters of black immigrants, alienated from British society, looked for heroes in the United States. The US provided the British with a critique of established norms and values and offered an alternative vision based on modernity, informality, consumerism and individualism. Some migrated to the United States, others adopted the clothes, demeanor and lifestyle of Americans they saw on screen and others still used either individual or collective effort to improve their economic position.

While British workers drew inspiration from the United States, the upper classes, middles-class intellectuals and partisans of the left and right, held negative opinions of US foreign policy, American economic and cultural influence on Britain, US society and the American people. The left criticized the US government for its willingness to use its military might on behalf of business interests in pursuit of the Cold War, American popular cultural exports for subduing class solidarity in Britain and American society for its free-market capitalism and racial and economic inequality. For conservatives, the upper classes and middle-class intellectuals, uncultured and materialistic Americans created an uncivilized society and with its tawdry cultural exports threatened Britain's elite cultural traditions. In the immediate postwar years, opposition to American cultural imports became a reflection of the anxiety felt most strongly by the middle and upper classes at the decline of Britain as a world power.

British views of the United States were far from static and have fluctuated over time partly due to events in America and partly due to changes in British society. While disaffection with British society made the United States look a superior alternative in the 1950s, an economically and culturally buoyant Britain helped the United States appear less inspiring in the 1960s and 1970s. Some Britons expressed dismay at American policy in Vietnam and the racially polarized nature of the United States but most criticism was directed at what seemed like the increasingly violent nature of society portrayed in Hollywood movies and in imported TV programs. In the 1980s, more and more Britons voiced criticisms of the nuclear brinkmanship of the US government and the serious social problems of American society, which many feared were coming to Britain with the help of a pro-American prime minister. National humiliation at being subservient to the United States, evident by American influence on British politics and society, ignited resentment against America in the 1990s, which would be repeated in response to Tony Blair's subservience to George W. Bush in the aftermath of September 11, 2001. The foreign policies of the George Bush government and the apparent difference in social values between the two countries helped to ignite hostility to the United States in the early years of the twenty-first century. Soon, however, this hostility was replaced by a growing indifference to American society and its people.

Probably the most important change that the United States brought to Britain was channeled through the two major political parties in Britain, Labour and the Conservatives. In the 1950s, the ideas of social democracy, partly derived from liberal influences in the United States, became the guiding ideology of the Labour Party while Bill Clinton and the Democrats became a formative influence on New Labour. British Conservatives were the section of society that changed its view of the United States the most. Previously, most Conservatives had seen America as a cultural wasteland and showed resentment toward America's rise to global dominance. But by the 1970s a new generation of Conservatives emerged who were far more appreciative of US society. The Labour Party's attempts to build a New Jerusalem in postwar Britain with extensive nationalization and a comprehensive welfare system made many Conservatives envious of the enterprise and free-market economy found in the United States. Margaret Thatcher, an early lover of American music and movies and an admirer of the US economy, privatized large sectors of British industry, weakened the welfare state, deregulated business and introduced a low-wage flexible labor market.

Britain in the twenty-first century is a different place than it was in the immediate postwar years and Britons have different concerns partly because of American influence. In the 1950s, Britain was a racially homogeneous isolated island cut off from Europe and with its focus firmly fixed on the United States. Slowly this changed with immigration, the development of the European Union, the growth of computer technology and digital communication, foreign travel and economic globalization, which made the United States vie with other countries to influence

Britain. When the Cold War ended, Britain had less need of American military support and the special relationship became less vital, which makes Tony Blair's close relationship with George Bush even harder to comprehend. Britons increasingly moved from a rather narrow view of the world, focusing on Britain and the United States, to a global view that brought influences from a much wider number of countries. As a result, prejudice against Americans still existed after George W. Bush left office and many British denounced aspects of American society, popular culture, and foreign policy but America no longer fueled the British imagination like it had in previous years.

This global interaction meant that in the twenty-first century, Britons imagined America in a different way than they did in earlier decades. The United States became more knowable through increased travel and the development of computer and digital technology, which revolutionized communications between the two countries. The United States no longer held the economic supremacy it enjoyed in previous decades or exerted the same cultural or political influence on Britain or the world. As long as the United States remains a major economic and political force in the world, however, American technology, movies, music, politics and television will continue to influence Britain and Britain's fascination with the giant across the Atlantic will continue. The extent of that fascination, and the way the United States is imagined in Britain, both positive and negative, will depend on developments in both the United States and Britain.

Notes

Introduction

1. *Tribune*, December 3, 1943, in Paul Anderson ed. *Orwell in Tribune* (London: Politico's, 2006), 57.
2. Margaret Tapster, WW2 People's War, an online archive of wartime memories contributed by members of the public and gathered by the BBC. The archive can be found at bbc.co.uk/ww2peopleswar. http://www.bbc.co.uk/history/ww2peopleswar/stories/65/a5827665.shtml Accessed May 30, 2013.
3. Paul Addison, *No Turning Back: The Peacetime Revolutions of Post-War Britain* (Oxford and New York: Oxford University Press, 2010); Peter Hennessy, *Having It So Good: Britain in the Fifties* (London: Allen Lane, 2006); David Kynaston *Austerity Britain, 1945–51* (London, Berlin and New York: Bloomsbury, 2007); David Kynaston, *Family Britain, 1951–1957* (London, Berlin, New York: Bloomsbury, 2009); Mark Donnelly, *Sixties Britain: Culture, Society and Politics* (Harlow: Pearson, 2005); Alwyn W. Turner, *Crisis? What Crisis? Britain in the 1970s* (London: Aurum Press, 2008); Andy Beckett, *When the Lights Went Out: Britain in the Seventies* (London: Faber and Faber, 2009); Dominic Sandbrook, *Seasons in the Sun: The Battle for Britain, 1974–1979* (London: Allen Lane, 2012); Alwyn W. Turner, *Rejoice! Rejoice! Britain in the 1980s* (London: Aurum, 2010) and Andy McSmith, *No Such Thing as Society: A History of Britain in the 1980s* (London: Constable, 2011).
4. British and European resistance to American culture is expounded by Dick Hebdige, *Subculture: The Meaning of Style* (London and New York: Routledge, 1979); Rob Kroes et al. *Cultural Transmissions and Receptions: American Mass Culture in Europe* (Amsterdam: VU University Press, 1993) and Rob Kroes, *If You've Seen One, You've Seen the Mall: Europeans and American Mass Culture* (Urbana, IL: University of Illinois Press, 1996). On a global level, Jan Nederveen Pieterse's, *Global Mélange: Globalization and Culture* (Lanham, MD: Rowman & Littlefield, 2003) and *Ethnicities and Global Multiculture: Pants for an Octopus* (Lanham, MD: Rowman & Littlefield, 2007) takes a similar position by emphasizing the development of hybrid cultures.
5. Richard Pells, *Not Like Us: How Europeans Have Loved, Hated, and Transformed American Culture since World War II* (New York: Basic Books, 1997), xiv and 333–334.
6. Adrian Horn, *Juke Box Britain: Americanisation and Youth Culture 1945–60* (Manchester and New York: Manchester University Press, 2009), 1.
7. Ibid., 186.
8. Victoria de Grazia, *Irresistible Empire: America's Advance through Twentieth-Century Europe* (Cambridge, MA: Belknap Press of Harvard University Press, 2005), 5.
9. H. L. Malchow, *Special Relations: The Americanization of Britain?* (Stanford, CA: Stanford University Press, 2011), 5.

10. Andrei S. Markovits, *Uncouth Nation: Why Europe Dislikes America* (Princeton and Oxford: Princeton University Press, 2007), 25. Other recent books that analyze cultural anti-Americanism include Barry Rubin and Judith Colp Rubin, *Hating America: A History* (Oxford and New York: Oxford University Press, 2004); Russell A. Berman, *Anti-Americanism in Europe: A Cultural Problem* (Stanford, CA: Hoover Institution Press, 2004); Jesper Gulddal, *Anti-Americanism in European Literature* (New York: Palgrave Macmillan, 2011); Jean Francois Revel, *Anti-Americanism* (New York: Encounter Books, 2003) and Barry A. Sanders, *American Avatar: The United States in the Global Imagination* (Washington DC: Potomac Books, 2011). See also Paul Hollander, *Anti-Americanism: Critiques at Home and Abroad, 1965–1990* (London and New York: Oxford University Press, 1992); Paul Hollander, ed. *Understanding Anti-Americanism: Its Origins and Impact at Home and Abroad* (Chicago: Ivan R. Dee, 2004) and Stephen Haseler, *The Varieties of Anti-Americanism: Reflex and Response* (Washington DC: Ethics and Public Policy Center, 1985).
11. Ziauddin Sardar and Merryl Wyn Davies, *Why Do People Hate America?* (Cambridge, UK: Icon Books, 2002); Richard Crockatt, *America Embattled: September 11, Anti-Americanism, and the Global Order* (London and New York: Routledge, 2003); Mark Hertsgaard, *The Eagle's Shadow: Why America Fascinates and Infuriates the World* (New York: Farrar, Straus, and Giroux, 2002) and Julia Sweig, *Friendly Fire: Losing Friends and Making Enemies in the Anti-American Century* (New York: Public Affairs, 2006). See also Ole R. Holsti, *To See Ourselves as Others See Us: How Publics Abroad View the United States After 9/11* (Ann Arbor, IL: University of Michigan Press, 2008); Andrew Ross and Kristin Ross, eds. *Anti-Americanism* (New York and London: New York University Press, 2004); Tony Judt and Denis Locorne, eds. *With US or against US. Studies in Global Anti-Americanism* (New York: Palgrave MacMillan, 2005) and Andrew Kohut and Bruce Stokes, *America Against the World: How We Are Different and Why We Are Disliked* (New York: Times Books, 2006). Max Paul Friedman, *Rethinking Anti-Americanism: The History of an Exceptional Concept in American Foreign Relations* (Cambridge, MA: Cambridge University Press, 2012) argues that the notion of a broad opposition to America and Americans is exaggerated and that the use of the concept "anti-American" only obscures valid criticisms of the role the United States plays in the world.
12. Giacomo Chiozza, *Anti-Americanism and the American World Order* (Baltimore, MD: The Johns Hopkins University Press, 2009) and Peter J. Katzenstein and Robert O. Keohane, eds. *Anti-Americanisms in World Politics* (Ithaca and London: Cornell University Press, 2007) see anti-Americanism as a multifaceted belief but divide the concept into too many phenomena to be really helpful.

Chapter 1

1. J. B. Priestley and Jacquetta Hawkes, *Journey Down a Rainbow* (New York: Harper and Brothers, 1955), xi.
2. Harry Hopkins, *The New Look: A Social History of the Forties and Fifties in Britain* (Boston, MA: Houghton Mifflin, 1964), 454.
3. James McMillan and Bernard Harris, *The American Take-Over of Britain* (London: Leslie Frewin, 1968), 32.
4. Paul Johnson, *A History of the Modern World from 1917 to the 1980s* (London: Weindenfeld and Nicolson, 1983), 693.
5. David Farber, *The Age of Great Dreams, America in the 1960s* (New York: Hill and Wang, 1994), 8.

6. "Evolution of National Nobel Prize Shares in the 20th Century," at http://www.idsia.ch/~juergen/nobelshare.html Accessed August 10, 2012.
7. Andrew Rosen, *The Transformation of British Life, 1950–2000* (Manchester and New York: Manchester University Press, 2003), 127 and Correlli Barnett, *The Lost Victory: British Dreams, British Realities, 1945–1950* (London: Pan Books, 1996).
8. Brian Harrison, *Seeking a Role: The United Kingdom, 1951–1970* (Oxford: Clarendon Press, 2009), 11.
9. Nicholas J. Cull, *The Cold War and the United States Information Agency: American Propaganda and Public Diplomacy, 1945–1989* (Cambridge and New York: Cambridge University Press, 2008).
10. Benn Steil, *The Battle of Bretton Woods: John Maynard Keynes, Harry Dexter White, and the Making of a New World Order* (Princeton and Oxford: Princeton University Press, 2013).
11. Robert J Donovan, *The Second Victory: Marshall Plan and the Postwar Revival of Europe* (New York: University Press of America, 1987).
12. Alan S. Milward and George Brennan *Britain's Place in the World: A Historical Enquiry into Import Controls, 1945–60* (London and New York: Routledge, 1996), 196–198.
13. Roy Porter, *London: A Social History* (Cambridge, MA: Harvard University Press, 1995), 325; McMillan and Harris, *The American Take-Over of Britain*, 7 and 14, and John H. Dunning, *U.S. Industry in Britain* (Boulder, CO: Westview Press, 1976), 9.
14. Peter Masson and Andrew Thorburn, "Advertising: the American Influence in Europe," in C. W. E. Bigsby, ed. *Superculture: American Popular Culture and Europe* (Bowling Green, OH: Bowling Green University Popular Press, 1975), 96–106.
15. Anthony Sampson, *Anatomy of Britain* (New York and Evanston, IL: Harper and Row, 1962), 584 and 580.
16. UK Telephone History, http://www.britishtelephones.com/histuk.htm Accessed December 28, 2012.
17. Stephen van Dulken, *Inventing the 20th Century: 100 Inventions that Shaped the World* (New York: New York University Press, 2000), 18, 30, 58, 64 and 138; Time-Life Books, *Inventive Genius* (New York: Time-Life Books, 1991), 99, and *The Guardian*, May 24, 2012, page 36.
18. Michele Brown, *The Little History of the Teddy Bear* (Stroud, OK: Tempus, 2006).
19. David Parlett, *The Oxford History of Board Games* (Oxford: Oxford University Press, 1999), 349–354 and 368–370.
20. A. H. Halsey with Josephine Webb eds. *Twentieth-Century British Social Trends* (London: Macmillan Press, 2000), 292.
21. Paul Addison, *No Turning Back: The Peacetime Revolutions of Post-War Britain* (Oxford and New York: Oxford University Press, 2010), 45, 171 and 56.
22. Elizabeth Roberts, *Women and Families: An Oral History, 1940–1970* (Oxford, UK and Cambridge, MA: Blackwell, 1995), 29.
23. Dominic Sandbrook, *Never Had It So Good: A History of Britain from Suez to the Beatles* (London: Abacas, 2005), 80.
24. Douglas Brinkley, *Wheels for the World: Henry Ford, His Company, and a Century of Progress 1903–2003* (New York: Viking, 2003), xxii.
25. Aldous Huxley, *Brave New World* (London: Chatto and Windus, 1932).
26. Robert Kanigel, *The One Best Way, Frederick Winslow Taylor and the Enigma of Efficiency* (Cambridge, MA: MIT Press, 2005); Jim Christy, *The Price of Power: A Biography of Charles Eugene Bedaux* (New York: Doubleday, 1984); Kevin Whitston, "Worker Resistance and Taylorism in Britain," *International Review of Social History* 42 (1997), 2, and C. R. Littler, *The Development of the Labour Process in Capitalist*

Societies: A Comparative Study of the Transformation of Work Organization in Britain, Japan and the USA (London: Heineman Educational Books, 1982), 114–115.

27. Lindy Woodhead, *Shopping, Seduction, and Mr Selfridge* (London: Profile Books, 2007), 8.
28. Bill Lancaster, *The Department Store: A Social History* (London and New York: Leicester University Press, 1995), Chapter 4 and David Frost and Michael Shea, *The Rich Tide: Men, Women, Ideas and Their Transatlantic Impact* (London: Collins, 1986), 214–219.
29. Stephen van Dulken, *Inventing the 20th Century: 100 Inventions that Shaped the World* (New York: New York University Press, 2000), 50.
30. Christina, Hardyment, *Slice of Life: The British Way of Eating since 1945* (London: BBC Books, 1995), 115.
31. Harrison, *Seeking a Role*, 335 and Gareth Shaw, Louise Curth and Andrew Alexander, "Selling Self-Service and the Supermarket: The Americanisation of Food Retailing in Britain, 1945–60," *Business History* 46 (October 2004): 568–582.
32. Hardyment, *Slice of Life*, 71, and 77–78.
33. Magnus Pyke, "The Influence of American Foods and Food Technology in Europe," in C. W. E. Bigsby ed. *Superculture: American Popular Culture and Europe* (Bowling Green, Ohio: Bowling Green University, 1975), 83–95.
34. *The Independent*, May 17, 2006, page 28.
35. Mark Kurlansky, *Birdseye: The Adventures of a Curious Man* (New York: Doubleday, 2012); "Clarence Birdseye" Bridget Travers (editor) *World of Invention* (London: Gale, 1994), 74 and *Daily Mirror*, September 26, 2005, page 8.
36. Charles Jennings, *Them and Us: The American Invasion of British High Society* (Gloucestershire: Sutton Publishing, 2007).
37. Kathryn A. Morrison, *English Shops and Shopping: An Architectural History* (New Haven and London: Yale University Press, 2003), 164.
38. H. L. Malchow, *Special Relations: The Americanization of Britain?* (Stanford, CA: Stanford University Press, 2011), 29–47 and Murray Fraser with Joe Kerr, *Architecture and the "Special Relationship": The American influence on Post-war British Architecture* (London and New York: Routledge, 2007), 5
39. Harrison, *Seeking a Role*, 163.
40. *The Times*, July 10, 2008, page 19.
41. Adrian Horn, *Juke Box Britain: Americanisation and Youth Culture 1945–60* (Manchester and New York: Manchester University Press, 2009), 169.
42. Hardyment, *Slice of Life*, 44–45.
43. John A. Walker, *America's Impact on British Art since 1945* (London: Pluto Press, 1998).
44. Christopher Simon Sykes, *David Hockney: The Biography, 1937–1975* (New York and London: Doubleday, 2012), 66 and 68.
45. *Best of British*, December 2006, pages 58–59.
46. Peter Fuller, *Beyond the Crisis in Art* (London: Writers and Readers, 1980), 78, 80 and 92.
47. John Lucas, *Next Year Will Be Better: A Memoir of England in the 1950s* (Nottingham: Five Leaves, 2011), 386–387.
48. Lucas, *Next Year Will Be Better*, 333.
49. Kingsley Amis, *Lucky Jim* (London: Victor Gollancz, 1954); John Braine, *Room at the Top* (London: Eyre and Spottiswoode, 1957); Alan Sillitoe, *Saturday Night and Sunday Morning* (London: W.H. Allen, 1958) and *The Loneliness of the Long Distance Runner* (London: W.H. Allen, 1959); Peter Lewis, *The Fifties* (New York: J. B.

Lippincott, 1978), 160 and James Gindin, *Postwar British Fiction: New Accents and Attitudes* (Berkeley and Los Angeles: University of California Press, 1963), Chapter 7.

50. Eric Hobsbawm, "Jazz Comes to Europe," in Eric Hobsbawn, ed. *Uncommon People: Resistance, Rebellion and Jazz* (New York: The New Press, 1998), 265–273; James J. Nott, *Music for the People: Popular Music and Dance in Interwar Britain* (Oxford: Oxford University Press, 2002); Jim Godbolt, *A History of Jazz in Britain 1919–50* (London and New York: Quartet Books, 1984); Jim Godbolt, *A History of Jazz in Britain 1950–70* (London and New York: Quartet Books, 1989) and George McKay, *Circular Breathing: The Cultural Politics of Jazz in Britain* (Durham, NC: Duke University Press, 2005).
51. Frances Rust, *Dance in Society* (London: Routledge and Kegan Paul, 1969), 89, 102–106 and 86.
52. Maureen Reynolds, *Voices in the Street: Growing Up in Dundee* (Edinburgh: Black and White Publishing, 2006), 213.
53. Hobsbawm, "Jazz Comes to Europe," 265–273; and Duncan Heining, *Trad Dads, Dirty Boppers and Free Fusioneers: British Jazz 1960–1975* (Sheffield: Equinox, 2012).
54. *Picture Post,* November 12, 1949, pages 24–25.
55. Number One's The 1950s. http://www.onlineweb.com/theones/1950_ones.htm Accessed February 26, 2010.
56. Richard Pells, *Modernist America: Art, Music, Movies and the Globalization of American Culture* (New Haven and London: Yale University Press, 2011), 180–186.
57. Georgina Boyes, *The Imagined Village: Culture, Ideology and the English Folk Revival* (Manchester and New York: Manchester University Press, 1993), 205.
58. Mike Brown, *The 1950s Look* (Kent: Sabrestorm, 2008), 5.
59. *Picture Post,* April 5, 1952, page 54, and May 3, 1952, page 6.
60. Kevin McManus, *"Nashville of the North": Country Music in Liverpool* (Liverpool: Institute of Popular Music, 1994).
61. *Mojo,* August 2013, page 65.
62. Brian Ward, " 'By Elvis and All the Saints' Images of the American South in the World of 1950s British Popular Music," in Joseph P. Ward ed. *Britain and the American South from Colonialism to Rock and Roll* (Jackson: The University Press of Mississippi, 2003), 187–213.
63. *Daily Mirror*, August 16, 1956, page 12.
64. Ibid.
65. Laura E. Cooper and B. Lee Cooper, "The Pendulum of Cultural Imperialism: Popular Music Interchanges Between the United States and Britain, 1943–1967," *Journal of Popular Culture* 27 (Winter 1993), 61–78.
66. *Mojo* (May 2013), page 126.
67. Greil Marcus, *Mystery Train* (New York: E. P. Dutton, 1975) and Charlie Gillett, *The Sound of the City* (New York: Outerbridge & Dienstfrey, 1970).
68. John Peel and Sheila Ravenscroft, *John Peel: Margrave of the Marshes* (Chicago: Review History, 2007 edition), 48.
69. Peter Guralnick, *Last Train to Memphis: The Rise of Elvis Presley* (New York: Little, Brown, 1994).
70. *Daily Mirror*, August 16, 1956, page 12.
71. Lewis, *The Fifties*, 132 and 134.
72. Presley never performed in Britain and it was always thought that he had never set foot in the country, except for when his plane briefly landed at Prestwick, Scotland, in March 1960 whilst en route from Germany where he served in the US Army. In 2008, however, English singer Tommy Steele

claimed that he had showed Elvis around London in 1958 when he had stopped off on his way to serve in Germany. *Daily Mail,* April 22, 2008, *Mail Online* at http://www.dailymail.co.uk/tvshowbiz/article-561170/Revealed—Elviss-secret-visit-London-little-help-rock-rival-Tommy-Steele.html Accessed June 22, 2012.

73. Cliff Richard, *My Life* (London: Headline Review, 2008), 21. See also Mo Foster, *Play Like Elvis: How British Musicians Bought the American Dream* (Bodmin: MPG Books, 2000).
74. Roberta Freund Schwartz, *How Britain Got the Blues: The Transmission and Reception of American Blues Style in the United Kingdom* (Aldershot, England: Ashgate, 2007); Bob Brunning, *Blues: The British Connection* (London: Helter Skelter, 2002), 12–20; David Williams, *The First Time We Met the Blues: A Journey of Discovery with Jimmy Page, Brian Jones, Mick Jagger and Keith Richards* (York, England: Mentor Books, 2009) and Bill Sykes, *Sit Down! Listen to This! The Roger Eagle Story* (Manchester: Empire Publications, 2012), 14–15.
75. Jonathon Green, *Days in the Life: Voices from the English Underground, 1961–1971* (London: Heinemann, 1988), 28.
76. Jim Dawson, *The Twist: The Story of the Song and Dance That Changed the World* (Boston and London: Faber and Faber, 1995).
77. Jeffrey Richards, *The Age of the Dream Palace: Cinema and Society in Britain 1930–1939* (London: Routledge and Kegan Paul, 1984), 11–12 and 395; David Atwell, *Cathedrals of the Movies: A History of British Cinemas and their Audiences* (London: Architectural Press, 1981), 167; Tom Ryall, *Britain and the American Cinema* (London: Sage, 2001) and Harrison, *Seeking a Role*, 395.
78. Kenneth and Valerie McLeish eds. *Long to Reign Over Us...Memories of Coronation Day and of Life in the 1950s* (London: Bloomsbury, 1992), 87.
79. Rowana Agajanian, "'Just for Kids?': Saturday Morning Cinema and Britain's Children's Film Foundation in the 1960s," *Historical Journal of Film, Radio and Television* 18 (August, 1998), 395–409.
80. The Theatres Trust, http://www.theatrestrust.org.uk/resources/theatres/show/2301-new-rainbow-astoria Accessed on May 27, 2010.
81. Robert Opie, *Remember When: A Nostalgic Trip Through the Consumer Era* (London: Mitchell Beazley, 1999), 65.
82. Sandbrook, *Never Had It So Good*, 135.
83. Paul Addison, *Now the War is Over: A Social History of Britain 1945–51* (London: BBC, 1985), 201.
84. Donald Spoto, *Marilyn Monroe: The Biography* (New York: Harper Collins, 1993).
85. Pete Frame, *The Restless Generation* (London: Rogan House, 2007), 125.
86. Colin MacFarlane, *Gorbals Diehards: A Wild Sixties Childhood* (Edinburgh and London: Mainstream, 2010), 107.
87. Nik Cohn, *Today There Are No Gentlemen: The Changes in Englishmen's Clothes since the War* (London: Weidenfeld and Nicolson, 1971), 18.
88. *Daily Mirror*, March 19, 1949, page 2.
89. Paul Gorman, *The Look: Adventures in Pop and Rock Fashion* (London: Sanctuary Publishing, 2001), 25, and Horn, *Juke Box Britain*, Chapter 5. For more on youth cultures see Bill Osgerby, *Youth in Britain since 1945* (Oxford: Blackwell, 1998).
90. *Picture Post,* June 4, 1955, page 37.
91. Mary Chamberlain, *Growing Up in Lambeth* (London: Virago, 1989), 79–80.
92. McLeish eds. *Long to Reign Over Us...*, 57.

93. Cilla Black, *What's It All About* (London: Ebury Press, 2003), 21 and 30.
94. Mae Stewart, *Dae Yeh Mind Thon Time?* (Edinburgh: Black and White Publishing, 2009), 167–168.
95. *Best of British Past and Present* (July 2003), 46.
96. Johnny Stuart, *Rockers* (London: Plexus, 1987), 108, 9 and 18.
97. Gareth Brown, *Mods and Rockers: The Origins and Era of a British Scene* (Shropshire: Independent Music Press, 2010).
98. Stuart, *Rockers*, 123 and 125.
99. Paul Rixon, *American Television on British Screens: A Story of Cultural Interaction* (Basingstoke: Palgrave Macmillan, 2006); Tim O'Sullivan, "Television Memories and Cultures of Viewing, 1950–65," in John Corner ed. *Popular Television in Britain: Studies in Cultural History* (London: BFI Publishing, 1991), 161, and David Buckingham et al. *Children's Television in Britain: History, Discourse and Policy* (London: British Film Institute, 1999), 21–29.
100. *The Independent,* March 21, 2010, http://www.independent.co.uk/voices/commentators/rupert-cornwell/rupert-cornwell-farewell-to-davy-crockett-ndash-and-the-wild-frontier-1924632.html Accessed May 14, 2012.
101. Bob Horlock, *I Remember When I Was Young: A Collection of Half a Century of People's Personal Memories from around Britain and Farther Afield* (Bloomington, IN: Unlimited Publishing, 2003), 282
102. John Walsh, *Are You Talking to Me? A Life Through the Movies* (London: HarperCollins, 2003), 82.
103. Julie Walters, *That's Another Story: The Autobiography* (London: Weidenfeld and Nicolson, 2008), 12.
104. Carolyn Kay Steedman, *Landscapes for a Good Woman: A Story of Two Lives* (New Brunswick, NJ: Rutgers University Press, 1987), 44.
105. Anthony Carew, *Labour under the Marshall Plan: The Politics of Productivity and the Marketing of Management Science* (Manchester: Manchester University Press, 1987), 242.
106. Kenneth O. Morgan, "Labour and the Anglo-American Alliance," in Antoine Capet, Aïssatou Sy-Wonyu eds. *The "special relationship" la relation speciale entre le royaume-uni et les etats-unis* (Rouen: Universitet' de Rouen, 2003), 176, and Harry Hopkins, *The New Look: A Social History of the Forties and Fifties in Britain* (Boston: Houghton Mifflin, 1964), 455.
107. Morgan, "Labour and the Anglo-American Alliance," 175. See also Stephen Brooke, "Atlantic Crossing? American Views of Capitalism and British Socialist Thought 1932–1962," *Twentieth Century British History* 2 (1991): 107–136 and Brian Brivati, *Hugh Gaitskell* (London: Richard Cohen Books, 1996), 148.
108. Harrison, *Seeking a Role*, 335 and Laura Mason, *Food Culture in Great Britain* (Westport, CT and London: Greenwood Press, 2004), 112.
109. Nick Tiratsoo, "Limits of Americanisation: The United States Productivity Gospel in Britain," in Becky Conekin, Frank Mort, and Chris Waters eds. *Moments of Modernity: Reconstructing Britain 1945–1964* (London and New York: Rivers Oram Press, 1999), 96–113; Jonathan Zeitlin and Gary Herrigel eds. *Americanization and Its Limits: Reworking US Technology and Management in Post-War Europe and Japan* (Oxford and New York: Oxford University Press, 2004); S. B. Saul, "The American Impact on British Industry, 1895–1914," *Business History* 3 (1967): 19–20 and David Brody, *In Labor's Cause: Main Themes on the History of the American Worker* (New York and Oxford: Oxford University Press, 1993), 229.
110. Sue Harper and Vincent Porter, *British Cinema of the 1950s: The Decline of Deference* (Oxford and New York: Oxford University Press, 2003), 248–253.

111. Screenline, http://www.screenonline.org.uk/film/id/1147086/ Accessed June 9, 2010.
112. George Orwell, *The Lion and the Unicorn: Socialism and the English Genius* (London: Secker and Warburg, 1941), 15.
113. Robert Opie, *Remember When: A Nostalgic Trip Through the Consumer Era* (London: Mitchell Beazley, 1999), 70–71 and 86 and Anthony McReavy, *The Toy story: The Life and Times of Inventor Frank Hornby* (London: Ebury, 2002).
114. Nott, *Music for the People*, 232–233.
115. Ian Whitcomb, *After the Ball* (New York: Limelight, 1986, first published in 1972), 177–179.
116. D. Richard Truman, *Mods, Minis and Madmen: A True Tale of Swinging London Culture in the 1960s* (Bloomington, IN: iUniverse, 2010), 107 and Peter Masson and Andrew Thorburn, "Advertising: the American Influence in Europe," in C. W. E. Bigsby, ed. *Superculture: American Popular Culture and Europe* (Ohio: Bowling Green University Popular Press, 1975), 96–106.
117. Peter Leese, *Britain since 1945: Aspects of Identity* (Hampshire: Palgrave Macmillan, 2006), 48 and Harrison, *Seeking a Role*, 2–4.
118. Hardyment, *Slice of Life*, 80.
119. Simon Webb, *A 1960s East End Childhood* (Gloucestershire: The History Press, 2012), 181.
120. Sampson, *Anatomy of Britain*, 575–576.
121. Harrison, *Seeking a Role*, 86.
122. Mike Brown, *The 1950s Look* (Kent: Sabrestorm, 2008), 55–57.
123. *New Musical Express*, February 15, 1963, page 9.
124. Harper and Porter, *British Cinema of the 1950s*, 245.
125. Mary Evans, *A Good School: Life at a Girls' Grammar School in the 1950s* (London: The Women's Press, 1991), 33.
126. Matthew Taylor, *The Association Game: A History of British Football* (London: Pearson Longman, 2008), 205–208
127. Gorman, *The Look*, 25.
128. Sheila Rowbotham, *Promise of a Dream: Remembering the Sixties* (London: Penguin Books, 2000), 5 and 24.
129. Joan Bakewell, *The Centre of the Bed: An Autobiography* (London: Hodder and Stoughton, 2003), 91
130. Terry Rawlings, *Mod A Very British Phenomenon* (London: Omnibus Press, 2000), 14. See also Richard Barnes, *Mods!* (London: Eel Pie, 1989); Paolo Hewitt, *The Soul Stylists: Forty Years of Modernism* (Edinburgh and London: Mainstream, 2000); Paolo Hewitt, *The Sharper Word: A Mod Anthology* (London: Helter Skelter, 2009); Paolo Hewitt and Mark Baxter, *The A to Z of Mod* (Munich, London and New York, Prestel, 2012) and Green, *Days in the Life*.
131. Gorman, *The Look*, 56.
132. Terry Rawlings, *Mod A Very British Phenomenon* (London: Omnibus Press, 2000), 20.
133. T. R. Fyvel, *Troublemakers: Rebellious Youth in an Affluent Society* (New York: Schocken Books, 1961), 59–60.
134. Colin MacInnes, *England, Half English* (New York, Random House, 1961), 154.
135. *New York Times*, October 14, 1959, page 48.
136. Janet Street-Porter, *Baggage: My Childhood* (London: Headline, 2004), 168–169 and 163.

Chapter 2

1. Paul Trynka, *David Bowie: Starman* (New York, Boston and London: Little, Brown and Company, 2011), 17 and 59; Marc Spitz, *Bowie: A Biography* (New York: Crown, 2009), 28; Kevin Cann, *David Bowie Any Day Now, The London Years: 1947–1974* (London: Adelita, 2010), 20; Peter and Leni Gillman, *Alias David Bowie* (New York: Henry Holt and Company, 1987), 69; Dylan Jones, *When Ziggy Played Guitar: David Bowie and Four Minutes That Shook the World* (London: Preface, 2012), 39 and Christopher Sandford, *Bowie: Loving the Alien* (New York: Da Capo Press, 1998), 24 and 36.
2. Raphael Samuel, ed. *Patriotism: The Making and Unmaking of British National Identity, Volume 1, History and Politics* (London and New York: Routledge, 1989), xxvi–xxvii and xxx–xxxi.
3. Meredith Veldman, *Fantasy, the Bomb, and the Greening of Britain: Romantic Protest, 1945–1980* (New York: Cambridge University Press, 1994), 202 and 306.
4. Mark Garnett and Richard Weight, *The A-Z Guide to Modern British History* (London: Jonathan Cape, 2003), 8.
5. Brian Harrison, *Seeking a Role: The United Kingdom, 1951–1970* (Oxford: Clarendon Press, 2009), 11 and David Farber, *The Age of Great Dreams, America in the 1960s* (New York: Hill and Wang, 1994), 8.
6. Doris and Edward L. Bernays, *What the British Think of Us: A Study of British Hostility to America and Americans and Its Motivation* (New York, English Speaking Union, 1958), 18.
7. Cited in Benn Steil, *The Battle of Bretton Woods: John Maynard Keynes, Harry Dexter White, and the Making of a New World Order* (Princeton and Oxford: Princeton University Press, 2013), 330.
8. Fred Vanderschmidt, *What the English Think of Us* (New York: Robert M McBride, 1948), 2.
9. *The Listener*, June 24, 1954, page 1100.
10. *Daily Mirror*, May 11, 1954, pages 8–9.
11. William Clark, *Less Than Kin: A Study of Anglo-American Relations* (Boston, MA: Houghton Mifflin, 1957), 161.
12. Martin Holmes et al. *British Security Policy and the Atlantic Alliance: Prospects for the 1990s* (Cambridge, MA: Pergamon-Brassey's International Defense, 1987), 100.
13. Simon Heffer, *Like the Roman: The Life of Enoch Powell* (London: Weidenfeld and Nicolson, 1998), 900–901.
14. *Daily Mirror*, March 4, 1957, page 2.
15. Margaret Thatcher, *The Path to Power* (London: HarperCollins, 1995), 89.
16. Sidney Smith, "Who Reads an American Book?" *Edinburgh Review* (January, 1820) Available at http://www.usgennet.org/usa/topic/preservation/epochs/vol5/pg144.htm Accessed November 7, 2012.
17. Rudyard Kipling, *From Sea to Sea: Letters of Trave*l (New York: Charles Scribner's Sons, 1899), 139.
18. F. R. Leavis, *Mass Civilisation and Minority Culture* (Cambridge, UK: Minority Pamphlets No. 1, 1930).
19. Frances Rust, *Dance in Society* (London: Routledge and Kegan Paul, 1969), 90.
20. Jeffrey Richards, *The Age of the Dream Palace: Cinema and Society in Britain 1930–1939* (London: Routledge and Kegan Paul, 1984), 59.
21. B. Seebohm Rowntree and G. R. Lavers in *English Life and Leisure: A Social Study* (London and New York: Longmans, Green and Co, 1951), 238, 239, 249, 256 and 314.

22. *The Times,* September 1956, page 4.
23. *Daily Express*, May 8, 1956, page 3.
24. *Daily Mail,* September 5, 1956. Quoted in Martin Cloonan, "Exclusive! The British Press and Popular Music, The Story So Far. . . ." in Steve Jones, ed. *Pop Music and the Press* (Philadelphia, PA: Temple University Press, 2002), 114–115.
25. Alwyn W. Turner, *Halfway to Paradise: The Birth of British Rock* (London: V&A Publishing, 2008), 74.
26. *Daily Mirror*, March 14, 1956, page 9.
27. Mary Evans, *A Good School: Life at a Girls' Grammar School in the 1950s* (London: The Women's Press, 1991), 33.
28. Barry Rubin and Judith Colp Rubin, *Hating America: A History* (Oxford and New York: Oxford University Press, 2004), 131.
29. *Daily Express,* December 13, 1960, page 6.
30. *Chicago Tribune,* May 17, 1957, page 1.
31. Jeremy Paxman, *The English: A Portrait of a People* (Woodstock and New York: The Overlook Press, 2000), 40.
32. Clark, *Less than Kin*, 168.
33. Nigel Nicolson ed. *Harold Nicolson: Diaries and Letters, 1945–1962* (London: Collins, 1968), page 243.
34. John Sheerin, "Do they like us?" *The Catholic World* (June 1953), 161.
35. Brian Magee, *Go West, Young Man* (London: Eyre and Spottiswoode, 1958), 15, 19, 20 and 21.
36. Henry Lee Munson, ed. *European Beliefs regarding the United States* (New York: Common Council for American Unity, 1949), 135.
37. H. D. Willcock, "Public Opinion: Attitudes towards America and Russia," *The Political Quarterly* 19 (1948), 68.
38. Jacques Freymond, "America through European Eyes," in *America through Foreign Eyes* special edition of *The Annals of the American Academy of Political and Social Science* 295 (September 1954), 38.
39. Pierangelo Isernia, "Anti-Americanism in Europe During the Cold War," in Peter J. Katzenstein and Robert O. Keohane, eds. *Anti-Americanisms in World Politics* (Ithaca and London: Cornell University Press, 2007), 73.
40. James M. McPherson, *Battle Cry of Freedom: The Civil War Era* (New York: Ballantine Books, 1988), 549.
41. G. D. Lillibridge ed. *The American Image: Past and Present* (Lexington, MA: D. C. Heath and Company, 1968), 6.
42. R. Laurence Moore, *European Socialists and the American promised Land* (New York: Oxford University Press, 1970); Stephen Brooke, "Atlantic Crossing? American Views of Capitalism and British Socialist Thought 1932–1962," *Twentieth Century British History* 2 (1991): 107–136; Roger Fagge, "'The Finest or the Damndest Country in the World?': The British Left and America in the 1930s," in Catherine Armstrong, Roger Fagge and Tim Lockley, eds. *America in the British Imagination* (Newcastle, UK: Cambridge Scholars, 2007), 168–181 and Hugh Wilford, "The South and the British Left, 1930–1960," in Joseph P. Ward, ed. *Britain and the American South from Colonialism to Rock and Roll* (Jackson, MS: The University Press of Mississippi, 2003), 163–186.
43. *Daily Herald*, December 14, 1945, page 2. See also R. H. S. Crossman, Michael Foot, and Ian Mikardo *Keep Left* (London: New Statesman, 1947): 30–45 and Henry Pelling, *America and the British Left: From Bright to Bevan* (New York: New York University, 1957), 150–151.

44. Philip M. Williams ed. *The Diary of Hugh Gaitskell, 1945–1956* (London: Jonathan Cape, 1983), 316 and 318.
45. Veldman, *Fantasy, the Bomb, and the Greening of Britain*, 306 and Barry Miles, *Peace: 50 Years of Protest* (New York: Readers Digest, 2008), 88 and 94.
46. Williams ed. *The Diary of Hugh Gaitskell*, 320.
47. Kingsley Martin, "The American Witch-Hunt," *The New Statesman and Nation,* July 5, 1952, pages 5–6.
48. Paul Hollander, *Anti-Americanism: Critiques at Home and Abroad, 1965–1990* (Oxford and New York: Oxford University Press, 1992), 374.
49. Francis Beckett, *Enemy Within: The Rise and Fall of the British Communist Party* (London: John Murray, 1995), 104–107.
50. Derek Kartun, *This Is America* (London: Thames Publications, 1948), 87.
51. Communist Party of Great Britain, *British Road to Socialism* (London: Communist Party, 1951), 7–8.
52. Derek Kartun, *America Go Home!* (London: Communist Party, 1951), 14.
53. Martin Barker, *A Haunt of Fears: The Strange History of the British Horror Comics Campaign* (Jackson, MS and London: University Press of Mississippi, 1984), 24–25.
54. Raymond Williams, *Britain in the Sixties: Communications* (Baltimore, MD: Penguin, 1962), 74–75.
55. Richard Hoggart, *The Uses of Literacy: Aspects of Working Class Life* (London: Chatto and Windus, 1957), 65.
56. Bertrand Russell et al. *The Impact of America on European Culture* (Boston, MA: The Beacon Press, 1951), 13–14.
57. Francis Williams, *The American Invasion* (London: Anthony Blond, 1962), 63.
58. Sue Harper and Vincent Porter, *British Cinema of the 1950s: The Decline of Deference* (Oxford and New York: Oxford University Press, 2003), 5–6.
59. Stephen Barnard, *On the Radio: Music Radio in Britain* (Milton Keynes and Philadelphia, PA: Open University Press, 1989), 4.
60. *BBC Variety Programmes Policy Guide for Writers and Producers* (London: BBC, 1948), 7–8, reprinted in Barry Took, *Laughter in the Air: An Informal History of British Radio Comedy* (London: Robson Books, 1976), 86–91.
61. Spencer Leigh, "Hello Me Ol' Mateys," http://www.spencerleigh.demon.co.uk/Feature_Satclub.htm Accessed June 6, 2011.
62. Valeria Camporesi, "There are no Kangaroos in Kent, The American 'Model' and the Introduction of Commercial Television in Britain, 1940–1954," in David E. Ellwood and Rob Kroes, eds. *Hollywood in Europe: Experiences of a Cultural Hegemony* (Amsterdam: VU University Press, 1994), 278–279 and *Time,* June 23, 1952, page 92.
63. Geoffrey Lealand, *American Television Programmes on British Screens* (London: Broadcasting Research Unit, 1984), 15–17 and 22.
64. *The Times,* March 10, 1952, 3.
65. Leon D. Epstein, *Uneasy Ally* (Chicago: University of Chicago Press, 1954), 128–148.
66. Michael Foot, "Socialists and the Atlantic Pact" *Tribune,* May 20, 1949, pages 6–8.
67. *Daily Express,* September 28, 1945, page 2, October 5, 1945, page 2 and October 31, 1945, page 1.
68. Richard Law, *Return from Utopia* (London: Faber and Faber, 1950), 75–76.
69. Morris Davis and Sidney Verba, "Party Affiliation and International Opinions in Britain and France, 1947–1956," *Public Opinion Quarterly* 24 (1960), 590–604 and Lloyd A. Free, *Six Allies and a Neutral: A Study of the International Outlooks of Political Leaders in the United States, Britain, France, West Germany, Italy, Japan and India* (Glencoe, IL: The Free Press, 1959), 58.

70. Epstein, *Uneasy Ally*, 196. See also Davis and Verba, "Party Affiliation and International Opinions in Britain and France," 590–604 for similar results.
71. Robert J. Wybrow, *Britain Speaks Out, 1937–87: A Social History as seen through the Gallup poll* (London: Macmillan, 1989), 33.
72. Valeria Camporesi, *Mass Culture and National Traditions: The B.B.C. and American Broadcasting, 1922–1954* (Italy: European Press Academic Publishing, 2000), 124 and 130.
73. *BBC Variety Programmes Policy Guide for Writers and Producers*, 7–8.
74. Paul Rixon, *American Television on British Screens: A Story of Cultural Interaction* (Basingstoke, UK: Palgrave Macmillan, 2006), 43.
75. Adrian Horn, *Juke Box Britain: Americanisation and Youth Culture 1945–60* (Manchester and New York: Manchester University Press, 2009), 78.
76. Vanderschmidt, *What the English Think of Us*, 2.
77. William Buchanan and Hadley Cantril, *How Nations See Each Other: A Study in Public Opinion* (Urbana: University of Illinois Press, 1953), 46.
78. Nigel Nicolson ed. *Harold Nicolson: Diaries and Letters, 1945–1962* (London: Collins, 1968), 397.
79. Ole R. Holsti, *To See Ourselves as Others See Us: How Publics Abroad View the United States after 9/11* (Ann Arbor, MI: University of Michigan Press, 2008), 193.
80. *The Listener,* June 17, 1954, page 1041.
81. *The Listener,* June 24, 1954, pages 1099–1100.
82. *Daily Mirror*, March 9, 1953, page 6.
83. *Picture Post,* July 12, 1952, page 8.
84. *Daily Mirror*, May 10, 1954, pages 8–9.
85. Richards, *The Age of the Dream Palace*, 15.
86. *Ibid.*, 24.
87. Joe Moran, *Queuing for Beginners: The Story of Daily Life from Breakfast to Bedtime* (London: Profile Books, 2007), 177.
88. Richards, *The Age of the Dream Palace*, 24.
89. Lulu, *I Don't Want to Fight* (London: Time Warner, 2002), 79 and 42.
90. J. P. Mayer, *British Cinemas and Their Audiences: Sociological Studies* (London: Dennis Dobson, 1948), 188.
91. Marcus Cunliffe, *In Search of America: Transatlantic Essays, 1951–1990* (Westport, CT, and London: Greenwood Press, 1991), 5.
92. Roderick McNeill interview with author, March 6, 2013.
93. Ross McKibbin, *Classes and Cultures: England 1918–1951* (Oxford and New York: Oxford University Press, 1998), 420.
94. Ian McLagan, *All the Rage: A Riotous Romp through Rock and Roll History* (New York: Billboard Books, 1998), 12–13.
95. Alan Lomax, "Skiffle: Where is it Going?" *Melody Maker*, September 7, 1957, page 5.
96. *The Guardian,* November 29, 2003, page 7.
97. *Time,* May 4, 1962, page 33.
98. *The Listener*, April 19, 1962, page 670.
99. *Time*, March 4, 1957, page 110 and *Time*, February 1, 1960, page 34.
100. Juliet Gardiner, "*Overpaid, Oversexed, and Over Here*" *The American GI in World War II Britain* (New York: Canopy Books, 1992), 108–110. See also Barbara G. Friedman, *Front the Battlefront to the Bridal Suite: Media Coverage of British War Brides, 1942–1946* (Columbia, MO: University of Missouri Press, 2007) and Helen D. Millgate, *Got Any Gum Chum? GIs in Wartime Britain, 1942–1945* (Gloucestershire: Sutton, 2001).

101. *Picture Post,* June 28, 1952, page 15.
102. *Daily Mirror*, April 28, 1948, page 4
103. McKibbin, *Classes and Cultures*, 395.
104. Pierangelo Isernia, "Anti-Americanism in Europe During the Cold War," 87.
105. Christine Paine interview with author April 28, 2013.
106. Mayer, *British Cinemas and Their Audiences*, 254, and 272.
107. Stacey, *Star Gazing: Hollywood Cinema and Female Spectatorship.*
108. Mayer, *British Cinemas and Their Audiences*, 218–219.
109. Stacey, *Star Gazing: Hollywood Cinema and Female Spectatorship.*
110. Julie Walters, *That's Another Story: The Autobiography* (London: Weidenfeld and Nicolson, 2008), 13.
111. Cilla Black, *What's It All About* (London: Ebury Press, 2003), 21 and 30.
112. Alan Clayson, *Ringo Starr* (London: Sanctuary, 2003 edition), 19.
113. Harrison, *Seeking a Role*, 14.
114. Andrew Rosen, *The Transformation of British Life, 1950–2000* (Manchester and New York: Manchester University Press, 2003), 13.
115. Colin MacFarlane, *The Real Gorbals Story: True Tales from Glasgow's Meanest Streets* (Edinburgh: Mainstream, 2007), 29–30.
116. Rosen, *The Transformation of British Life*, 13.
117. Julie Walters, *That's Another Story: The Autobiography* (London: Weidenfeld and Nicolson, 2008), 10.
118. Rosen, *The Transformation of British Life*, 14.
119. Bernays, *What the British Think of Us*, 12 and 19.
120. Paul Wood interview with author April 28, 2013.
121. Mary Minnock interview with author, July 29, 2012.
122. *Daily Mirror*, May 28, 1949, page 5, *Daily Mirror*, July 2, 1949, page 8, *Daily Mirror*, February 23, 1950, page 6, *Daily Mirror*, July 28, 1951, page 8, *Daily Mirror*, April 19, 1951, page 8, *Daily Mirror*, July 18, 1953, page 8, *Daily Express*, January 8, 1955, page 7 and *Daily Mirror*, January 28, 1956 page 10.
123. *Daily Express,* September 7, 1961, page 12.
124. *Daily Mirror*, January 24, 1952, page 2.
125. *Commentary,* December 1952, 558–559.
126. *Record Collector,* March 2011, page 8.
127. BBC News, http://news.bbc.co.uk/2/hi/health/2545747.stm Accessed October 29, 2010.
128. Sting, *Broken Music* (New York: Dial Press, 2003), 63.
129. Paolo Hewitt, *The Soul Stylists: Forty Years of Modernism* (Edinburgh and London: Mainstream, 2000), 50.
130. David Kamp, "The British Invasion: The Oral History," *Vanity Fair,* November 2002, 261.
131. Ray Gosling, *Personal Copy: A Memoir of the Sixties* (London and Boston: Faber and Faber, 1980), 25.
132. W. A. C. Stewart, *Higher Education in Postwar Britain* (London: Macmillan, 1989), 280.
133. Richards, *The Age of the Dream Palace*, 245–246.
134. Samantha Lay, *British Social Realism: From Documentary to Brit-grit* (New York: Columbia University Press, 2002), 15.
135. Adam Faith, *Acts of Faith: The Autobiography* (London and New York: Bantam Press, 1996), 21.
136. Mayer, *British Cinemas and Their Audiences*, 118–119.

137. Ken Worpole, *Dockers and Detectives* (London: Verso, 1983), 30.
138. *The Times*, Weekend Section, January 25, 1997, page 1.
139. Michael Caine, *The Elephant to Hollywood* (New York: Henry Holt and Company, 2010), 22–23; Michael Caine, *What's It All About? An Autobiography* (New York: Turtle Bay Books, 1992), 28–29 and Michael Freedland, *Michael Caine* (London: Orion, 1999), 32–33 and 70.
140. Bernays, *What the British Think of Us*, 11 and 19.
141. *Chicago Tribune*, July 27, 2007, Section 7, page 1.
142. Graham Smith, *When Jim Crow Met John Bull: Black American Soldiers in World War II Britain* (New York: St Martin's Press, 1987), 122.
143. Henry Lee Munson, ed. *European Beliefs Regarding the United States* (New York: Common Council for American Unity, 1949), 135.
144. Andre Visson, *As Others See Us* (New York: Doubleday, 1948), 94.
145. Alan Stepney interviewed by author June 18, 2013.
146. Wilford, "The South and the British Left, 1930–1960," 176.
147. Val Wilmer, *Mama Said There'd Be Days like This: My Life in the Jazz World* (London: The Women's Press, 1989), 18.
148. Peter Noble, *The Negro in Films* (New York: Arno Press, 1970), 8.
149. Edward Mapp, *Blacks in American Films: Today and Yesterday* (Metuchen, NJ: Scarecrow Press, 1972), 66.
150. Daniel Snowman, *Britain and America: An Interpretation of their Culture, 1945–1975* (New York: New York University Press, 1977).
151. Paul Swann, *The Hollywood Feature Film in Postwar Britain* (London and Sydney: Croom Helm, 1987), 43.
152. Peter Clarke, *Hope and Glory: Britain 1900–2000* (London: Penguin, 2004), 248–249.
153. *Commentary* (December 1952), 558–559 and Rixon, *American Television on British Screens*, 41.
154. Mayer, *British Cinemas and Their Audiences*, 33 and 31.
155. Rowntree and Lavers, *English Life and Leisure*, 249–250.
156. Adam Faith, *Acts of Faith: The Autobiography* (London and New York: Bantam Press, 1996), 13.
157. Wybrow, *Britain Speaks Out, 1937–87*, 49.
158. *2010 Yearbook of Immigration Statistics* (Washington DC: Office of Immigration Statistics, US Department of Homeland Security, August 2011), 8–10.
159. Ferdynand Zweig, *The Worker in an Affluent Society: Family Life and Industry* (New York: Free Press, 1961), 68.
160. *1951 Conservative Party General Election Manifesto* available at *ConservativeManifest.com.* http://conservativemanifesto.com/1951/1951-conservative-manifesto.shtml Accessed August 30, 2012.
161. David Kynaston, *Family Britain, 1951–1957* (London, Berlin, New York: Bloomsbury, 2009), 480.
162. Vernon Bogdanor, "Britain in the 20th Century: The Conservative Reaction, 1951—1965," available at http://www.gresham.ac.uk/lectures-and-events/britain-in-the-20th-century-the-conservative-reaction-1951-1965 Accessed August 6, 2012.

Chapter 3

1. Francis Williams, *The American Invasion* (London: Anthony Blond, 1962), 16.
2. John H. Dunning, *U.S. Industry in Britain* (Boulder, CO: Westview Press, 1976), 9.

3. James McMillan and Bernard Harris, *The American Take-Over of Britain* (London: Leslie Frewin, 1968), 4.
4. *Encounter,* April 1967, page 74.
5. McMillan and Harris, *The American Take-Over of Britain*, 6.
6. Brian Harrison, *Seeking a Role: The United Kingdom, 1951–1970* (Oxford: Clarendon Press, 2009), 464–465 and McMillan and Harris, *The American Take-Over of Britain*, 188–192.
7. Thomas J. Carbery, "The Americanisation of British Politics," *The Journal of Politics*, 27 (February 1965), 183
8. Martin Rosenbaum, *From Soapbox to Soundbite: Party Political Campaigning in Britain since 1945* (London: Macmillan Press, 1997), quote on page 93.
9. H. L. Malchow, *Special Relations: The Americanization of Britain?* (Stanford, CA: Stanford University Press, 2011).
10. Malchow, *Special Relations*, 95.
11. Harold Evans, *They Made America: From the Steam Engine to the Search Engine: Two Centuries of Innovators* (New York: Back Bay, 2006), 130.
12. *Daily Star*, July 4, 2012, page 6.
13. Paul Gorman, *The Look: Adventures in Pop and Rock Fashion* (London: Sanctuary Publishing, 2001), 91–92 and Graham Marsh and J. P. Gaul, *The Ivy Look* (London: Frances Lincoln Ltd, 2010).
14. Brian Viner, *Nice to See It, to See It, Nice: The 1970s in Front of the Telly* (London: Simon and Schuster, 2009), 222–223.
15. Terry Christian, *Reds in the Hood* (London: Andre Deutsch, 1999), 81.
16. Alan Davies, *My Favourite People and Me 1978–1988* (London: Penguin, 2009), 13 and 14.
17. Ray Kennedy interview with author July 31, 2011.
18. Gary Kemp, *I Know This Much: From Soho to Spandau* (London: Fourth Estate, 2009), 8.
19. British Film Institute, http://www.bfi.org.uk/features/mostwatched/1970s.html Accessed December 16, 2010.
20. *Birmingham Post*, September 13, 1999, page 15,
21. Sarah Street, *British National Cinema* (London and New York: Routledge, 1997), 20–21.
22. Patrick Mills interview with author February 8, 2013.
23. Philip Norman, *John Lennon: The Life* (New York: HarperCollins, 2008), 82.
24. Ray Coleman, *Lennon* (New York: McGraw-Hill, 1984), 187.
25. Alan Clayson, *Ringo Starr* (London: Sanctuary, 2003 edition), 28.
26. Brian Ward, " 'By Elvis and All the Saints' Images of the American South in the World of 1950s British Popular Music," in Joseph P. Ward ed. *Britain and the American South from Colonialism to Rock and Roll* (Jackson, MS: The University Press of Mississippi, 2003), footnote 55 page 265.
27. Bill Harry, *The Ringo Starr Encyclopedia* (London: Virgin Books, 2004), 32 and 299–307.
28. Ray Coleman, *McCartney Yesterday and Today* (Los Angeles, CA: Dove Books, 1996), 26 and Howard Sounes, *Fab: An Intimate Life of Paul McCartney* (Cambridge, MA: Da Capo Press, 2010), 5–6.
29. *The Word,* March 2012, page 65.
30. *Uncut,* February 2012, page 9.
31. *The Word,* March 2012, page 67.
32. *Melody Maker*, January 9, 1965, page 3.
33. Ian MacDonald, *Revolution in the Head: The Beatles' Records and the Sixties* (Chicago: Chicago Review Press, third edition, 2007).

34. Barbara Charone, *Keith Richards* (London: Futura, 1979), 18–19. See also Phillip Norman, *The Stones* (London: Elm Tree Books, 1984).
35. Keith Richards with James Fox, *Life* (New York and London: Little, Brown and Company, 2010), 58.
36. *Uncut,* June 2010, page 105.
37. Richards with Fox, *Life*, 149.
38. *The Guardian,* G2 section, October 3, 2005, page. 22.
39. *Uncut,* January 2012, page 66.
40. Dave Marsh, *Before I Get Old: The Story of the Who* (New York: St Martin's Press, 1983) and Tim Ewbank and Stafford Hildred, *Roger Daltrey: The Biography* (London: Portrait, 2004).
41. Barry Lazell and Dafydd Rees, *Illustrated Book of Rock Records* (New York: Delilah Books, 1982), 92, 102 and 104.
42. Jon Savage, *England's Dreaming: Anarchy, Sex Pistols, Punk Rock, and Beyond* (New York: St Martin's Griffin, revised edition, 2001); Dave Laing, *One Chord Wonders: Power and Meaning in Punk Rock* (Milton Keynes: Open University Press, 1985); Greil Marcus, *Lipstick Traces: A Secret History of the Twentieth Century* (Harvard: Harvard University Press, 1990) and Roger Sabin, ed. *Punk Rock: So What? The Cultural Legacy of Punk* (London and New York: Routledge, 1999).
43. Richard Hell, *I Dreamed I Was a Very Clean Tramp: An Autobiography* (New York: HarperCollins, 2013).
44. Jon Savage, *England's Dreaming: Anarchy, Sex Pistols, Punk Rock, and Beyond* (New York: St Martin's Griffin, revised edition, 2001), 184.
45. Will Hermes, *Love Goes to Buildings on Fire: Five Years in New York That Changed Music Forever* (New York: Faber and Faber, 2011), 180–181.
46. John Robb, *Punk Rock: An Oral History* (London: Ebury Press, 2006), 198–202 and Stephen Colegrave and Chris Sullivan, *Punk: The Definitive Record of a Revolution* (London: Cassell, 2001), 212.
47. Dave Haslam, *Adventures on the Wheels of Steel: The Rise of the Superstar DJs* (London: Fourth Estate, 2001), 60.
48. Keith Rylatt and Phil Scott, *CENtral 1179: The Story of the Twisted Wheel Club* (London: Bee Cool, 2001), 36.
49. *The Independent,* October 20, 2004, page 34 and Dave Godin interviewed by Bill Brewster September 21, 1998, http://www.djhistory.com/interviews/dave-godin Accessed May 28, 2012.
50. Mark "Snowboy" Cotgrove, *From Jazz Funk and Fusion to Acid Jazz: The History of the UK Jazz Dance Scene* (London: Chaser, 2009), 15.
51. Paul Rambali, "The English Pub, Death by Disco," *The Face* (November, 1984) and Sarah Thornton, *Club Cultures: Music, Media and Subcultural Capital* (Hanover and London: Wesleyan University Press, 1996). For studies on disco in America see Albert Goldman, *Disco* (New York: Hawthorn Books, 1978); Alice Echols, *Hot Stuff: Disco and the Remaking of American Culture* (New York and London: WW Norton, 2010); Peter Shapiro, *Turn the Beat Around: The Secret History of Disco* (New York: Faber and Faber; Revised edition 2007) and Tim Lawrence, *Love Saves The Day: A History of American Dance Culture 1970–1979* (Durham, NC: Duke University Press, 2003).
52. Robert Elms, *The Way We Wore* (London: Picador, 2005), 110–115, quote on page 113.

53. Gary Kemp, *I Know This Much: From Soho to Spandau* (London: Fourth Estate, 2009), 84.
54. Lazell and Rees, *Illustrated Book of Rock Records*, 92.
55. Mike Ritson and Stuart Russell, *The In Crowd: The Story of the Northern & Rare Soul Scene* (London: Bee Cool 1999); Rylatt and Scott, *CENtral 1179*; David Nowell, *Too Darn Soulful: The Story of Northern Soul* (London: Robson Books, 2001); Reg Stickings, *Searching for Soul* (London: SAF Publishing, 2008) and Andy Wilson, *Northern Soul: Music, Drugs and Subcultural Identity* (Devon: Willan Publishing, 2007).
56. Bill Brewster and Frank Broughton, *The Record Players: DJ Revolutionaries* (London: DJ History.com, 2010), 94.
57. Stuart Maconie, *Cider with Roadies* (London: Ebury Press, 2004), 62–63.
58. Ritson and Russell, *The In Crowd*, 209.
59. Neil Rushton, *Northern Soul Stories* (Staffordshire, UK: Soulvation, 2009), 109.
60. Brewster and Broughton, *The Record Players*, 107–108.
61. Russ Winstanley and David Nowell, *Soul Survivors: The Wigan Casino Story* (London: Robson Books, 1996), 55 and 1. See also Tim Brown, *The Wigan Casino Years: The Essential Story 1973–81* (Alcester: Outta Sight Ltd, 2010) and Dave Shaw, *Casino: Wigan 30th Anniversary Edition* (London: Bee Cool, 2000).
62. Peter Leese, *Britain since 1945: Aspects of Identity* (Hampshire: Palgrave Macmillan, 2006), 49 and 89.
63. W. W. Daniel, *Racial Discrimination in England* (Middlesex: Penguin, 1968), 209 and 47.
64. Cyrille Regis, *My Story: The Autobiography of the First Black Icon of British Football* (London: Andre Deutsch, 2010), 96–97 and 127.
65. Chris Mullard, *Black Britain* (London: George Allen and Unwin, 1973), 7.
66. Errol Christie with Tony McMahon, *No Place to Hide: How I Put the Black in the Union Jack* (London: Aurum, 2010), 82.
67. Sara Maitland ed. *Very Heaven: Looking Back at the 1960s* (London: Virago Press, 1988), 33.
68. Mike Phillips and Trevor Phillips, *Windrush: The Irresistible Rise of Multi-Racial Britain* (London: HarperCollins, 1998), 232.
69. Mike Sewell, "British Responses to Martin Luther King Jr and the Civil Rights Movement, 1954–68," in Brian War and Tony Badger eds. *The Making of Martin Luther King and the Civil Rights Movement* (New York: New York University Press, 1996), 194–212.
70. Michael Abdul Malik, *From Michael de Freitas to Michael X* (London: Andre Deutsch, 1968) and Dilip Hiro, *Black British White British: A History of Race Relations in Britain* (London: Grafton Books, 1991)
71. See Stokely Carmichael and Charles V. Hamilton, *Black Power: The Politics of Liberation in America* (New York: Random House, 1967); Robert Lee Scott and Wayne Brockriede, eds. *The Rhetoric of Black Power* (New York: Harper and Row, 1969); William L. Van Deburg, *New Day in Babylon: The Black Power Movement and American Culture, 1965–1975* (Chicago and London: University of Chicago Press, 1992), 40–51; Daniel Wynn, *The Black Protest Movement* (New York: Philosophical Library, 1974), chapter 6 and Allen J. Matusow, *The Unraveling of American: A History of Liberalism in the 1960s* (New York: Harper and Row, 1984), chapter 12.
72. Charles E. Jones, ed. *The Black Panther Party* (Baltimore, MD: Black Classics Press, 1998).

73. Malik, *From Michael de Freitas to Michael X*.
74. Obi Egbuna, *Destroy This Temple: The Voice of Black Power in Britain* (New York: William Morrow and Company, 1971) and Anne-Marie Angelo, "The Black Panthers in London, 1967–1972: A Diasporic Struggle Navigates the Black Atlantic," *Radical History Review* 103 (Winter 2009): 17–35.
75. Don Letts with David Nobakht, *Culture Clash: Dread Meets Punk Rockers* (London: SAF Publishing, 2007), 39.
76. Letts with Nobakht, *Culture Clash*, 41.
77. Pauline Black, *Black by Design: A 2-Tone Memoir* (London: Serpent's Tail, 2011), 63 and 66.
78. Black, *Black by Design*, 73–75 and 76–77.
79. Huffington Post, February 1, 2009, http://www.huffingtonpost.com/johann-hari/hanif-kuresihi-on-the-cou_b_162968.html Accessed December 15, 2012.
80. Hanif Kureishi, *My Beautiful Laundrette and the Rainbow Sign* (London and Boston: Faber and Faber, 1986), 13.
81. A. H. Halsey with Josephine Webb eds. *Twentieth-Century British Social Trends* (London: Macmillan Press, 2000), 449 and 640.
82. Dominic Sandbrook, *State of Emergency: The Way We Were: Britain, 1970–1974* (London: Penguin, 2010), 19 and 347.
83. Bernard Nossiter, *Britain: A Future That Works* (Boston, MA: Houghton Mifflin, 1978), 105.
84. *The Independent*, March 17, 2004, page 12.
85. Paul Addison, *No Turning Back: The Peacetime Revolutions of Post-War Britain* (Oxford and New York: Oxford University Press, 2010), 197.
86. Harrison, *Seeking a Role*, 480–481.
87. Addison, *No Turning Back*, 197–215.
88. Martin Goldsmith, *The Beatles Come to America* (Hoboken, NJ: John Wiley, 2004).
89. Philip Norman, *Shout: The Beatles in Their Generation* (New York: Fireside, 1981) and Hunter Davies, *The Beatles: The Authorized Biography* (New York: McGraw-Hill 1968).
90. David Kamp, "The British Invasion: The Oral History," *Vanity Fair*, November 2002, page 261.
91. Charlie Gillett, "Big Noise from Across the Water: The American Influence on British Popular Music," in Allen F. Davis ed. *For Better or Worse: The American Influence in the World* (Westport, CT and London: Greenwood Press, 1981), 63.
92. Tony Visconti, *Bowie, Bolan and the Brooklyn Boy* (London, HarperCollins, 2007), 17 and 21.
93. *New Musical Express*, August 6, 1965, page 10.
94. *Time*, April 15, 1966, pages 30–34.
95. Sally Hewitt, *I Can Remember the 1960s* (London and Sydney: Franklin Watts, 2003), 23.
96. Charles Hamblett and Jane Deverson, *Generation X* (Greenwich, CT: Gold Medal Books, 1964), 137.
97. Bill Wyman, *Stone Alone: The Story of a Rock n Roll Band* (London and New York: NY, USA: Viking, 1990.), 227.
98. Pete Townshend, *Who I Am* (New York: HarperCollins, 2012), 123.
99. Twiggy Lawson with Penelope Dening, *Twiggy in Black and White* (London: Simon and Schuster, 1997), 2.

100. Steven D Stark, *Meet the Beatles: A Cultural History of the Band That Shook Youth, Gender, and the World* (New York: HarperCollins, 2005), 26.
101. Sewell, "British Responses to Martin Luther King Jr and the Civil Rights Movement," 194–212.
102. *Daily Mirror,* September 16, 1963, page 1.
103. *Daily Express,* May 23, 1961, page 1.
104. *Melody Maker*, November 21, 1964, page 3.
105. Hazel Erskine, "The Polls: World Opinion of U.S. Racial Problems," *Public Opinion Quarterly* 32 (Summer 1968): 299–312.
106. Robert J. Wybrow, *Britain Speaks Out, 1937–87: A Social History as seen through the Gallup poll* (London: Macmillan, 1989), 77, 81 and 108.
107. Ibid.
108. Michael Tanner, *Ali in Britain* (Edinburgh and London: Mainstream, 1995), 96.
109. Mike Marqusee, *Redemption Song: Muhammad Ali and the Spirit of the Sixties* (London and New York: Verso, second edition, 2005, originally published in 1999), 207.
110. *Daily Record*, December 13, 1999, page 7.
111. *The Guardian*, October 15, 2008, http://www.guardian.co.uk/commentisfree/2008/oct/15/blackhistorymonth-muhammad-ali Accessed March 12, 2012.
112. Gary Younge interview with author February 8, 2013.
113. Christie with McMahon, *No Place to Hide*, 77 and 264.
114. Helen Taylor, *Circling Dixie: Contemporary Southern Culture through a Transatlantic Lens* (New Brunswick, NJ and London: Rutgers University Press, 2001), 70.
115. *The Observer*, March 25, 2007, page 18.
116. Peter Hitchens, *The Abolition of Britain: From Winston Churchill to Princess Diana* (San Francisco, CA: Encounter Books, 2000), 155.
117. Ray Kennedy Interview with author July 31, 2011.
118. Peter O'Neill interview with author August 12, 2012.
119. Christine Paine interview with author April 28, 2013. See also David Nunnerley, *President Kennedy and Britain* (New York: St Martin's Press, 1972).
120. David Farber, *The Age of Dreams, America in the 1960s* (New York: Hill and Wang, 1994), 111.
121. Maurice Isserman and Michael Kazin, *America Divided, The Civil War of the 1960s* (New York: Oxford University Press, 2000), 199 and William L. O'Neill, *Coming Apart: An Informal History of America in the 1960s* (Chicago: Quadrangle Books, 1971), 170–173, 176–177.
122. Simon Heffer, *Like the Roman: The Life of Enoch Powell* (London: Weidenfeld and Nicolson, 1998), 467.
123. Alwyn W. Turner, *Crisis? What Crisis? Britain in the 1970s* (London: Aurum Press, 2008), 31.
124. Jeremy Seabrook, *City Close-Up* (Indianapolis and New York: Bobbs-Merrill, 1971), 116 and 166.
125. Stuart Hall et al. *Policing the Crisis: Mugging, the State, and Law and Order* (New York: Holmes and Meier, 1978), 22 and 3.
126. Steve Chibnall, *Law-and-Order News: An Analysis of Crime Reporting in the British Press* (London: Tavistock, 1977), 123 and 126.
127. Seabrook, *City Close-Up*, 167.
128. *Daily Express*, October 29, 1977, page 4.
129. *Daily Mirror,* September 17, 1969, page 16

130. *Daily Express,* February 27, 1969, page 9.
131. Alison Pressley, *The Seventies: Good Times, Bad Taste* (London: Index Books, 2002), 44.
132. *Daily Express,* February 6, 1975, page 11.
133. Brian O' Sullivan interview with author July 23, 2012.
134. Derek Tait, *A 1970s Childhood: From Glam Rock to Happy Days* (Gloucestershire: The History Press, 2011), 136.
135. Roderick McNeill interview with author March 6, 2013.
136. Viner, *Nice to See It, to See It,* 73.
137. *The New York Times* Online Blog, http://cityroom.blogs.nytimes.com/2007/07/09/remembering-the-77-blackout/?apage= 2#comments Accessed September 18, 2010.
138. *Daily Express,* July 26, 1977, page 6.
139. Rubin, *How Others Report Us: America in the Foreign Press* (Washington DC: The Center for Strategic and International Studies, Georgetown University, 1979), 34.
140. Colin Seymour-Ure, *The British Press and Broadcasting since 1945* (Oxford: Blackwell, second edition, 1996), 160 and Sylvia Ellis, *Britain, America, and the Vietnam War* (Westport, CT and London: Praeger, 2004).
141. Rubin, *How Others Report Us,* 16.
142. Anthony King, ed. *British Political Opinion 1937–2000 The Gallup Polls* (London: Politico's, 2001), 328–329.
143. Nick Thomas, "Protests against the Vietnam War in 1960s Britain: The Relationship between Protesters and the Press," *Contemporary British History* 22 (September 2008): 335–354.
144. King, ed. *British Political Opinion 1937–2000,* 329.
145. Steven K. Smith and Douglas A. Wertman, *US-West European Relations During the Reagan Years: The Perspective of West European Publics* (New York: St Martin's Press, 1992), 267.
146. Viner, *Nice to See It, to See It, Nice,* 129.
147. Philip Agee, *Inside the Company: CIA Diary* (London: Penguin, 1975) and Philip Agee, *On the Run* (Secaucus, NJ: Lyle Stuart, 1987).
148. Tony Benn, *Against the Tide: Diaries 1973–1976* (London: Hutchinson, 1989), 225, 318–319, 332 and 692.
149. Julie Burchill and Tony Parsons, "*The Boy Looked at Johnny*": *The obituary of Rock and Roll* (London: Pluto Press, 1978), 59, 66 and 72.
150. Burchill and Parsons, "*The Boy Looked at Johnny,*" 59, 66 and 72.
151. *New Musical Express,* December 22, 1979, page 43.
152. Ibid. page 78.
153. Hiro, *Black British White British.*
154. Letts with Nobakht, *Culture Clash,* 60.
155. Jon Denton interview with author August 23, 2012.

Chapter 4

1. Stuart Hall, "The Great *Moving Right* Show," *Marxism Today* (January, 1979), 14–20; Shirley Robin Letwin, *The Anatomy of Thatcherism* (London: Fontana, 1992); E. H. H. Green, *Thatcher* (London: Hodder Arnold, 2006); E. H. H. Green, *Ideologies of Conservatism: Conservative Political Ideas in the Twentieth Century* (Oxford: Oxford University Press, 2002); Peter Clarke, *A Question of Leadership. From Gladstone to*

Thatcher (London: Hamish Hamilton, 1991); Arthur Aughey, "Mrs Thatcher's Political Philosophy," *Parliamentary Affairs* 36 (1983): 389–398 and Ian Gilmour, *Dancing with Dogma: Britain Under Thatcherism* (London: Simon and Schuster, 1992), 9 and 13.

2. Eric J. Evans, *Thatcher and Thatcherism* (London and New York: Routledge, 1997).
3. Richard Vinen, *Thatcher's Britain: The Politics and Social Upheaval of the Thatcher Era* (London: Simon and Schuster, 2009).
4. "Radio Interview for BBC Radio 4 *Desert Island Discs*," February 1, 1978, Margaret Thatcher Foundation (Hereafter MTF). http://www.margaretthatcher.org/document/103509 Accessed December 15, 2010. The best biographies of Thatcher are John Campbell, *Margaret Thatcher: Volume One: The Grocer's Daughter* (London: Pimlico, 2001); John Campbell, *Margaret Thatcher: Volume Two: The Iron Lady* (London: Pimlico, 2004) and Hugo Young, *One of Us: A Biography of Margaret Thatcher* (London: Macmillan, 1989).
5. Campbell, *Margaret Thatcher: Volume One*, 25.
6. Margaret Thatcher, *The Path to Power* (London: HarperCollins, 1995), 14–15.
7. *Smash Hits*, March 25, 1987, page 18.
8. "*Smash Hits* interview conducted on March 2, 1987," *Margaret Thatcher Complete Public Statements*, UDN: 87_063.
9. Thatcher, *The Path to Power*, 14–15.
10. Claire Berlinkski, "*There Is No Alternative*" *Why Margaret Thatcher Matters* (New York: Basic Books, 2008), 311.
11. Thatcher, *The Path to Power*, 32.
12. "Speech to U.S. Congress," February 20, 1985 in Robin Harris, ed. *The Collected Speeches of Margaret Thatcher* (New York, HarperCollins, 1997), 237.
13. Thatcher, *The Path to Power*, 153–154. See Giles Scott-Smith, " 'Her Rather Ambitious Washington Program': Margaret Thatcher's International Visitor Program Visit to the United States in 1967," *British Contemporary History* 17 (Winter 2003): 65–86.
14. Margaret Thatcher, *Statecraft: Strategies for a Changing World* (New York: HarperCollins, 2002), 20.
15. Margaret Thatcher, *The Downing Street Years* (New York: HarperCollins, 1993), 784.
16. *Time*, June 22, 1987, page 38.
17. "Speech at Pilgrims Dinner," January 29, 1981, *Margaret Thatcher Complete Public Statements*, UDN: 81_021.
18. "Party Political Broadcast on BBC Radio 4," March 5, 1985, *Margaret Thatcher Complete Public Statements*, UDN: 75_102; "Speech to Finchley Conservative Women," March 12, 1959, MTF http://www.margaretthatcher.org/document/101014 Accessed February 2, 2012, and Clare Beckett, *Thatcher* (London: Haus, 2006), 53.
19. *Vanity Fair*, (June 1989), page 174. See also "Speech to the Fraser Institute," November 8, 1993, *Margaret Thatcher Complete Public Statements*, UDN: 93_017.
20. David Frost and Michael Shea, *The Rich Tide: Men, Women, Ideas and Their Transatlantic Impact* (London: Collins, 1986), 355.
21. Martin Holmes et al. *British Security Policy and the Atlantic Alliance: Prospects for the 1990s* (Cambridge, MA and Washington DC, Institute for Foreign Policy Analysis, 1987), 103.
22. "Margaret Thatcher TV Interview for CBS *60 Minutes*," February 15, 1985, MTF http://www.margaretthatcher.org/document/105964, Accessed August 14, 2011.
23. Thatcher, *The Path to Power*, 594.
24. Frost and Shea, *The Rich Tide*, 355.

25. *The Independent*, May 7, 1994, page 18.
26. Bill Hagerty, "Paul Dacre: The Zeal Thing," *British Journalism Review* 13 (2002): 11–22.
27. Hagerty, "Paul Dacre: The Zeal Thing," 16.
28. "Speech to Westminster Catholic Parents Association," May 1, 1970, MTF http://www.margaretthatcher.org/document/ 101742 Accessed September 3, 2011.
29. "Speech to National Association of Head Teachers Conference," May 25, 1970, MTF http://www.margaretthatcher.org/document/101752 Accessed September 3, 2011.
30. Thatcher, *The Downing Street Years*, 14.
31. Richard Cockett, *Thinking the Unthinkable: Think-Tanks and the Economic Counter-Revolution 1931–1983* (London: HarperCollins, 1994), 282–283.
32. Campbell, *Margaret Thatcher: Volume One*, 372.
33. Young, *One of Us*, 22 and Campbell, *Margaret Thatcher: Volume One*, 60.
34. Campbell, *Margaret Thatcher: Volume One*, 372.
35. Lanny Ebenstein, *Milton Friedman: A Biography* (New York: Palgrave Macmillan, 2009).
36. Campbell, *Margaret Thatcher: Volume One*, 372; Cockett, *Thinking the Unthinkable*, 173–174 and Brian Harrison, "Mrs Thatcher and the Intellectuals," *Twentieth Century British History* 5 (1994), 206–245.
37. Cockett, *Thinking the Unthinkable*, 236–242.
38. David Smith, *The Rise and Fall of Monetarism* (Middlesex: Penguin, 1987), 47.
39. Dominic Sandbrook, *Seasons in the Sun: The Battle for Britain, 1974–1979* (London: Allen Lane, 2012), 227.
40. George A. Boyne, *Public Choice Theory and Local Government: A Comparative Analysis of the UK and the USA* (London: Macmillan, 1998); Colin Robinson, *Arthur Seldon: A Life for Liberty* (London: Profile Books, 2009), 129–135 and Daniel Stedman Jones, *Masters of the Universe: Hayek, Friedman, and the Birth of Neoliberal Politics* (Princeton and Oxford: Princeton University Press, 2012), 129.
41. Ben Jackson and Robert Saunders eds. *Making Thatcher's Britain* (Cambridge: Cambridge University Press, 2012), 5–6.
42. Margaret Thatcher, "Reflections on Liberty," *Hofstra Law Review* 28 (Summer 2000), 870.
43. Stedman Jones, *Masters of the Universe*, 167.
44. *Time*, February 3, 1986, page 16.
45. David P. Dolowitz, "British Employment Policy in the 1980s: Learning from the American Experience," *Governance 10* (January 1997), 23–42, Thatcher quote on page 29; David P. Dolowitz, *Learning from America: Policy Transfer and the Development of the British Workfare State* (Brighton, Sussex: Academic Press, 1998), quote on page 174, and David P. Dolowitz with Rob Hulme, Mike Nellis and Fiona O'Neill, *Policy Transfer and British Social Policy: Learning from the USA?* (Buckingham and Philadelphia: Open University Press, 2000).
46. Rob Hulme, "Education: Post-Compulsory Education in England and Wales," in David P. Dolowitz with Rob Hulme, Mike Nellis and Fiona O'Neill, *Policy Transfer and British Social Policy: Learning from the USA?* (Buckingham and Philadelphia: Open University Press, 2000), 77–97.
47. "Margaret Thatcher Speech at dinner to President Reagan (80th birthday)," February 6, 1991, MTF http://www.margaretthatcher.org/document/108260 Accessed August 14, 2011.
48. Campbell, *Margaret Thatcher: Volume One*, 357.

49. Ronald Reagan, *An American Life* (New York: Simon and Schuster, 1990), 204.
50. Thatcher, *The Path to Power*, 372.
51. Thatcher, *The Downing Street Years*, 157.
52. "Speech to U.S. Congress," February 20, 1985 in Harris, ed. *The Collected Speeches of Margaret Thatcher*, 242.
53. Richard Aldous, *Reagan and Thatcher: The Difficult Relationship* (New York and London: W. W. Norton and Co, 2012), 288; Nicholas Wapshott, *Ronald Reagan and Margaret Thatcher: A Political Marriage* (London: Sentinel, 2007); John Nott, *Here Today, Gone Tomorrow: Recollections of an Errant Politician* (London: Politico's, 2002), 270–271; Geoffrey Howe, *Conflict of Loyalty* (New York: St. Martin's Press, 1994), 325–337; Reagan, *An American Life*, 454, and Young, *One of Us*, 255–257, 346, 394–395, 398–400 and 479–481.
54. Nigel Lawson, "Economy: The New Conservatism *(Lecture to the Bow Group)*" August 4, 1980, MTF http://www.margaretthatcher.org/document/ 109505 Accessed September 3, 2011
55. "Radio Interview for Radio New Zealand," August 10, 1982, *Margaret Thatcher Complete Public Statements*, UDN: 82_231.
56. "Radio Interview for BBC Radio 4 program: Mrs Thatcher's Enlightenment: Two Hundred Years of Adam Smith," July 15, 1990, *Margaret Thatcher Complete Public Statements*, UDN: 90_177.
57. "Speech to Conservative Party Conference," October 8, 1976, *Margaret Thatcher Complete Public Statements*, UDN: 76_270.
58. "Speech to U.S. Congress," February 20, 1985 in Harris, ed. *The Collected Speeches of Margaret Thatcher*, 242.
59. Nigel Lawson, *The View from No. 11: Memoirs of a Tory Radical* (London: Bantam Press, 1992), 64.
60. Tony Benn, *The End of an Era: Diaries 1980–90* edited by Ruth Winstone (London: Hutchinson, 1992), 44.
61. *Socialist Review* (December 12, 1979–January 16, 1980), page 6.
62. Barry Miles, *Peace: 50 Years of Protest* (New York: Readers Digest, 2008), 194 and 199.
63. Tom Bromley, *Wired for Sound: Now That's What I Call an 80s Music Childhood* (London: Simon and Schuster, 2012), 190.
64. Miles, *Peace*, 199–217.
65. Stephen Foster, *From Working Class Hero to Absolute Disgrace: An Eighties Memoir* (London: Short Books, 2009), 203.
66. Andy McSmith, *No Such Thing as Society* (London: Constable, 2010), 47.
67. Alwyn W. Turner, *Rejoice! Rejoice! Britain in the 1980s* (London: Aurum, 2010), 97.
68. Louise Wener, *Different for Girls: My True-Life Adventures In Pop* (London: Ebury Press, 2010), 79 and 81.
69. Bruce Russett and Donald R. Deluca, "Theater Nuclear Forces: Public Opinion in Western Europe," *Political Science Quarterly* 98 (Summer 1983), 188; Steven K. Smith and Douglas A. Wertman, *US-West European Relations During the Reagan Years: The Perspective of West European Publics* (New York: St Martin's Press, 1992), 60 and Graham Stewart, *Bang! A History of Britain in the 1980s* (London: Atlantic Books, 2013), 204.
70. Holmes et al. *British Security Policy and the Atlantic Alliance*, 114–115.
71. Roger Fieldhouse, *Anti-Apartheid: A History of the Movement in Britain: A Study in Pressure Group Politics* (London: Merlin Press, 2005), 180–199.

72. Michael Palin, *Halfway to Hollywood: Diaries 1980–1988* (New York: Thomas Dunne Books, 2011), 431.
73. *New Musical Express*, December 21/28, 1985, page 33.
74. Fieldhouse, *Anti-Apartheid: A History of the Movement in Britain*, 302–303.
75. Foster, *From Working Class Hero to Absolute Disgrace*, 100.
76. Bromley, *Wired for Sound*, 255.
77. Fieldhouse, *Anti-Apartheid: A History of the Movement in Britain*, 121 and 433.
78. Holmes et al. *British Security Policy and the Atlantic Alliance*, 112–113 and 115.
79. *The New York Times*, November 13, 1983, Section 4, page 21.
80. Palin, *Halfway to Hollywood*, 417.
81. *The New York Times*, November 29, 1983, page A3.
82. Jorgen Rasmussen and James M. McCormick, "British Mass Perceptions of the Anglo-American Special Relationship," *Political Science Quarterly* 108 (Fall 1993).
83. Zachary Leader ed. *The Letters of Kingsley Amis* (London: HarperCollins, 2000), 967.
84. *Daily Express*, October 27, 1983, page 8.
85. *The New York Times*, November 29, 1983, page 3.
86. *Daily Express*, October 27, 1983, page 7.
87. E P Thompson, "Letter to Americans," in Mary Kaldor and Paul Anderson eds. *Mad Dogs: The US Raids on Libya* (London: Pluto Press, 1986), 13.
88. *New Musical Express*, December 20/29, 1986, page 30.
89. *Daily Express*, October 27, 1983, pages 6–7.
90. *The Guardian*, December 24, 1985, page 8.
91. John O' Farrell, *Things Can Only Get Better: Eighteen Miserable Years in the Life of a Labour Supporter 1979–1997* (London and New York: Doubleday, 1998), 32.
92. Steve Bell, *If . . . Only Again* (London: Methuen, 1984).
93. *New Musical Express*, December 21/28, 1985, page 41.
94. Russett and Deluca, "Theater Nuclear Forces: Public Opinion in Western Europe," 184.
95. Smith, *Reagan and Thatcher*, 242.
96. Lyrics Mode, http://www.lyricsmode.com/lyrics/c/collide/the_lunatics_have_taken_over_the_asylum.html Accessed June 26, 2012.
97. *The New York Times*, October 8, 1986, Section C, page 26 and *The New York Times*, January 16, 1987, Section C, page 6.
98. Chris Mullin, *A Very British Coup* (London: Hodder and Stoughton, 1982), 22 and 160, 24–25 and 161.
99. *The Sunday Times*, October 13, 1985, page 15.
100. *The Sunday Times*, November 10, 1985, page 26.
101. *The Independent*, May 30, 1990, page 11.
102. *Daily Express*, October 21, 1982, page 3.
103. *The Times*, July 10, 1986, page 33.
104. *The Guardian*, August 9, 1986, page 15.
105. Mike Lyons interview with author June 16, 2012.
106. *The Times*, August 12, 1985, page 8.
107. *The Times*, January 19, 1987, page 10 and January 20, 1987, page 10.
108. Sally Hewitt, *I Can Remember the 1980s* (London and Sydney: Franklin Watts, 2005), 8.
109. *The Washington Post*, Style Section, May 28, 1980, page 1.
110. Cheryl Buckley and Hilary Fawcett, *Fashioning the Feminine: Representation and Women's Fashion from the Fin de Siecle to the Present* (London and New York: I. B. Tauris, 2002), 132–133.

111. Mary Lyons interview with author June 27, 2012.
112. Patricia McManus interview with author September 2, 2012.
113. Geoffrey Lealand, *American Television Programmes on British Screens* (London: Broadcasting Research Unit, 1984), 77.
114. Mary Lyons interview with author June 27, 2012.
115. Peter O'Neill interview with author August 12, 2012.
116. Gareth Rowlands interview with author March 13, 2013.
117. Lindsay Brook et al. *British Social Attitudes Cumulative Sourcebook: The First Six Surveys* (Aldershot: Gower, 1992), A-10, A-11 and A-15.
118. *Christian Science Monitor,* March 3, 1986, page 27 and Robert J. Wybrow, *Britain Speaks Out, 1937–87: A Social History as Seen through the Gallup poll* (London: Macmillan, 1989), 134.
119. Smith and Wertman, *US-West European Relations During the Reagan Years,* 106–107.
120. *The New York Times,* September 30, 1985, page 1.
121. *The Guardian,* August 9, 1988, page 16.
122. *The Independent,* May 3, 1989, page 19.
123. *The New York Times,* Section 4, May 17, 1987, page 2.
124. *The Independent,* March 21, 1989, page 16.
125. *The Guardian,* December 28, 1988, page 9.
126. Mary Lyons interview with author June 27, 2012.
127. *Newsweek,* February 28, 1983, page 79.
128. Holmes et al., *British Security Policy and the Atlantic Alliance,* 107–108 and 116.
129. *Christian Science Monitor,* March 3, 1986, page 27.
130. *The Guardian,* October 22, 1987, page 14.
131. *The Times,* Weekend Section, January 25, 1997, page 2.
132. *The New York Times,* June 15, 1988, page 16.
133. *Daily Express,* June 5, 1986, page 26.
134. Bill Buford, *Among the Thugs* (New York: Vintage Books, 1990), 26.
135. *A Bit of Fry and Laurie: The Complete Collection... Every Bit!* (BBC, 2007).
136. Smith, *Reagan and Thatcher,* 266.
137. Brook et al. *British Social Attitudes Cumulative Sourcebook,* D-2.
138. Holmes et al., *British Security Policy and the Atlantic Alliance,* 113.

Chapter 5

1. *The Guardian,* September 16, 2000, page C3.
2. Jesper Gulddal, *Anti-Americanism in European Literature* (New York: Palgrave Macmillan, 2011), 167.
3. Andrew Kohut and Bruce Stokes, *American against the World* (New York: Owl Books, 2006), 1.
4. Birmingham Post, September 8, 2005, page 8.
5. *Chronicle of Higher Education,* November 21, 2003, page A34.
6. *The Observer,* January 23, 2000, page 18.
7. Jeremy Tunstall, "The United Kingdom" in Mary Kelly, Gianpietro Mazzoleni, and Denis McQuail eds. *The Media in Europe: The Euromedia Handbook* (London: Sage Publications Ltd; 3rd edition, 2004), 265.
8. Richard Pells, *Not like Us: How Europeans Have Loved, Hated, And Transformed American Culture since World War II* (New York: Basic Books, 1997), 231.

9. Jane Stokes, "Anglo-American Attitudes: Affirmations and Refutations of 'Americanicity' " in British Television Advertising, in Yahya R. Kamalipour ed. *Images of the U.S. around the World: A Multicultural Perspective* (Albany, NY: State University of New York Press, 1999), 147–156.
10. Kamalipour ed. *Images of the U.S. Around the World: A Multicultural Perspective*, xxvi.
11. Benjamin Barber, *Jihad vs. McWorld: How Globalism and Tribalism Are Reshaping the World* (New York: Times Book, 1995), 102.
12. Steven Daly and Nathaniel Wice, "London is Dead" *New Republic*, June 14, 1993, 11–12.
13. Johnny Ryan, *A History of the Internet and the Digital Future* (London: Reaktion Books, 2010), 55 and 115.
14. A. H. Halsey with Josephine Webb eds. *Twentieth-Century British Social Trends* (London: Macmillan Press, 2000), 640.
15. Ryan, *A History of the Internet and the Digital Future*, 125.
16. Cinema Exhibitors' Association (CEA) Website, http://www.cinemauk.org.uk/ukcinemasector/admissions/annualukcinemaadmissions1935–2010/ Accessed June 17, 2011.
17. Eddie Dyja, *Studying British Cinema: The 1990s* (Leighton Buzzard: Auteur, 2010), 94–95.
18. Pells, *Not Like Us*, 229.
19. Peter Todd, "The British Film Industry in the 1990s," in Robert Murphy ed. *British Cinema of the 90s* (London: BFI Publishing, 2000), 22 and Geoff Brown, "Something for Everyone: British Film Culture in the 1990s," in Robert Murphy ed. *British Cinema of the 90s* (London: BFI Publishing, 2000), 31.
20. Dyja, *Studying British Cinema*, 234.
21. Brown, "Something for Everyone," 33.
22. David Puttnam with Neil Watson, *Movies and Money* (New York: Alfred A. Knopf, 1998), 245–256.
23. Dyja, *Studying British Cinema*.
24. *Evening Standard*, May 18, 1993, pages 14 and 15.
25. Bakari Kitwana, *Why White Kids Love Hip-Hop: Wankstas, Wiggers, Wannabes, and the New Reality of Race in America* (New York: Basic Books, 2005); Jeff Chang, *Can't Stop Won't Stop: A History of the Hip-Hop Generation* (New York: Picador, 2005); Eithne Quinn, *Nuthin' but a "G" Thang: The Culture and Commerce of Gangsta Rap* (New York: Columbia University Press, 2005); Robin D. G. Kelley, *Race Rebels: Culture, Politics and the Black Working Class* (New York: Free Press, 1994) and David Toop, *Rap Attack 2: African Rap to Global Hip Hop* (London: Serpent's Tail, 1991).
26. Daly and Wice, "London is Dead," 11.
27. *The Sunday Times,* December 5, 1993, page 7.
28. Brown, "Something for Everyone," 32.
29. Anna Quindlen, *Imagined London: A Tour of the World's Greatest Fictional City* (Washington, DC: National Geographic, 2004), 141.
30. Dave Haslam, *Adventures on the Wheels of Steel: The Rise of the Superstar DJs* (London: Fourth Estate, 2001).
31. Bill Brewster and Frank Broughton, *The Record Players: DJ Revolutionaries* (London: DJ History.com, 2010), 251.
32. Matthew Collin, *Altered States: The Story of Ecstasy and Acid House* (London: Serpent's Tail, 1997); Sheryl Garratt, *Adventures in Wonderland: A Decade of Club Culture*

(London: Headline: 1998) and Bill Brewster and Frank Broughton, *Last Night A DJ Saved My Life* (London: Headline, 1999).

33. Mark Yarm, *Everybody Loves Our Town: An Oral History of Grunge* (New York: Crown Archetype, 2011)
34. Halsey with Webb eds. *Twentieth-Century British Social Trends*, 640.
35. Alwyn W. Turner, *Rejoice! Rejoice! Britain in the 1980s* (London: Aurum, 2010), 335.
36. NFL London, http://www.nfllondon.net/history.html Accessed March 10, 2011.
37. Barber, *Jihad vs. McWorld* 101.
38. Karen DeBres, "Burgers for Britain; A Cultural Geography of McDonald's UK," *The Journal of Cultural Geography* 22 (Spring/Summer, 2005), 124.
39. Pells, *Not Like Us*, 296–297.
40. Quezi.com, http://quezi.com/5940 Accessed June 18, 2011.
41. Mike Storry and Peter Childs eds. *British Cultural Identities* (London and New York: Routledge, 1997), 69 and Murray Fraser with Joe Kerr, *Architecture and the "Special Relationship": The American influence on Post-war British Architecture* (London and New York: Routledge, 2007), 466.
42. Laura Mason, *Food Culture in Great Britain* (Westport, CT, and London: Greenwood Press, 2004), 112.
43. Cherie Blair, *Speaking for Myself: My Life from Liverpool to Downing Street* (New York and London: Little, Brown and Company, 2008), 93.
44. Francis Beckett, *Gordon Brown: Past, Present and Future* (London: Haus Publishing, 2007).
45. Tony Blair, *A Journey: My Political Life* (New York and Toronto: Alfred A. Knopf, 2010), xii.
46. *The Guardian,* May 7, 2003, page 7.
47. Tom Bower, *Gordon Brown* (London: HarperCollins, 2004). Gordon Brown chose no American songs on his appearance on the BBC radio show *Desert Island Discs* on March 3, 1996 see http://www.bbc.co.uk/radio4/features/desert-island-discs/castaway/539e19df#p0093nrg Accessed on May 22, 2011. Tony Blair, in contrast picked Bruce Springsteen and blues artist Robert Johnson when he appeared on *Desert Island Discs* on November 24, 1996 see http://www.bbc.co.uk/radio4/features/desert-island-discs/castaway/ca0f2a43#p0093n5f Accessed on May 22, 2011.
48. Stanley B. Greenberg, *Dispatches from the War Room: In the Trenches with Five Extraordinary Leaders* (New York: Thomas Dunne Books, 2009), 180.
49. Greenberg, *Dispatches from the War Room*, chapters 4 and 5, and Philip Gould, *The Unfinished Revolution: How the Modernisers Saved the Labour Party* (London: Abacus, 1999), 172–177.
50. James Naughtie, *The Rivals: The Intimate Story of a Political Marriage* (London: Fourth Estate, 2001), 214–215 and Peter Riddell, *The Unfulfilled Prime Minister: Tony Blair's Quest for a Legacy* (London: Politico, updated and revised edition, 2006), 8.
51. *Tribune*, January 29, 1993, page 5.
52. John Rentoul, *Tony Blair Prime Minister* (London: Little, Brown and Company, 2001), 192–194.
53. Anthony Seldon, *Blair* (London: Free Press, 2004), 124 and Greenberg, *Dispatches from the War Room*, 186.
54. Trevor Jones and Tim Newburn, *Policy Transfer and Criminal Justice: Exploring U.S Influence Over British Crime Control Policy* (Maidenhead: Open University Press, 2005).

55. *Tribune*, January 29, 1993, page 5.
56. Martin Pugh, *Speak for Britain! A New History of the Labour Party* (London: The Bodley Head, 2010), 393.
57. Naughtie, *The Rivals*, 214–215; Donald Macintyre, *Mandelson and the Making of New Labour* (London: HarperCollins, 1999), 368–369 and Riddell, *The Unfulfilled Prime Minister*, 24–25.
58. Claire Short, *An Honorable Deception? New Labour, Iraq, and the Misuse of Power* (London: Simon and Schuster, 2004), 2.
59. *The Times,* June 10, 2002, page 16. See also Richard Heffernan, *New Labour and Thatcherism: Political Change in Britain* (London: Macmillan, 2000).
60. Tony Benn, *More Time for Politics Diaries 2001–2007* selected and edited by Ruth Winstone (London: Hutchinson, 2007), 111.
61. Desmond King and Mark Wickham-Jones, "From Clinton to Blair: The Democratic (Party) Origins of Welfare to Work," *Political Quarterly* 70 (1999), 72; Jamie Peck, *Workfare States* (New York and London, Guildford Press, 2001), 4, and Anne Daguerre and Peter Taylor-Gooby, "Neglecting Europe: Explaining the Predominance of American Ideas in New Labour's Welfare Policies since 1997," *Journal of European Social Policy* 14 (February 2004): 25–39.
62. Bower, *Gordon Brown*, 102, 104, 232–233 and 344 and King and Wickham-Jones, "From Clinton to Blair: The Democratic (Party) Origins of Welfare to Work," 62–74.
63. Conn Coughlin, *American Ally: Tony Blair and the War on Terror* (New York: HarperCollins, 2006), 7; Philip Stephens, *Tony Blair: The Making of a World Leader* (New York: Penguin, 2004), 71 and James Naughtie, *The Rivals: The Intimate Story of a Political Marriage* (London: Fourth Estate, 2001), 218.
64. Blair, *A Journey*, 231.
65. James Naughtie, *The Accidental American: Tony Blair and the Presidency* (New York: Public Affairs, 2004), 47 and Naughtie, *The Rivals*, 223–229.
66. Ole R. Holsti, *To See Ourselves as Others See Us: How Publics Abroad View the United States after 9/11* (Ann Arbor, MI: University of Michigan Press, 2008), 30
67. Francis Fukuyama, *The End of History and the Last Man* (New York: Free Press, 1992).
68. Steven Kull, "Culture Wars? How Americans and Europeans View Globalization," *Brookings Review* 19 (Fall 2001), 18–21.
69. *The Observer,* January 23, 2000, page 18.
70. John Goodwin ed. *Peter Hall's Diaries* (London: Oberon Books, originally published in 1982, second edition 2000), 13.
71. *The Sunday Times*, May 12, 1991, page 7.
72. Nigel Copsey, *Contemporary British Fascism: The British National Party and the Quest for Legitimacy* (Basingstoke: Palgrave Macmillan, 2004).
73. Jeremy Black, *Britain since the Seventies: Politics and Society in the Consumer Age* (London: Reaktion, 2004), 155, 200, 209 and 215; Richard Weight, *Patriots: National Identity in Britain 1940–2000* (London: Macmillan, 2002) and The *Sun*, April 23, 1999, "100 Reasons Why It's Great to Be English" supplement.
74. *Best of British,* November 2004, pages 4–5.
75. Jeremy Black, *Modern British History since 1900* (London: Macmillan, 2000), 350 and 356.
76. Eddie Dyja, *Studying British Cinema: The 1990s* (Leighton Buzzard: Auteur, 2010).
77. *The Financial Times*, February 24, 2001, page 24.
78. *Daily Express*, January 26, 1998, page 27.
79. Andrei S. Markovits, *Uncouth Nation: Why Europe Dislikes America* (Princeton and Oxford: Princeton University Press, 2007), 88–89 and 104 and *Daily Express,* February 7, 2001, page 75.

80. *The Sunday Times*, Section 10, May 8, 1994, page 13.
81. *The Observer*, January 23, 2000, page 18.
82. *Daily Mail*, March 20, 1999, page 40.
83. King and Wickham-Jones, "From Clinton to Blair: The Democratic (Party) Origins of Welfare to Work," 73.
84. *The Scotsman*, February 3, 1998, page17.
85. Anthony Seldon, *Blair* (London: Free Press, 2004), 123.
86. Naomi Klein, *No Logo* (New York: Picador, 1999).
87. Karen DeBres, "Burgers for Britain: A Cultural Geography of McDonald's UK," *The Journal of Cultural Geography* 22 (Spring/Summer, 2005), 124. See also George Ritzer, *The McDonaldization of Society* (Newbury Park, CA: Pine Forge Press, 1993).
88. John Vidal, *McLibel: Burger Culture on Trial* (New York: The New Press, 1997).
89. Steven Kull, "Culture Wars? How Americans and Europeans View Globalization," *Brookings Review* 19 (Fall 2001), 18–21.
90. "Britain Turning against Globalisation," October 11, 2001, Ipsos MORI website http://www.ipsos-mori.com/researchpublications/researcharchive/1270/Britain-Turning-Against-Globalisation.aspx Accessed October 17, 2012.
91. "Letter from London," *The American Spectator*, January 1998, pages 52–53.
92. *Sunday Express*, October 8, 2000, page 40
93. *The Independent*, November 9, 1996, page 3, *The Times*, May 16, 1997, page 19, and *The Independent*, October 22, 1997, page 10.
94. "*Americana* 'Dumb' Part One" YouTube http://www.youtube.com/watch?v=4wXzz K5R__g Accessed June 9, 2011.
95. *Evening Standard*, July 2, 1993, page 22.
96. *The Guardian*, August 16, 1991, page 8.
97. *Daily Mail*, January 29, 1993, page 39.
98. David P. Farrington, Patrick A. Langan, and Michael Tonry eds. *Cross-National Studies in Crime and Justice* (Washington, DC: U.S. Department of Justice, 2004), iv.
99. BBC News, http://news.bbc.co.uk/2/hi/uk_news/810522.stm Accessed December 7, 2012.
100. *The Toronto Star*, November 9, 1997, page A1.
101. "Letter from London," *The American Spectator*, January 1998, pages 52–53.
102. Susan Marling, *American Affair: The Americanisation of Britain* (London: Boxtree, 1993), 7.
103. Jonathan Freedland, *Bring Home the Revolution: The Case for a British Republic* (London: Fourth Estate, 1998), 3.
104. *Daily Mail*, November 11, 2000, page 5.
105. *The Scotsman*, July 4, 1998, page 13; and Freedland, *Bring Home the Revolution*
106. *The Observer*, July 5, 1998, page 18.
107. *The Times*, Weekend Section, January 25, 1997, page 2.
108. *The Sunday Times*, December 5, 1993, page 7.
109. *The Irish Times*, February 8, 1997, page 5.
110. John Harris, *Britpop! Cool Britannia and the Spectacular Demise of English Rock* (Cambridge, MA: Da Capo Press, 2004), 79.
111. Harris, *Britpop!*, 77.
112. *Select*, April 1993.
113. Harris, *Britpop!*, 72–73.
114. Alex James, *Bit of a Blur* (London: Little, Brown, 2007), 98. *Bad Vibes: Britpop and My Part in Its Downfall* (London: William Heinemann, 2009) by the Auteurs singer Luke Haines and the wonderful *Different for Girls: My True-Life Adventures in Pop* (London: Ebury Press, 2010) by Sleeper singer Louise Wener demonstrate the shallowness of the Britpop scene.

115. Harris, *Britpop!*, 79.
116. Paul Anderson and Nyta Mann, *Safety First: The Making of New Labour* (London: Granta Books, 1997), 384–385.
117. King and Wickham-Jones, "From Clinton to Blair: The Democratic (Party) Origins of Welfare to Work," 68.
118. Anderson and Mann, *Safety First: The Making of New Labour*, 16.
119. Stephen Driver and Luke Martell, *New Labour: Politics After Thatcherism* (Cambridge: Polity Press, 1998), 23–24.
120. *The Age,* September 7, 2010 at http://www.theage.com.au/opinion/politics/oxford-days-with-my-friend-tony-20100906-14xgj.html Accessed June 29, 2011.
121. Driver and Martell, *New Labour*, 23 and 109.
122. Halsey with Josephine Webb eds. *Twentieth-Century British Social Trends*, 640.
123. BBC News, http://news.bbc.co.uk/2/hi/8424597.stm Accessed July 25, 2012.
124. Andrew Geddes, *Britain and the European Union* (Basingstoke: Palgrave MacMillan, 2013)
125. Brian Harrison, *Finding a Role? The United Kingdom, 1970–1990* (Oxford: Clarendon Press, 2010), 18.
126. Karen O'Reilly, *The British on the Costa del Sol: Transnational Identities and Local Communities* (London and New York: Routledge, 2000).
127. Collin, *Altered States* Garratt, *Adventures in Wonderland*; Simon Reynolds, *Energy Flash: Journey through Rave Music and Dance Culture* (London: Picador, 1998) and Brewster and Broughton, *Last Night A DJ Saved My Life*.
128. Turner, *Rejoice! Rejoice!*, 331.
129. Hunter Davies, *London to Loweswater: A Journey through England at the End of the Twentieth Century* (Edinburgh and London: Mainstream Publishing, 1999), 14.
130. Christina Hardyment, *Slice of Life: The British Way of Eating since 1945* (London: BBC Books, 1995), 136.
131. Michael H. Fisher et al. *A South-Asian History of Britain: Four Centuries of Peoples from the Indian Sub-Continent* (Oxford and Westport, CT: Greenwood, 2007), 198–204.
132. *The Times*, April 26, 2008, page 98

Chapter 6

1. Andrew Kohut and Bruce Stokes, *American against the World* (New York: Owl Books, 2006), 165.
2. *London Review of Books,* October 4, 2001, page 20.
3. *New Statesman*, September 17, 2001, page 4.
4. Anna Kiernan ed. *Voices for Peace: An Anthology* (London: Scribner, 2001), 5–6 and 201.
5. *The Guardian*, January 16, 2003, page 22. http://www.guardian.co.uk/stage/2003/jan/16/theatre.artsfeatures1?INTCMP= SRCH Accessed January 12, 2013.
6. *Daily Express,* November 18, 2003, page 12.
7. *The Sunday Times,* July 4, 2004, page 7.
8. *The Weekly Standard,* May 31, 2004, page 23.
9. *The Economist,* November 6, 2003, page 12.
10. Paul Davis, *Us and Them: What the Americans Think of the British, What the British Think of the Americans* (New York: Princeton Architectural Press, 2004), 13, 31 and 51.

11. *The Economist*, March 29, 2008, pages 71–73.
12. *Wall Street Journal*, May 19, 2010, page 19.
13. Julia E. Sweig, *Friendly Fire: Losing Friends and Making Enemies in the Anti-American Century* (New York: Public Affairs, 2006), 110.
14. *The Guardian*, November 29, 2003, page 7.
15. *The New York Times*, February 4, 2002, page 23.
16. *New Statesman*, July 22, 2002, page 11.
17. T. R. Reid, *The United States of Europe: The New Superpower and the End of American Supremacy* (New York: Penguin Press, 2004), 7–11.
18. Kohut and Stokes, *American against the World*, 32.
19. Francis Beckett, *Gordon Brown: Past, Present and Future* (London: Haus Publishing, 2007), 203.
20. Kohut and Stokes, *American against the World*, 174.
21. *Daily Mirror*, November 4, 2004, pages 6–7.
22. Brian Eno et al. *Not One More Death* (London and New York: Verso, 2006), 67.
23. Public Diplomacy, http://www.publicdiplomacy.org/41.htm Accessed December 20, 2012.
24. BBC News, http://news.bbc.co.uk/2/hi/uk/4881474.stm Accessed June 3, 2012.
25. *Christian Science Monitor*, October 15, 2009, page 9.
26. Carol Gould, *Don't Tread On Me: Anti-Americanism Abroad* (New York and London: Encounter Books, 2009), xiv and 24–26.
27. BBC News, http://news.bbc.co.uk/2/hi/uk/4881474.stm Accessed June 3, 2012.
28. *The Guardian*, October 18, 2004, http://www.guardian.co.uk/world/2004/oct/18/usa.guardianletters Accessed September 14, 2012.
29. Ibid.
30. Amazon, http://www.amazon.com/Dont-Tread-Me-Anti-Americanism-Abroad/dp/1594032394 Accessed November 23, 2012.
31. Alexei Lalo, "Borat as Tragicomedy of Anti US-Americanism," *Comparative Literature and Culture* 11 (2009), http://vdocs.lib.purdue.edu/cgi/viewcontent.cgi?article=1468&context= clcweb Accessed May 22, 2012.
32. *The Guardian*, January 31, 1998, page 1 and *The Scotsman*, February 21, 1998, page 13.
33. Facebook LFC Reds, http://www.facebook.com/pages/Thanks-but-NO-YANKS/262589086647 Accessed June 11, 2011 and Fox Soccer, http://msn.foxsports.com/foxsoccer/worldcup/story/american-flag-burning-by-liverpool-fans-should-incense-yanks Accessed June 12, 2011.
34. George W. Bush, *Decision Points* (New York: Crown Publications, 2010), 230–231.
35. Tony Blair, *A Journey: My Political Life* (New York and Toronto: Alfred A. Knopf, 2010), 392.
36. Bush, *Decision Points*, 140 and 230–231.
37. Blair, *A Journey*, 507.
38. Blair, *A Journey*, 399.
39. John Burton and Eileen McCabe, *We Don't Do God: Blair's Religious Belief and its Consequences* (London: Continuum, 2009).
40. Peter Riddell, *Hug Them Close: Blair, Clinton, Bush and the 'Special Relationship'* (London, Politico's, 2003), 2.
41. Claire Short, *An Honorable Deception? New Labour, Iraq, and the Misuse of Power* (London: Simon and Schuster, 2004), 272
42. James Naughtie, *The Rivals: The Intimate Story of a Political Marriage* (London: Fourth Estate, 2001), 223–229; James Naughtie, *The Accidental American: Tony Blair and*

the Presidency (New York: Public Affairs, 2004); Sweig, *Friendly Fire*, 107–114, and Philip Stephens, *Tony Blair: The Making of a World Leader* (New York: Penguin, 2004), Chapters 9–12.

43. Blair, *A Journey*, 409.
44. Patrick Deer, "The Dogs of War: Myths of British Anti-Americanism," in Andrew Ross and Kristin Ross eds. *Anti-Americanism* (New York and London: New York University Press, 2004), 158–178.
45. *The Times*, March 18, 2003, page 1.
46. *The Observer*, November 16, 2003, page 17.
47. MacRumors, http://forums.macrumors.com/showthread.php?t= 243926 Accessed May 19, 2012.
48. *NME Rock 'n' Roll Yearbook*, 2006, page 6
49. Paul Wood interview with author April 28, 2013.
50. Braggtopia, http://www.braggtopia.com/songs/bushwar-words.htm Accessed September 8, 2012.
51. Lyrics Mode, http://www.lyricsmode.com/lyrics/g/george_michael/shoot_the_dog.html Accessed September 8, 2012.
52. Lyrics Mode, http://www.lyricsmode.com/lyrics/p/pet_shop_boys/#share Accessed September 8, 2012.
53. MacRumors, http://forums.macrumors.com/showthread.php?t= 243926 Accessed May 19, 2012.
54. *The Daily Telegraph*, July 3, 2006, page 10.
55. Andrei S. Markovits, *Uncouth Nation: Why Europe Dislikes America* (Princeton and Oxford: Princeton University Press, 2007), 1.
56. Sweig, *Friendly Fire*, x.
57. Giacomo Chiozza, *Anti-Americanism and the American World Order* (Baltimore, MD: The Johns Hopkins University Press, 2009), 31.
58. Jesper Gulddal, *Anti-Americanism in European Literature* (New York: Palgrave Macmillan, 2011), 168.
59. Phillip Dick interview with author May 7, 2013.
60. GfK Roper, http://www.gfk.com/group/press_information/press_releases/008789/index.en.html Accessed July 5, 2012.
61. BBC News, http://www.bbc.co.uk/news/world-middle-east-11069261 Accessed June 13, 2011.
62. *The Guardian*, March 29, 2010, page 11.
63. *The Telegraph* April 19, 2010, http://www.telegraph.co.uk/comment/columnists/maryriddell/7607847/General-Election-2010-If-nothing-else-Nick-Clegg-has-held-up-a-mirror-to-David-Camerons-defects.html Accessed June 29, 2012.
64. *The Sunday Times,* March 14, 2010, page 31.
65. *The Daily Telegraph*, July 26, 2012, page 16.
66. Nile Gardiner, "Mind the Gap: Is the Relationship Still Special?" *World Affairs,* March/April 2011, http://www.worldaffairsjournal.org/article/mind-gap-relationship-still-special.
67. *The Telegraph,* March 11, 2010, http://blogs.telegraph.co.uk/news/alexsingleton/100029555/why-barack-obama-has-made-me-boycott-america/ Accessed October 11, 2012.
68. Nik Skeat interview with author May 16, 2013
69. Sophie Meunier, "The Dog that Did Not Bark: Anti-Americanism and the 2008 Financial Crisis in Europe," (2011), http://euce.org/eusa/2011/papers/9h_meunier.pdf Accessed December 22, 2012.

70. *The Guardian*, January 24, 2009, page 4, and *The Daily Express*, April 24, 2009, page 38.
71. *Evening Standard*, January 8, 2008, page 32.
72. BBC World Service Poll, http://www.worldpublicopinion.org/pipa/pipa/pdf/apr10/BBCViews_Apr10_rpt.pdf Accessed August 13, 2012 and http://www.bbc.co.uk/pressoffice/pressreleases/stories/2007/01_january/23/us.shtml Accessed August 13, 2012.
73. Pew Research Center, http://www.pewglobal.org/2012/06/13/global-opinion-of-obama-slips-international-policies-faulted/ Accessed November 10, 2012.
74. "Global Attitudes Project," Pew Research Center http://www.pewglobal.org/files/2012/06/Pew-Global-Attitudes-U.S.-Image-Report-FINAL-June-13-2012.pdf, page 61, Accessed November 10, 2012.
75. Jan Nederveen Pieterse, *Global Mélange: Globalization and culture* (Lanham, MD: Rowman & Littlefield, 2003) and Jan Nederveen Pieterse, *Ethnicities and Global Multiculture: Pants for an Octopus* (Lanham, MD: Rowman & Littlefield, 2007).
76. William H. Marling, *How "American" Is Globalization?* (Baltimore: The Johns Hopkins University Press, 2006), 77.
77. *Chicago Tribune*, April 18, 2013, page 23.
78. Peter Marsh, *The New Industrial Revolution: Consumers, Globalization and the End of Mass Production* (New Haven and London: Yale University Press, 2012), 237–238.
79. *Time*, February 25, 2013, page 9.
80. *The Economist*, January 12–18, 2013, page 55.
81. Fareed Zakaria, *The Post-American World* (New York and London: W. W. Norton and Co, 2008).
82. The number of books devoted to the financial crisis is voluminous. Among the best are George Cooper, *The Origin of Financial Crises: Central Banks, Credit Bubbles, and the Efficient Market Fallacy* (New York: Vintage, 2008); Joseph E. Stiglitz, *Freefall: America, Free Markets and the Sinking of the World Economy* (New York: WW Norton, 2010) and Michael Lewis, *The Big Short: Inside the Doomsday Machine* (New York: W. W. Norton, 2010).
83. *The Economist*, September 8, 2012, page 59.
84. Harold Evans, *They Made America: From the Steam Engine to the Search Engine: Two Centuries of Innovators* (New York: Back Bay, 2006), 13 and Robert Atkinson and Stephen Ezell, *Innovation Economics: The Race for Global Advantage* (New Haven, CT: Yale University Press, 2012).
85. World Intellectual Property Organization, http://www.wipo.int/pressroom/en/articles/2012/article_0001.html Accessed November 12, 2012.
86. "Global Attitudes Project," Pew Research Center, page 78, http://www.pewglobal.org/files/2012/06/Pew-Global-Attitudes-U.S.-Image-Report-FINAL-June-13-2012.pdf Accessed November 10, 2012.
87. Zakaria, *The Post-American World*, 36.
88. *Newsweek*, August 9, 2010, http://www.thedailybeast.com/newsweek/2010/08/09/post-anti-americanism.html Accessed October 12, 2012.
89. Mary Lyons interview with author June 27, 2012.
90. *The Globe and Mail*, July 22, 2010, page A15.
91. Kohut and Stokes, *American against the World*, 35.
92. *Daily Mail*, May 10, 2012, http://www.dailymail.co.uk/news/article-1275878/Three-quarters-Britons-want-emigrate-Australia-popular-destination.html Accessed November 10, 2012.

93. Breaking Travel News, http://www.breakingtravelnews.com/news/article/88-want-to-leave-broken-britain-for-new-life-abroad/ Accessed November 10, 2012.
94. Peter Todd, "The British Film Industry in the 1990s," in Robert Murphy ed. *British Cinema of the 90s* (London: BFI Publishing, 2000), 22.
95. John Fitzgerald, *Studying British Cinema: 1999–2009* (Leighton Buzzard: Auteur, 2010).
96. Marling, *How "American" Is Globalization?*, 18 and 25.
97. *Daily Mirror,* July 7, 2008, page 7.
98. BBC News, http://news.bbc.co.uk/2/hi/8424597.stm Accessed July 25, 2012
99. *The Independent,* January 11, 2011, page 6.
100. Official Chart Company, http://www.officialcharts.com/chart-news/the-first-ever-official-singles-chart-revisited-1708/ and http://www.officialcharts.com/search-results-chart/_/2012/11/17 Accessed July 15, 2013.
101. BBC Radio 1 Newsbeat, http://www.bbc.co.uk/newsbeat/20754852 Accessed June 14, 2013.
102. *Sunday Chicago Tribune*, Section 4, June 10, 2012, page 10 and *Chicago Tribune,* Section 5, June 15, 2012, page 9.
103. *New York Times,* Arts and Leisure section, August 26, 2012, page 16.
104. Football Fan Cast, http://www.footballfancast.com/premiership/foreign-ownership-in-the-premier-league-why-so-much-and-what-does-it-mean-2 Accessed December 21, 2012.
105. David Conn, *Richer Than God: Manchester City, Modern Football and Growing Up* (London: Quercus, 2012)
106. *The Independent on Sunday,* November 20, 2005, page 60.
107. *The Times*, May 25, 2012, page 49.
108. Laura Mason, *Food Culture in Great Britain* (Westport, Connecticut, and London: Greenwood Press, 2004), 171–172.
109. The Student Room website, http://www.thestudentroom.co.uk/showthread.php?t=1459535&page=7&page=7 Accessed September 9, 2012.
110. *The Telegraph,* October 21, 2009, http://www.telegraph.co.uk/finance/6396381/10-foreign-takeovers-of-UK-companies-in-the-past-decade.html Accessed September 6, 2012.
111. *Times of India,* December 6, 2006, http://articles.timesofindia.indiatimes.com/2006-12-06/international-business/27822767_1_second-biggest-investor-indian-investors-foreign-direct-investment-agency Accessed September 6, 2012.
112. *The Scotsman*, May 4, 2012, page 40.
113. *Daily Mail*, April 13, 2012, http://www.dailymail.co.uk/news/article-2129507/Britain-sale-Uniquely-world-Britain-sold-half-companies-foreigners-And-paying-price.html Accessed September 6, 2012.
114. *Daily Express*, October 28, 2010, page 46.
115. *Daily Express,* December 16, 2011, page 79.
116. *Daily Star*, July 4, 2012, page 6.
117. *Daily Express,* June 29, 2011, page 26.
118. Tim Bale, *The Conservative Party from Thatcher to Cameron* (Cambridge: Polity, 2010), 161 and 226.
119. *The Scotsman*, April 14, 2010, page 1.
120. *Time*, April 14, 2010, http://content.time.com/time/world/article/0,8599,1981915,00.html
121. *2010 Yearbook of Immigration Statistics* (Washington DC: Office of Immigration Statistics, US Department of Homeland Security, August 2011), 8–10 and 70.

122. Wendy D. Roth, "United Kingdom," in Mary C. Waters and Reed Ueda with Helen B. Marrow. eds. *The New Americans: A Guide to Immigration since 1965* (Cambridge, MA: Harvard University Press, 2007), 642.
123. Pierangelo Isernia, "Anti-Americanism in Europe During the Cold War," in Peter J. Katzenstein and Robert O. Keohane eds. *Anti-Americanisms in World Politics* (Ithaca and London: Cornell University Press, 2007), 64.
124. Office for National Statistics, "Detailed country of birth and nationality analysis from the 2011 Census of England and Wales," May 2013, page 8, at http://www.ons.gov.uk/ons/dcp171776_310441.pdf.
125. *Sunday Chicago Tribune,* April 15, 2012, page 16.
126. Visit Britain website, http://www.visitbritain.org/insightsandstatistics/inboundtourism facts/ Accessed May 28, 2013.
127. Office for National Statistics, http://www.ons.gov.uk/ons/rel/family-spending/family-spending/family-spending-2011-edition/sum-consumer-durables-nugget.html Accessed April 30, 2013.
128. *Chicago Tribune,* Section 2, December 7, 2012, page 1.
129. *The Guardian,* May 16, 2012, page 13.
130. *New York Times,* Sunday Review Section, April 21, 2013, pages 1 and 6.
131. Raymond Johnston interview with author April 28, 2013.
132. Patricia McManus interview with author September 2, 2012.
133. Brian O' Sullivan interview with author July 23, 2012.
134. Mike Penny interview with author March 13, 2013
135. Gareth Rowlands interview with author March 13, 2013
136. *The Guardian,* December 27, 2012, http://www.guardian.co.uk/commentisfree/2012/dec/27/piers-morgan-gun-laws Accessed January 15, 2013.
137. Anglotopia.net http://www.anglotopia.net/british-identity/humor/15-way-to-not-look-and-act-like-an-idiot-american-in-britain/ Accessed November 10, 2012.
138. Liz Fiorani interview with author April 28, 2013.
139. Mike Penny interview with author March 13, 2013
140. Peter O'Neill interview with author August 12, 2012.

Conclusion

1. *The Minority Report,* http://mrjanari.wordpress.com/2011/04/13/ownership-of-english-premier-league-clubs/ Accessed July 8, 2011.

Bibliography

Interviews

Jon Denton, August 23, 2012.
Phillip Dick, May 7, 2013.
Liz Fiorani, April 28, 2013.
James Graham, June 19, 2013.
Raymond Johnston, April 28, 2013.
Ray Kennedy, July 31, 2011.
Mary Lyons, June 27, 2012.
Michael Lyons, June 16, 2012.
Patricia McManus, September 2, 2012.
Roderick McNeill, March 6, 2013.
Patrick Mills, February 8, 2013.
Mary Minnock, July 29, 2012.
Davina Neal, July 30, 2012.
Peter O'Neill, August 12, 2012.
Brian O'Sullivan, July 23, 2012.
Christine Paine, April 28, 2013.
Michael Penny, March 13, 2013.
Gareth Rowlands, March 13, 2013.
Nik Skeat, May 16, 2013.
Barbara Smith, March 24, 2013.
Sheryl Smithson, February 25, 2013.
Alan Stepney, June 18, 2013.
Paul Wood, April 28, 2013.
Gary Younge, February 8, 2013.

Newspapers and magazines

The American Spectator
Best of British Past and Present
Birmingham Post
Chicago Tribune
Christian Science Monitor
Chronicle of Higher Education
Commentary
Daily Express
Daily Herald

Daily Mirror
Daily Mail
Daily Record
Daily Star
Daily Telegraph
The Economist
Encounter
Evening Standard
The Financial Times
The Globe and Mail
The Guardian
The Independent
The Irish Times
Life
The Listener
London Review of Books
Melody Maker
Mojo
The Nation
New Musical Express
New Republic
The New Statesman and Nation
Newsweek
The New York Times
The Observer
Picture Post
Record Collector
The Scotsman
Socialist Review
The Sun
Time
The Times
The Toronto Star
Tribune
Uncut
U. S. News and World Report
Wall Street Journal
The Washington Post
The Weekly Standard
The Word

Autobiographies, Diaries and Memoirs

Agee, Philip. *Inside the Company: CIA Diary*. London: Penguin, 1975.
———. *On the Run*. Secaucus, NJ: Lyle Stuart, 1987.
Bakewell, Joan. *The Centre of the Bed: An Autobiography*. London: Hodder and Stoughton, 2003.
The Beatles. *The Beatles Anthology*. San Francisco: Chronicle Books, 2000.
Benn, Tony. *Against the Tide: Diaries 1973–1976*. London: Hutchinson, 1989.

———. *The End of an Era: Diaries 1980–1990* edited by Ruth Winstone. London: Hutchinson, 1992.

———- *Free at Last!: Diaries 1991–2001* edited by Ruth Winstone. London: Hutchinson, 2002.

———. *More Time for Politics Diaries 2001–2007* edited by Ruth Winstone. London: Hutchinson, 2007.

Black, Cilla. *What's It All About.* London: Ebury Press, 2003.

Black, Pauline. *Black By Design: A 2-Tone Memoir.* London: Serpent's Tail, 2011.

Blair, Cherie. *Speaking for Myself: My Life from Liverpool to Downing Street.* New York and London: Little, Brown and Company, 2008.

Blair, Tony. *A Journey: My Political Life.* New York and Toronto: Alfred A. Knopf, 2010.

Boyson, Rhodes. *Speaking My Mind: The Autobiography of Rhodes Boyson.* London and Chester Springs, Peter Owen, 1995.

Bromley, Tom. *Wired for Sound: Now That's What I Call an 80s Music Childhood.* London: Simon and Schuster, 2012.

Bush, George W. *Decision Points.* New York: Crown Publications, 2010.

Caine, Michael. *What's It All About? An Autobiography.* New York: Turtle Bay Books, 1992.

———. *The Elephant to Hollywood.* New York: Henry Holt and Company, 2010.

Campbell, Alastair. *The Blair Years: Extracts from the Alastair Campbell Diaries.* New York: Alfred A. Knopf, 2007.

Chamberlain, Mary. *Growing Up in Lambeth.* London: Virago, 1989.

Childs, Rosie, with Diane Taylor, *Catch Me Before I Fall.* London: Virgin, 2006.

Christian, Terry. *Reds in the Hood.* London: Andre Deutsch, 1999.

Christie, Errol with Tony McMahon. *No Place to Hide: How I Put the Black in the Union Jack.* London: Aurum, 2010.

Clapton, Eric. *Clapton: The Autobiography*. New York, Broadway Books, 2007.

Collins, Andrew. *Where Did It All Go Right? Growing Up Normal in the 70s.* London: Ebury Press, 2003.

Collins, Andrew. *Heaven Knows I'm Miserable Now: My Difficult 80s.* London: Ebury Press, 2004.

Conn, David. *Richer Than God: Manchester City, Modern Football and Growing Up.* London: Quercus, 2012

Davies, Alan. *My Favourite People and Me 1978–1988.* London: Penguin, 2009.

Deegan, Frank. *There's No Other Way: An Autobiography.* Liverpool, Toulouse Press, 1980.

Denton, Diane. *Monochrome to Colour: My Place in Time.* London: Pen Press, 2004.

Diski, Jenny. *The Sixties.* 2009.

Douglas, Robert. *Night song of the Last Tram: A Glasgow Memoir.* London: Hodder and Stoughton, 2005.

Douglas, Robert. *Somewhere to Lay My Head.* London: Hodder and Stoughton, 2007.

Elms, Robert. *The Way We Wore.* London: Picador, 2005.

Evans, Mary. *A Good School: Life at a Girls' Grammar School in the 1950s.* London: The Women's Press, 1991.

Faith, Adam. *Acts of Faith: The Autobiography.* London and New York: Bantam Press, 1996.

Feeney, Paul. *A 1950s Childhood: From Tin Baths to Bread and Dripping.* Gloucestershire: The History Press, 2009.

———. *A 1960s Childhood: From Thunderbirds to Beatlemania.* Gloucestershire: The History Press, 2010.

Foster, Stephen. *From Working Class Hero to Absolute Disgrace: An Eighties Memoir.* London: Short Books, 2009.

Goodwin, John. ed. *Peter Hall's Diaries*. London: Oberon Books, originally published in 1982, second edition 2000.

Gosling, Ray. *Personal Copy: A Memoir of the Sixties*. London and Boston: Faber and Faber, 1980.

Gould, Carol. *Don't Tread On Me: Anti-Americanism Abroad.* New York and London: Encounter Books, 2009.

Green, Jonathan. *Days in the Life: Voices from the English Underground, 1961–1971*. London: Heinemann, 1988.

Haines, *Luke. Bad Vibes: Britpop and My Part in its Downfall.* London: William Heinemann, 2009.

Hell, Richard. *I Dreamed I was a Very Clean Tramp: An Autobiography*. New York: Harper Collins, 2013.

Heron, Liz, ed. *Truth, Dare or Promise: Girls Growing Up in the Fifties*. London, Virago, 1985.

Hewitt, Sally. *I Can Remember the 1960s*. London and Sydney: Franklin Watts, 2003.

———. *I Can Remember the 1980s*. London and Sydney: Franklin Watts, 2005.

Hobbs, May. *Born to Struggle*. London: Quartet Books, 1973.

Hitchens, Christopher. *Hitch-22 A Memoir.* New York and Boston, Twelve, 2010.

Horlock, Bob. *I Remember When I Was Young: A Collection of half a Century of People's Personal Memories from Around Britain and Farther Afield.* Bloomington, Indiana: Unlimited Publishing, 2003.

Howe, Geoffrey. *Conflict of Loyalty*. New York: St. Martin's Press, 1994.

Hughes, Don. *Friday on my Mind.* London, Armadillo, 2010.

James, Alex. *Bit of a Blur.* London: Little, Brown, 2007.

Johnson, Michael A. *A 1980s Childhood: From He-Man to Shell Suits*. Gloucestershire: The History Press, 2012.

Jordan, Terry. *Growing Up in the 50s*. London: Optima, 1990.Kelly, Stephen F. *'You've Never Had It So Good:' Recollections of Life in the 1950s*. Gloucestershire: The History Press, 2012.

Kemp, Gary. *I Know This Much: From Soho to Spandau*. London: Fourth Estate, 2009.

Kipling, Rudyard. *From Sea to Sea: Letters of Trave*l. New York: Charles Scribner's Sons, 1899.

Kureishi, Hanif. *My Beautiful Laundrette and the Rainbow Sign*. London and Boston: Faber and Faber, 1986.

Landau, Cecile. *Growing Up in the Sixties*. London: Macdonald Optima, 1991.

Lawson, Nigel. *The View From No. 11: Memoirs of a Tory Radical.* London: Bantam Press, 1992.

Lawson, Twiggy with Penelope Dening. *Twiggy in Black and White*. London: Simon and Schuster, 1997.

Leader, Zachary ed. *The Letters of Kingsley Amis*. (London: HarperCollins, 2000).

Letts, Don, with David Nobakht. *Culture Clash: Dread Meets Punk Rockers*. London: SAF Publishing, 2007.

Lucas, John. *Next Year Will Be Better: A Memoir of England in the 1950s*. Nottingham: Five Leaves, 2011.

Lulu, *I Don't Want to Fight*. London: Time Warner, 2002.

MacFarlane, Colin. *The Real Gorbals Story: True Tales From Glasgow's Meanest Streets*. Edinburgh and London: Mainstream, 2007.

———. *Gorbals Diehards: A Wild Sixties Childhood.* Edinburgh and London: Mainstream, 2010.

Maconie, Stuart. *Cider With Roadies*. London: Ebury Press, 2004.

Magee, Brian. *Go West, Young Man.* London: Eyre and Spottiswoode, 1958.
Maitland, Sara ed. *Very Heaven: Looking Back at the 1960s.* London: Virago Press, 1988.
Malik, Michael Abdul. *From Michael de Freitas to Michael X.* London: Andre Deutsch, 1968.
Manzoor, Sarfraz, *Greetings From Bury Park: Race, Religion and Rock 'n' Roll.* London, Bloomsbury, 2007.
McLagan, Ian. *All the Rage: A Riotous Romp Through Rock and Roll History.* New York: Billboard Books, 1998.
McLeish, Kenneth and Valerie. eds. *Long to Reign Over Us . . . Memories of Coronation Day and of Life in the 1950s.* London: Bloomsbury, 1992.
Nicolson, Nigel. ed. *Harold Nicolson: Diaries and Letters, 1945–1962.* London: Collins, 1968.
Nott, John. *Here Today, Gone Tomorrow: Recollections of an Errant Politician.* London: Politico's, 2002.
O' Farrell, John. *Things Can Only Get Better: Eighteen Miserable Years in the Life of a Labour Supporter 1979–1997.* London and New York: Doubleday, 1998.
Palin, Michael. *Halfway to Hollywood: Diaries 1980–1988.* New York: Thomas Dunne Books, 2011.
Peel, John, and Sheila Ravenscroft. *John Peel: Margrave of the Marshes.* Chicago: Review History, 2007.
Pressley, Alison. *The Seventies: Good Times, Bad Taste.* London: Index Books, 2002.
Radcliffe, Mark. *Reelin' in the Years: The Soundtrack of a Northern Life.* London, Simon and Schuster, 2011.
Reagan, Ronald. *An American Life.* New York: Simon and Schuster, 1990.
Regis, Cyrille. *My Story: The Autobiography of the First Black Icon of British Football.* London: Andre Deutsch, 2010.
Reynolds, Maureen. *Voices in the Street: Growing Up in Dundee.* Edinburgh: Black and White Publishing, 2006.
Richard, Cliff. *My Life.* London: Headline Review, 2008.
Richards, Keith, with James Fox. *Life.* New York and London: Little, Brown and Company, 2010.
Robb, John. *Punk Rock: An Oral History.* London: Ebury Press, 2006.
Roberts, Elizabeth. *Women and Families: An Oral History, 1940–1970.* Oxford UK and Cambridge USA: Blackwell, 1995.
Rowbotham, Sheila. *Promise of a Dream: Remembering the Sixties.* London: Penguin Books, 2000.
Rushton, Neil. *Northern Soul Stories.* Staffordshire, UK: Soulvation, 2009.
Sardar, Ziauddin. *Balti Britain: A Journey Through the British Asian Experience.* London: Grant, 2008.
Staple, Neville. *Original Rude Boy: From Borstal to the Specials.* London, Aurum. 2010.
Steedman, Carolyn Kay. *Landscapes for a Good Woman: A Story of Two Lives.* New Brunswick, New Jersey: Rutgers University Press, 1987.
Steel, Mark. *Reasons to be Cheerful: From Punk to New Labour through the Eyes of a Dedicated Troublemaker.* London: Scribner, 2001.
Steele, Tommy.*Bermondsey Boy: Memories of a South London Blitz Childhood.* London: Penguin, 2006.
Stewart, Mae. *Dae Yeh Mind Thon Time?* Edinburgh: Black and White Publishing, 2009.
Stewart, Rod. *Rod.* New York: Crown Archetype, 2012.
Stickings. Reg. *Searching For Soul.* London: SAF Publishing, 2008.
Sting. *Broken Music.* New York: Dial Press, 2003.
Street-Porter, Janet. *Baggage: My Childhood.* London: Headline, 2004.

Tait, Derek. *A 1970s Childhood: From Glam Rock to Happy Days.* Gloucestershire: The History Press, 2011.

Thatcher, Margaret. *The Downing Street Years.* London: HarperCollins, 1993.

———. *The Path to Power.* London: HarperCollins, 1995.

Thompson, Brian. *Clever Girl: Growing Up in the 1950s.* London: Atlantic Books, 2007.

Thorn, Tracey. *Bedsit Disco Queen: How I Grew Up and Tried to Be a Pop Star.* London, Virago, 2013.

Townshend, Pete. *Who I Am.* New York: HarperCollins, 2012.

Truman, D. Richard. *Mods, Minis and Madmen: A True Tale of Swinging London Culture in the1960s.* Bloomington, IN: iUniverse, 2010.

Viner, Brian. *Nice to See It, To See It, Nice: The 1970s in Front of the Telly.* London: Simon and Schuster, 2009.

Waddell, Sid. *The Road Back Home: A Northern Childhood.* Ebury Press, London, 2009.

Walsh, John. *Are You Talking to Me? A Life Through the Movies.* London: HarperCollins, 2003.

Walters, Julie. *That's Another Story: The Autobiography.* London: Weidenfeld and Nicolson, 2008.

Webb, Simon. *A 1960s East End Childhood.* Gloucestershire: The History Press, 2012.

———. *A 1970s Teenager: From Bell-Bottoms to Disco Dancing.* Gloucestershire: The History Press, 2013.

Wener, Louise. *Different for Girls: My True-Life Adventures In Pop.* London: Ebury Press, 2010.

Williams, David. *The First Time WeMet the Blues: A journey of Discovery with Jimmy Page, Brian Jones, Mick Jagger and Keith Richards.* York, England: Mentor Books, 2009.

Williams, Philip M. ed. *The Diary of Hugh Gaitskell, 1945–1956.* London: Jonathan Cape, 1983.

Wilmer, Val. *Mama Said There'd be days Like This: My Life in the Jazz World.* London: The Women's Press, 1989.

Wobble, Jah. *Memoirs of a Geezer: Music, Life, Mayhem.* London: Serpent's Tail, 2009.

Wood, Ronnie. *Ronnie: The Autobiography.* New York, St Martin's Press, 2007.

Worth, Jennifer. *The Midwife: A Memoir of Birth, Joy, and Hard Times.* London: Penguin, 2009.

Wyman, Bill. *Stone Alone: The Story of a Rock n Roll Band.* London and New York: Viking, 1990.

Yarm, Mark. *Everybody Loves Our Town: An Oral History of Grunge.* New York: Crown Archetype, 2011.

Films, TV Programs and Videos

A Bit of Fry and Laurie (BBC, 1989-1995)

Americana (Channel 4, 1992)

Borat (20th Century Fox, 2006)

Bragg on America (ITV, 1997)

Bruno (Universal Studios, 2009)

Defense of the Realm (MGM, 1985)

Edge of Darkness (BBC, 1985)

I'm Afraid of Americans (David Bowie video, 1997)

Local Hero (Channel 4, 1983)

Shoot the Dog (George Michael video, 2002)

Spitting Image (ITV,1984-1996)

Novels

Amis, Kingsley. *Lucky Jim*. London: Victor Gollancz, 1954.
Braine, John. *Room at the Top*. London: Eyre and Spottiswoode, 1957.
Huxley, Aldous. *Brave New World*. London: Chatto and Windus, 1932.
Lodge, David. *Changing Places: A Tale of Two Campuses*. London: Secker & Warburg, 1975.
MacInnes, Colin. *Absolute Beginners*. London: MacGibbon & Kee, 1959.
Mullin, Chris. *A Very British Coup*. London: Hodder and Stoughton, 1982.
Sillitoe Alan. *Saturday Night and Sunday Morning*. London: W.H. Allen, 1958.
———. *The Loneliness of the Long Distance Runner*. London: W.H. Allen, 1959.

Books and Journal Articles

Addison, Paul. *Now the War is Over: A Social History of Britain 1945–1951*. London: BBC, 1985.
———. *No Turning Back: The Peacetime Revolutions of Post-War Britain*. Oxford and New York: Oxford University Press, 2010.
Agajanian, Rowana. " 'Just for Kids?': Saturday Morning Cinema and Britain's Children's Film Foundation in the 1960s." *Historical Journal of Film, Radio and Television* 18 (August, 1998): 395–409.
Aldous, Richard. *Reagan and Thatcher: The Difficult Relationship*. New York and London: W. W. Norton and Co, 2012.
Anderson, Paul ed. *Orwell in Tribune*. London: Politico's, 2006.
Anderson Paul, and Nyta Mann. *Safety First: The Making of New Labour*. London: Granta Books, 1997.
Angelo, Anne-Marie. "The Black Panthers in London, 1967–1972: A Diasporic Struggle Navigates the Black Atlantic." *Radical History Review* 103 (Winter 2009): 17–35.
Arieti, James et al., *Kazaam! Splat! Ploof!: The American Impact on European Popular Culture Since 1945*. Lanham, MD: Rowman & Littlefield, 2002.
Atkinson, Robert, and Stephen Ezell. *Innovation Economics: The Race for Global Advantage*. New Haven, Conn: Yale University Press, 2012.
Atwell, David. *Cathedrals of the Movies: A History of British Cinemas and their Audiences*. London: Architectural Press, 1981.
Aughey, Arthur. "Mrs Thatcher's Political Philosophy." *Parliamentary Affairs* 36 (1983): 389–398.
Bale, Tim. *The Conservative Party From Thatcher to Cameron*. Cambridge: Polity, 2010.
Barber, Benjamin. *Jihad vs. McWorld: How Globalism and Tribalism Are Reshaping the World*. New York: Times Book, 1995.
Barker, Martin. *A Haunt of Fears: The Strange History of the British Horror Comics Campaign*. Jackson and London: University Press of Mississippi, 1984.
Barnard, Stephen. *On the Radio: Music Radio in Britain*. Milton Keynes and Philadelphia: Open University Press, 1989.
Barnes, Richard. *Mods!* London: Eel Pie, 1989.
Barnett, Correlli. *The Lost Victory: British Dreams, British Realities, 1945–1950*. London: Pan Books, 1996.
Beckett, Andy. *When the Lights Went Out: Britain in the Seventies*. London: Faber and Faber, 2009.
Beckett, Francis. *Gordon Brown: Past, Present and Future*. London: Haus Publishing, 2007.
———. *Enemy Within: The Rise and Fall of the British Communist Party*. London: John Murray, 1995.

Bell, Steve. *If... Only Again.* London: Methuen, 1984
Berlinkski, Claire. *"There Is No Alternative" Why Margaret Thatcher Matters.* New York: Basic Books, 2008.
Berman, Russell A. *Anti-Americanism in Europe: A Cultural Problem.* Stanford, CA: Hoover Institution Press, 2004.
Bernays, Doris and Edward L. *What the British Think of Us: A Study of British Hostility to America and Americans and its Motivation.* New York: English Speaking Union, 1958.
Black, Jeremy. *Modern British History Since 1900.* London: Macmillan, 2000.
———. *Britain Since the Seventies: Politics and Society in the Consumer Age.* London: Reaktion, 2004.
Bogdanor, Vernon. "Britain in the 20th Century: The Conservative Reaction, 1951–1965," available at http://www.gresham.ac.uk/lectures-and-events/britain-in-the-20th-century-the-conservative-reaction-1951–1965
Bower, Tom. *Gordon Brown.* London: HarperCollins, 2004.
Boyes, Georgina. *The Imagined Village: Culture, Ideology and the English Folk Revival.* Manchester and New York: Manchester University Press, 1993.
Boyne, George A. *Public Choice Theory and Local Government: A Comparative Analysis of the UK and the USA.* London: Macmillan, 1998.
Brewster, Bill, and Frank Broughton. *Last Night A DJ Saved My Life.* London: Headline, 1999.
———. *The Record Players: DJ Revolutionaries.* London: DJ History.com, 2010.
Brinkley, Douglas. *Wheels for the World: Henry Ford, His Company, and a Century of Progress1903–2003.* New York: Viking, 2003.
Brivati, Brian. *Hugh Gaitskell.* London: Richard Cohen Books, 1996.
Brody, David. *In Labor's Cause: Main Themes on the History of the American Worker.* New York and Oxford: Oxford University Press, 1993.
Brook, Lindsay et al. *British Social Attitudes Cumulative Sourcebook: The First Six Surveys.* Aldershot: Gower, 1992.
Brooke, Stephen. "Atlantic Crossing? American Views of Capitalism and British Socialist Thought 1932–1962." *Twentieth Century British History* 2 (1991): 107–136.
Brown, Gareth. *Mods and Rockers: The Origins and Era of a British Scene.* Shropshire: Independent Music Press, 2010.
Brown, Geoff. "Something for Everyone: British Film Culture in the 1990s." In Robert Murphy ed. *British Cinema of the 90s.* London: BFI Publishing, 2000.
Brown, Michele. *The Little History of the Teddy Bear.* Stroud: Tempus, 2006.
Brown, Mike. *The 1950s Look.* Kent: Sabrestorm, 2008.
Brown, Tim. *The Wigan Casino Years: The Essential Story 1973–1981.* Alcester: Outta Sight Ltd, 2010.
Brunning, Bob. *Blues: The British Connection.* London: Helter Skelter, 2002.
Buchanan, William, and Hadley Cantril. *How Nations See Each Other: A Study in Public Opinion.* Urbana: University of Illinois Press, 1953.
Buckingham, David et al. *Children's Television in Britain: History, Discourse and Policy.* London: British Film Institute, 1999.
Buckley, Cheryl, and Hilary Fawcett. *Fashioning the Feminine: Representation and Women's Fashion from the Fin de Siecle to the Present.* London and New York: I. B. Tauris, 2002.
Buford, Bill. *Among the Thugs.* New York: Vintage Books, 1990.
Burchill, Julie, and Tony Parsons. *"The Boy Looked at Johnny": The Obituary of Rock and Roll.* London: Pluto Press, 1978.
Burton, John, and Eileen McCabe. *We Don't Do God: Blair's Religious Belief and its Consequences.* London: Continuum, 2009.

Campbell, John. *Margaret Thatcher: Volume One: The Grocer's Daughter.* London: Pimlico, 2001.

———. *Margaret Thatcher: Volume Two: The Iron Lady.* London: Pimlico, 2004.

Campbell, Neil et al. *Issues in Americanisation and Culture.* Edinburgh: Edinburgh University Press, 2004.

Camporesi, Valeria. "There are no Kangaroos in Kent, The American 'Model' and the Introduction of Commercial Television in Britain, 1940–1954." In David E. Ellwood and Rob Kroes eds. *Hollywood in Europe: Experiences of a Cultural Hegemony.* Amsterdam: VU University Press, 1994.

Camporesi, Valeria. *Mass Culture and National Traditions: The B.B.C. and American Broadcasting, 1922–1954.* Italy: European Press Academic Publishing, 2000.

Cann, Kevin. *David Bowie Any Day Now, The London Years: 1947–1974.* London: Adelita, 2010.

Carbery, Thomas J. "The Americanisation of British Politics." *The Journal of Politics* 27 (February 1965): 178–184.

Carew, Anthony. *Labour under the Marshall Plan: The Politics of Productivity and the Marketing of Management Science.* Manchester: Manchester University Press, 1987.

Carmichael, Stokely, and Charles V. Hamilton. *Black Power: The Politics of Liberation in America.* New York: Random House, 1967.

Chang, Jeff. *Can't Stop Won't Stop: A History of the Hip-Hop Generation.* New York: Picador, 2005.

Charone, Barbara. *Keith Richards.* London: Futura, 1979.

Chibnall, Steve. *Law-and-Order News: An Analysis of Crime Reporting in the British Press.* London: Tavistock, 1977.

Chiozza, Giacomo. *Anti-Americanism and the American World Order.* Baltimore, MD: The Johns Hopkins University Press, 2009.

Christy, Jim. *The Price of Power: A Biography of Charles Eugene Bedaux.* New York: Doubleday, 1984.

Clark, William. *Less than Kin: A Study of Anglo-American Relations.* Boston: Houghton Mifflin, 1957.

Clarke, Peter. *A Question of Leadership. From Gladstone to Thatcher.* London: Hamish Hamilton, 1991.

———. *Hope and Glory: Britain 1900–2000.* London: Penguin, 2004.

Clayson, Alan. *Ringo Starr.* London: Sanctuary, 2003.

Cloonan, Martin. "Exclusive! The British Press and Popular Music, The Story So Far . . . ." In Steve Jones ed. *Pop Music and the Press.* Philadelphia: Temple University Press, 2002, 114–133.

Cockett, Richard. *Thinking the Unthinkable: Think-Tanks and the Economic Counter-Revolution 1931–1983.* London: HarperCollins, 1994.

Cohn, Nik. *Today There Are No Gentlemen: The Changes in Englishmen's Clothes Since the War.* London: Weidenfeld and Nicolson, 1971.

Colegrave, Stephen, and Chris Sullivan. *Punk: The Definitive Record of a Revolution.* London: Cassell, 2001.

Coleman, Ray. *Lennon.* New York: McGraw-Hill, 1984.

———. *McCartney Yesterday and Today.* Los Angeles, CA: Dove Books, 1996.

Collin, Matthew. *Altered States: The Story of Ecstasy and Acid House.* London: Serpent's Tail, 1997.

Collins, Christopher ed. *Margaret Thatcher Complete Public Statements CD-ROM, 1945–1990.* Oxford: Oxford University Press, 1998–2000.

Communist Party of Great Britain. *British Road to Socialism.* London: Communist Party, 1951.

Cooper, George. *The Origin of Financial Crises: Central Banks, Credit Bubbles, and the Efficient Market Fallacy.* New York: Vintage, 2008.

Cooper Laura E., and B. Lee Cooper, "The Pendulum of Cultural Imperialism: Popular Music Interchanges Between the United States and Britain, 1943–1967." *Journal of Popular Culture* 27 (Winter 1993): 61–78.

Copsey, Nigel. *Contemporary British Fascism: The British National Party and the Quest forLegitimacy.* Basingstoke: Palgrave Macmillan, 2004.

Cotgrove, Mark "Snowboy." *From Jazz Funk and Fusion to Acid Jazz: The History of the UK Jazz Dance Scene.* London: Chaser, 2009.

Coughlin, Conn. *American Ally: Tony Blair and the War on Terror.* New York: HarperCollins, 2006.

Crockatt, Richard. *America Embattled: September 11, Anti-Americanism, and the Global Order.* London and New York: Routledge, 2003.

Crosland, C. A. R. *The Future of Socialism.* New York: Macmillan, 1957.

Crossman, R. H. S. Michael Foot, and Ian Mikardo. *Keep Left.* London: New Statesman, 1947.

Cull, Nicholas. J. *The Cold War and the United States Information Agency: American Propaganda and Public Diplomacy, 1945–1989.* Cambridge and New York: Cambridge University Press, 2008.

Cunliffe, Marcus. *In Search of America: Transatlantic Essays, 1951–1990.* Westport, Connecticut and London: Greenwood Press, 1991.

Daguerre, Anne, and Peter Taylor-Gooby. "Neglecting Europe: Explaining the predominance of American ideas in New Labour's Welfare Policies Since 1997." *Journal of European Social Policy* 14 (February 2004): 25–39.

Daniel, W. W. *Racial Discrimination in England.* Middlesex: Penguin, 1968.

Davies, Hunter. *The Beatles: The Authorized Biography.* New York: McGraw-Hill 1968.

———. *London to Loweswater: A Journey Through England at the End of the Twentieth Century.* Edinburgh and London: Mainstream Publishing, 1999.

Davis, Morris, and Sidney Verba. "Party Affiliation and International Opinions in Britain and France, 1947–1956." *Public Opinion Quarterly* 24 (1960): 590–604.

Davis, Paul. *Us and Them: What the Americans Think of the British, What the British Think of the Americans.* New York: Princeton Architectural Press, 2004.

Dawson, Jim. *The Twist: The Story of the Song and Dance That Changed the World.* Boston and London: Faber and Faber, 1995.

de Grazia, Victoria. *Irresistible Empire: America's Advance through Twentieth-Century Europe.* Cambridge: Belknap Press of Harvard University Press, 2005.

Deer, Patrick. "The Dogs of War: Myths of British Anti-Americanism." In Andrew Ross and Kristin Ross eds. *Anti-Americanism.* New York and London: New York University Press, 2004, 158-178.

DeBres, Karen. "Burgers for Britain; A Cultural Geography of McDonald's UK." *The Journal of Cultural Geography* 22 (Spring/Summer, 2005): 115–188.

Dolowitz, David P. "British Employment Policy in the 1980s: Learning from the American Experience." *Governance* 10 (January 1997): 23–42.

———. *Learning From America: Policy Transfer and the Development of the British Workfare State.* Brighton, Sussex: Academic Press, 1998.

———. with Rob Hulme, Mike Nellis and Fiona O'Neill. *Policy Transfer and British SocialPolicy: Learning from the USA?* Buckingham and Philadelphia: Open University Press, 2000.

Donnelly, Mark. *Sixties Britain: Culture, Society and Politics.* Harlow: Pearson, 2005.

Donovan, Robert J. *The Second Victory: Marshall Plan and the Postwar Revival of Europe.* New York: University Press of America, 1987.

Driver, Stephen and Luke Martell. *New Labour: Politics After Thatcherism.* Cambridge: PolityPress, 1998.

Dunning, John H. *U.S. Industry in Britain.* Boulder, Colorado: Westview Press, 1976.

Dyja, Eddie. *Studying British Cinema: The 1990s.* Leighton Buzzard: Auteur, 2010.

Ebenstein, Lanny. *Milton Friedman: A Biography.* New York: Palgrave Macmillan, 2009.

Echols, Alice. *Hot Stuff: Disco and the Remaking of American Culture.* New York and London: WW Norton, 2010.

Egbuna, Obi. *Destroy This Temple: The Voice of Black Power in Britain.* New York: William Morrow and Company, 1971.

Ellis, Sylvia. *Britain, America, and the Vietnam War.* Westport, Connecticut and London: Praeger, 2004.

Eno, Brian et al. *Not One More Death.* London and New York: Verso, 2006.

Epstein, Leon D. *Uneasy Ally.* Chicago: University of Chicago Press, 1954.

Erskine, Hazel. "The Polls: World Opinion of U.S. Racial Problems." *Public Opinion Quarterly* 32 (Summer 1968): 299–312.

Evans, Eric J. *Thatcher and Thatcherism.* London and New York: Routledge, 1997.

Evans, Harold. *They Made America: From the Steam Engine to the Search Engine: Two Centuries of Innovators.* New York: Back Bay, 2006.

"Evolution of National Nobel Prize Shares in the 20th Century" at http://www.idsia.ch/~juergen/nobelshare.html.

Ewbank, Tim, and Stafford Hildred. *Roger Daltrey: The Biography.* London: Portrait, 2004.

Fagge, Roger. "'The Finest or the Damndest Country in the World?': The British Left and America in the 1930s." In Catherine Armstrong, Roger Fagge and Tim Lockley. eds. *America in the British Imagination.* Newcastle: Cambridge Scholars, 2007, 168–181.

Farber, David. *The Age of Great Dreams, America in the 1960s.* New York: Hill and Wang, 1994.

Farrington, David P. Patrick A. Langan, and Michael Tonry eds. *Cross-National Studies in Crime and Justice.* Washington DC: US Department of Justice, 2004.

Fieldhouse, Roger. *Anti-Apartheid A History of the Movement in Britain: A Study in Pressure Group Politics.* London: Merlin Press, 2005.

Fisher, Michael H. et al. *A South-Asian History of Britain: Four Centuries of Peoples from the Indian Sub-Continent.* Oxford and Westport, Connecticut: Greenwood, 2007.

Fitzgerald, John. *Studying British Cinema: 1999–2009.* Leighton Buzzard: Auteur, 2010.

Foster, Mo. *Play Like Elvis: How British Musicians Bought the American Dream.* Bodmin: MPG Books, 2000.

Frame, Pete. *The Restless Generation.* London: Rogan House, 2007.

Fraser, Murray with Joe Kerr. *Architecture and the "Special Relationship": The American influence on Post-war British Architecture.* London and New York: Routledge, 2007.

Free, Lloyd A. *Six Allies and a Neutral: A Study of the International Outlooks of Political Leaders in the United States, Britain, France, West Germany, Italy, Japan and India.* Glencoe, IL: The Free Press, 1959.

Freedland, Jonathan. *Bring Home The Revolution: The Case for a British Republic.* London: Fourth Estate, 1998.

Freedland, Michael. *Michael Caine.* London: Orion, 1999.

Freymond, Jacques. "America Through European Eyes." *America Through Foreign Eyes* special edition of *The Annals of the American Academy of Political and Social Science* 295 (September 1954).

Friedman, Barbara G. *Front the Battlefront to the Bridal Suite: Media Coverage of British War Brides, 1942–1946.* Columbia: University of Missouri Press, 2007.

Friedman, Max Paul. *Rethinking Anti-Americanism: The History of an Exceptional Concept in American Foreign Relations.* Cambridge: Cambridge University Press, 2012.

Frost, David, and Michael Shea. *The Rich Tide: Men, Women, Ideas and Their Transatlantic Impact.* London: Collins, 1986.

Fukuyama, Francis. *The End of History and the Last Man.* New York: Free Press, 1992.

Fuller, Peter. *Beyond the Crisis in Art.* London: Writers and Readers, 1980.

Fyvel, T. R. "Realities Behind British 'Anti-Americanism': The Minority Leading the National Pastime." *Commentary* (December 1952): 558–559.

———. *Troublemakers: Rebellious Youth in an Affluent Society.* New York: Schocken Books, 1961.

Gallup, George H. *The Gallup International Public Opinion Polls, Great Britain 1937–1975 Volume 1 1937–1964.* New York: Random House, 1976.

Gardiner, Juliet. *"Overpaid, Oversexed, and Over Here" The American GI in World War II Britain.* New York: Canopy Books, 1992.

Gardiner, Nile. "Mind the Gap: Is the Relationship Still Special?" *World Affairs,* March/April 2011 at http://www.worldaffairsjournal.org/article/mind-gap-relationship-still-special.

Garnett, Mark, and Richard Weight. *The A-Z Guide to Modern British History.* London: Jonathan Cape, 2003.

Garratt, Sheryl. *Adventures In Wonderland: A Decade Of Club Culture.* London: Headline: 1998.

Geddes, Andrew. *Britain and the European Union.* Basingstoke: Palgrave MacMillan, 2013.

Gillett, Charlie. *The Sound of the City.* New York: Outerbridge & Dienstfrey, 1970.

———. "Big Noise from Across the Water: The American Influence on British Popular Music." In Allen F. Davis ed. *For Better or Worse: The American Influence in the World.* Westport Connecticut and London: Greenwood Press, 1981.

Gillman, Peter and Leni. *Alias David Bowie.* New York: Henry Holt and Company, 1987.

Gilmour, Ian. *Dancing with Dogma: Britain Under Thatcherism.* London: Simon and Schuster, 1992.

Gindin, James. *Postwar British Fiction: New Accents and Attitudes.* Berkeley and Los Angeles: University of California Press, 1963.

Godbolt, Jim. *A History of Jazz in Britain 1919–1950.* London and New York: Quartet Books, 1984.

———. *A History of Jazz in Britain 1950–1970.* London and New York: Quartet Books, 1989.

Goldman, Albert. *Disco.* New York: Hawthorn Books, 1978.

Goldsmith, Martin. *The Beatles Come to America.* Hoboken, NJ : John Wiley and sons, 2004.

Gorman, Paul. *The Look: Adventures in Pop and Rock Fashion.* London: Sanctuary, 2001.

Gould, Philip. *The Unfinished Revolution: How the Modernisers Saved the Labour Party.* London: Abacus, 1999.

Green, E. H. H. *Ideologies of Conservatism: Conservative Political Ideas in the Twentieth Century.* Oxford: Oxford University Press, 2002.

———. *Thatcher.* London: Hodder Arnold, 2006.

Greenberg, Stanley B. *Dispatches from the War Room: In the Trenches with Five Extraordinary Leaders.* New York: Thomas Dunne Books, 2009.

Gulddal, Jesper. *Anti-Americanism in European Literature.* New York: Palgrave Macmillan, 2011.

Guralnick, Peter. *Last Train to Memphis: The Rise of Elvis Presley.* New York, Little, Brown, 1994.

Hagerty, Bill. "Paul Dacre: The Zeal Thing." *British Journalism Review* 13 (2002): 11–22.
Hall, Stuart et al. *Policing the Crisis: Mugging, the State, and Law and Order.* New York: Holmes and Meier, 1978.
———. "The Great *Moving Right* Show." *Marxism Today* (January, 1979): 14–20.
Halsey A. H. with Josephine Webb eds. *Twentieth-Century British Social Trends.* London: Macmillan Press, 2000.
Hamblett, Charles, and Jane Deverson. *Generation X*. Greenwich, Conn: Gold Medal Books, 1964.
Hardyment, Christina. *Slice of Life: The British Way of Eating Since 1945.* London: BBC Books, 1995.
Harper, Sue, and Vincent Porter. *British Cinema of the 1950s: The Decline of Deference.* Oxford and New York: Oxford University Press, 2003.
Harris, John. *Britpop! Cool Britannia and the Spectacular Demise of English Rock.* Cambridge, MA: Da Capo Press, 2004.
Harris, Robin. ed. *The Collected Speeches of Margaret Thatcher.* New York, HarperCollins, 1997.
Harrison, Brian. "Mrs Thatcher and the Intellectuals." *Twentieth Century British History* 5 (1994): 206–245.
———. *Seeking a Role: The United Kingdom, 1951–1970.* Oxford: Clarendon Press, 2009.
Harry, Bill. *The Ringo Starr Encyclopedia.* London: Virgin Books, 2004.
Haseler, Stephen. *The Varieties of Anti-Americanism: Reflex and Response.* Washington DC: Ethics and Public Policy Center, 1985.
Haslam, Dave. *Adventures on the Wheels of Steel: The Rise of the Superstar DJs.* London: Fourth Estate, 2001.
Hebdige, Dick. *Subculture: The Meaning of Style.* London and New York: Routledge, 1979.
Heffer, Simon. *Like the Roman: The Life of Enoch Powell.* London: Weidenfeld and Nicolson, 1998.
Heffernan, Richard. *New Labour and Thatcherism: Political Change in Britain.* London: Macmillan, 2000.
Heining, Duncan. *Trad Dads, Dirty Boppers and Free Fusioneers: British Jazz 1960–1975.* Sheffield: Equinox, 2012.
Hennessy, Peter. *Having It So Good: Britain in the Fifties.* London: Allen Lane, 2006.
Hermes, Will. *Love Goes to Buildings on Fire: Five Years in New York that Changed MusicForever.* New York: Faber and Faber, 2011.
Hertsgaard, Mark. *The Eagle's Shadow: Why America Fascinates and Infuriates the World.* New York: Farrar, Straus, and Giroux, 2002.
Hewitt, Paolo. *The Soul Stylists: Forty Years of Modernism.* Edinburgh and London: Mainstream, 2000.
———. *The Sharper Word: A Mod Anthology*. London: Helter Skelter, 2009.
———, and Mark Baxter. *The A to Z of Mod.* Munich, London and New York: Prestel, 2012.
Hiro, Dilip. *Black British White British: A History of Race Relations in Britain.* London: Grafton Books, 1991.
Hitchens, Peter. *The Abolition of Britain: From Winston Churchill to Princess Diana.* San Francisco: Encounter Books, 2000.
Hobsbawm, Eric. *Uncommon People: Resistance, Rebellion and Jazz.* New York: The New Press, 1998.
Hoggart, Richard. *The Uses of Literacy: Aspects of Working Class Life.* London: Chatto and Windus, 1957.
Hollander, Paul. *Anti-Americanism: Critiques at Home and Abroad, 1965–1990.* London and New York: Oxford University Press, 1992.

———. ed. *Understanding Anti-Americanism: Its Origins and Impact at Home and Abroad.* Chicago: Ivan R. Dee, 2004.

Holmes, Martin et al. *British Security Policy and the Atlantic Alliance: Prospects for the 1990s.* Cambridge, Mass.: Pergamon-Brassey's International Defense, 1987.

Holsti, Ole R. *To See Ourselves as Others See Us: How Publics Abroad View the United States After 9/11.* Ann Arbor: University of Michigan Press, 2008.

Hopkins, Harry. *The New Look: A Social History of the Forties and Fifties in Britain.* Boston: Houghton Mifflin, 1964.

Horn, Adrian. *Juke Box Britain: Americanisation and Youth Culture 1945–1960.* Manchester and New York: Manchester University Press, 2009.

Hulme, Rob. "Education: Post-Compulsory Education in England and Wales." In David P. Dolowitz with Rob Hulme, Mike Nellis and Fiona O'Neill eds. *Policy Transfer and British Social Policy: Learning from the USA?* Buckingham and Philadelphia: Open University Press, 2000: 77–97.

Huxley, Aldous. *Brave New World.* New York: Harper, 1958.

Isernia, Pierangelo. "Anti-Americanism in Europe During the Cold War." In Peter J. Katzenstein and Robert O. Keohane eds. *Anti-Americanisms in World Politics.* Ithaca and London: Cornell University Press, 2007.

Isserman, Maurice, and Michael Kazin. *America Divided, The Civil War of the 1960s.* New York: Oxford University Press, 2000.

Jackson, Ben, and Robert Saunders eds. *Making Thatcher's Britain.* Cambridge: Cambridge University Press, 2012.

Jennings, Charles. *Them and Us: The American Invasion of British High Society.* Gloucestershire: Sutton Publishing, 2007.

Johnson, Paul. *A History of the Modern World from 1917 to the 1980s.* London: Weindenfeld and Nicolson, 1983.

Jones, Charles E. ed. *The Black Panther Party.* Baltimore: Black Classics Press, 1998.

Jones, Dylan. *When Ziggy Played Guitar: David Bowie and Four Minutes That Shook the World.* London: Preface, 2012.

Jones, Trevor, and Tim Newburn. *Policy Transfer and Criminal Justice: Exploring U.S Influence Over British Crime Control Policy.* Maidenhead: Open University Press, 2005.

Judt, Tony, and Denis Locorne eds. *With US or Against US. Studies in Global Anti-Americanism.* New York: Palgrave MacMillan, 2005.

Kamalipour, Yahya R. ed. *Images of the U.S. Around the World: A Multicultural Perspective.* Albany: State University of New York Press, 1999.

Kamp, David. "The British Invasion: The Oral History." *Vanity Fair.* November 2002.

Kanigel, Robert. *The One Best Way, Frederick Winslow Taylor and the Enigma of Efficiency.* Cambridge, Massachusetts: MIT Press, 2005.

Kartun, Derek. *This is America.* London: Thames publications, 1948.

———. *America Go Home!* London: Communist Party, 1951.

Katzenstein, Peter J., and Robert O. Keohane eds. *Anti-Americanisms in World Politics.* Ithaca and London: Cornell University Press, 2007.

Kelley, Robin D. G. *Race Rebels: Culture, Politics and the Black Working Class.* New York: Free Press, 1994.

Kiernan. Anna ed. *Voices for Peace: An Anthology.* London: Scribner, 2001.

King, Anthony ed. *British Political Opinion 1937–2000 The Gallup Polls.* London: Politico's, 2001.

King, Desmond, and Mark Wickham-Jones. "From Clinton to Blair: The Democratic (Party) Origins of Welfare to Work." *The Political Quarterly,* (January 1999): 62–74.

Kitwana, Bakari. *Why White Kids Love Hip-Hop: Wankstas, Wiggers, Wannabes, and the New Reality of Race in America.* New York: Basic Books, 2005.

Klein, Naomi. *No Logo.* New York: Picador, 1999.

Kohut, Andrew, and Bruce Stokes. *America Against the World: How We Are Different and Why We are Disliked.* New York: Times Books, 2006.

Kroes, Rob et al., *Cultural Transmissions and Receptions: American Mass Culture in Europe.* Amsterdam: VU University Press, 1993.

———. *If You've Seen one, you've Seen the Mall: Europeans and American Mass Culture.* Urbana: University of Illinois Press, 1996.

———, and Rossem, Maarten van, eds. *Anti-Americanism in Europe.* Amsterdam: Free University Press, 1986.

Kull, Steven. "Culture Wars? How Americans and Europeans View Globalization." *Brookings Review* 19 (Fall 2001): 18–21.

Kurlansky, Mark. *Birdseye: The Adventures of a Curious Man.* New York: Doubleday, 2012.

Kynaston, David. *Austerity Britain, 1945–1951.* London, Berlin and New York: Bloomsbury, 2007.

———. *Family Britain, 1951–1957.* London, Berlin, New York: Bloomsbury, 2009.

Laing, Dave. *One Chord Wonders: Power and Meaning in Punk Rock.* Milton Keynes: Open University Press, 1985.

Lalo, Alexei. "Borat as Tragicomedy of Anti US-Americanism." *Comparative Literature and Culture* 11 (2009), http://docs.lib.purdue.edu/cgi/viewcontent.cgi?article=1468&context=clcweb

Lancaster, Bill. *The Department Store: A Social History.* London and New York: Leicester University Press, 1995.

Law, Richard. *Return from Utopia.* London: Faber and Faber, 1950.

Lawrence, Tim. *Love Saves The Day: A History of American Dance Culture 1970–1979.* Durham: Duke University Press, 2003.

Lay, Samantha. *British Social Realism: From Documentary to Brit-grit.* New York: Columbia University Press, 2002.

Lazell, Barry, and Dafydd Rees *Illustrated Book of Rock Records.* New York: Delilah Books, 1982.

Lealand, Geoffrey. *American Television Programmes on British Screens.* London: Broadcasting Research Unit, 1984.

Leavis, F. R. *Mass Civilisation and Minority Culture.* Cambridge: Minority Pamphlets No. 1, 1930.

Leese, Peter. *Britain Since 1945: Aspects of Identity.* Hampshire: Palgrave Macmillan, 2006.

Leigh, Spencer. "Hello Me Ol' Mateys." available at http://www.spencerleigh.demon.co.uk/Feature_Satclub.htm

Letwin, Shirley Robin. *The Anatomy of Thatcherism.* London: Fontana, 1992.

Lewis, Michael. *The Big Short: Inside the Doomsday Machine.* New York: W. W. Norton, 2010.

Lewis, Peter. *The Fifties.* New York: J. B. Lippincott, 1978.

Lillibridge, G. D. ed. *The American Image: Past and Present.* Lexington, MA: D. C. Heath and Company, 1968.

Littler, C. R. *The Development of the Labour Process in Capitalist Societies: A Comparative Studyof the Transformation of Work Organization in Britain, Japan and the USA.* London: Heineman Educational Books, 1982.

MacDonald, Ian. *Revolution in the Head: The Beatles' Records and the Sixties.* Chicago: Chicago Review Press, third edition, 2007.

MacInnes, Colin. *England, Half English.* New York: Random House, 1961.

Macintyre, Donald. *Mandelson and the Making of New Labour.* London: HarperCollins, 1999.

Malchow, H. L. *Special Relations: The Americanization of Britain?* Stanford, CA: Stanford University Press, 2011.

Mapp, Edward. *Blacks in American Films: Today and Yesterday.* Metuchen, NJ: Scarecrow Press, 1972.

Marcus, Greil. *Mystery Train.* New York: E. P. Dutton, 1975.

———. *Lipstick Traces: A Secret History of the Twentieth Century.* Harvard: Harvard University Press, 1990.

Markovits, Andrei S. *Uncouth Nation: Why Europe Dislikes America.* Princeton and Oxford: Princeton University Press, 2007.

Marling, Susan. *American Affair: The Americanisation of Britain.* London: Boxtree, 1993.

Marling, William H. *How "American" Is Globalization?* Baltimore: The Johns Hopkins University Press, 2006.

Marqusee, Mike. *Redemption Song: Muhammad Ali and the Spirit of the Sixties.* London and New York: Verso, second edition, 2005, originally published in 1999.

Marsh, Dave. *Before I Get Old: The Story of the Who.* New York: St Martin's Press, 1983.

Marsh, Graham, and J. P. Gaul, *The Ivy Look.* London: Frances Lincoln Ltd, 2010.

Marsh, Peter. *The New Industrial Revolution: Consumers, Globalization and the End of Mass Production.* New Haven and London: Yale University Press, 2012.

Mason, Laura. *Food Culture in Great Britain.* Westport, Connecticut, and London: Greenwood Press, 2004.

Masson, Peter, and Andrew Thorburn. "Advertising: The American Influence in Europe." In C. W. E. Bigsby, ed. *Superculture: American Popular Culture and Europe.* Bowling Green, Ohio: Bowling Green University Popular Press, 1975, 96–106.

Matusow, Allen J. *The Unraveling of American: A History of Liberalism in the 1960s.* New York: Harper and Row, 1984.

Mayer, J. P. *British Cinemas and their Audiences*: Sociological Studies. London: Dennis Dobson, 1948.

McKay, George. *Circular Breathing: The Cultural Politics of Jazz in Britain.* Durham NC: Duke University Press, 2005.

McKibbin, Ross. *Classes and Cultures: England 1918–1951.* Oxford and New York: Oxford University Press, 1998.

McManus, Kevin. *"Nashville of the North": Country Music in Liverpool.* Liverpool: Institute of Popular Music, 1994.

McMillan, James, and Bernard Harris. *The American Take-Over of Britain.* London: Leslie Frewin, 1968.

McPherson, James M. *Battle Cry of Freedom: The Civil War Era.* Ballantine Books: New York, 1988.

McReavy, Anthony. *The Toy story: The Life and Times of Inventor Frank Hornby.* London: Ebury, 2002.

McSmith, Andy. *No Such Thing as Society: A History of Britain in the 1980s.* London: Constable, 2011.

Meunier, Sophie. "The dog that did not bark: Anti-Americanism and the 2008 financial crisis in Europe." 2011. http://euce.org/eusa/2011/papers/9h_meunier.pdf.

Miles, Barry. *Peace: 50 Years of Protest.* New York: Readers Digest, 2008.

Millgate, Helen D. *Got Any Gum Chum? GIs in Wartime Britain, 1942–1945.* Gloucestershire: Sutton, 2001.

Milward, Alan S., and George Brennan. *Britain's Place in the World: A Historical Enquiry into Import Controls, 1945–1960.* London and New York: Routledge, 1996.

Moore, R. Laurence. *European Socialists and the American promised Land.* New York: Oxford University Press, 1970.
Moran, Joe. *Queuing for Beginners: The Story of Daily Life from Breakfast to Bedtime.* London: Profile Books, 2007.
Morgan, Kenneth O. "Labour and the Anglo-American Alliance." In Antoine Capet and Aïssatou Sy-Wonyu eds. *The "special relationship" la relation speciale entre le royaume-uni et les etats-unis.* Rouen: Universitet' de Rouen, 2003, 169–184.
Morrison, Kathryn. A. *English Shops and Shopping: An Architectural History.* New Haven and London: Yale University Press, 2003.
Mullard, Chris. *Black Britain.* London: George Allen and Unwin, 1973.
Munson, Henry Lee. ed. *European Beliefs regarding the United States.* New York: Common Council for American Unity, 1949.
Naughtie, James. *The Rivals: The Intimate Story of a Political Marriage.* London: Fourth Estate, 2001.
———. *The Accidental American: Tony Blair and the Presidency.* New York: Public Affairs, 2004.
Nederveen Pieterse, Jan. *Global Mélange: Globalization and culture.* Lanham, MD: Rowman & Littlefield, 2003.
———. *Ethnicities and Global Multiculture: Pants for an Octopus.* Lanham, MD: Rowman & Littlefield, 2007.
1951 Conservative Party General Election Manifesto available at ConservativeManifest.com. \http://conservativemanifesto.com/1951/1951-conservative-manifesto.shtml
Noble, Peter. *The Negro in Films.* New York: Arno Press, 1970.
Norman, Philip. *Shout: The Beatles in Their Generation.* New York: Fireside, 1981.
———. *The Stones.* London: Elm Tree Books, 1984.
———. *John Lennon: The Life.* New York: Harper Collins, 2008.
Nossiter, Bernard. *Britain: A Future That Works.* Boston: Houghton Mifflin, 1978.
Nott, James J. *Music For the People: Popular Music and Dance in Interwar Britain.* Oxford: Oxford University Press, 2002.
Nowell, David. *Too Darn Soulful: The Story of Northern Soul.* London: Robson Books, 2001.
Nunnerley, David. *President Kennedy and Britain.* New York: St. Martin's Press, 1972.
Opie, Robert. *Remember When: A Nostalgic Trip Through the Consumer Era.* London: Mitchell Beazley, 1999.
Orwell, George. *The Lion and the Unicorn: Socialism and the English Genius.* London: Secker and Warburg, 1941.
Osgerby, Bill. *Youth In Britain Since 1945.* Oxford: Blackwell, 1998.
O'Neill, William L. *Coming Apart: An Informal History of America in the 1960s.* Chicago: Quadrangle Books, 1971.
O'Reilly, Karen. *The British on the Costa del Sol: Transnational Identities and Local Communities.* London and New York: Routledge, 2000.
O'Sullivan, Tim. "Television Memories and Cultures of Viewing, 1950–1965." In John Corner, ed. *Popular Television in Britain: Studies in Cultural History.* London: BFI Publishing, 1991.
Parlett, David. *The Oxford History of Board Games.* Oxford: Oxford University Press, 1999.
Paxman, Jeremy. *The English: A Portrait of a People.* Woodstock and New York: The Overlook Press, 2000.
Peck, Jamie. *Workfare States.* New York and London, Guildford Press, 2001.
Pelling, Henry. *America and the British Left: From Bright to Bevan.* New York: New York University, 1957.

Pells, Richard. *Not Like Us: How Europeans Have Loved, Hated, And Transformed American Culture Since World War II.* New York: Basic Books, 1997.

———. *Modernist America: Art, Music, Movies and the Globalization of American Culture.* New Haven and London: Yale University Press, 2011.

Phillips, Mike, and Trevor Phillips. *Windrush: The Irresistible Rise of Multi-Racial Britain.* London: Harper Collins, 1998.

Porter, Roy. *London: A Social History.* Cambridge Mass: Harvard University Press, 1995.

Priestley, J. B., and Jacquetta Hawkes. *Journey Down a Rainbow.* New York: Harper and Brothers, 1955.

Pugh, Martin. *Speak for Britain! A New History of the Labour Party.* London: The Bodley Head, 2010.

Puttnam, David, with Neil Watson. *Movies and Money.* New York: Alfred A. Knopf, 1998.

Pyke, Magnus. "The Influence of American Foods and Food Technology in Europe." In C. W. E. Bigsby ed. *Superculture: American Popular Culture and Europe.* Ohio: Bowling Green University, 1975, 83–95.

Quindlen, Anna. *Imagined London: A Tour of the World's Greatest Fictional City.* Washington DC: National Geographic, 2004.

Quinn, Eithne. *Nuthin' but a "G" Thang: The Culture and Commerce of Gangsta Rap.* New York: Columbia University Press, 2005.

Rambali, Paul. "The English Pub, Death by Disco." *The Face* (November, 1984).

Rasmussen, Jorgen, and James M. McCormick. "British Mass Perceptions of the Anglo-American Special Relationship." *Political Science Quarterly* 108 (Fall 1993): 515–541.

Rawlings, Terry. *Mod A Very British Phenomenon.* London: Omnibus Press, 2000.

Reid, T. R. *The United States of Europe: The New Superpower and the End of American Supremacy.* New York: Penguin Press, 2004.

Rentoul, John. *Tony Blair Prime Minister.* London: Little, Brown and Company, 2001.

Revel, Jean Francois. *Anti-Americanism.* New York: Encounter Books, 2003.

Reynolds, Simon. *Energy Flash: Journey Through Rave Music and Dance Culture.* London: Picador, 1998.

Richards, Jeffrey. *The Age of the Dream Palace: Cinema and Society in Britain 1930–1939.* London: Routledge and Kegan Paul, 1984.

Riddell, Peter. *Hug Them Close: Blair, Clinton, Bush and the "Special Relationship."* London, Politico's, 2003.

———. *The Unfulfilled Prime Minister: Tony Blair's Quest for a Legacy.* London: Politico, updated and revised edition, 2006.

Ritson, Mike, and Stuart Russell. *The In Crowd The Story of the Northern & Rare Soul Scene.* London: Bee Cool, 1999.

Ritzer, George. *The McDonaldization of Society.* Newbury Park, CA: Pine Forge Press, 1993.

Rixon, Paul. *American Television on British Screens: A Story of Cultural Interaction.* Basingstoke: Palgrave Macmillan, 2006.

Robinson, Colin. *Arthur Seldon: A Life for Liberty.* London: Profile Books, 2009.

Rosen, Andrew. *The Transformation of British Life, 1950–2000.* Manchester and New York: Manchester University Press, 2003.

Rosenbaum, Martin. *From Soapbox to Soundbite: Party Political Campaigning in Britain Since 1945.* London: Macmillan Press, 1997.

Ross, Andrew, and Ross, Kristin. eds. *Anti-Americanism.* New York: New York University Press, 2004.

Roth, Wendy D. "United Kingdom." In Mary C. Waters and Reed Ueda with Helen B. Marrow, eds. *The New Americans: A Guide to Immigration Since 1965.* Cambridge, MA: Harvard University Press, 2007.

Rowntree, B. Seebohm, and G. R. Lavers. *English Life and Leisure: A Social Study.* London and New York: Longmans, Green and Co, 1951.

Rubin, Barry. *How Others Report Us: America in the Foreign Press.* Washington D.C.: The Center for Strategic and International Studies, Georgetown University, 1979.

Rubin, Barry, and Judith Colp Rubin. *Hating America: A History.* Oxford and New York: Oxford University Press, 2004.

Russell, Bertrand et al. *The Impact of America on European Culture.* Boston: The Beacon Press, 1951.

Russett, Bruce, and Donald R. Deluca. "Theater Nuclear Forces: Public Opinion in Western Europe." *Political Science Quarterly* 98 (Summer 1983): 179–196.

Rust, Frances. *Dance in Society.* London: Routledge and Kegan Paul, 1969.

Ryall, Tom. *Britain and the American Cinema.* London: Sage, 2001.

Ryan, Johnny. *A History of the Internet and the Digital Future.* London: Reaktion Books, 2010.

Rylatt, Keith, and Phil Scott. *CENtral 1179: The Story of the Twisted Wheel Club.* London: Bee Cool, 2001.

Sabin, Roger ed. *Punk Rock: So What? The Cultural Legacy of Punk.* London and New York: Routledge, 1999.

Sampson, Anthony. *Anatomy of Britain.* New York and Evanston: Harper and Row, 1962.

Samuel, Raphael ed. *Patriotism: The Making and Unmaking of British National Identity, Volume 1, History and Politics.* London and New York: Routledge, 1989.

Sandbrook, Dominic. *Never Had It So Good: A History of Britain From Suez to the Beatles.* London: Abacas, 2005.

——— *White Heat: A History of Britain in the Swinging Sixties.* London: Little, Brown, 2006.

——— *State of Emergency: The Way We Were: Britain, 1970–1974.* London: Penguin, 2010.

———. *Seasons in the Sun: The Battle for Britain, 1974–1979.* London: Allen Lane, 2012.

Sanders, Barry A. *American Avatar: The United States in the Global Imagination.* Washington DC: Potomac Books, 2011.

Sandford, Christopher. *Bowie: Loving the Alien.* New York: Da Capo Press, 1998.

Sardar, Ziauddin and Merryl Wyn Davies. *Why Do People Hate America?* Cambridge: Icon Books, 2002.

Saul, S. B. "The American Impact on British Industry, 1895–1914." *Business History* 3 (1967): 19–38.

Savage, Jon. *England's Dreaming: Anarchy, Sex Pistols, Punk Rock, and Beyond.* New York: St. Martin's Griffin, revised edition, 2001.

Schwartz, Roberta Freund. *How Britain Got the Blues: The Transmission and Reception of American Blues Style in the United Kingdom.* Aldershot, England: Ashgate, 2007.

Scott, Robert Lee, and Wayne Brockriede. eds. *The Rhetoric of Black Power.* New York: Harper and Row, 1969.

Scott-Smith, Giles. "'Her Rather Ambitious Washington Program': Margaret Thatcher's International Visitor Program Visit to the United States in 1967." *British Contemporary History* 17 (Winter 2003): 65–86.

Seabrook, Jeremy. *City Close-Up.* Indianapolis and New York: Bobbs-Merrill, 1971.

Seldon, Anthony. *Blair.* London: Free Press, 2004.

Sewell, Mike. "British Responses to Martin Luther King Jr and the Civil Rights Movement, 1954–1968." In Brian Ward and Tony Badger eds. *The Making of Martin Luther King and the Civil Rights Movement.* New York: New York University Press, 1996, 194–212.

Seymour-Ure, Colin. *The British Press and Broadcasting Since 1945.* Oxford: Blackwell, second edition, 1996.

Shapiro, Peter. *Turn the Beat Around: The Secret History of Disco.* New York: Faber and Faber; Revised edition 2007.

Shaw, Dave. *Casino: Wigan 30th Anniversary Edition.* London: Bee Cool, 2000.

Shaw, Gareth, Louise Curth and Andrew Alexander. "Selling Self-Service and the Supermarket: The Americanisation of Food Retailing in Britain, 1945–1960." *Business History* 46 (October 2004): 568–582.

Sheerin, John. "Do they like us?" *The Catholic World* (June 1953).

Short, Claire. *An Honorable Deception? New Labour, Iraq, and the Misuse of Power.* London: Simon and Schuster, 2004.

Simon Sykes, Christopher. *David Hockney: The Biography, 1937–1975.* New York and London: Doubleday, 2012.

Smith, David. *The Rise and Fall of Monetarism.* Middlesex: Penguin, 1987.

Smith, Graham. *When Jim Crow Met John Bull: Black American Soldiers in World War II Britain.* New York: St Martin's Press, 1987.

Smith, Geoffrey. *Reagan and Thatcher.* (New York and London: W. W. Norton, 1991).

Smith, Sidney. "Who Reads an American Book?" *Edinburgh Review* (January, 1820).

Smith, Steven K. and Douglas A. Wertman. *US-West European Relations During the Reagan Years: The Perspective of West European Publics.* New York: St. Martin's Press, 1992.

Snowman, Daniel. *Britain and America: An Interpretation of their Culture, 1945–1975.* New York: New York University Press, 1977.

Sounes, Howard. *Fab: An Intimate Life of Paul McCartney.* Cambridge MA: Da Capo Press, 2010.

Spitz, Marc. *Bowie: A Biography.* New York: Crown, 2009.

Spoto, Donald. *Marilyn Monroe: The Biography.* New York: Harper Collins, 1993.

Stacey, Jackie. *Star Gazing: Hollywood Cinema and Female Spectatorship.* London and New York: Routledge, 1994.

Stark, Steven D. *Meet the Beatles: A Cultural History of the Band That Shook Youth, Gender, and the World.* New York: Harper Collins, 2005.

Stedman Jones, Daniel. *Masters of the Universe: Hayek, Friedman, and the Birth of Neoliberal Politics.* Princeton and Oxford: Princeton University Press, 2012.

Steil, Benn. *The Battle of Bretton Woods: John Maynard Keynes, Harry Dexter White, and the Making of a New World Order.* Princeton and Oxford: Princeton University Press, 2013.

Stephens, Philip. *Tony Blair: The Making of a World Leader.* New York: Penguin, 2004.

Stewart, Graham. *Bang! A History of Britain in the 1980s.* London: Atlantic Books, 2013.

Stewart, W.A.C. *Higher Education in Postwar Britain.* London: Macmillan, 1989.

Stiglitz. Joseph E *Freefall: America, Free Markets and the Sinking of the World Economy.* New York: WW Norton, 2010.

Stokes, Jane. "Anglo-American Attitudes: Affirmations and Refutations of 'Americanicity' in British Television Advertising." In Yahya R. Kamalipour ed. *Images of the U.S. Around the World: A Multicultural Perspective.* Albany: State University of New York Press, 1999.

Storry, Mike, and Peter Childs. eds. *British Cultural Identities.* London and New York: Routledge, 1997.

Street, Sarah. *British National Cinema.* London and New York: Routledge, 1997.

Stuart, Johnny. *Rockers.* London: Plexus, 1987.

Swann, Paul. *The Hollywood Feature Film in Postwar Britain.* London and Sydney: Croom Helm, 1987.

Sweig, *Friendly Fire: Losing Friends and Making Enemies in the Anti-American Century.* New York: Public Affairs, 2006.

Sykes, Bill. *Sit Down! Listen to This! The Roger Eagle Story.* Manchester: Empire Publications, 2012.

Tanner, Michael. *Ali in Britain.* Edinburgh and London: Mainstream, 1995.

Taylor, Helen. *Circling Dixie: Contemporary Southern Culture Through a Transatlantic Lens.* New Brunswick, New Jersey and London: Rutgers University Press, 2001.

Taylor, Matthew. *The Association Game: A History of British Football.* London: Pearson Longman, 2008.

———. "Reflections on Liberty." *Hofstra Law Review* 28 (Summer 2000), 869–875.

———. *Statecraft: Strategies for a Changing World.* New York: HarperCollins, 2002.

Thomas, Nick. "Protests Against the Vietnam War in 1960s Britain: The Relationship between Protesters and the Press." *Contemporary British History* 22 (September 2008): 335–354.

Thompson, E P. "Letter to Americans." In Mary Kaldor and Paul Anderson eds. *Mad Dogs: The US Raids on Libya.* London: Pluto Press, 1986.

Thornton, Sarah. *Club Cultures: Music, Media and Subcultural Capital.* Hanover and London: Wesleyan University Press, 1996.

Time-Life Books, *Inventive Genius.* New York: Time-Life Books, 1991.

Tiratsoo, Nick. "Limits of Americanisation: The United States Productivity Gospel in Britain." In Becky Conekin, Frank Mort, and Chris Waters eds. *Moments of Modernity: Reconstructing Britain 1945–1964.* London and New York: Rivers Oram Press, 1999, 96–113.

Todd, Peter. "The British Film Industry in the 1990s." In Robert Murphy ed. *British Cinema ofthe 90s.* London: BFI Publishing, 2000.

Took, Barry. *Laughter in the Air: An Informal History of British Radio Comedy.* London: Robson Books, 1976.

Toop, David. *Rap Attack 2: African Rap to Global Hip Hop.* London: Serpent's Tail, 1991.

Travers, Bridget. ed. *World of Invention.* London: Gale, 1994.

Trynka, Paul. *David Bowie: Starman.* New York, Boston and London: Little, Brown and Company, 2011.

Tunstall, Jeremy. "The United Kingdom." In Mary Kelly, Gianpietro Mazzoleni, and Denis McQuail eds. *The Media in Europe: The Euromedia Handbook.* London: Sage Publications Ltd, 3rd edition, 2004.

Turner, Alwyn W. *Crisis? What Crisis? Britain in the 1970s.* London: Aurum Press, 2008.

———. *Halfway to Paradise: The Birth of British Rock.* London: V&A Publishing, 2008.

———. *Rejoice! Rejoice! Britain in the 1980s.* London: Aurum, 2010.

2010 Yearbook of Immigration Statistics. Washington DC: Office of Immigration Statistics, US Department of Homeland Security, August 2011.

Vanderschmidt, Fred. *What The English Think of Us.* New York: Robert M McBride, 1948.

Van Deburg, William L. *New Day in Babylon: The Black Power Movement and American Culture, 1965–1975.* Chicago and London: University of Chicago Press, 1992.

Van Dulken, Stephen. *Inventing the 20th Century: 100 Inventions that Shaped the World.* New York: New York University Press, 2000.

Veldman, Meredith. *Fantasy, the Bomb, and the Greening of Britain: Romantic Protest, 1945–1980.* New York: Cambridge University Press, 1994.

Vidal, John. *McLibel: Burger Culture on Trial.* New York: The New Press, 1997.

Vinen, Richard. *Thatcher's Britain: The Politics and Social Upheaval of the Thatcher Era.* London: Simon and Schuster, 2009.

Visconti, Tony. *Bowie, Bolan and the Brooklyn Boy.* London: HarperCollins, 2007.
Visson, Andre. *As Others See Us.* New York: Doubleday, 1948.
Walker, John A. *America's Impact on British Art Since 1945.* London: Pluto Press, 1998.
Wapshott, Nicholas. *Ronald Reagan and Margaret Thatcher: A Political Marriage.* London: Sentinel, 2007.
Ward, Brian. "'By Elvis and All the Saints' Images of the American South in the World of 1950s British Popular Music." In Joseph P. Ward ed. *Britain and the American South From Colonialism to Rock and Roll.* Jackson: The University Press of Mississippi, 2003.
Weight, Richard. *Patriots: National Identity in Britain 1940–2000.* London: Macmillan, 2002.
Whitcomb, Ian. *After the Ball.* New York: Limelight, 1986, first published in 1972.
Whitston, Kevin. "Worker Resistance and Taylorism in Britain." *International Review of Social History* 42 (1997): 1–24.
Willcock, H. D. "Public Opinion: Attitudes Towards America and Russia." *The Political Quarterly* 19 (1948).
Wilford, Hugh."The South and the British Left, 1930–1960." In Joseph P. Ward ed. *Britain and the American South From Colonialism to Rock and Roll.* Jackson: The University Press of Mississippi, 2003, 163–186.
Williams, Francis. *The American Invasion.* London: Anthony Blond, 1962.
Williams, Raymond. *Britain in the Sixties: Communications.* Baltimore, Maryland: Penguin, 1962.
Wilson, Andy. *Northern Soul: Music, Drugs and Subcultural Identity.* Devon: Willan Publishing, 2007.
Winstanley, Russ, and David Nowell. *Soul Survivors: The Wigan Casino Story.* London: Robson Books, 1996.
Woodhead, Lindy. *Shopping, Seduction, and Mr Selfridge.* London: Profile Books, 2007.
Worpole, Ken. *Dockers and Detectives.* London: Verso, 1983.
Wybrow, Robert J. *Britain Speaks Out, 1937-1987: A Social History as seen through the Gallup poll.* London: Macmillan, 1989.
Wynn, Daniel. *The Black Protest* Movement. New York: Philosophical Library, 1974.
Young, Hugo. *One of Us: A Biography of Margaret Thatcher.* London: Macmillan, 1989.
Zakaria, Fareed. *The Post-American World.* New York and London: W. W. Norton and Co, 2008.
Zeitlin, Jonathan, and Gary Herrigel eds. *Americanization and Its Limits: Reworking US Technology and Management in Post-War Europe and Japan.* Oxford and New York: Oxford University Press, 2004.
Zweig, Ferdynand. *The Worker in an Affluent Society: Family Life and Industry.* New York, NY: Free Press, 1961.

Websites

The Age. http://www.theage.com
Amazon. http://www.amazon.com
Anglotopia.net at http://www.anglotopia.net
BBC News. http://news.bbc.co.uk
Braggtopia. http://www.braggtopia.com
Breaking Travel News. http://www.breakingtravelnews.com
British Film Institute. http://www.bfi.org.uk/features/mostwatched/1970s.html
Cinema Exhibitors' Association. http://www.cinemauk.org.uk

Desert Island Discs. http://www.bbc.co.uk
Facebook LFC Reds. http://www.facebook.com
Football Fan Cast. http://www.footballfancast.com
Fox Soccer. http://msn.foxsports.com
GfK Roper. http://www.gfk.com
The Guardian. http://www.guardian.co.uk
Huffington Post. http://www.huffingtonpost.com
The Independent. www.independent.co.uk
Ipsos MORI. http://www.ipsos-mori.com
Lyrics Mode. http://www.lyricsmode.com.
MacRumors. http://forums.macrumors.com
Mail Online. http://www.dailymail.co.uk
Margaret Thatcher Foundation. http://www.margaretthatcher.org/document/103509
NFL London. http://www.nfllondon.net
The New York Times Online Blog. http://cityroom.blogs.nytimes.com
Office for National Statistics at http://www.ons.gov.uk
Pew Research Center. http://www.pewglobal.org
Public Diplomacy. http://www.publicdiplomacy.org
Quezi.com. http://quezi.com/5940
Screenline. http://www.screenonline.org.uk
Sixty Years of British Number Ones. http://www.onlineweb.com/theones/
DJ History. http://www.djhistory.com
The Student Room. http://www.thestudentroom.co.uk
The Telegraph. http://www.telegraph.co.uk
The Theatres Trust. http://www.theatrestrust.org.uk
Times of India. http://articles.timesofindia.indiatimes.com
UK Telephone History. http://www.britishtelephones.com
Visit Britain. http://www.visitbritain.org
World Intellectual Property Organization. http://www.wipo.int
WW2 People's War. bbc.co.uk/ww2peopleswar

Index

Note: Letter 'n' followed by the locator refers to notes

Printed in Dunstable, United Kingdom

67673777R00159